T0091532

Intelligent Information Systems – Vol. 6

Recommender Systems
Advanced Developments

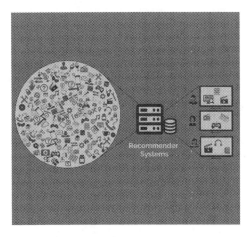

INTELLIGENT INFORMATION SYSTEMS

ISSN: 1793-4990

Series Editor: Jie Lu *(University of Technology, Sydney, Australia)*

Published

Intelligent Information Systems – Vol. 6

Recommender Systems
Advanced Developments

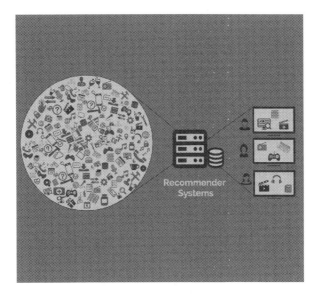

Jie Lu
Qian Zhang
Guangquan Zhang

University of Technology Sydney, Australia

 **World Scientific**

NEW JERSEY · LONDON · SINGAPORE · BEIJING · SHANGHAI · HONG KONG · TAIPEI · CHENNAI · TOKYO

Published by

World Scientific Publishing Co. Pte. Ltd.

5 Toh Tuck Link, Singapore 596224

USA office: 27 Warren Street, Suite 401-402, Hackensack, NJ 07601

UK office: 57 Shelton Street, Covent Garden, London WC2H 9HE

British Library Cataloguing-in-Publication Data
A catalogue record for this book is available from the British Library.

Intelligent Information Systems — Vol. 6
RECOMMENDER SYSTEMS
Advanced Developments

Copyright © 2021 by World Scientific Publishing Co. Pte. Ltd.

All rights reserved. This book, or parts thereof, may not be reproduced in any form or by any means, electronic or mechanical, including photocopying, recording or any information storage and retrieval system now known or to be invented, without written permission from the publisher.

For photocopying of material in this volume, please pay a copying fee through the Copyright Clearance Center, Inc., 222 Rosewood Drive, Danvers, MA 01923, USA. In this case permission to photocopy is not required from the publisher.

ISBN 978-981-122-462-1 (hardcover)
ISBN 978-981-122-463-8 (ebook for institutions)
ISBN 978-981-122-464-5 (ebook for individuals)

For any available supplementary material, please visit
https://www.worldscienti ic.com/worldscibooks/10.1142/11947#t=suppl

Printed in Singapore

Jie Lu dedicates this book to her parents, Zesheng Lu and Yunxia Zhao, with love and gratitude.

You are the greatest factor contributing to my academic accomplishments.

Preface

This monograph systematically presents state-of-the-art theoretical and methodological developments of recommender systems, and chiefly presents successful application developments and how the recommender system is implemented in real-world practice. The content is primarily based on the authors' research results in the recommender system field during the past ten years, which have been published in more than 70 journal and conference publications (which are marked with * in Bibliography) and involved five Australian national and industrial research projects.

Why We Wrote This Monograph

Recommender systems aim to provide users (individuals and businesses) with personalized recommendations on the most relevant products or services (called items), as an effective strategy to overcome the increasing overload of online information in e-service and also to drive business sales. The key technique of recommender systems is to automatically predict and identify users' preferences for particular items. At the early stages in this field, a recommender system was considered solely as a specific type of information filtering technique that presented user-relevant information. Today, recommender systems are one of the most successful and widespread applications of machine learning and computational intelligence techniques.

Recent developments in recommender systems comprise: advanced learning models to improve user preference prediction accuracy; new computational intelligent tools to deal with the cold start/new user issue, data sparsity issue and user preference uncertainty issue; more effective frameworks to generate recommendations in complex situations such as group recommender systems and tree-structured items; and more powerful methods to integrate machine learning into recommendation process such as cross-domain recommendation and user preference drift-aware recommendation. By taking advantage of the greater opportunities available in the real-world, recommender systems are now being successfully applied in e-commence, e-business, e-government, e-learning and e-tourism, as well as other business domains.

Since recommender system study has entered a new era of more powerful learning and computation capability and is facing more complex environments such as involving uncertain, dynamic and massive data, there has been greater interest in exploring advanced recommender system techniques and applications more recently. Therefore, we believe now is the right time to provide a systematic overview of recommender systems and to disseminate the latest results of theoretical research, technological development, and practical applications in the field. Our aim and motivation were to write an instructive monograph in which not only is there up-to-date advanced theoretical research in recommender systems but also recent practical developments.

The Advantages of This Monograph

This monograph is timely in that it reflects recent recommender system advancements and presents sophisticated real-world applications in the field. It offers the following advantages:

- It systematically presents in their entirety recommender system theories, methods, algorithms and applications. Not only are advanced recommendation models and prediction algorithms covered in detail, but also real-world applications with software systems, including all the important aspects of implementing recommender systems in practice.
- It focuses on challenging issues in recommender system research, such as when an item has to be described as a tree; when a user's profile has to be described in linguistic terms; when users' preference patterns have un-predicable drift; when users are in a group; and when a recommendation generation process needs to be visualized and provide advanced solutions.
- It reflects the latest academic research progress and state-of-the-art development throughout, as well as results from our widely published research in the recommender system field. It doesn't attempt to provide exhaustive coverage of every fact and all the research result that exist.

This monograph has a total of 15 chapters divided into three parts.

- Part I: Recommender System: Introduction
- Part II: Recommender System: Methods and Algorithms
- Part III: Recommender System: Software and Applications

Part I, from Chapters 1 to 3, covers concepts, basic content-based, collaborative filtering-based and knowledge-based recommendation methods, and the seven main application domains of recommender systems. This part provides fundamental knowledge for Parts II and III.

Part II, from Chapters 4 to 11, presents in detail a set of advanced frameworks, methods and algorithms of recommender systems. Chapter 4 reports how social networks can provide more user relationships by using a graph ranking technique to help predict new user preferences to handle the cold start issue. Chapter 5 illustrates how tag data can enhance prediction and recommendation accuracy. Chapter 6 explores how fuzzy techniques can deal with uncertainties and therefore enhance the performance of recommendation methods. Chapter 7 presents a comprehensive similarity measure and recommendation method for tree-structured items and tree-structured user requirements. Chapter 8 provides a solution for generating recommendations for a group of people and presents a web-based tourism group recommender system prototype called GroTo. Chapter 9 presents new developments in cross-domain recommender systems aimed at handling the sparsity issue. Chapter 10 focuses on how user preference drift is identified and how a user preference drift-aware recommender system can provide accurate recommendations in a dynamic environment. Chapter 11 presents how visualization techniques can enhance users' trust in recommender systems, especially for group recommender systems.

Part III, from Chapters 12 to 15, shows the real-world application developments of recommender systems by using the methods presented in the previous chapters. These applications include customer retention in telecommunications; connecting small and medium-size business (SMB) business partners; learning activity recommendation in e-learning; and property investment recommendation in the real estate industry. All these chapters cover the background to the real-world application, data collection, system design and software interfaces.

Who Should Read This Monograph

This monograph is for current and aspiring recommender system researchers and practitioners who are looking forward to implementing solutions to real-world personalized recommendation problems. Therefore, our potential readers include (1) organizational managers and practicing professionals, who can use the provided methods and software to solve their e-service recommendation problems; (2) scientists and researchers in the area of recommender systems and related areas of business intelligence, machine learning and decision support systems; and (3) students at the advanced undergraduate or master's level in information systems, management business administration, or application of computer science programs. Since we do not describe how to write recommendation algorithms from scratch, but instead focus on how to understand and use the algorithms given, the monograph is geared towards the more advanced student.

Acknowledgments

Without the help and support of a group of people, this monograph would never have existed. We wish to thank Australian Research Council, as the work presented in this monograph was partially supported under ARC discovery project grants; co-workers who have advised and conducted research, and whose results are included in this monograph; many researchers who have worked in recommender systems and related areas, and whose significant insights have been referenced in the monograph; our team members Dr. Dianshuang Wu, Dr. Mingsong Mao, Dr. Wei Wang and Dr. Peng Hao, who have completed their PhDs in our lab in the area of recommender systems, and with whom we have some joint publications that are referenced in the monograph; the researchers and students in the Decision System and e-Service Intelligence (DeSI) laboratory, Center for Artificial Intelligence at University of Technology Sydney, who suffered through several versions of the recommender system methods and algorithms shown in this monograph; Camilla Davis who proofread the main part of this book; and the editors and production staff at World Scientific, who helped us to ensure the book is as good as we are capable of making it.

Jie Lu
Qian Zhang
Guangquan Zhang
University of Technology Sydney, Australia
April 2020

Foreword

I still remember the first time I met Professor Jie Lu in Xiamen, China in 2008. It was when she was the co-chair of the conference ISKE2008, in which I gave a keynote talk. I learned a great deal by talking to her at the time, and most of all I was very delighted to know that she is a foremost expert in recommender systems. Her teams work has been presented at top conferences such as the International Joint Conference on Artificial Intelligence (IJCAI), Association for the Advancement of Artificial Intelligence (AAAI) and top journals such as the journal of Artificial Intelligence (AIJ) and IEEE Transactions on Neural Networks and Learning Systems (IEEE TNNLS), which featured only top-notch research innovations in the world. As the president of IJCAI (2017-2019) and an active researcher in recommender systems areas myself, I have been tracking her team's work in recommender system field closely. This book contains ten years' work by her and her team, some of which were published in more than 50 published theoretical or applications papers.

As the book introduces, a recommender system includes a combination of technologies to provide personalized e-services to end-users. It is not just about algorithms as a form of information filtering, it is also about the methodologies and software systems to support government agencies, companies, educators, and many online service organizers to drive their business values and improve marketing and customer relationship management. As the book mentioned, a recommender system can support a small business to select the most suitable telecommuting package, support a learner to select the most suitable subjects for his career, and support a real estate investor to find the most suitable property.

In recent years, artificial intelligence has been widely and successfully applied in recommender systems and significantly enhanced their performance. As a result, companies seize the opportunities to start bringing AI approaches to their online service systems. In this way, intelligent decision support and personalized online services are emphasized as key tasks of business strategies and are brought to a new stage of development. After more than 10 years of work in this area, Professor Lu made a great effort to bring these AI-driven research methods and innovative software applications together to present a whole picture of the latest developments and trends in recommender systems. I believe that with AI's power, with the effort such as that of Professor Lu's team, recommender systems will continue to be one of the most important AI and IT innovations and business intelligence techniques for many years to come.

This book provides a valuable perspective on recommender systems through the presentation of advanced research results, techniques and systems in the broad field of recommender systems. It covers the necessary contents from basic recommender system methods to new AI-enhanced developments. For example, as a researcher in transfer learning field, an important subfield of machine learning, I really appreciate that cross-domain recommender systems enhances the ability of recommender systems in transferring knowledge between application domains. This is a critical technology to solve data sparsity and cold start issues in generating personalized recommendations. This book also proposes user preference drift-aware recommender systems through concept drift adaptation techniques to handle the issue that users' preferences are dynamically changing. If one only exploits past behavior of users in designing recommendation models, the models may not be tailored to a user's personal and current preferences. Fuzzy technique-enhanced recommender systems are presented in this book to handle uncertainties in data, learning and recommendation process. Likewise, recommendation visualization methods introduced in the book is a promising solution to overcome this weakness, which can also reduce users' concerns on privacy and improve users' confidence. Advanced techniques such as federated recommender systems, a technology my research team has spearheaded, are also described as a future direction with a purpose to bridge data repositories without compromising data security and privacy. In this new age of AI applications and online services, it is a good timing to provide researchers and practitioners from academia and industry state-of-the-art knowledge about recommender systems. This book presents a great step in that direction.

I am confident that readers can receive great benefits from reading this book. This book not only focuses on an introduction of recommender systems, but also helps readers quickly enter the frontier of the advances in recommender systems and applications. For practitioners, the applications shown in the book are developed by the authors. The first-hand experience of the authors can provide valuable guidance for the readers in developing their own recommender systems.

Qiang Yang
Chief AI Officer, WeBank,
Chair Professor at Hong Kong University of Science and Technology,
AAAI Fellow, IEEE Fellow, ACM Fellow, AAAS Fellow,
CAAI (Chinese AI) Fellow, IAPR Fellow,
Founding Editor in Chief of ACM Transactions on Intelligent Systems
and IEEE Transactions on Big Data
April 10, 2020

About the Authors

Jie Lu is a Distinguished Professor and Director of the Australian Artificial Intelligence Institute at the University of Technology Sydney. Notably, she is an Australian Laureate Fellow, IEEE Fellow, and IFSA Fellow. Distinguished Professor Lu's research interests include fuzzy transfer learning, concept drift, DSS and recommender systems. She has published six books and more than 500 papers; delivered 25 keynote speeches at conferences; won ten Australian Research Council Discovery projects; led 15 industry projects; and received several prestigious awards, including the 2019 UTS Medal for Research Excellence, the 2019 IEEE Transactions on Fuzzy Systems Outstanding Paper Award, and the 2019 Australian Most Innovative Engineer Award.

Qian Zhang is a Postdoctoral Research Fellow and core member of the Decision Systems and e-Service Intelligent Research Laboratory of the Australian Artificial Intelligence Institute at the University of Technology Sydney. Dr Zhang's research interests include recommender systems, fuzzy recommender systems, and cross-domain recommender systems. She has published close to 20 papers in the area of recommender systems, and developed recommender systems for real-world applications.

Guangquan Zhang is a Research Associate Professor and Director of the Decision Systems and e-Service Intelligent Research Laboratory of the Australian Artificial Intelligence Institute at the University of Technology Sydney. His research interests include fuzzy measure, fuzzy optimization, fuzzy decision and recommender systems. Professor Zhang has authored nine books and more than 500 papers, including over 240 articles in international journals. He was awarded an Australian Research Council (ARC) QEII Fellowship, and nine ARC Discovery Projects; and served as an editorial board member for several international journals and guest editor for eight special issues of IEEE Transactions and other journal.

Contents

PART 2

Recommender Systems: Methods and Algorithms   **63**

PART 3

Recommender Systems: Software and Applications   235

PART 1
Recommender Systems: Introduction

Chapter 1

Recommender System Concepts

The rapid growth of web information provides excellent opportunities for developing various e-services applications in many domains. However, it has also caused information overload problems, whereby users are unable to efficiently locate relevant information to meet their needs when using the current Internet search tools. To help users retrieve the most relevant information from a massive amount of online information, thereby providing personalized services, recommender systems are proposed. A recommender system aims to recommend the most suitable items (products or services) to a particular user (individual or business) by predicting the user's interest in an item based on user historical records. Recommender systems provide users with personalized online information, product and service recommendations, assisting them to make decisions. Since the mid-1990s, various recommender system frameworks, methods and tools have been proposed and applied in e-commerce, e-business, e-government and other areas.

This chapter will present the basic concepts of recommender systems. The background on information overload and personalization are first introduced in Section 1.1. Then the recommender system definition, characteristics and types are discussed in Section 1.2. A general recommender system framework is given in Section 1.3. Section 1.4 presents the design and development of recommender systems, including industrial applications and the benefits of developing recommender systems. Section 1.5 summarizes this chapter.

1.1   Information Overload and Personalization

In current web systems, a huge amount of information is provided to users when they are making decisions about any kind of product or e-service. Usually, users are unwilling to explore the vast amount of information offered by companies in relation to their products and services and, choose a product or service in which they are truly interested. Thus, in this fiercely competitive marketplace it is crucial for a company to help its customers deal with information overload in decision-making so as to retain their loyalty [Schafer *et al.* (1999)]. Providing personalized e-services to customers is an appropriate approach to handle the information overload problem and improve user's experience. In this way, services to different users are customized, making it easy for customers to find what they need.

Providing customized products and services to customers, while they are basically being passive, is known as personalization, and is becoming a key factor for a company to satisfy their customers. This is where recommender systems come in. Using recommender systems to provide personalized e-services has become the most commonly used technique to solve the information overload problem that has been brought about by Web 2.0 [Adomavicius and Tuzhilin (2005)]. The recommendation process predicts a user's potential interest (user's preference) in items that they haven't previously bought, according to the user's historical records, thus creating a personalized list from which users can choose.

Recommender systems were first applied in e-commerce to solve the infor-mation overload problem, and were quickly expanded to the personalization of e-government, e-business, e-learning and e-tourism [Lu *et al.* (2015b)]. Nowadays, recommender systems are an indispensable part of Internet websites such as Amazon.com, YouTube, Netflix, Yahoo, Facebook, Last.fm and Meetup.

1.2   Definition, Characteristics and Types of Recommender Systems

In this Section we provide the definition of a recommender system. Then we list its characteristics. Finally we introduce the four different types of recommender systems.

1.2.1   *Definition*

A recommender system can be defined as a set of programs that attempt to recommend the most suitable items to particular users by predicting a user's interest in an item based on the information about the items, the users and the interactions between items and users [Bobadilla *et al.* (2013)]. The users could be individuals or businesses, such as book buyers, job seekers or small businesses who want to find a potential partner. The items could be either products or services, such as a book, a movie or a package of mobile services, as shown in Fig. 1.1.

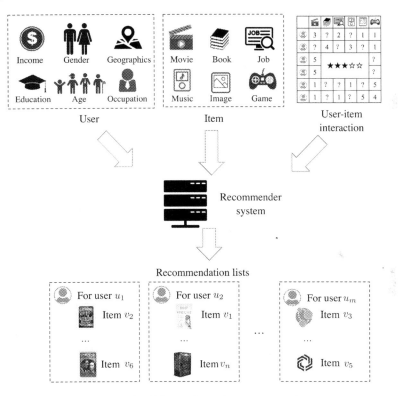

Fig. 1.1: A graphical illustration of a recommender system.

In brief, recommender systems are designed to estimate the utility of an item and predict whether it is worth recommending. The core part of recommender systems is a function to define the utility of a specific item to a user [Adomavicius and Tuzhilin (2005)]:

$$f : \mathcal{U} \times \mathcal{V} \to \mathcal{D} \tag{1.1}$$

This is a function to define the utility of a specific item $v \in \mathcal{V}$ to a user $u \in \mathcal{U}$. $\mathcal{D}$ is the final recommendation list containing a set of items in a ranked order. This list is ranked according to the utility of all the items the user has not consumed.

The key purpose of most recommendation methods is to find an item for the user so as to maximize the utility function, formulated as follows:

$$\forall u \in \mathcal{U}, \; \underset{v \in \mathcal{V}}{\operatorname{argmax}} \, f(u, v) \qquad (1.2)$$

A final recommendation list, containing a set of items in a ranked order, will then be provided. Essentially, the utility of an item is presented as ratings of a user. A rating given by user u to an item v is $r_{u,v}$. With the number of users M and the number of items N, the rating matrix is $R \in \mathbb{R}^{M \times N}$. The recommendation task is to either fill in the rating matrix or give a ranking score for each user-item pair. Thus the items that the user has not seen before can be ranked and the Top-K items will be recommended. Predicting the utility of items to a particular user varies in different recommendation methods. Also, other information, for example item attribute information, user-generated information and user social information, have been used in different methods.

1.2.2   *Characteristics*

According to the definition of recommender systems and their various applications, we list the main characteristics of a recommender system below:

(1) It mainly deals with information overload problem;
(2) It supports both individual and group users in decision making;
(3) It provides users with personalized services;
(4) It usually generates recommendation without additionally requiring information from users;
(5) It supports a variety of business use cases and scenarios such as data uncertain and data sparsity;
(6) It can access a wide variety of data sources across multiple domains simultaneously;

With these characteristics, we can develop different types of recommender systems, use different estimation and prediction models, and apply them in different domains for various users to help them make decisions.

1.2.3   *Types*

Recommendation methods are the key to implementing a recommender system. In principle, the methods can be classified into four types: collaborative filtering (CF)-based, content-based, knowledge-based and hybrid recommendation method. Each recommendation method has both advantages and limitations. For example, CF-based methods require the rating of user data and so it is hard to deal with new users or users who do not have enough rating data (known as cold start or data sparsity problem). However, advanced developments in recommender systems to overcome disadvantages and provide better user experiences are growing each year. Here we give a brief overview of the four recommendation method types. More detail can be found in Chapter 2.

(1) CF-based recommendation methods

CF-based recommendation methods help users to make choices based on the opinions of other users who share similar interests. The CF-based methods can be divided into memory-based CF and model-based CF. Memory-based CF methods contain user-based and item-based CF [Sarwar *et al.* (2001)]. In the user-based CF, a user will receive recommendations of items liked by similar users. In the item-based CF, a user will receive recommendations of items that are similar to those they have loved in the past. The similarity between users or items can be calculated by different measures.

With the development of machine learning techniques, model-based CF methods are built on the basis of optimizing an objective function between the model prediction and the true label. The model-based CF is more superior, as it benefits from various artificial intelligence (AI) techniques. To overcome the disadvantages of prediction in one way, multi-criteria CF has also been developed.

(2) Content-based recommendation methods

Content-based recommendation methods focus on recommending items that are similar to items previously preferred by a specific user [Ricci *et al.* (2010)]. The basic principles of content-based recommender systems are: (1) To analyze the description of the items preferred by a particular user so as to determine the principal common attributes (preferences) that can be used to distinguish these items. These preferences are stored in a user profile. (2) To compare each item's attributes with the user profile so that only items that have a high degree of similarity with the user profile will be recommended.

Content-based recommender systems generate recommendations heuristically using traditional information retrieval methods such as the cosine similarity measure. Also, they generate recommendations using statistical learning and machine learning methods, which are capable of learning users' interests from the historical data of users. One disadvantage of content-based recommendation methods is overspecialization, since any recommendation is provided based on the user's historical consumption records. Details of content-based recommendation methods will be discussed in Chapter 2.

(3) Knowledge-based recommendation methods

Knowledge-based recommendation methods offer items to users based on external knowledge about the users, items and/or their relationships. Usually, knowledge-based recommendation methods retain a functional knowledge base that describes how a particular item meets a specific user's need. This is performed based on inferences about the relationship between a user's need and a possible recommendation. Case-based reasoning (CBR) is a common expression of knowledge-based recommendation methods in which items are represented as cases and recommendations are generated by retrieving the most similar cases to the user's query or profile [Brusilovski *et al.* (2007)]. Ontology, as a formal knowledge representation method, represents the domain concepts and the relationships between those concepts. It also has been used to express domain knowledge in recommender systems. The most obvious disadvantage of the knowledge-based recommendation method is the human intervention required to acquire the knowledge and build the knowledge base.

(4) Hybrid recommendation methods

To overcome the disadvantages of using only one type of recommendation method, various hybrid recommendation methods, which combine two or more recommendation methods, have been developed [Burke (2002)]. The most common practice is the combination of CF-based and content-based methods, including user-based CF with content-based and item-based CF with content-based. Knowledge-based recommendation methods have also been widely combined with CF-based and content-based recommendation methods.

1.3   Framework of Recommender Systems

The framework of recommender systems contains three main components: data sources (input), recommendation engine (core technique) and recommendation generation (output). A recommender system can use data from various sources. This means the information about a user, an item and the interaction between them can be taken care of by recommender systems as shown in Fig. 1.2. Then, the recommendation engine processes and generates results to fit diverse requirements. The output of the recommender system varies in accordance with the application scenarios.

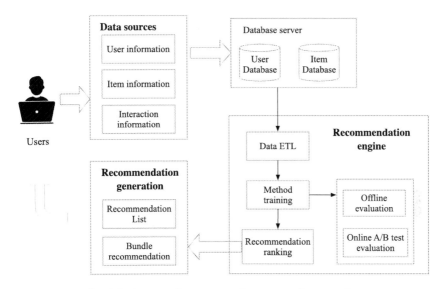

Fig. 1.2: A general recommender system framework.

1.3.1 *Data sources*

Data about users, items and their interactions come from different sources and can be in various forms. We will first give a detailed description of the data the recommender system can make use of.

Users have different preferences and various purposes. In order to provide users with personalized recommendation, the recommender system needs to profile each user using the user's related information. For example, when a user is selecting a movie on a website, the available information of that user includes: demographic information such as age, gender, nationality, the language he/she speaks, search history, clicked movies, watched movies, user social relations or user generated tags or comments. All of the above can be used to profile the user's preferences. The process of data selection and the way the data is used vary based on the recommendation method. Also, users can be individuals or something more complex such as a group or a business. For example, a user can be a channel group for online videos or a company where each member may have different purposes.

Items refer to anything that needs to be recommended to users. The attributes of an item are not just text descriptions, but also comprise images or knowledge graph between a set of items. The attributes of an item can greatly affect the recommendation methods. For example, groceries can be recommended to users repetitively and music or news can be consumed in large quantity. On the other hand, luxuries, such as a mobile phone or a house, may be consumed by a user with careful considerations. Additionally, some complicated items where knowledge and rules accounted for a large proportion in recommendation such as jobs, hotels or insurance policies.

The interaction between users and items contains all the information the user has left behind after browsing the web or using an App. This information can be in different forms such as ratings, tags or free-text comments. In a broad sense, the user feedbacks can be divided into explicit feedbacks and implicit feedbacks:

(1) Explicit feedbacks refer to the rating stars given by the user as $\star$ to $\star\star\star\star\star$ as the ordinal rating $\{1,2,3,4,5\}$. In such case, the rating contains both positive and negative feedback from the users.
(2) Implicit feedbacks refer to the binary values given by user behaviors such as whether the user has viewed, clicked or bought an item or not. The implicit feedbacks only represent positive feedbacks - users' negative feedbacks are not collected.

1.3.2 *Recommendation engine*

The recommendation engine is the core part of the recommender system. First, data from various sources need to be processed by data extract, transform and load (ETL). Then structured data, such as user features and item features, are stored in the database. After data are processed, the engine is to train the recommendation methods. The recommendation engine contains recommendation methods that take those input data to classify, measure and match users or items; predict a score indicating preferences; and generate recommendation lists.

We now describe the two kinds of evaluations for the recommendation engine: (1) Offline evaluation: Data engineering techniques and recommendation methods are validated and evaluated with offline data where they are selected for online serving according to their performance on offline evaluation criteria. (2) Online A/B test evaluation: Except for offline evaluation, online A/B test is also needed for a new recommendation method before it is deployed. Two groups of users (corresponding to A and B) are randomly selected and are provided with recommendations generated by two different methods. The feedbacks of users from group A and B are collected and the significance of the difference is statistically analyzed as a "two-sample hypothesis test" to evaluate which recommendation method is more effective.

1.3.3 *Recommendation generation*

Recommendation results are usually generated as a ranked list of items and are presented to users to help them make decisions. Moreover, some recommender systems can bundle related items and give a package for the users to choose from [Zhu *et al.* (2014)]. The bundle recommendation can not only improve the sales of items, but also integrate price strategy where users are offered diverse choices and discount promotions. All in all, recommender systems can be used in various scenarios and situations to offer customers better experiences and companies commercial value through their ability to filter information.

1.4 Design and Development of Recommender Systems

Almost every website is powered by a recommender system. It has become an indispensable part of e-commerce in industry. In this section, we introduce the design and development of recommender systems in industry. Firstly, we give a general introduction about the industrial application of recommender systems. Then the benefits of developing recommender systems are listed.

1.4.1 *Applications*

Recommender systems are adopted in many industrial companies with applications in different areas. The business target is decided by the uniqueness of each application area. As a result, the constructed recommender systems vary according to the different users, items, contexts and business problems. In this Section, we give a general system design of the recommender system used in industry, ignoring the techniques applied. Also, we review several well-known applications in industry, as examples of how recommendation methods help to build the system and how industry benefits by building recommender systems.

The first application of the recommender system in a large company was at Amazon [Linden *et al.* (2003)]. The item-based CF method is employed in Amazon as part of its online shopping system, and deployment of the recommender system has helped Amazon increase its profits around 30% (analyzed by McKinsey & Company in 2017). The success in Amazon has attracted other e-commerce companies to attach importance to the application of recommender systems, including eBay [Schafer *et al.* (1999)] and Tmall [Wang *et al.* (2018a)]. Embedding and graph embedding techniques are applied to process the huge amount of items and complex relationships between them. The recommender system is now an indispensable part of online shopping websites.

E-entertainment followed the step of e-commerce with the well-known Netflix Prize [Bennett and Lanning (2007)]. Video recommendation taking various data sources from structured meta data such as actors, titles to unstructured data such as images and videos are applied in YouTube [Davidson *et al.* (2010)]. Similarly, the music genome project is launched where features are extracted containing information about the music artists, band, albums, genre, style and emotion are extracted. These features are integrated with the CF recommendation method which generates music play lists for users. Also, social platforms, such as Twitter and Facebook, connect users with artists and their friends. Spotify deployed Echo Nest for powering the recommendation in its music streaming platform in 2014 [Eriksson *et al.* (2019)]. With Apple Music entering the competitive market, music platforms all recommend a play list for users once they launch the App or website. These e-entertainment items can be repetitively consumed by users, particularly for music, and recommender systems are developed to fit this requirement.

Recommender systems are also directly connected and widely used with ad promotions. The click through rate is the metric that is directly linked with the profits from advertising revenues. Facebook uses logistic regression and boosted decision trees to improve the click through rate in ad recommendation [He *et al.* (2014)]. LinkedIn provides personalized feed to users to improve user participation on the activities [Agarwal *et al.* (2015)]. The click through rate is also a crucial indicator for evaluation on news recommendation, which is used by Google and Yahoo [Das *et al.* (2007)].

Except for recommender systems on single domain, some companies also develop cross-domain recommender systems. The cross-domain recommender systems can leverage a source domain containing rich information to alleviate data sparsity problem. They can also help to promote a combination of items from several domains and increase the diversity of consumption. Microsoft has developed cross-domain recommender systems by using Apps and News together with Movie/TV on Xbox to generate recommendation to users [Elkahky *et al.* (2015)].

Current development in the industry shows that recommender systems have become one of the most important business intelligence techniques. Because of the opportunities they have provided in the area of promotions, recommender systems are connected with the profit of companies. At the same time, recommender systems play a crucial role in improving user experience.

1.4.2 *Benefits*

The advantages of recommender systems for both customers and companies are summarized below.

(1) Personalized services.

One of the key benefits recommender systems provide is a personalized service for users. Since users are limited to their own knowledge and experience, the personalized service of a recommender system can help users quickly find what they need while discovering new items which they did not know about previously. This reduces the amount of time the user needs to spend searching and exploring.

(2) Improved user profile.

If recommender systems have the ability to give users personalized recommendation, users need to be profiled accurately. The recommender systems can assimilate the various pieces of information about a user, including demographic information, browsing history, user preference interactions and business knowledge, to create user profiles. These user profiles can then be utilized for business analysis.

(3) Retain the loyalty of users.

Recommender systems provide a guide for users when they are browsing the website. They can make it easier for customers to find what they need and limit the time spent completing an order. In such case, users' needs are satisfied and their experience of using the website or service are improved. This can encourage users to stick with the service based on it being user-friendly and helpful. The user experience is crucial to companies in keeping user loyalty and capturing market share.

(4) Increase the revenue.

Recommender systems provide a guide for users when they are browsing the website. They can make it easier for customers to find what they need and limit the time spent completing an order. Users can be swamped by the excessive number of product choices, particularly when there are long-tail products. Users are more likely to discover diverse range of items that they are more likely to be interested in.

(5) Understanding market trends.

A secondary but integral benefit of the recommender system is to provide reports on sales direction and market trends. These reports and analysis can help a company make decisions about the direction to drive the market.

1.5   Summary

The development of recommender systems aims to provide personalized items (products and services) to users (business or individual). Recommender systems, as one of the hottest areas in artificial intelligence, have brought great profits to companies who are prompting frontier development with more sophisticated techniques to support consumers. This chapter presents the definitions, types of recommendation methods and the general framework of the recommender system. It also presents the design and development of recommender systems in practice.

Chapter 2

Basic Recommendation Methods

Recommender systems can be seen as a decision-making strategy for users under complex information environments and also as a tool for products/service providers to understand users' interest and preference. The most important characteristic of a recommender system is its ability to "guess" a user's preferences and interests, and not ask, in order to generate personalized commodity/service recommendations. The ability to "guess" users' preference comes from the recommendation methods, which contain a set of measure, analysis and prediction algorithms.

Before we introduce the recommendation methods, we give here the following concepts that are used throughout the book:

- User: who has experience of purchasing products or/and services online. Users can be either individuals or groups; consumers or businesses; give feedbacks such as ratings, reviews or tags.
- Target user: who is the user a recommender system is trying to provide recommendations to.
- Items: the products or services to be recommended to users such as a movie, a house, a meet-up activity, a health policy, *etc.*

As shown in Chapter 1, recommendation methods are categorized in four types. Here in Chapter 2, we first introduce CF-based recommendation methods in Section 2.1. Followed by content-based recommendation methods in Section 2.2. Then knowledge-based recommendation methods are presented in Section 2.3 and finally hybrid recommendation methods in Section 2.4. A comprehensive comparison of these basic methods is given in Section 2.5, then in Section 2.6 we present evaluations of recommendation methods. Finally, Section 2.7 summarizes this chapter.

2.1   CF-based Recommendation Methods

Collaborative filtering (CF)-based recommendation methods infer the utility of an item according to other users' ratings. The term "collaborative filtering" was first used in Tapestry [Goldberg *et al.* (1992)], one of the first systems to implement the CF-based recommendation method. CF has been widely researched in academia and has been rapidly applied in industry.

The basic assumption underpinning CF is that users who share similar interests will consume similar items. Therefore, a system using the CF method relies on other users who share similar preferences to the given user. How are the preferences of users expressed and collected? On one side, users gave product/service ratings, indicating how satisfied they were with their consumption. These ratings are known as explicit feedback. On the other side, users left viewing, clicking or purchasing history that the web server records as a log file or to a database. This information is collected as implicit feedback about user actions.

A classic scenario in CF is to predict a target user's ratings on his/her unconsumed items. As shown in Fig. 2.1 (a), a user-item rating matrix is a representative of explicit feedback containing five users u_1 to u_5 and six items v_1 to v_6. It suggests that user u_1 likes v_1 but does not like v_4. u_1 has no interaction with item v_3 and the rating value is missing for this item. As shown in Fig. 2.1 (b), a user-item indicator matrix is a representative of implicit feedback. The first line indicates that user u_1 has consumed items v_1, v_2, v_4 and v_5 but not v_3.

	v_1	v_2	v_3	v_4	v_5	v_6
u_1	5	2	-	1	3	?
u_2	4	3	2	-	2	2
u_3	5	1	-	1	3	1
u_4	1	-	4	5	3	5
u_5	3	4	5	3	2	2

	v_1	v_2	v_3	v_4	v_5	v_6
u_1	1	1	-	1	1	?
u_2	1	1	1	-	1	1
u_3	1	1	-	1	1	1
u_4	1	-	1	1	1	1
u_5	1	1	1	1	1	1

(a) A rating matrix with explicit feedback.   (b) A rating matrix with implicit feedback.

Fig. 2.1: An example of rating matrixes.

CF-based recommendation methods are classified into two types [Breese *et al.* (1998)]: memory-based CF and model-based CF. The example in Fig. 2.1 on explicit and implicit feedbacks will be used throughout Section 2.1.

2.1.1 *Memory-based CF*

Memory-based CF is an early generation of CF using heuristic algorithms to calculate similarity values between users or between items, and can be divided into two types: user-based CF and item-based CF.

Here in Fig. 2.2 we give an example to show the intuition behind the memory-based CF from both the user and the item side. Emma is the target user. From the user side, Emma has similar tastes to Angela. They have watched similar movies and have given these movies similar ratings. This implies Angela is a similar user of Emma. Emma did not watch the movie "Little Women", but Angela did, and she likes this movie. It is highly probable that Emma will like it too. From the item side, the movie "Downton Abbey" and the movie "Jane Eyre" have been rated by lots of users, all of whom gave the same rating. This implies that these two movies are very similar items. Therefore, there is a big chance that Emma will like the movie "Downton Abbey" as well.

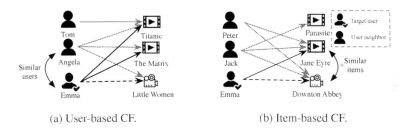

(a) User-based CF.   (b) Item-based CF.

Fig. 2.2: An example of CF.

Based on the above, both the user-based and the item-based CF share the basic assumption: similar users share similar preferences or similar items are preferred by similar users. The core part in the memory-CF is to find similar users or items through the nearest neighbor algorithm. Rating is then predicted through aggregation of similar users/items, and finally items are sorted according to their predicted ratings as a ranked list for the target user. The memory-based CF method is well accepted because of its simplicity, efficiency and ability to produce accurate results. Both user-based CF and item-based CF are implemented using similar steps: similarity calculation, rating prediction and top-K recommendation. But the first two steps are in different dimensions, just as the same user-based CF and item-based CF imply in user and item dimensions. We will introduce these two methods separately with examples in Fig. 2.1.

(1) User-based CF

In Fig. 2.1, we want to know whether recommending v_6 is appropriate for u_1 or not. We do not have the rating of u_1 currently, but we have other user's ratings on v_6. User u_3 is a user neighbor (similar user) with user u_1, as they have both gave v_1 and v_4 the same rating. The assumption of CF leads to the conclusion that u_1 may also give v_6 a similar rating as u_3. The rating prediction may not be accurate if we only use one user neighbor, but it will be more reliable if we use a set of user neighbors. This is also known as collective intelligence.

There are three steps in the user-based CF recommendation method. The first step is that the similarities between the target user and the other users are calculated to find the neighbors of the target user. Next, ratings are predicted with the help of user neighbors and then, finally, the top-K items are selected by ranking the rating predictions. The details are as follows:

Step 1: Calculate user similarities.

The historical records of the target user can help us to find other users who have similar preferences. The similarities between two users can be calculated based on their ratings on co-rated items (items that are rated by both users). This step is vital for the final accuracy of the recommendation. Different measuring methods can be applied in this step. In this part, cosine similarity and Pearson correlation coefficient (PCC) similarity will be used to calculate the similarities between users [Sarwar *et al.* (2001)]. Example is given on calculating similarity between u_1 and u_2.

Let the rating matrix be $\boldsymbol{R} \in \mathbb{R}^{M \times N}$, suggesting that M users and N items are in the matrix. Two users u_i and u_j can be represented by the ratings on each item in a vector. Cosine similarity is calculated as:

$$S_{u_i,u_j}^{cos} = \frac{\sum_{v \in \mathcal{V}_{u_i} \cap \mathcal{V}_{u_j}} r_{u_i,v} \times r_{u_j,v}}{\sqrt{\sum_{v \in \mathcal{V}_{u_i} \cap \mathcal{V}_{u_j}} r_{u_i,v}^2} \times \sqrt{\sum_{v \in \mathcal{V}_{u_i} \cap \mathcal{V}_{u_j}} r_{u_j,v}^2}} \tag{2.1}$$

where $\mathcal{V}_{u_i}$ is the item set rated by user u_i, and $\mathcal{V}_{u_j}$ is the item set rated by user u_j. $\mathcal{V}_{u_i} \cap \mathcal{V}_{u_j}$ represents items that are co-rated by u_i and u_j. $r_{u_i,v}$ and $r_{u_j,v}$ are the ratings of user u_i and user u_j on item v respectively.

We give a detailed example of user similarity calculation of u_1 and u_2 in Fig. 2.1. First we need to clarify that only when users have rated v_6, they can be helpful in rating prediction of u_1 on v_6. If u_2 did not rate v_6, then there is no need to calculate the similarity of u_1 and u_2. If an item has been rated only by one of the users, it has no contribution on numerator in Eq. (2.1). The user vectors in this calculation are $u_1 = (5, 2, 3)$ and $u_2 = (4, 3, 2)$. According to Eq. (2.1), the similarity between u_1 and u_2 is:

$$
\begin{aligned}
S_{u_1,u_2}^{cos} &= \frac{\sum_{v \in \mathcal{V}_{u_1} \cap \mathcal{V}_{u_2}} r_{u_1,v} \times r_{u_2,v}}{\sqrt{\sum_{v \in \mathcal{V}_{u_1} \cap \mathcal{V}_{u_2}} r_{u_1,v}^2} \times \sqrt{\sum_{v \in \mathcal{V}_{u_1} \cap \mathcal{V}_{u_2}} r_{u_2,v}^2}} \\
&= \frac{5 \times 4 + 2 \times 3 + 3 \times 2}{\sqrt{5^2 + 2^2 + 3^2} \times \sqrt{4^2 + 3^2 + 2^2}} \\
&= 0.9640.
\end{aligned}
$$

The cosine similarity of the target user u_1 with other users are shown in Table 2.1. Cosine similarity has its shortcomings because it fails to take into consideration the differences in means and variances between users' rating scales. This is considered in PCC, a more popular measurement method. Both similarity calculation methods have their own application scenarios. The PCC similarity between two users u_i and u_j is calculated by:

$$
S_{u_i,u_j}^{PCC} = \frac{\sum_{v \in \mathcal{V}_{u_i} \cap \mathcal{V}_{u_j}} (r_{u_i,v} - \bar{r}_{u_i}) \times (r_{u_j,v} - \bar{r}_{u_j})}{\sqrt{\sum_{v \in \mathcal{V}_{u_i} \cap \mathcal{V}_{u_j}} (r_{u_i,v} - \bar{r}_{u_i})^2} \times \sqrt{\sum_{v \in \mathcal{V}_{u_i} \cap \mathcal{V}_{u_j}} (r_{u_j,v} - \bar{r}_{u_j})^2}} \tag{2.2}
$$

where $\mathcal{V}_{u_i}$ and $\mathcal{V}_{u_j}$ are the item sets that are rated by users u_i and u_j, $\mathcal{V}_{u_i} \cap \mathcal{V}_{u_j}$ represents items that are co-rated by user u_i and user u_j together. $\bar{r}_{u_i}$ and $\bar{r}_{u_j}$ are the average ratings of user u_i and user u_j on all the items in $\mathcal{V}_{u_i} \cap \mathcal{V}_{u_j}$, respectively.

Similar to cosine similarity, only co-rated items contribute to the PCC similarity calculation. The average rating of each user is then calculated on the co-rated items of the user pairs. They have co-rated items v_1, v_2 and v_5. The user vectors in this calculation are $u_1 = [5, 2, 3]$ and $u_2 = [4, 3, 2]$. According to Eq. (2.2), the similarity of u_1 and u_2 is:

$$
\begin{aligned}
S_{u_1,u_2}^{PCC} &= \frac{\sum_{v \in \mathcal{V}_{u_1} \cap \mathcal{V}_{u_2}} (r_{u_1,v} - \bar{r}_{u_1}) \times (r_{u_2,v} - \bar{r}_{u_2})}{\sqrt{\sum_{v \in \mathcal{V}_{u_1} \cap \mathcal{V}_{u_2}} (r_{u_1,v} - \bar{r}_{u_1})^2} \times \sqrt{\sum_{v \in \mathcal{V}_{u_1} \cap \mathcal{V}_{u_2}} (r_{u_2,v} - \bar{r}_{u_2})^2}} \\
&= \frac{(5 - 3.33) \times (4 - 3) + (2 - 3.33) \times (3 - 3) + (3 - 3.33) \times (2 - 3)}{\sqrt{(5 - 3.33)^2 + (2 - 3.33)^2 + (3 - 3.33)^2} \times \sqrt{(4 - 3)^2 + (3 - 3)^2 + (2 - 3)^2}} \\
&= 0.6547.
\end{aligned}
$$

PCC similarities of the target user u_1 with other users are shown in Table 2.1.

Step 2: Rating prediction.

After the user-user similarity matrix is calculated, the rating of a target user on a specific item can be predicted. In user-based CF with a cosine similarity, the

Table 2.1: User cosine similarity between each user and target user u_1.

	u_1	u_2	u_3	u_4	u_5
u_1 Cosine similarity	1	0.9640	0.9875	0.5429	0.8312
u_1 PCC similarity	1	0.6547	0.9683	-1.0000	-0.2390

prediction $\hat{r}_{u_i,v}$ of user u_i on item v is:

$$\hat{r}_{u_i,v} = \frac{\sum_{u_j \in \mathcal{U}_v} r_{u_j,v} \times S_{u_i,u_j}}{\sum_{u_j \in \mathcal{U}_v} |S_{u_i,u_j}|} \quad (2.3)$$

In user-based CF with a PCC similarity, the prediction $\hat{r}_{u_i,v}$ of user u_i on item v is:

$$\hat{r}_{u_i,v} = \bar{r}_{u_i} + \frac{\sum_{u_j \in \mathcal{U}_v} (r_{u_j,v} - \bar{r}_{u_j}) \times S_{u_i,u_j}}{\sum_{u_j \in \mathcal{U}_v} |S_{u_i,u_j}|} \quad (2.4)$$

where S_{u_i,u_j} is the similarity between target user u_i and another user u_j, and $\mathcal{U}_v$ is the user set consisting of all the users who have rated item v.

For a detailed example in Fig. 2.1, the rating prediction of u_1 on v_6 on user-based cosine similarity is:

$$\hat{r}^{cos}_{u_1,v_6} \quad \frac{\sum_{u_j \in \mathcal{U}_{v_6}} r_{u_j,v_6} \times S_{u_1,u_j}}{\sum_{u_j \in \mathcal{U}_{v_6}} |S_{u_1,u_j}|}$$

$$= \frac{2 \times 0.9640 + 1 \times 0.9875 + 4 \times 0.5429 + 2 \times 0.8312}{0.9640 + 0.9875 + 0.5429 + 0.8312}$$

$$= 2.0295.$$

The rating prediction of u_1 on v_6 on user-based PCC similarity is:

$$\hat{r}^{PCC}_{u_1,v_6} = \bar{r}_{u_1} + \frac{\sum_{u_j \in \mathcal{U}_{v_6}} (r_{u_j,v_6} - \bar{r}_{u_j}) \times S_{u_1,u_j}}{\sum_{u_j \in \mathcal{U}_{v_6}} |S_{u_1,u_j}|}$$

$$= 2.75 + \frac{\begin{array}{c}(2 - 2.75) \times 0.6547 + (1 - 2.5) \times 0.9683 + \\ (4 - 3.25) \times (-1) + (2 - 3.4) \times (-0.2390)\end{array}}{0.6547 + 0.9683 + 1 + 0.2390}$$

$$= 1.9258.$$

The rating predictions on both similarities are similar and how to evaluate which is better is introduced in Section 2.6. In this example, each user who has rated the target item is included in the rating prediction. That is, we have used every neighbor of the target user in the user-set to predict ratings. There are two problems that using each user's data may cause: (1) If the user-set is large, say 10,000 users, the computation is expensive; and (2) If some users' similarities with the target user are very low, the contribution of those users are limited and may mislead the prediction. To solve these two problems noted, the number of neighbors is set to a prefixed number or a threshold for the similarity is set.

Step 3: Top-K recommendation.

After ratings are predicted for target users, the recommendation is given by ranking the predicted ratings of items that users have never purchased before. The rating predictions are sorted in decreasing order and the Top-K items are chosen to form the recommendation list.

(2) Item-based CF

Item-based CF, for easy understanding, can be treated as a transposed version of user-based CF. In an ideal scenario where the rating matrix is full, the two methods are the same. In the following part, we only give the PCC similarity and omit cosine similarity because item-based CF is very similar to user-based CF. Similar to user-based CF, item-based CF has three main steps.

Step 1: Calculate item similarities.

With the previous notations in user-based CF, the PCC similarity between two items v_i and v_j is:

$$S_{v_i,v_j}^{PCC} = \frac{\sum_{u \in \mathcal{U}_{v_i} \cap \mathcal{U}_{v_j}} (r_{u,v_i} - \bar{r}_{v_i}) \times (r_{u,v_j} - \bar{r}_{v_j})}{\sqrt{\sum_{u \in \mathcal{U}_{v_i} \cap \mathcal{U}_{v_j}} (r_{u,v_i} - \bar{r}_u)^2} \times \sqrt{\sum_{u \in \mathcal{U}_{v_i} \cap \mathcal{U}_{v_j}} (r_{u,v_j} - \bar{r}_{v_j})^2}} \quad (2.5)$$

where $\mathcal{U}_{v_i}$ and $\mathcal{U}_{v_j}$ are the user sets who rated items v_i and v_j. $\mathcal{U}_{v_i} \cap \mathcal{U}_{v_j}$ represents users who have co-rated item v_i and item v_j together. $\bar{r}_{v_i}$ and $\bar{r}_{v_j}$ are the average ratings of item v_i and item v_j rated by all the users in $\mathcal{U}_{v_i} \cap \mathcal{U}_{v_j}$ respectively.

We give a detailed example of item similarity calculation between v_6 and v_1 in Fig. 2.1. The item vectors in this calculation are $v_6 = [2, 1, 4, 3]$ and $v_1 = [4, 5, 1, 3]$. According to Eq. (2.5), the similarity of v_1 and v_6 is:

$$
\begin{aligned}
S_{v_1,v_6}^{PCC} &= \frac{\sum_{u \in \mathcal{U}_{v_1} \cap \mathcal{U}_{v_6}} (r_{u,v_1} - \bar{r}_{v_1}) \times (r_{u,v_6} - \bar{r}_{v_6})}{\sqrt{\sum_{u \in \mathcal{U}_{v_1} \cap \mathcal{U}_{v_6}} (r_{u,v_1} - \bar{r}_u)^2} \times \sqrt{\sum_{u \in \mathcal{U}_{v_1} \cap \mathcal{U}_{v_6}} (r_{u,v_6} - \bar{r}_{v_6})^2}} \\
&= \frac{\begin{array}{c}(4 - 3.25) \times (2 - 2.25) + (5 - 3.25) \times (1 - 2.25) \\ + (1 - 3.25) \times (4 - 2.25) + (3 - 3.25) \times (2 - 2.25)\end{array}}{\begin{array}{c}\sqrt{(4 - 3.25)^2 + (5 - 3.25)^2 + (1 - 3.25)^2 + (3 - 3.25)^2} \\ \times \sqrt{(2 - 2.25)^2 + (1 - 2.25)^2 + (4 - 2.25)^2 + (2 - 2.25)^2}\end{array}} \\
&= -0.9695.
\end{aligned}
$$

PCC similarities of the target item v_6 with other items are shown in Table 2.2. Note that the similarity between v_3 and v_6 is not calculated here because v_3 was not rated by u_1. And it is not helpful on the prediction of u_1 rating on v_6.

Table 2.2: User PCC similarity between each item and target item v_6.

	v_1	v_2	v_3	v_4	v_5	v_6
v_6	-0.9695	0.9449	$-$	0.9820	0.2294	1

Step 2: Rating prediction.

After the item-item similarity matrix is calculated, the rating of a target user on a specific item can be predicted depending on the neighbors of the target item. In item-based CF with a PCC similarity, the prediction $\hat{r}_{u,v_i}$ of user u on item v_i is calculated as:

$$\hat{r}^{PCC}_{u,v_i} = \bar{r}_{v_i} + \frac{\sum_{v_j \in \mathcal{V}_u} (r_{u,v_j} - \bar{r}_{v_j}) \times S_{v_i,v_j}}{\sum_{v_j \in \mathcal{V}_u} |S_{v_i,v_j}|} \qquad (2.6)$$

where $\mathcal{V}_u$ is the item set containing all the other items that user u has rated, and S_{v_i,v_j} is the similarity between target item v_i and another item v_j whose rating is known.

For a detailed example in Fig. 2.1, the rating prediction of u_1 on v_6 on item-based PCC similarity is:

$$
\begin{aligned}
\hat{r}^{PCC}_{u_1,v_6} &= \bar{r}_{v_6} + \frac{\sum_{v_j \in \mathcal{V}_{u_1}} (r_{u_1,v_j} - \bar{r}_{v_j}) \times S_{v_6,v_j}}{\sum_{v_j \in \mathcal{V}_{u_1}} |S_{v_6,v_j}|} \\
&= 2.25 + \frac{\begin{array}{c}(5 - 3.25) \times (-0.9695) + (2 - 2.6667) \times 0.9449 \\ + (1 - 3) \times 0.9820 + (1 - 3) \times 0.2294\end{array}}{0.9695 + 0.9449 + 0.9820 + 0.2294} \\
&= 2.1167.
\end{aligned}
$$

Step 3: Top-K recommendation.

After ratings are predicted, the calculation of the item-based CF will be the same as user-based CF. In general, the item-based CF method is more scalable, since the items stay in the market for longer time and are comparatively stable than users.

Here, two similarity measurements are presented in memory-based CF, cosine similarity and PCC similarity. Other measurements can also be chosen such as Euclidean distance and Jaccard coefficient. Cosine similarity places emphasis on the angels between two vectors but ignores the length of vectors. In comparison, PCC is more widely used since it considers the impact of the rating average. Similar to PCC, adjusted cosine similarity is proposed as another measurement option [Sarwar *et al.* (2001)]. For cosine similarity, the value ranges in $[0, 1]$ where $S = 1$ represents strong correlation between two vectors and $S = 0$ represents no correlation between two vectors. For PCC similarity, the value ranges in $[-1, 1]$ where $S = 1$ and $S = 0$ have the same meaning as cosine similarity. But $S = -1$ means that two vectors are negatively correlated. Obviously, if $S = 0$, it means two vectors are not correlated and they are not helpful for rating prediction. But for both positive and negative correlation, they are useful for the rating prediction.

2.1.2 Model-based CF

The model-based CF method builds a model to predict a user's rating on items using machine learning or data mining methods rather than the heuristic methods, which were discussed in Section 2.1.1. In addition to the user-item rating matrix, other side information such as user locations, user contributed tags, social network and item contents, can be used. Matrix factorization is the most widely used technique in the model-based CF due to its high accuracy, and it is very easy to combine side information with matrix factorization. In this section, we focus on the matrix factorization-based recommendation methods. As we mentioned at the start of this section, feedbacks of users on items are divided into explicit ratings and implicit feedback. We will introduce matrix factorization on both kinds.

(1) Matrix factorization on explicit feedback

Matrix factorization was first used in recommendation methods as probabilistic latent semantic analysis (pLSA), which is also known as latent factor models [Paterek (2007)] or singular value decomposition (SVD) [Koren *et al.* (2009)]. Matrix factorization emanated from the Netflix Prize competition. It projects both user space and item space onto the same latent factor space so that they are comparable.

A typical matrix factorization method involves two matrixes: one is a user latent matrix $U \in \mathbb{R}^{M \times K}$ and the other is an item latent matrix $V \in \mathbb{R}^{N \times K}$, where K is a relatively smaller number compared with the number of users M and the number of items N. The matrix factorization form is to predict ratings in user-item rating matrix R with multiplication of latent matrixes, as $\hat{R} = UV^T$. Specifically, for a prediction $\hat{r}_{u_i, v_j}$, user latent vector is u_i as the i-th row in U and item latent vector is v_j as the j-th row in V.

$$U = \begin{bmatrix} - & u_1 & - \\ & \vdots & \\ - & u_M & - \end{bmatrix}, V = \begin{bmatrix} - & v_1 & - \\ & \vdots & \\ - & v_N & - \end{bmatrix}.$$

The rating prediction is the inner product between the user and item latent vectors as $\hat{r}_{u_i, v_j} = u_i v_j^T$. The prediction can be improved by adding the average rating and the user/item bias. For a rating matrix in one recommender system, there exists some preference tendency in the whole data set as well as for users and items. Some users tend to give higher ratings and some items tend to receive higher ratings. This phenomenon may affect the fitting of the matrix factorization; therefore, it will be adjusted by bias factors first to eliminate the floating on the average. We denote the overall rating average as $\bar{r}$, user bias as b_{u_i} and item bias as b_{v_j}. For example, the overall rating average is 3.5. For the user Emily, a critical user who tends to give a lower rating on movies she has seen, the user bias is 0.3. The movie "The Godfather" is a very popular and famous movie and the item bias for this movie is 0.8. As a result, the average of Emily's rating on "The Godfather" is $3.5 - 0.3 + 0.8 = 4.0$. User bias and item bias are two parameters for each user and item. Together with the user latent vector and item latent vector, we have:

$$\hat{r}_{u_i,v_j} = \bar{r} + b_{u_i} + b_{v_j} + \boldsymbol{u}_i \boldsymbol{v}_j^T \tag{2.7}$$

where $\hat{r}_{u_i,v_j}$ is the predicted rating of user u_i on item v_j, $\bar{r}$ is the overall rating average, b_{u_i} is the user bias for user u_i, b_{v_j} is the item bias for item v_j, $\boldsymbol{u}_i$ is the user latent vector and $\boldsymbol{v}_j$ is the item latent vector. A user latent vector $\boldsymbol{u}_i$ and a user bias b_{u_i} need to be trained for user u_i. Also, an item latent vector $\boldsymbol{v}_j$ and an item bias b_{v_j} need to be trained for item v_j. The goal of matrix factorization is to complete the rating matrix $\boldsymbol{R}$. The matrix completion forms an optimization problem:

$$min \sum_{r_{u_i,v_j} \neq 0} (r_{u_i,v_j} - \hat{r}_{u_i,v_j})^2 + \lambda \mathcal{R}(\hat{r}_{u_i,v_j}) \tag{2.8}$$

where $\mathcal{R}(\hat{r}_{u_i,v_j})$ is the regularization of the parameters, and λ is the parameter that controls how much the regularization affects the optimization.

To solve the optimization problem, we can use stochastic gradient descent. Suppose for each rating, the error is $e_{u_i,v_j} = \hat{r}_{u_i,v_j} - r_{u_i,v_j}$. We update the parameters with learning rate η in the opposite direction of the gradient as:

$$b_{u_i} = b_{u_i} - \eta(e_{u_i,v_j} + \lambda \cdot b_{u_i})$$
$$b_{v_j} = b_{v_j} - \eta(e_{u_i,v_j} + \lambda \cdot b_{v_j})$$
$$\boldsymbol{u}_i = \boldsymbol{u}_i - \eta(e_{u_i,v_j} \cdot \boldsymbol{v}_j + \lambda \cdot \boldsymbol{u}_i)$$
$$\boldsymbol{v}_j = \boldsymbol{v}_j - \eta(e_{u_i,v_j} \cdot \boldsymbol{u}_i + \lambda \cdot \boldsymbol{v}_j).$$

With the above parameters learned, the ratings can be predicted by Eq. (2.7) and top-K recommendation can be generated.

(2) Matrix factorization on implicit feedback

Instead of explicit ratings in Fig. 2.1 (a), only $0, 1$ values are available in the rating matrix for implicit feedback as shown in Fig. 2.1 (b). The prediction can be treated as a binary classification problem. Many machine learning methods, such as support vector machines, are capable of discriminating the data into two classes and achieving high accuracy. But these methods fail to provide a good solution for recommendation on implicit feedback. This is because only data in positive class (where rating values is 1) are available. If the user u_1 has not clicked the item v_2, where $r_{1,2} = 0$ in the rating matrix, it may be either that u_1 "dislikes" the item v_2 or u_1 has not seen it before. In this section, we introduce a classic method for implicit feedback, Bayesian personalized ranking (BPR) [Rendle *et al.* (2009)].

The training of BPR is based on pair-wise ranking optimization criterion. The assumption is that for each user, the observed item (with value 1) is preferred to the unobserved item (with value 0). For example, as shown in Fig. 2.1, user u_1 has observed v_1, v_2, v_4, v_5. For two items v_1 and v_3, u_1 will prefer item v_1 to v_3. But for two items v_1 and v_2, we do not know the preference of user u_1. For a user u, if u prefers item v_i to v_j, we formally represent it as $v_i >_u v_j$. For user u, the item set the u has observed is $\mathcal{V}_u^+$ and not observed is $\mathcal{V}_u^-$. If $v_i \in \mathcal{V}_u^+$ and $v_j \in \mathcal{V}_u^-$, then $v_i >_u v_j$.

Usually, negative items are not given in the dataset. For one observed item v_i in the dataset, all the unobserved items can formulate a pair as $v_i >_u v_j$. Then, the model is trained on the dataset $T = \{(u, v_i, v_j) | u \in \mathcal{U}, v_i >_u v_j\}$. There are two drawbacks to using all the combinations of pairs: (1) The training set will be excessive on the whole combination of observed and unobserved pair; and (2) The unobserved items contain those items that users are interested in but have not found yet, so treating all of them as negative items is not reasonable. If one item is treated as a negative sample and is used to train the model in multiple pairs, this item will not be recommended to any users. In such case, negative sampling strategies are applied to balance the impact that users may be interested in unobserved items but did not have the time to discover them. Model parameters are updated slightly by one sample compared with millions or billions of training samples. Therefore, random sampling on negative items can alleviate the impact on training the model. For each item pair $v_i >_u v_j$, the negative item v_j is randomly selected from the unobserved items of user u.

Each user has an ideal item ranking list which is unavailable because the user cannot consume or view each item in the item set. The ideal user ranking list for user u is $Ranking(u) : v_a > \cdots > v_b$. The target of the recommendation method is to maximize the posterior probability of the ideal ranking list:

$$p\big(\Theta|Ranking(u)\big) \propto p\big(Ranking(u)|\Theta\big)p(\Theta)$$

where Θ represents the parameters of this method to predict the ranking scores of this user on items (for example, matrix factorization). The training set for all users is $T = \{(u, v_i, v_j)|u \in \mathcal{U}, v_i >_u v_j\}$. The user-specific likelihood can be written as a combination of item-pairs according to whether these items are observed or not, and it can be easily expanded to a combination of all users in user set:

$$\prod_{u\in\mathcal{U}} p\big(Ranking(u)|\Theta\big) = \prod_{(u,v_i,v_j)\in T} p(v_i >_u v_j|\Theta). \qquad (2.9)$$

In BPR model, the probability that a user u prefers item v_i to v_j is specifically calculated as:

$$p(v_i >_u v_j|\Theta) = \sigma(\hat{x}_{u,v_i,v_j}(\Theta)) \qquad (2.10)$$

where σ is the sigmoid function $\sigma(x) = \frac{1}{1+e^{-x}}$, $\hat{x}_{u,v_i,v_j}(\Theta)$ is a function with model parameters Θ to represent the relationship of user u prefer item v_i to v_j.

Usually, $\hat{x}_{u,v_i,v_j}(\Theta)$ is defined as $\hat{x}_{u,v_i,v_j}(\Theta) = \hat{x}_{u,v_i}(\Theta) - \hat{x}_{u,v_j}(\Theta)$. $\hat{x}_{u,v_i}(\Theta)$ and $\hat{x}_{u,v_j}(\Theta)$ are predicted ranking scores of user u on items v_i and v_j. These predictions can be made through any rating prediction methods such as matrix factorization. The argument Θ in $\hat{x}_{u,v_i,v_j}(\Theta)$ will be omitted in the following part for simplicity.

For the prior density $p(\Theta)$, generally, it is assumed to be standard normal distribution as:

$$p(\Theta) \sim N(0, \sigma_\Theta)$$

where $\sigma_\Theta = \lambda_\Theta I$ for simplicity, and λ_Θ is the regularization parameter.

The maximum posterior estimator for the ideal item ranking list is:

$$
\begin{aligned}
E &= \ln \prod_{u\in\mathcal{U}} p\big(Ranking(u)|\Theta\big)p(\Theta) \\
&= \ln \prod_{(u,v_i,v_j)\in T} p(v_i >_u v_j|\Theta)p(\Theta) \\
&= \ln \prod_{(u,v_i,v_j)\in T} \sigma(\hat{x}_{u,v_i,v_j})p(\Theta) \\
&= \sum_{(u,v_i,v_j)\in T} \ln \sigma(\hat{x}_{u,v_i,v_j}) + \ln p(\Theta) \\
&= \sum_{(u,v_i,v_j)\in T} \ln \sigma(\hat{x}_{u,v_i,v_j}) - \lambda_\Theta ||\Theta||_2.
\end{aligned}
$$

To solve the maximum optimization, stochastic gradient decent is used over each $(u, v_i, v_j) \in T$ updating Θ by $\Theta \leftarrow \Theta + \eta \frac{\partial E}{\partial \Theta}$, specifically as:

$$\Theta \leftarrow \Theta + \eta (\frac{1}{1 + e^{\hat{x}_{u,v_i,v_j}}} \cdot \frac{\partial}{\partial \Theta} \hat{x}_{u,v_i,v_j} - \lambda_\Theta \cdot \Theta) \qquad (2.11)$$

where η is the learning rate.

There are three advantages of matrix factorization that contribute to its popularity. Firstly, the dimension of the user-item rating matrix can be reduced significantly, so the scalability of the system employing matrix factorization is secured. Secondly, users who only have a few ratings can acquire relatively more accurate recommendation through matrix factorization, which is a significant improvement compared with memory-based methods. Thirdly, matrix factorization is highly suitable for integrating various side information. This helps to profile user preferences and improves the performance of recommendation methods. We will give more methods on extending matrix factorization with side information in Chapter 4.

2.2 Content-based Recommendation Methods

Content-based recommendation methods are dependent on the user's own historical records and independent of other users, making it different from the CF-based recommendation methods. As the name suggests, content-based recommendation methods aim to recommend items whose contents are similar to those in which a specific user was interested in previously [Shardanand and Maes (1995)]. The content-based recommendation methods derive from information retrieval and focus on items with text information such as documents, news or Web pages. For example, users who liked articles that have discussed "recommender systems" and "database" will prefer articles with the same topics.

The basic steps of content-based recommendation methods are: (1) To represent items with attributes and features that are important and discriminative; (2) To analyze the description of the items preferred by a particular user to determine the principal common attributes (preferences) that can be used to distinguish these items. These preferences are stored in a user profile; and (3) To compare each item's attributes with the user profile so that only items that have a high degree of similarity with the user profile will be recommended.

(1) Learning item content representation

Different item properties are extracted from documents and descriptions. These properties are referred to as "attributes", "characteristics", "fields" or "variables".

For instance, a movie can be represented by attributes such as genres, directors, writers, actors, storyline, *etc.* In document recommendation, vector space model is used for representing items with words. Rather than using the whole set of words in the corpus, stop words are removed and stemming is recommended. Another way is to use keywords in the documents instead of whole word sets. For each word, there are many different ways to determine its weights, among which is the well-known term frequency-inverse document frequency (TF-IDF) [Salton and Buckley (1988)]. The frequency of one term t in document d is $f_{t,d}$, calculated by the raw count of term t in d divided by the total number of words of d as:

$$\text{TF}_{t,d} = \frac{f_{t,d}}{\sum_{t \in d} f_{t,d}}.$$

The inverse document frequency is to measure how much information the word provides in the corpus D. It represents whether the word is common or rare; whether the word is useful to distinguish the document to be relevant or not. It is defined as:

$$\text{IDF}_{t,D} = \ln \frac{|D|}{n_t}$$

where $|D|$ is the total number of documents in the corpus D, n_t is the number of documents that contains term t. The TF-IDF is the multiplication of the above two terms. The weight of term t in document d of corpus D is:

$$w_{t,d} = \text{TF}_{t,d} \times \text{IDF}_{t,D}.$$

The document d_i is represented as $\text{Content}(d_i) = (w_{1,d_i}, w_{2,d_i})$. As shown in Table 2.3, we give an example of word count in documents and the five documents form a corpus. The weight of each word is in Table 2.4. The document content profile is built on word weight. Item v_1 has content profile: $\text{Content}(v_1) = (0, 0.2061, 0, 0, 0, 0, 0, 0.0021, 0, 0)$.

Table 2.3: An example of word count for documents.

	t_1	t_2	t_3	t_4	t_5	t_6	t_7	t_8	t_9	t_{10}	total
v_1	5	230	0	0	10	0	0	1	3	0	249
v_2	4	35	2	0	2	0	0	0	90	80	213
v_3	5	150	0	1	50	1	1	0	1	1	210
v_4	1	0	0	5	35	4	3	100	5	70	223
v_5	3	4	0	3	30	22	2	200	10	2	276

Table 2.4: An example of item content profile.

	t_1	t_2	t_3	t_4	t_5	t_6	t_7	t_8	t_9	t_{10}
v_1	0	0.2061	0	0	0	0	0	0.0021	0	0
v_2	0	0.0367	0.0151	0	0	0	0	0	0	0.0838
v_3	0	0.1596	0	0	0	0.0024	0.0024	0	0	0.0011
v_4	0	0	0	0	0	0.0092	0.0069	0.2291	0	0.0700
v_5	0	0.0032	0	0	0	0.0407	0.0037	0.3702	0	0.0016

(2) Establishing user profile

To build a user profile Content(u) in the same form as the item profile, we need to map the user preference to a word vector or whatever the item profile representation is. User profile is built based on whether the user has liked the item or not. For implicit ratings, if the user has viewed items v_1 and v_2, a simple strategy to profile the user is an aggregation as Content(v_1) + Content(v_2). For explicit ratings, the preference can simply be as if rating is above the average and dislike below. For example, we can build profile of user u_1 as a combination of Content(v_1) and Content(v_5) in Table 2.4 as u_1 has rated them no less than 3.

(3) Filtering and recommendation

With established user profile, the recommendation method calculates the similarity between item profile and user profile to find the most relevant items and form the recommendation list. Content-based recommendation is a filtering and matching process between the item representation and the user profile. The similarity calculation can be either cosine similarity like Eq. (2.1) or other measurements. Items are ranked through these similarities and then a final recommendation list is generated. The performance of recommendation methods is dependent on the accuracy of the item's representation and the user's profile.

Also, it is possible to provide recommendation without user profile establishment. One way is to consider the item profile built in Step 1 as features, and the like or dislike of the user as labels. We can build an item classification model on each user. The other way is to calculate the similarities between the unrated items and the rated items on the item profile. Then the rating prediction is similar to the item-based CF method, with the difference that item-based CF uses item ratings to calculate the item similarity while the content-based method uses item profiles.

2.3 Knowledge-based Recommendation Methods

Knowledge-based recommendation methods are not commonly reported in literature, but they are very important for some specific domains. CF and content-based
methods are suitable for items that are repetitively consumed and items whose
attributes are usually constant.   Knowledge-based recommendation methods
take advantage of user preference inference from user history records and user
requirements. For example, when considering buying a car, it is very hard to
collect ratings from customers and then build recommender system on the ratings.
The characteristics of cars are very complex, ranging from a car's capacity, the
fuel usage of the car, the appearance design of the car to price and insurance
costs. CF and content-based methods are not capable of handling all these item
characters, let alone the requirements of users they potentially should consider.
Domains like cars, properties, computers or phones are suitable for knowledge-
based recommendation methods, as one or several characteristics below are likely
to apply:

(1) Users do not consume items frequently;
(2) The content or features of the items are complex, or domain knowledge is
     very important;
(3) Users raise specific requirements during recommendations.

   Knowledge-based recommendation methods offer items to users based on
knowledge about the users and items. Usually, a knowledge-based recommender
system retains a functional knowledge base that describes how a particular item
meets a specific user's requirements, which can be performed based on inferences
about the relationship between a user's need and a possible recommendation.
   CBR is a common example of knowledge-based recommendation methods
[Brusilovski *et al.* (2007)]. CBR systems rely on the idea of using the past
problem-solving experiences as a primary source to solve a new problem. It is
represented by a four-step (4Rs) cycle: retrieve, reuse, revise and retain. The past
problem solutions are stored in a database as cases, and each case is typically made
up of two parts: the specification part and the solution part. The specification part
describes the problem at hand, whereas the solution part describes the solution
that was used to solve the problem. A new problem is solved by retrieving a
case with similar specifications to the current problem and then fitting the attained
solution to match the current problem. Case-based recommendation methods
represent items as cases and generate the recommendations by retrieving the most
similar cases to the user's query or profile. In these systems, items are described

in terms of a well-defined set of features (e.g., price, color, make). Case-based recommendation methods borrow heavily from the core concepts of retrieval and similarity in CBR.

The case-based recommendation methods can be seen as a special type of content-based recommendation methods. There are two important ways in which case-based recommendation methods can be distinguished from other types of content-based recommendation methods: (1) the manner in which products are represented; and (2) the way in which product similarity is assessed. Case-based recommendation methods rely on structured representations of item content, which is often called semantic knowledge. The semantic knowledge about items consists of the attributes of the items, the relation between items, and the relation between items and the meta-information. Taxonomies and ontologies, as the major source of semantic information, can be taken advantage of in recommender systems, since they provide a means of discovering and classifying new information about the items to recommend, user profiles and even the context of use. For example, product taxonomies have been presented in several recommender systems to utilize the relevant semantic information to improve recommendation quality. In a business environment, product categories are used to evaluate the semantic similarity between businesses [Shambour and Lu (2012)].

The second important distinguishing feature of case-based recommendation methods relates to their use of various sophisticated approaches to similarity measurement when it comes to judging which cases to retrieve in response to a user query. An ontology is a conceptualization of a domain into a format that is understandable to humans, but at the same time is a machine-readable format consisting of entities, attributes, relationships and axioms. Ontology, as a formal knowledge representation method, represents the domain concepts and the relationships between those concepts. It has been used to express domain knowledge in recommender systems. The semantic similarity between items can be calculated based on the domain ontology. Ontology-based recommendation methods, which are typical knowledge-based recommendation methods, classify items using ontological classes, represent user profiles in terms of ontological terms, use ontological inference to improve user profiling, and use ontological knowledge to bootstrap a recommender system and support profile visualization to improve profiling accuracy. The semantic similarity between items can be calculated based on the domain ontology. The usage of the semantic information can provide additional explanation about why particular items have or have not been recommended, and provide better recommendation effectiveness than current CF methods, particularly in cases where little or no rating information is available.

The knowledge-based recommendation method is of great application value, especially for house sales, financial services or health decision support. These services are characterized by their specific domain knowledge and the unique situation of each case.

2.4 Hybrid Recommendation Methods

All the methods introduced above are summarized in Table 2.5. To achieve higher performance and overcome the drawbacks of each recommendation method, a hybrid recommendation method that combines the best features of two or more recommendation methods into one has been proposed. Two or more methods can be combined to overcome the limitation of any individual one, and the most common practice within the existing hybrid recommendation methods is to combine the CF recommendation with the others. According to [Burke (2002)], there are seven basic hybridization mechanisms of different recommendation method combinations.

(1) Weighted: scores of each of the recommendation methods are combined numerically to produce a new prediction;
(2) Mixed: results from different recommendation methods are presented together, either in a separated presentation or combined in one list;
(3) Switching: one of the recommendation methods is selected to make the prediction when certain criteria are met using decision criteria;
(4) Feature combination: a single prediction algorithm is provided with features from different recommendation methods;
(5) Feature augmentation: the output from one recommendation method is fed to another;
(6) Cascade: one recommendation method refines another recommendation method;
(7) Meta-level: the entire model produced by one recommendation method is used by another.

2.5 Comparison of Recommendation Methods

There are five issues in recommendation methods, which first we list here and then identify with each of the different methods:

(1) Cold start: For a new user or a new item, there isn't enough data to make accurate recommendations.

(2) Scalability: In some environments in which a recommender system makes recommendations, there are millions of users and items. Thus, a large amount of computation power is often necessary to calculate recommendations.

(3) Sparsity: The most active users have only rated a small subset of the overall database. Thus, some items have very few ratings from users, even the most popular items.

(4) Serendipity: Recommended items are popular for every user or very similar to items a user usually consumes. The user is already familiar with the recommended items, therefore is unsatisfied with the recommender system.

(5) Transparency: If appropriate explanations are not given to users, the recommendation results make users worried about their privacy.

Compared with content-based methods, CF has its own advantages. Firstly, the content information is not always available with content-based methods. Without this limitation, CF-based recommendation methods have a wider application. Secondly, the CF-based recommendation methods are easily implemented. They can be applied to any online e-commerce website with a rating system. Thirdly, CF methods contribute to the serendipity of recommendation methods, which is the main reason that they are applied to websites such as Netflix or Amazon. This serendipity helps users to find items that are hidden in the long tail but very attractive to them, thus they support the user's decision making and improve the supplier's profits.

Although memory-based CF is well known for its easy implementation and relatively effective application in practice, it still has some not-so-insignificant drawbacks. Two of these include the fact that CF cannot deal with the inevitable cold start problem and the problem of data sparsity. Therefore, the coverage and accuracy of recommendation is limited. The third problem is scalability. The heuristic process takes a long time to give a recommendation result, especially when the dimension of the user-item rating matrix is high. This problem is partly solved by a pre-calculated and pre-stored weighting matrix in item-based CF. Model-based CF also suffers with scalability problem, as once the model is trained and stored, the only way to update it is to re-train it.

By comparison, content-based recommendation methods have several advantages. Firstly, content-based recommendation is based on item representation, so it is user independent. As a result, this kind of system does not suffer from the same data sparsity problem as CF-based recommendation methods, as discussed previously. Secondly, content-based recommendation methods are able to recommend new items to users, so the system can solve the new item cold start problem. Lastly, content-based recommendation methods can provide a clear explanation of the recommendation result. The transparency of this kind of system is a great advantage compared to other methods in real-world applications.

However, content-based recommendation methods also have several limitations. To begin with, although the new item problem can be solved or alleviated by using content-based recommendation methods, they suffer from the new user problem as a lack of user profile information can seriously affect the accuracy of the recommendation result. Furthermore, a content-based system will always choose similar items for users, leading to overspecialization in recommendation. A user tends to become bored with similar recommendation lists, since most users want to learn about new and fashionable items rather than being limited to items similar to those they have previously used or purchased. Finally, items sometimes cannot easily be represented in the specific form required by content-based recommendation methods. Therefore, this kind of system is more suitable for articles or news recommendation rather than movies or music.

The knowledge-based recommendation methods have some advantages when compared with both content-based and CF-based recommendation methods. As knowledge-based recommendation methods exploit deep knowledge about the product or service domain, they are able to support intelligent explanations and product recommendations, which are determined by a set of explicitly defined constraints [Felfernig *et al.* (2006)]. One advantage of knowledge-based recommendation methods is that the new item or user problem does not exist, since prior knowledge is acquired and stored in the knowledge base. A knowledge-based recommender system generates recommendations by computing the similarities between the existing cases and the user's request, so it doesn't require the user to rate or purchase many items in order to generate good recommendations. Another advantage is that the user can set up constraints on the recommendation result.

A knowledge-based recommendation method does, however, have some drawbacks too. It requires extensive effort to acquire, maintain and retain the knowledge or information about items and users for making recommendations. It also requires more feedback and involvement from a target user in order to make an appropriate recommendation for the user. The recommendations generated can be monotonous, because they already existed in the knowledge base as an old case. The recommendations generated by knowledge-based recommendation methods lack serendipity.

2.6   Evaluation in Recommendation Methods

Evaluation of recommendation methods is to assess the quality of recommendation methods with off-line data and to help to improve their performance before

Table 2.5: Comparison of recommendation methods.

Method	Basic Description	Representative Techniques	Advantages	Drawbacks
CF-based	Recommendations are based on other users who have similar tastes.	Memory-based: Neighbor-based CF Top-K CF Model-based: Latent factor model Graph-based CF Context-aware CF	1. No content needed 2. Easy implementation 3. Serendipity	1. cold start 2. Sparsity 3. Scalability
Content-based	Recommendations are based on the content of the item which the user preferred before.	Vector Space Model TF-IDF Bayes Network Decision Trees	1. User independent 2. New item can be recommended 3. Transparency	1. New user problem 2. Over-specialization 3. Content-dependent
Knowledge-based	Recommendations are based on user's needs and item's function.	CBR Ontology-based Semantic web	1. cold start 2. Reasonable recommendation that meet specific needs	1. Serendipity 2. Complex knowledge database management

they are running online. We have introduced off-line evaluation methods in this section and classified them in four types: metrics on prediction, metrics on classification, metrics on ranking and metrics on diversity. Metrics on prediction is for explicit feedback, and the other three are for implicit feedback.

2.6.1 *Metrics on prediction*

Some recommendation methods predict the missing ratings of a user to an unseen item, then rank all the candidate items according to the predictions. For these systems, it is necessary to evaluate whether the predicted ratings are accurate. If a recommendation method successfully predicts a rating for a user u on item v, and the predicted rating is denoted as $\hat{r}_{u,v}$, the deviation/error between $\hat{r}_{u,v}$ and the actual rating $r_{u,v}$ in the test set is used to evaluate the prediction accuracy of this recommendation method. Two widely used metrics mean absolute error (MAE) and root mean square error (RMSE) are introduced below:

$$\text{MAE} = \sum_{u,v,r_{u,v} \in Y} \frac{|\hat{r}_{u,v} - r_{u,v}|}{|Y|}$$

$$\text{RMSE} = \sqrt{\sum_{u,v,r_{u,v} \in Y} \frac{(\hat{r}_{u,v} - r_{u,v})^2}{|Y|}}$$

where r_{uv} and $\hat{r}_{uv}$ are the true and predicted ratings, Y is the test set and $|Y|$ is the number of the test set. The smaller the errors, the better the performance.

2.6.2   *Metrics on classification*

Before the ranked item list is generated, some recommendation methods can be understood as a classifier to guess the preferred or not-preferred items for a particular user in the test set. Thus, the classification evaluation metrics precision, recall and F1 are introduced in this section. The precision indicates the percentage of relevant items given in the recommendation list from the total recommended items. The recall indicates the percentage of relevant items given in the recommendation list from the total relevant items. Generally, precision is the fraction of the relevant items among the retrieved items while recall is the fraction of retrieved relevant items among the total relevant items. F1 is a combination of precision and recall, indicating a comprehensive performance.

Let the recommendation list be a top-K list and the recommendation list is denoted as X, the length of recommendation for each user is K, U_Y is the set containing users in the test set and $|U_Y|$ is the number of users in the test set. For user u in U_Y, the recommendation list generated for this user is X_u, and the ground truth for this user in test set is Y_u. The relevant items for user u is denoted as X_u^{rel} and $X_u^{rel} \subset X_u$. X_u^{rel} represents the predicted relevant items for user u. If the recommendation method predicts the numerical rating of the items, X_u^{rel} contains items whose predicted rating is higher than a threshold θ. If the recommendation method classifies the items, X_u^{rel} contains items in the class that is preferred by users. Besides Y_u^{rel} represents the actual relevant items for user u. Usually, it is items with positive rating in the test set Y_u.

$$\text{precision} = \frac{1}{|U_Y|} \sum_{u \in U_Y} \frac{|X_u^{rel}|}{|X_u|}$$

$$\text{recall} = \frac{1}{|U_Y|} \sum_{u \in U_Y} \frac{|X_u^{rel}|}{|Y_u^{rel}|}$$

$$\text{F1} = \frac{2 \times \text{precision} \times \text{recall}}{\text{precision} + \text{recall}}$$

The receiver operating characteristic (ROC) curve is well known in evaluation classification methods, which is a recall (true positive rate) against fallout (false positive rate) curve. A perfect ROC curve goes straight up towards 1.0 recall with 0.0 fallout and then straight right towards 1.0 fallout. In such case, the area under the curve (AUC) is 1. AUC is also used in recommendation to reflect the quality of the recommendation list [Schröder *et al.* (2011)]. For the perfect ROC curve, the recommender system retrieves all the relevant items for a user and leaves out all the irrelevant items. Usually in recommender systems, AUC is connected with the pair-wise learning-to-rank recommendation method. AUC is designed particularly for implicit feedback and is based on pair-wise comparisons.

$$\text{AUC} = \frac{1}{|U_Y|} \sum_{u \in U_Y} \frac{1}{|E(u)|} \sum_{(v_i, v_j) \in E(u)} \delta(\hat{r}_{u,v_i} > \hat{r}_{u,v_j})$$

where $E(u) = \{(v_i, v_j) | (u, v_i) \in Y \wedge (u, v_j) \notin (R \cup Y)\}$. Concretely, the $E(u)$ contains all the user-item pairs that one is observed and the other is not observed. In other words, we calculate the fraction of times that the "observed" items v_i are preferred over "non-observed" item v_j.

2.6.3 *Metrics on ranking*

Some recommendation methods do not predict the rating values of users to items, but directly output a sorted list of items based on unique utility scores. The metrics of ranking plays a particularly important role when the recommendation list is short and the first few items are crucial to users. The metric normalized discounted cumulative gain (NDCG) is introduced below.

First, for each user u, discounted cumulative gain (DCG) over first recommended k items is defined as:

$$\text{DCG}@k = \sum_{i=1}^{k} \frac{2^{\hat{r}_{ui}} - 1}{log_2(i + 1)}$$

where $\hat{r}_{ui}$ denotes the utility score of recommended item at position i for user u. The NDCG@k is the normalized version of DCG@k and averaged over all test users, as defined by:

$$\text{NDCG}@k = \frac{1}{|U_Y|} \sum_{u \in U_Y} \frac{\text{DCG}@k}{\text{IDCG}@k}$$

where IDCG@k is the DCG of the ideal ranking order, i.e., the ranking order based on the actual ratings in test set. Higher values of NDCG@k are more desirable as they indicate that the user favored items in their predicted lists.

2.6.4 *Metrics on diversity*

Personalization, also named inter-user diversity, considers the uniqueness of different users' recommendation lists. Given two users u_i and u_j, the different between their recommendation lists can be measured by the inter-list distance:

$$h_{ij}(K) = 1 - \frac{q_{ij}(K)}{K}$$

where $q_{ij}(K)$ is the number of common items in the top K places of the both lists: if the two lists are identical, $h_{ij}(K) = 0$ whereas completely different lists lead to $h_{ij}(K) = 1$.

By averaging $h_{ij}(K)$ over all pairs of users we obtain the mean distance $h(K)$, for which the larger the distance is, the more diverse the recommendation lists are.

2.7 Summary

Before going into descriptions of advanced recommendation methods, this chapter reviews the basic types of recommendation methods: CF-based, content-based, knowledge-based and hybrid recommendation methods. Then the comparison between these methods are given. Off-line recommendation evaluation is then introduced. Given that the anticipated recommendation should always meet user requirements, while also gaining a better understanding of what interests a broad range of users, several advanced developments, such as group recommendation methods, fuzzy recommendation methods, will be introduced in detail in Part II of this book.

Chapter 3

Recommender System Applications

With the development of recommendation methods and algorithms, more and more practical recommender systems have been developed and implemented in real-world applications to provide personalized services to both individuals and groups. The application of recommender systems is wide ranging with them being used by companies to recommend movies, music, learning materials, television programs, books, documents, houses, business partners, websites, conferences, tourism scenic spots, products, financial services, learning materials, *etc.* Notable successful commercial recommender systems include Netflix, Pandora and Amazon, but there are many more. At the core of these real-world applications are the recommendation methods and algorithms, which are incorporated by software developers into the software to become "recommender systems".

To help readers understand the development process and to assist developers in their applicable recommender system development, this chapter presents the typical applications of recommender systems, which have been grouped in seven main service types: e-government, e-business, e-commerce/e-shopping, e-library, e-learning, e-tourism and e-entertainment. This chapter also systematically examines the recommender systems through four dimensions: recommendation methods, recommender systems software, real-world application domains and application platforms. Some significant new topics are also identified and listed as new directions. In principle, this chapter provides a general introduction to recommender systems in the main application fields, with a more detailed exploration given in the Part III of this book.

In Section 3.1 to Section 3.7 of this chapter, we present the seven main application domains of recommender systems and their implementation. The four-dimensional comprehensive analysis of recommender system applications is presented in Section 3.8. The summary of this chapter is presented in Section 3.9.

3.1   E-government Recommender Systems

Electronic government (E-government) refers to the use of the Internet to support governments effectively in providing information and services to citizens and businesses. However, the rapid growth of e-government has caused information overload, leaving businesses and citizens unable to make effective choices from the range of information to which they are exposed. Recommender systems can overcome this problem through providing personalized service and have been adopted in e-government applications [Guo and Lu (2007)], which include government-to-citizen (G2C) and government-to-business (G2B) services.

G2C service recommendations aim to support government agencies to provide citizens personalized services. Many applications have been developed to implement the personalized services supplied by public administration offices. For example, a multi-agent system can help government agencies and citizens simultaneously by constructing and handling profiles of citizens and services in [De Meo *et al.* (2008)]. Except the construction of profiles, decision making process is also enhanced by recommender systems. To assist voters to make decisions in the e-election process, a recommender system was proposed [Terán and Meier (2010)], which uses fuzzy clustering methods and provides information about candidates close to voters' preferences. To provide personalized exercises to patients with low back pain problems and to offer recommendations for their prevention, a recommender system called Tplufib-web was presented in [Esteban *et al.* (2014)]. The system can be used in people travel and staffing costs. Besides, an e-government recommendation method can be improved with combination of probabilistic matrix factorization, which shows superior performance than the memory-based method.

In G2B services, many items from a business perspective are one-time items, such as business exhibitions or other events. An effective recommendation method, which handles an attribute-considered recommendation issue in G2B event recommendation, by integrating the semantic similarity techniques with the item-based CF, was proposed in [Guo and Lu (2007)]. A recommender system called Smart Trade Exhibition Finder, which suggests suitable trade exhibitions to businesses, has been developed. To flexibly reflect graded/uncertain information in the G2B domain, Cornelis et al. modeled user and item similarities as fuzzy relations [Cornelis *et al.* (2005)]. They also proposed a novel hybrid CF and content-based method to further improve the performance of the Smart Trade Exhibition Finders recommender system. A hybrid fuzzy logic-based recommendation framework was also developed to improve the trade exhibition recommender system for e-government. To support government to effectively recommend proper business partners (e.g., international buyers, agents, distributors, and retailers) to individual businesses (e.g., exporters), a recommender system called BizSeeker was developed [Lu *et al.* (2010)]. Business users can obtain a recommendation list of potential business partners from BizSeeker (more details will be described in Chapter 13).

3.2 E-business Recommender Systems

This type of recommender systems usually aims to assist businesses with personalized e-services. For businesses, there are two types of recommender systems: one type of recommender systems focus on the generation of recommendations to individual consumers, which are business-to-consumer systems, while the other type aims to provide recommendations about products and services to business users, which are business-to-business systems. This section mainly focuses on business-to-business recommender systems, the business-to-customer is mainly about e-commerce/e-shopping recommender systems which will be presented in the next section.

To help catalog administrators in business-to-business marketplaces maintain up-to-date product databases, an ontology-based recommender system was presented [Lee *et al.* (2006)], in which keyword-based, ontology and Bayesian belief network techniques were used to generate recommendations. To help business users select trusted online auction sellers, a recommender system was designed [Wang and Chiu (2008)] in which trading relationships were used to calculate the level of recommendations. To help private bankers provide suitable investment portfolios to their clients, a multi-investment recommender system PB-ADVISOR was presented [Gonzalez-Carrasco *et al.* (2012)]. The system used both semantic technologies and fuzzy logic to improve recommendation quality. The semantic characterization of the investments and their characteristics enabled the private banker to recommend a wide spectrum of products with very diverse characteristics. Because the market is changing, the temporal behavior pattern is also considered by constructing a temporal graph as the knowledge representation of each business in [Yang *et al.* (2017b)].

Another application is to support telecommunication companies in recommending suitable products and services to their business and individual customers. A telecommunication recommender system has been developed to improve small and medium-size business (SMB) customer satisfaction [Zhang *et al.* (2013)]. A personalized recommendation method and a software system called fuzzy-based telecom product recommender system is designed and implemented to generate service plan and package recommendations for customers (e.g. SMB). The details of this recommender systems and how this system improved prediction accuracy will be discussed in Chapter 12.

In e-business recommender systems, the knowledge-based methods, such as knowledge-base, CBR, ontology and semantic techniques, are widely integrated with CF and content-based recommendation methods. The main reason for this is that e-businesses have a high need for business domain knowledge to assist their recommendations.

3.3   E-commerce/E-shopping Recommender Systems

E-shopping is a specialized and highly popular field of e-commerce. In the last few years, a number of e-shopping recommender systems have been developed to provide guidelines to online customers. Rating is a common function in e-shopping systems, especially for electronic products. For example, in the iTunes store[1], customers are able to provide feedback by allocating a value, such as between 1 and 5, to purchased items. These rating data can subsequently be used to make recommendations. Tagging is another way to connect user-item data. For example, users of the movie review site Movielens [Resnick *et al.* (1994)] are able to assign tags freely to a movie by using simple words. Correspondingly, CF and social tag analysis are two effective methods in such systems when used separately or collectively with both ratings and tags to enhance recommendation performance.

Many e-commerce websites, such as Amazon and eBay, have used recommender systems to help their customers finding suitable products to purchase. In these e-commerce websites, products can be recommended based on the top overall sellers, customer demographics, or an analysis of the past buying behaviors of the customer as a prediction for future buying behavior. Some knowledge-based analyses are usually employed in systems where it is difficult to collect user rating data. For example, the Wasabi Personal Shopper is a domain-independent database browsing tool designed for online information access, particularly for electronic product catalogs [Burke (1999)]. Wasabi Personal Shopper is based on a line of academic research called the FindMe system. FindMe is built in several different languages, and uses custom-built ad-hoc databases and knowledge retrieval. A fuzzy-based recommender system for products made up of different components was developed [Cao and Li (2007)]. When buying a laptop, for instance, shoppers may consider the individual performance of each component, such as the CPU, motherboard, memory, *etc.* In this application, the weights of a

---

[1] www.apple.com/itunes

shopper's needs on each component are collected and the most satisfied candidates are then generated according to a fuzzy similarity measure model. More recently, virtual reality is also adopted in helping decision making in recommender systems, which allows online collaboration among users in a 3-D virtual space [Contreras *et al.* (2018)].

A content-based book recommender system was developed which utilized information extraction and machine-learning algorithms for text categorization [Mooney and Roy (2000)]. A naive Bayesian text classifier is used to train the data abstracted from the web to build features of books and profiles of customers and find the best matched books for a target customer. In some music sharing websites such as the Last.fm system, the music social community is made up of various types of music and customer relations. To better utilize the rich social information, a hypergraph model is introduced in the music recommendation method [Tan *et al.* (2011)] to treat the rich social media information. Certain shopping assistant systems have an interest in explaining the recommendations made to users. For example, when buying expensive goods, buyers expect to be skillfully steered through the options by well-informed sales assistants who are capable of balancing the user's various requirements. To provide an equivalent virtual recommendation explanation such as "why product A is better than B", a shopping assistant website called Qwikshop.com was developed where compound critiques were used as explanations [McCarthy *et al.* (2004)]. A set of critique patterns is generated by comparing each remaining case to the current recommended case; the relative feature differences make up the critique pattern. The best candidate products, for example those with the highest cost-performance ratio, will be recommended to users. Another issue is the purchase of a bundle of items or bundle promotion. The one-product-at-a-time search method used in "shopbot" (a shopping search engine) considers purchasing plans for a bundle of items [Garfinkel *et al.* (2006)]. This recommender system leverages bundle-based pricing and promotional deals frequently offered by online merchants to extract substantial savings.

With the increasing use of mobile phones and the advances in wireless networks, recommender systems are not only available for web users but are also being provided to mobile users as mobile-based recommender systems. A mobile-based recommender system was designed to suggest new products to supermarket shoppers [Lawrence *et al.* (2001)]. It used personal digital assistants to compose and transmit their orders to the store where they are assembled for subsequent pickup. The association mining method is used to determine relationships among product classes for use in characterizing the appeal of individual products. Clustering is used to identify groups of shoppers with similar spending histories.

Cluster-specific lists of popular products are then used as input to a matching process of customers and products to generate recommendations. Alibaba has developed mobile-based recommender system for the largest online platform in China with a graph embedding method [Wang *et al.* (2018a)]. The system is designed for the scalability of the large amount of items in Alibaba and enhanced with side information to solve the data sparsity problem.

In general, e-shopping recommender systems (web-based or mobile-based) are widely implemented in online purchasing for both digital products (such as music, movies, *etc.*) and physical goods (such as books, bags, *etc.*).

3.4   E-learning Recommender Systems

E-learning recommender systems have become increasingly popular in various learning and teaching systems. This type of recommender systems usually aims to assist learners to choose courses, subjects and learning materials that interest and suitable for them, as well as support their learning activities (such as in-class lecture or online study group discussion).

Many practicable e-learning recommender systems have been developed. For example, a software agent is proposed that uses data mining techniques to construct a model that represents online user behaviors, and used this model to recommend activities or shortcuts [Zaíane (2002)]. The recommended shortcuts assist learners to better navigate online material by finding most relevant resources more quickly. A personalized e-learning material recommender system was proposed in [Lu (2004)]. A recommender system that utilizes web usage mining to recommend the links in an adaptive web-based educational system was proposed in [Romero *et al.* (2009)]. A web mining tool and a recommendation engine were developed and applied into the "Adaptive Hypermedia for All" system to help an instructor to carry out the whole web mining process. In the personalized courseware recommender system, a fuzzy item response theory is proposed to initially collect a learner's preferences, following which the learner provides a fuzzy response as a percentage of their understanding of the learned courseware [Chen and Duh (2008)]. The system framework of contains both online and off-line modules. The online modules provide the evaluations of a learner's preference and the matching process between learners and courseware. The off-line module provides a courseware management agent to assess the level of difficulty of each course, in support of the matching process. To recommend learning goals and generate learning experiences for learners, a recommendation methodology was defined and a recommender system prototype component was developed for integration into a commercial adaptive e-learning system called IWT [Capuano *et al.* (2014)]. The recommendation method applies a hybrid recommendation method which consists of three steps: concept mapping, concept utility estimation and upper level learning goals utility estimation. Once the utility of each upper level learning goals is estimated for a learner, the ones with the greater utility can be suggested to the learner. To adapt to the learning objectives of different learners, an e-learning recommender system integrating the content matching and the style of learners is also developed [Gope and Jain (2017)].

In another e-learning recommender system, CourseAgent, students are able to provide feedback in implicit and explicit ways [Farzan and Brusilovsky (2006)]. They can directly evaluate courses in respect of their relevance to each career goal as well as the difficulty level of the course. They can also provide implicit feedback when they plan or register for a course. The basic and evident benefit of the system to students is that it offers a course management system that retains the information about courses they have taken and facilitates communication with their advisors. This work is a good attempt at providing social navigation support and community-based recommendations which generate benefit to users and therefore offer encouragement to use the system. In addition to implicitly mining from web usage or explicitly obtaining recommendations through a response/feedback system, relevant pedagogical rules should also be considered. Pedagogical rules describe pedagogy-oriented relations between the characteristics of learners and their learning activities. A recommender system of pedagogical patterns was developed to help lecturers choose a proper pedagogical pattern and define the best teaching strategies. It defined an ontology to represent the pedagogical patterns and their interaction with the fundamentals of the educational process, and applies a unified hybrid model which combines content and CF to make recommendations. To extend web-based educational systems with personalized support, a user-centered design method was proposed and applied to the Willow system [Santos *et al.* (2014)]. This study indicated that building personalized e-learning environments is a process that must consider learners' needs throughout the e-learning life cycle. It also reported that the e-learning life cycle can be used to design and evaluate personalization support through recommendations in web-based educational systems. The corresponding ontologies of learners and learning objectives were also discussed in the literature. A technical solution for a personalized search of learning objects on the web was proposed using a comparison of learner profiles and learning object descriptions [Biletskiy *et al.* (2009)]. This comparison was based not only on the values of the attributes of learner profiles and learning object descriptions, but also on the importance of these attributes for the learner. In the framework, a comparator was proposed to evaluate the "matching score" between learners and learning objectives, based on comparison rules. Also, bag-of-words was applied in recommender systems to help users find the right learning materials with user queries in [Mbipom *et al.* (2018)].

In e-learning recommender systems, knowledge-based pedagogical rules play a more important role in making recommendations than they do in other recommender systems, because of the insufficient historical datasets for CF or content-based recommendation methods. We also would like to indicate that the architecture of an e-learning recommender system usually consists of three parts: (1) Collect learners' profiles and identify their personalized demands using web analysis techniques; (2) Collect the metadata of learning objectives to identify the features; (3) Acquire related pedagogical knowledge to evaluate the matching degree between learners and learning objectives.

3.5   E-library Recommender Systems

Recommender systems have been used in digital library (e-library) applications to help users effectively locate and select information and knowledge source. For example, Fab, a part of the Stanford University Digital Library Project, was a recommender system through combining both the content-based and CF recommendation techniques [Balabanović and Shoham (1997)]. To provide better personalized e-library services, a system called Cyclades[2], was subsequently presented [Renda and Straccia (2005)]. Cyclades provides an integrated environment for individual users and group users (communities) in a highly personalized and flexible way. The recommendation methods rely on both personalized information organization and users' opinions and use content-based and CF methods separately and in combination. A recommender system to recommend research resources in university digital libraries was proposed [Porcel and Herrera-Viedma (2010)]. A fuzzy linguistic recommender system was proposed in which multi-granular fuzzy linguistic modeling was used to represent and handle flexible information by means of linguistic labels, and a hybrid recommender system that combines both content-based and CF methods was presented. Based on the above research, Serrano-Guerrero et al. presented a recommender system which can incorporate Google Wave technology in university digital libraries [Serrano-Guerrero *et al.* (2011)]. A decision support system assisting academic staff to increase the feasibility of academic digital library is proposed by integrating several decision rules [Cabrerizo *et al.* (2015)]. A more advanced method was proposed to allow multiple recommendation methods to work in the same platform

---

[2]www.ercim.org/cyclades

and accommodate the requirement of different types of users including internal users, digital library users, academic users, active users and passive users [Guan *et al.* (2019)].

In the e-library recommender systems, the hybrid recommendation methods which combine content-based, CF and/or knowledge-based methods are widely used. They can take advantage of the merits of several different recommendation techniques and overcome data sparsity problems. Fuzzy techniques, such as multi-granular fuzzy linguistic modeling, are used to represent and handle the flexible information of linguistic labels.

3.6 E-tourism Recommender Systems

Internet and mobile devices provide tourists with great opportunities to access tourism information, but the dramatic increase in the number of available tourism choices make it difficult for tourists to choose which option they prefer. E-tourism recommender systems are designed to provide personalized suggestions for tourists. Some systems focus on attractions and destinations, while others offer tour plans that include transportation, restaurant and accommodation.

There are several restaurant recommender systems. Burke et al. proposed a recommender system called Entrée to recommend restaurants based on knowledge-based methods [Burke *et al.* (1996)]. The knowledge was collected from users and retrieved by Entrée to find similar choices by refining such search criteria as price and taste. Entrée was improved by incorporating CF into knowledge-based, which meant that apart from restaurant features, the assessments of users also became criteria [Burke (2002)]. Another restaurant recommender system, REstaurants of JAén hybridizes CF and knowledge-based methods [Martinez *et al.* (2009)]. The recommendations can be provided by the CF method when the system is able to construct a user profile according to the user's ratings. When the system has insufficient information about a user, a CBR method is executed.

As we mentioned before, mobile devices provide opportunities for the development of mobile-based recommender systems and the best application is in E-tourism recommendation. For example, Tung and Soo designed a system to suggest restaurants for tourists in Taipei [Tung and Soo (2004)]. This system is a content-based recommender system which allows users to obtain real time suggestions from a mobile application. CATIS is a context-aware recommender system which recommends tourist accommodation, restaurants and attractions. The context information (e.g., location and wireless device features) is dynamically collected by a context manager. A collection of web services provided by an application server was used to gather user context information. The recommendations are generated by combining the user query and the user context information from the application server.

A sightseeing planning system, which is used to aid tourists to find a personalized tour plan in the city of Oporto, Portugal, was developed in [Lucas *et al.* (2013)]. To avoid the shortcomings of current recommender systems, such as scalability, sparsity, first-rater and gray sheep problems, a hybrid recommendation method was proposed. The proposed hybrid recommendation method employed CF and content-based methods, combined a clustering technique and an associative classification algorithm, and also used fuzzy logic to enhance the quality of recommendations. SigTur/E-Destination [Moreno *et al.* (2013)] was designed to provide personalized recommendations of tourism activities in the region of Tarragona. To make proper recommendations, the SigTur/E-Destination integrated several types of information and recommendation methods. The information used in the recommender includes demographic data, details that define the context of the travel, geographical aspects, information provided explicitly by the user and implicit feedback deduced from the interaction of the user with the system. The SigTur/E-Destination employs many recommendation methods, such as the use of stereotypes (standard tourist segments), content-based and CF methods, and some artificial intelligence tools including automatic clustering algorithms, ontology management, and the definition of new similarity measures between users, based on complex aggregation operators.

SmartMuseum, a mobile-based recommender system, presents users with recommendations for sites and objects on those sites on their mobile phones [Ruotsalo *et al.* (2013)]. In this system, an ontology-based personalization, annotation, and information filtering framework was developed. The contextual data, whether input by users or captured by the built-in sensors of mobile devices, are mapped to the concepts defined in the ontologies. The filtering framework introduced ontology-based query expansion for triples, feature balancing, and result clustering, which led to significant improvements in the accuracy of information filtering. iTravel, another mobile-based recommender system, was developed to provide tourists with on-tour attraction recommendation [Yang and Hwang (2013)]. In this system, CF-based recommendation method and mobile peer-to-peer communication were combined. To utilize the information of other tourists with similar interests in mobile tourism, three data exchange methods for users to exchange their ratings of attractions they had visited were proposed. In [Braunhofer *et al.* (2013)], a mobile-based tourism recommender system was designed by adding the weather information as context.

Moleskiing is a website for assisting community users to plan their skiing activities [Avesani *et al.* (2005)]. This recommender system allows users to share their opinions and experiences of particular sites as well as the trust degrees for specific users. People who are going skiing can exploit the snow condition information to personalize a safe route. DIETORECS is a CBR recommender system which creates a complete plan for tourists [Fesenmaier *et al.* (2003)]. Users can utilize the system in different ways according to their experience. The experienced user can make detailed preferences for attractions, while the less-experienced user can simply make a list of attractions of interest. An on-board recommender system for drivers called Mastrocaronte utilizes knowledge-based methods to recommend attractions, restaurants, and hotels [Console *et al.* (2003)]. It utilizes context information to suggest appropriate items to drivers such as restaurants at meal time or nearby fuel stations when fuel is exhausted.

The SPETA system uses the knowledge of a user's current location, preferences, and the history of past locations to recommend the services that tourists expect from a human tour guide [García-Crespo *et al.* (2009)]. It combines social networks, Semantic web, and context-awareness in pervasive systems to improve tourists' experiences. It offers a personalized guide and solves the problem of tourism service disintegration in respect of searching, finding and presenting personalized services by means of semantic, geo-location, and social technologies. Traveller is proposed to provide package holidays and tours [Schiaffino and Amandi (2009)]. It builds an agent which combines CF with content-based and demographic recommendation methods.

Attractions, accommodation and restaurants are often recommended to groups in tourism group recommender systems, and their features are used to form group recommendation lists. Xplorer is a recommender system developed for both individuals and groups on mobile platform [Logesh *et al.* (2019)]. Pocket restaurant finder is a group recommender system that locates a restaurant for a group of people [McCarthy (2002)]. Every member presents their opinions, stipulating such conditions as distance, price and so on. This group recommender system builds a group preference model and evaluates each restaurant according to the model. The final recommendations are produced as a list. Content-based recommendation methods are mainly used to produce personal preferences. The collaborative advisory travel system was proposed in [McCarthy *et al.* (2006)] to recommend a plan for ski holidays for a group of friends. Users present their explicit critiques for the features of the plan and negotiate to reach agreement on those critiques, called the group user model. The system produces recommendations according to this model. INTRIGUE is a tourism group recommender system that is also based on aggregating recommendation methods [Ardissono *et al.* (2003)]. The group is first divided into several subgroups according to the demographic information (e.g., number of children). Recommendations are generated for each subgroup and the final result is built by taking into consideration the influence of subgroups (e.g., people with disabilities). Personalized electronic tourist guides provide a solution for personalized route generation based on the profile and constraints of a group of tourists [Garcia *et al.* (2009)]. The solution is integrated by three aspects: demographic information, route information and specified preference. With each aspect, a group preference model is constructed and recommendations are added to a candidate list.

E-tourism generates recommendations about personalized tourist tours in the city of Valencia (Spain) for a single person or a group of tourists [Garcia *et al.* (2011)]. In the e-tourism system, group preferences are elicited from individual preferences through the application of intersection and aggregation mechanisms. Instead of making recommendations that directly match the group preferences, e-tourism also applies a hybrid recommendation method by combining demographic, content-based recommendation and likes-based filtering, which ensures that e-tourism is always able to offer a recommendation, even when the user profile contains very little information. In [Lorenzi *et al.* (2008)], a multi-agent recommender system for tourism was developed based on the cooperation of two types of agent: user agent and recommender agent. The user agent stores the user preference information and the recommender agent stores the travel information locally. The recommendations are produced by the exchange of information between these two types of agent. For users who want to plan a vacation together but find it difficult to negotiate face to face, the tourism group recommender system also takes negotiation support into consideration. A system called Travel Decision Forum was proposed to help groups to plan a vacation using an asynchronous communication mechanism [Jameson (2004)]. Users in a group can view and even copy other members' preferences. After the users have reached agreement, the system aggregates individual preferences with the median strategy. The features predefined by the system for both resorts and accommodation are critiqued by members. All the feedback is aggregated and the recommendations most likely to satisfy the group as a whole are generated. Different strategies for group tourism recommendation were also implemented in [Herzog and Wörndl (2019)], including strategies that allow groups to split temporarily and rejoin later or combines the various individual to form a sequence of recommendation.

In summary, various recommendation methods are applied in e-tourism recommender systems according to the degree of complexity and requirements of their recommended items. For recommending relatively simple items, such as restaurants, content-based and CF-based methods are usually applied. For recommending more complex items, such as travel routes and time schedules, knowledge-based and hybrid recommendation methods with domain knowledge are utilized. For recommending items with real time requirements, such as fuel stations, context-aware recommendation methods are used.

3.7 E-entertainment Recommender Systems

The E-entertainment mentioned here refers to content such as videos, music and documents which is uploaded by users. Some recommender system users share sources to the Internet so that other users can access the resources that interest them. This section focuses on several typical applications of recommender systems in entertainment services: TV program, web page, news, document, movie, music and tag recommendation.

3.7.1 TV program recommendation

TV programs can be seen as a special type of Entertainment released by broadcasters. A large increase in the number of TV channels and programs has been seen in recent years due to the growth of interactive and two-way TV. Even with an electronic program guide, it is difficult for viewers to find interesting programs from the hundreds or thousands of options. A TV program recommender system is required to help viewers to choose programs that interest them.

Content information for TV programs can be described by features (e.g., genre, actor), so the content-based recommendation method is commonly used; where the TV mode allows the user to give feedback (e.g., ratings), the CF recommendation method is well applied. In PTV [3], viewers rate programs through a web system to specify their preferences [Smyth and Cotter (2000b)]. After the system has collected explicit data from viewers, both CF and content-based recommendation methods are used to find similar programs according to the ratings given by viewers and the program information.

With the development of smart TV sets, viewers are allowed to give ratings on TV, which has resulted in TV-based recommender systems. TiVo allows viewers to rate programs using the remote control, and CF is utilized to suggest suitable programs [Ali and Van Stam (2004)]. The implicit feedback, such as whether the program is being recorded, is taken into account in addition to the explicit ratings from viewers. Requiring users to respond to programs is tedious and raises privacy issues, so some systems try to collect the required data in the background. User preferences are built using program attributes such as program title, genre,

---

[3] www.ptv.ie

subgenre, channel, and actors in [Bjelica (2010)]. TV programs are recommended by comparing the features of the past viewing set with current programs. A novel similarity method that applies raw moment-based similarity was proposed and used in memory-based CF methods to address such shortcomings as cold start and high calculating cost [Kwon and Hong (2011)]. The application queveo.tv combines the content-based method and item-based CF method to address the problems of gray sheep, cold start and first rating [Barragáns-Martínez *et al.* (2010)]. The dimensionality reduction technique, singular value decomposition, is incorporated to solve sparsity and scalability problems. Except for the efficiency and effectiveness of the recommendation methods, the user interface and user requirements are also considered in [Abreu *et al.* (2018)].

TV program recommendation has been developed and is important not only for individual personalization but also for group adaptation, such as when family members watch programs together. A challenge in making TV program recommendation different from other web-based group recommender systems is that it is difficult to identify the members in a group because the group could be dynamic, with members able to join and leave the group at any time. In the family interactive TV system reported in [Goren-Bar and Glinansky (2004)], viewers are modeled according to their stereotypes and the probability of preferred watching time for each type. The programs are recommended according to the combined probability.TV4M identifies members by providing a login function [Yu *et al.* (2006)]. The preferences are aggregated by minimizing the feature distance. Model-based CF recommendation methods are also utilized in TV program recommendation. A recommender system was built for a family by supporting vector machine and made suggestions using a knowledge-based method [Vildjiounaite *et al.* (2009)].

3.7.2 Web page, news and document recommendation

Suggesting web pages, news and documents is a traditional area for recommender systems because such resources grow rapidly. In most instances, textual content such as news, emails, documents and web pages are described as a list of keywords, which can be extracted from historic data, URLs and search engines, and many recommender systems are designed on the basis of analyzing keywords. Probabilistic models such as the information retrieval technique are common in this area. Contextual resources are transformed to a vector, with each element representing a keyword which takes frequency and location (title or plain text) into account. The recommendations are generated by retrieving resources that are similar to the user patterns. For example, Amalthaea [Moukas and Maes

(1998); Moukas (1997)] draws keywords from URLs by examining the hot-list and browsing history, and investigates the interest shown by users by information retrieval. Content-based methods are adopted in ifweb to measure the similarity between pages [Asnicar and Tasso (1997)]. CF is feasible if systems can collect information about whether users evaluate the content by ratings. For instance, News Dude [Billsus and Pazzani (2000)], a news recommender system, uses CF to model users' short term interests. Other examples of systems in which CF is used are the joke recommender system Eigentaste [Goldberg *et al.* (2001)] and the Usenet news recommender system GroupLens [Resnick *et al.* (1994); Konstan *et al.* (1997)]. In addition to News Dude [Billsus and Pazzani (2000)], which builds long-term preferences through Bayesian methods, other model-based systems have also been proposed, such as Foxtrot [Middleton *et al.* (2004)], which uses k-nearest classification. Graph-based clustering was adopted in WinPUM [Jalali *et al.* (2010)], in which the authors transformed websites into graphs and classified user navigation patterns according to users' session information. Recently, Nguyen et al. suggested that by integrating ontology and semantic knowledge, which are used to analyze session data, the system could navigate more accurately [*Nguyen *et al.* (2013)]. In Eigentaste [Goldberg *et al.* (2001)], principal component analysis is adopted to deduce the dimension of a keywords matrix to accelerate the process of user clustering and the computation of recommendations.

Apart from the keywords taken from the textual content, implicit and explicit feedback from users is also taken into account. Lifestyle Finder [Krulwich (1997)] uses demographic information to model the user and provide webpage recommendations. ACR News Vectors [Mobasher *et al.* (2000)] are built based on implicit feedback and viewing frequency for webpages. The clustering model is then trained and pages are recommended by a content-based method on related clusters. In ArgueNet [Chesnevar and Maguitman (2004)], another webpage recommender system, users are allowed to address such criteria as the trustworthiness of websites. The user preferences are modeled by keywords along with these criteria to generate personalized recommendations. With the demand of users of fast-paced life, the recommendation is developing from webpage to news recommendation on mobiles. The system named Lumi is to provide personalized content recommendations by leveraging the social and location information [Kazai *et al.* (2016)].

Many group recommender systems are designed to recommend books, documents and web pages. GRec-OC is a book recommender system developed for an online community [Kim *et al.* (2010)]. Their intention is to satisfy the small number of group members who are likely to be ignored although the majority of the community is satisfied. They adopt two levels of filtering mechanism, content-based and CF-based recommendation methods, to generate candidate books by CF according to the group preference, and eliminate candidate books if any member's compatibility score is below the threshold. To augment browsing activities, Context Aware Proxy-based System was proposed to collect the frequency and dwell time for pages, which works as a proxy for browsers without requiring the user to input data actively [Sharon *et al.* (2003)]. The repositories for a group of collaborative members and ranks for pages are built to augment other members' browsing and searching activity. StoryTime is a book recommendation website for a group of users (children) that caters children preference and teacher's suggestions [Milton *et al.* (2019)].

3.7.3 Movie and music recommendation

With the extensive usage of mobile devices in recent years, a particularly rapid growth in movie, video and music resources has taken place. However, users experience frustration when searching for content that interests them on mobile devices. To solve the problem, many movie recommender systems, such as PocketLens, CinemaScree and movie recommender system in smart phone, and music recommender systems such as Flycasting, Smart Radio, RACOFI, Foafing the Music and Moodplay, have been developed. Because most of these systems allow users to rate resources, CF recommendation methods are commonly used in these recommender systems. In some systems, such as Flycasting [Hauver and French (2001)], users cannot rate music directly, so this system first translates historical listening information into ratings and then carries out CF. To address the cold start and sparsity problems of CF methods, content-based methods are incorporated to overcome the sparsity and first-rate problem. CinemaScreen used a content-based method to solve cold start problems in movie recommendation [Salter and Antonopoulos (2006)]. One feature of movie and music recommender systems is that it is not easy to obtain the content and navigation history from multimedia resources. These resources contain such features as artist and genre, and how to extract the underlying correlations is an important issue in this area. Model-based methods like semantic analysis and social network are also integrated into CF. RACOFI utilizes semantic web techniques [Anderson *et al.* (2003)]. Foafing the Music maintains friend of friend profiles which work in a similar way to social networks [Celma and Serra (2008)]. CoFoSIM, a mobile music recommender system, utilizes multi-criteria decision-making techniques to analyze the implicit feedback and partial listening records, and aggregates them into a composed preference [Lee *et al.* (2010)]. An interesting aspect of music recommender systems is that some systems use implicit feedback to augment or replace the explicit ratings from users. For example, both CoFoSIM and Smart Radio use the listening history to infer their user ratings [Lee *et al.* (2010); Hayes and Cunningham (2001)]. Also, visual interface is designed and developed in [Andjelkovic *et al.* (2016)] to improve user experience.

Recommender systems are also developed for a group of users to share music and movie. Some music recommender systems automatically broadcast music to users without user selection; these are referred to as radio-based recommender systems. For example, MusicFX is a group recommender system that recommends music to all the people in a gym [McCarthy and Anagnost (1998)]. Members' preferences are stored in the system, and the recommended music is generated according to personal preferences and played for members without further selection. Flytrap is another group recommender system that selects music to be played in a public room [Crossen *et al.* (2002)]. Instead of collecting personal preferences by asking, Flytrap automatically collects meta information about the music that the user is listening to. Genres and artists are used to build a network with edges between network nodes representing the similarity between them. The play list is ultimately determined by a voting mechanism, with some constraints predefined by the system. Like a threshold on rating to measure a particular kind of music, the similarity combined related threshold can also be used to measure preference. In [Chao and Forrest (2003)], adaptive radio is proposed to broadcast songs to people who share the radio. The system adopts a simple mechanism whereby rejected songs, or other songs which are similar to the rejected ones, will not be played, whereas recommendations will be broadcast and played automatically.

PolyLens, which supports group creation and management, is extended from MovieLens and is designed for movie recommendation for a relatively small group [O'connor *et al.* (2001)]. It considers the nature of the group, the group's formation and evolution, privacy, group recommendation generation and interfaces. PolyLens merges the recommendations generated for individual users by nearest neighbor methods and sorts the merged list according to the lowest ratings ascribed to the movie; it can therefore provide more information to both individuals and the group. Also, a group recommender system with CF and content-based hybrid strategies can solve the group conflicts of these two strategies is proposed [Kaššák *et al.* (2016)].

Features of users and items can be collected to measure the relevancy between multimedia resources and users and therefore generate highly accurate group recommendations. Knowledge from domains has also been incorporated into recommendation methods. Recio-Garcia et al. took the member personality composition into account [Recio-Garcia *et al.* (2009)]. A Thomas-Kilmann Conflict Mode Instrument test, which is common in the human resource domain, is implemented for every member, and two measures are generated to depict member behavior patterns, assertiveness and cooperativeness. Then the conflict mode weight method is proposed which incorporates CF to generate recommendations and improves the recommendation quality tested by MovieLens.

3.7.4 Tag recommendation

Tags are arbitrary words specified by users to label and manage the resources that are uploaded to the Internet. Users want tags to be personalized and convenient to enable the easy sharing of resources, but it is often difficult for users to select appropriate tags from the wide range of possibilities. Tag recommender systems thus become increasingly important for making tag selection easy and personalized.

Folksonomies, which contain tag recommender systems, are web-based systems that allow users to upload their resources (e.g., documents, pictures), and to label them with tags. Folksonomies can be seen as three-part systems comprised of resources, users and tags. A folksonomy recommender system based on CF is implemented [Zheng and Li (2011)]. It exploited the tag and time effects in the recommendation procedure. Instead of utilizing the rating matrix in traditional CF, they built matrixes based on tag and time relations. Three strategies, tag-weight, time-weight and tag-time-mixed, are used to calculate the similarities based on corresponding matrixes. The recommendations are predicted by neighbors who are identified based on new similarities.

Another tag recommendation method, FolkRank, was proposed in [Jäschke *et al.* (2007)], in which the tags are recommended by calculating the distance from the uploaded resource. ENTAGREC++ is designed to recommend tag for software questions, which leverages the information of users, and an initial set of tags that a user may provide for tag recommendation [Wang *et al.* (2018b)]. It uses the Bayesian inference model latent Dirichlet allocation to predict the probability of tags of software objects.

In general, these entertainment service recommender systems aim to organize and manage this type of web service content and save users from performing tedious searches. In the tag domain, the CF method is the dominant recommendation method. For TV programs, intelligent techniques such as Bayesian classifier [Xuan *et al.* (2019)], decision tree and semantic analysis are integrated with CF and content-based recommendation methods to implement recommender systems. Recommending contextual content, such as web pages and documents, is a traditional application area of content-based and CF methods, as well as memory-based methods, and model-based methods, such as Bayesian and clustering techniques, are all utilized. Social and context-aware recommendation methods play an increasingly important role alongside traditional content-based and CF recommendation methods in movie and music recommendation.

3.8 Comprehensive Analysis of Recommender System Applications

Recommender systems and their applications discussed above are summarized in this section. For each application domain, the number of reviewed recommender systems and the recommendation methods used in the systems are summarized and presented in Table 3.1[4]. The following important findings can be extracted:

(1) CF, content-based and knowledge-based, still play a dominant role in almost all kinds of application, but hybrid recommender systems are more popular than single recommendation method-based systems for avoiding the drawbacks of individual recommendation methods;
(2) To our best knowledge, of the seven main recommender system application domains, e-entertainment recommender systems have been the most-reported, and systems for individual users constitute the majority;
(3) Compared to other domains, e-learning recommender systems have relatively applied more knowledge-based methods, while e-entertainment recommender systems use more CF methods;
(4) Some new recommendation methods, such as the social network-based recommendation, context awareness-based recommendation and more currently cross-domain recommendation, have played an increasingly important role in recent application developments;
(5) Some computational intelligence techniques, such as fuzzy logic, have been applied in various kinds of recommender system application domains. This chapter reports 27 successful recommender systems that use various computational intelligence techniques;
(6) Some new application platforms (not traditional web-based platforms) of recommender systems, such as mobile, TV and radio platforms, have emerged only recently. This chapter lists the 12 newest mobile-based recommender systems, 14 TV-based recommender systems and 4 radio-based recommender systems.

The details of each recommender system application reviewed in this chapter,

---

[4] In this table, CI is for Computational Intelligence, CB is for content-based recommendation and KB is for knowledge-based recommendation methods.

including its application domain, the applied recommendation methods, application platforms, user types and periods of use, are listed in Table 3.2.

Table 3.1: Summary of recommendation methods in applications.

	CB	CF	KB	Hybrid	CI	Social network	Context aware	No. of references
E-government	1	6	1	5	4			9
E-business	1		3	2	4	1		5
E-commerce	4	3	4	1	4	2		10
E-learning	5		10		2			11
E-library	3	3		3	1			5
E-tourism	9	9	9	9	4	2	3	24
E-entertainment	19	15	6	17	8	1	12	43
Total	42	36	33	37	27	6	15	107

3.9   Summary

In this chapter, we provide researchers and practical professionals with the state-of-the-art knowledge on development of recommender system applications and provide guidelines about how to develop and apply recommender systems in different domains to support users in various decision activities. This chapter mainly targets and focuses the real-world application development of recommender systems, and systematically examines the reported recommender systems through four dimensions: recommendation methods (such as CF), recommender systems software (such as BizSeeker), real-world application domains (such as e-business) and application platforms (such as mobile-based and TV-based platforms).

Table 3.2: Summary of recommender systems developed, the methods applied and user type.

Reference	Application domain	Method	Application platform	User type	Period
[Terán and Meier (2010)]	E-government	Fuzzy clustering	Web-based	Individual	2010
[De Meo et al. (2008)]	E-government	KB	Web-based	Individual	2005
[Esteban et al. (2014)]	E-government	Fuzzy linguistic modeling, hybrid	Web-based	Individual	2014
[Adadi et al. (2015)]	E-government	CF, Ontology	Web-based	Individual	2015
[Xu et al. (2019)]	E-government	CF	Web-based	Individual	2019
[Guo and Lu (2007)]	E-government	CF, hybrid	Web-based	Business	2007
[Cornelis et al. (2005)]	E-government	CF, hybrid, fuzzy logic	Web-based	Business	2007
[Lu et al. (2010)]	E-government	CF, hybrid	Web-based	Business	2010
[Wu et al. (2014b)]	E-government	CF, hybrid, fuzzy logic	Web-based	Business	2014
[Lee et al. (2006)]	E-business	KB, Bayesian belief network	Web-based	Business	2006
[Wang and Chiu (2008)]	E-business	Social network analysis	Web-based	Business	2008
[Gonzalez-Carrasco et al. (2012)]	E-business	Fuzzy logic, KB	Web-based	Business	2012
[Yang et al. (2017b)]	E-business	Probabilistic graphical model	Web-based	Business	2017
[Zhang et al. (2013)]	E-business	CB, KB, hybrid, fuzzy sets	Web-based	Business	2013
[Nanopoulos et al. (2009)]	E-commerce	Social tag, CF, hybrid	Web-based	Individual	2010
[Burke (1999)]	E-commerce	CB, KB	Web-based	Individual	1999
[Cao and Li (2007)]	E-commerce	KB, CI, fuzzy techniques	Web-based	Individual	2007
[Contreras et al. (2018)]	E-commerce	CB, CF, virtual reality	Web-based	Individual	2018
[Mooney and Roy (2000)]	E-commerce	CB	Web-based	Individual	2000
[Tan et al. (2011)]	E-commerce	Social network, CI	Web-based	Individual	2011
[McCarthy et al. (2004)]	E-commerce	KB	Web-based	Individual	2004
[Garfinkel et al. (2006)]	E-commerce	KB, CI	Web-based	Individual	2006
[Lawrence et al. (2001)]	E-commerce	CB, CI	Mobile-based	Individual	2001
[Wang et al. (2018a)]	E-commerce	Graph embedding, CF	Mobile-based	Individual	2018
[Zaïane (2002)]	E-learning	KB, rule-mining	Web-based	Individual	2002
[Lu (2004)]	E-learning	CB, KB	Web-based	Individual	2004

Reference	Application domain	Method	Application platform	User type	Period
[Romero et al. (2009)]	E-learning	Web usage mining	Web-based	Individual	2009
[Chen et al. (2004)]	E-learning	KB, CB, fuzzy item response theory	Web-based	Individual	2004
[Chen and Duh (2008)]	E-learning	KB, CB, fuzzy item response theory	Web-based	Individual	2008
[Capuano et al. (2014)]	E-learning	KB	Web-based	Individual	2014
[Gope and Jain (2017)]	E-learning	KB, CB	Web-based	Individual	2019
[Farzan and Brusilovsky (2006)]	E-learning	KB	Web-based	Individual	2006
[Santos et al. (2014)]	E-learning	KB	Web-based	Individual	2014
[Biletskiy et al. (2009)]	E-learning	KB, CB	Web-based	Individual	2009
[Mbipom et al. (2018)]	E-learning	KB, bag of words	Web-based	Individual	2019
[Balabanović and Shoham (1997)]	E-library	CB, CF, hybrid	Web-based	Individual	1997
[Renda and Straccia (2005)]	E-library	CB, CF, hybrid	Web-based	Individual	2005
[Porcel (2009b)]	E-library	Hybrid fuzzy linguistic modeling	Web-based	Individual	2009-11
[Cabrerizo et al. (2015)]	E-library	Decision rules	Web-based	Individual	2015
[Guan et al. (2019)]	E-library	CB, CF, location-based	Web-based	Individual	2019
[Martinez et al. (2009)]	E-tourism	CB, KB	Web-based	Individual	2009
[Burke et al. (1996)]	E-tourism	KB	Web-based	Individual	1996
[Burke (2002)]	E-tourism	KB, CF	Web-based	Individual	2002
[Tung and Soo (2004)]	E-tourism	Context-aware	Mobile-based	Individual	2004
[Pashtan et al. (2003)]	E-tourism	Context-aware	Mobile-based	Individual	2003
[Braunhofer et al. (2013)]	E-tourism	Context-aware	Mobile-based	Individual	2013
[Lucas et al. (2013)]	E-tourism	CF, CB, clustering	Web-based	Individual	2013
[Moreno et al. (2013)]	E-tourism	CF, CB, context	Web-based	Individual	2013
[Ruotsalo et al. (2013)]	E-tourism	Ontology context, CF	Web-based	Individual	2013
[Yang and Hwang (2013)]	E-tourism	CF, context	Web-based	Individual	2013
[Fesenmaier et al. (2003)]	E-tourism	KB	Web-based	Individual	2003
[Avesani et al. (2005)]	E-tourism	Trust	Web-based	Individual	2005
[Console et al. (2003)]	E-tourism	KB, context-aware	Web-based	Individual	2003
[García-Crespo et al. (2009)]	E-tourism	social networks, context-aware	Web-based	Individual	2009

Reference	Application domain	Method	Application platform	User type	Period
[Schiaffino and Amandi (2009)]	E-tourism	CB, CF	Web-based	Individual	2009
[Logesh et al. (2019)]	E-tourism	CI, context-aware	Mobile-based	Both	2019
[McCarthy (2002)]	E-tourism	CB	Web-based	Group	2002
[McCarthy et al. (2006)]	E-tourism	CB	Web-based	Group	2006
[Ardissono et al. (2003)]	E-tourism	Weighted average	Web-based	Group	2003-05
[Garcia et al. (2009)]	E-tourism	CB, CF, demographic	Web-based	Group	2009
[Garcia et al. (2011)]	E-tourism	CB, demographic	Web-based	Group	2011
[Lorenzi et al. (2008)]	E-tourism	Agent	Web-based	Group	2008
[Jameson (2004)]	E-tourism	Asynchronous	Web-based	Group	2004
[Herzog and Wörndl (2019)]	E-tourism	CF, context-aware	Mobile-based	Group	2019
[Smyth and Cotter (2000b)]	E-entertainment	CB, CF	Web-based	Individual	2000
[Ali and Van Stam (2004)]	E-entertainment	Clustering, CF	TV-based	Individual	2004
[Bjelica (2010)]	E-entertainment	Information retrieval clustering	TV-based	Individual	2010
[Kwon and Hong (2011)]	E-entertainment	CF	TV-based	Individual	2011
[Barragáns-Martínez et al. (2010)]	E-entertainment	CB, CF	TV-based	Individual	2010
[Abreu et al. (2018)]	E-entertainment	CB	TV-based	Individual	2018
[Goren-Bar and Glinansky (2004)]	E-entertainment	CB	TV-based	Group	2004
[Yu et al. (2006)]	E-entertainment	CB	TV-based	Group	2006
[Vildjiounaite et al. (2009)]	E-entertainment	Classifier	TV-based	Group	2009
[Moukas and Maes (1998)]	E-entertainment	Information filtering and retrieval	Web-based	Individual	1997-98
[Asnicar and Tasso (1997)]	E-entertainment	CB	Web-based	Individual	1997
[Billsus and Pazzani (2000)]	E-entertainment	Bayesian classifier	Web-based	Individual	1999
[Goldberg et al. (2001)]	E-entertainment	CF, dimension reduction	Web-based	Individual	2001
[Resnick et al. (1994)]	E-entertainment	CF	Web-based	Individual	1994-97
[Middleton et al. (2004)]	E-entertainment	K-nearest classification	Web-based	Individual	2004
[Jalali et al. (2010)]	E-entertainment	Graph based clustering	Web-based	Individual	2010
[*Nguyen et al. (2013)]	E-entertainment	Ontology KB	Web-based	Individual	2013
[Krulwich (1997)]	E-entertainment	Demographic information	Web-based	Individual	1997

Reference	Application domain	Method	Application platform	User type	Period
[Mobasher et al. (2000)]	E-entertainment	CB, clustering	Web-based	Individual	2000
[Chesnevar and Maguitman (2004)]	E-entertainment	CB	Web-based	Individual	2004
[Kazai et al. (2016)]	E-entertainment	CB, context-aware	Mobile-based	Individual	2016
[Kim et al. (2010)]	E-entertainment	CB, CF	Web-based	Group	2010
[Sharon et al. (2003)]	E-entertainment	CB	Web-based	Group	2003
[Milton et al. (2019)]	E-entertainment	CB	Web-based	Group	2019
[Miller et al. (2004)]	E-entertainment	CF	Web-based	Individual	2004
[Salter and Antonopoulos (2006)]	E-entertainment	CF, CB	Web-based	Individual	2006
[Kim and Moon (2012)]	E-entertainment	CF, genre	Mobile-based	Individual	2012
[Hauver and French (2001)]	E-entertainment	CF	Mobile-based	Individual	2001
[Hayes and Cunningham (2001)]	E-entertainment	CF	Radio-based	Individual	2001
[Anderson et al. (2003)]	E-entertainment	Semantic web, CF	Web-based	Individual	2003
[Celma and Serra (2008)]	E-entertainment	Social network, CB	Mobile-based	Individual	2005
[Melville et al. (2002)]	E-entertainment	CF, CB	Web-based	Individual	2002
[Lee et al. (2010)]	E-entertainment	CF, multi-criteria decision making	Mobile-based	Individual	2010
[Andjelkovic et al. (2016)]	E-entertainment	CF, CB, hybrid, visualization	Web-based	Individual	2016
[McCarthy and Anagnost (1998)]	E-entertainment	CB	Radio-based	Group	1998
[Crossen et al. (2002)]	E-entertainment	CB	Radio-based	Group	2002
[Chao and Forrest (2003)]	E-entertainment	CF	Radio-based	Group	2005
[O'connor et al. (2001)]	E-entertainment	CF	Web-based	Group	2002
[Recio-Garcia et al. (2009)]	E-entertainment	CF, TKI	Web-based	Group	2009
[Kaššák et al. (2016)]	E-entertainment	CF, CB, hybrid	Web-based	Group	2016
[Zheng and Li (2011)]	E-entertainment	CF	Web-based	Individual	2011
[Jäschke et al. (2007)]	E-entertainment	CF, CB	Web-based	Individual	2006-07
[Wang et al. (2018b)]	E-entertainment	CB, LDA	Web-based	Individual	2018

PART 2

Recommender Systems: Methods and Algorithms

Chapter 4

Social Network-based Recommender Systems

With the dramatic growth of social networking data and tools, user-to-user relationships are emerging as an additional source of information for amalgamating users' preferences, which can be incorporated into CF-based recommendation models to alleviate the data sparsity. If we place users and items into a graph as nodes, then the recommendation problem can be transferred to a ranking problem on the graph data. On the graph, social network is represented as edges between users. The recommendation problem can be represented naturally as a graph ranking problem that seeks an optimal ranking order of the candidate items (vertices) for target users. Advanced graph ranking techniques have been utilized in the field of recommender systems, such as multipartite graph, multigraph and hypergraph. Of these, it is the hypergraph graph structure that is most widely used, because it can theoretically handle all types of information entities and high-order relationships.

In this chapter we use graph ranking techniques to enhance the recommender systems by obtaining information from social networks, particularly the social network information used for recommendation generation, to deal with context information. First we introduce the social network-based recommender system in Section 4.1. Then graph ranking techniques in recommender systems are introduced in Section 4.2. Two social network-based recommendation methods are then presented: a multi-relational social recommendation method by multigraph ranking in Section 4.3, which handles different types of user relationships, and in Section 4.4 a multi-objective recommendation method by hypergraph ranking, which improves accuracy and is able to satisfy the complex demands of users. Finally, Section 4.5 summarizes the chapter.

4.1   User Relationships in Social Networks

Various types of social network correlations between users have been incorporated to recommender systems to enhance their performance, including similarity calculation and user neighbor identification. There are three different types of user relationships from which a social network can be established:

(1) User preference similarity relationship. Similarity relationships can be generated from users' rating behaviors based on the assumption that similar users hold similar opinions consistently. Here, user preference similarity is different from the rating similarity that we calculated in Chapter 2. For example, in the ItemRank rating similarity, a correlation network of items is built using the binary user-rating-item information [Gori and Pucci (2007)]. A network based on the user preference similarity is established and an indirect relationship is inferred using network propagation. The enriched similarity can also be integrated with rating similarities.

(2) Explicit social relationship. Increasingly, online Web/Apps involve social network tools, in the form of online friendships, interest groups, *etc.*, to enable users to interact with each other directly. Usually users ask their friends for suggestions for online commodities/services, therefore the explicit social relationship can be used to find neighbor users. For example, in the FilmTrust recommender system users are required to provide a friendship trust rating in a range of $[0, 1]$ when a new person is added to the friends list [Golbeck and Hendler (2006)]. However, unlike this example, the majority of social network-enabled systems only provide binary relationships between users. Also, with these binary relationships graph searching techniques employed for network propagation, indirect friendship relationship is inferred from direct relationships.

(3) Implicit user relationship. Implicit correlation networks of users can be derived from broader user behavior such as bookmark, view, tag or comment. Users are connected if they share common characteristics or have engaged in similar behaviors. For example, in the academic collaboration recommender system, "Co-citation" and "co-author" relationship of users is constructed to help scientists to find potential opportunities for cooperation.

More diverse correlations of users can be extracted as new resource to enhance CF, particularly for handling the data sparsity problem. Representative relationships in the above three types of user relationships are used in this chapter as similarity relationship, friendship relationship and tagging relationship.

Incorporating social networks with conventional CF methods has gained much attention and can be categorized in three ways:

(1) Post hoc combination. With post hoc combination each input resource is investigated in separate recommendation approaches. The results are then combined and then, usually, the post hoc validation parameters are fine-tuned.
(2) Neighborhood integration. In contrast to post hoc combinations, with neighborhood integration social networks can be aggregated at an earlier stage to establish a union neighborhood to perform traditional CF methods.
(3) Unified models. Unified models are usually applied for systems with complex networks of users, items and/or context information. Examples include the multipartite graph models, hypergraph models and cross domain multi-relational models.

In general, post hoc combines the outputs of any two techniques using a weighting function such as Arithmetic Mean and Harmonic Mean to aggregate the results. Neighborhood integration emphasizes on the preprocessing of social network information before the CF. Unified models is the way to extend the model-based CF with social network information and establish new algorithms and methods. But user relations are merged into a union network using linear or nonlinear weighting methods, where structural information is ignored. Therefore, multigraphs and hypergraphs are needed to handle high-order and various user-user and user-item relationships. Also, the hypergraphs are also suitable for providing multi-objective recommendations [Mao *et al.* (2019)], where recommender systems consider a user's different preferences in specific situations, such as time and location.

4.2 Graph Ranking Techniques in Recommender Systems

In this section, we introduce some basic graph ranking techniques including random walk for social network propagation and random walk for hypergraphs.

4.2.1 *Random walk model for social network propagation*

Trust transitivity in social networks has been widely accepted. Three aspects of this user relationship were introduced in the last section. Two users can be connected through a third user even when they do not have co-rated items. Formally, all users in a recommender system form a simple graph, defined as:

Definition 4.1 (User single graph). In a recommender system, a user single graph is denoted as $G = \{\mathcal{U}, E\}$, where $\mathcal{U}$ is the entire user set and each user

$u \in \mathcal{U}$ treated as a graph vertex and $E \subseteq \mathcal{U} \times \mathcal{U}$ is a set of edges where a directed pair of users $[u_i, u_j] \in E$ indicates a social connection from user u_i to user u_j.

The relationships in a graph can be directed or undirected, weighted or binary. To be consistent, an undirected relationship can be decomposed to two one-way directed relationships. Also, a binary social network can be treated as a special weighted network in which every edge has equal weighting. For a normalized and weighted network, the edges are natively associated with a weighting function $w : E \rightarrow [0, 1]$. For a binary network, however, a weighting function is assumed to be $w : E \rightarrow 1$ which gives a constant weight to every visible edge. In this chapter, we use $[u_i, u_j]$ to denote a directed path from vertex u_i to vertex u_j. We then denote a weighting adjacency matrix $\boldsymbol{W}$ for a social network $G = \{\mathcal{U}, E\}$ with $\boldsymbol{W}_{ij} = w([u_i, u_j])$ if the directed path $[u_i, u_j]$ exists and 0 otherwise.

The random walk to infer the missing edges in a social network is as follows: Given a source user u_{sou} and a target user u_{tar}, for whom $[u_{\text{sou}}, u_{\text{tar}}] \notin E$, i.e., there is no edge from u_{sou} to u_{tar} in the original social network, a single random walk is started from the source user to reach the target user to infer their indirect relationship, which is denoted as $\tilde{w}([u_{\text{sou}}, u_{\text{tar}}])$. While the runner is walking, it is the walking part in this random walk. At a time t, assuming the runner has reached a certain user u_i, the runner can choose to keep moving to another node or terminate this walk, which is called selection part. To summarize, the walking action performs the search of similar users in the network while the selection action polls the suggestions of the reached user's opinion. In the selection part, the runner has two options:

Option 1. With probability ϕ_t, the walking is terminated and return the value of $w([u_i, u_{\text{tar}}])$ as the result. If u_i is not connected to u_{tar}, zero is returned.

Option 2. With probability $1 - \phi_t$, the walking continues and another node connected by u_i will be randomly reached at the next step.

Here, the notation ϕ_t is the termination probability with regard to walking time/step t. In the walking process, the transition probability of moving from a current user u_i to another user u_j is $p(u_j|u_i) = \frac{W_{ij}}{d(u_i)}$, where $d(u_i)$ denotes the vertex degree of user u_i calculated as $d(u_i) = \sum_{j=1}^{|U|} W_{ij}$.

A diagonal matrix $\boldsymbol{D}$ can be constructed with $\boldsymbol{D}_{ii} = d(u_i)$. We define a row vector $\boldsymbol{p}^{(t)}$ presenting the visiting probability distribution over all users at a certain time t, i.e., the i-th element $p_i^{(t)}$ denotes the probability of that the i-th user u_i is being visited at this time. With these settings, the transition matrix of this random walk is $\boldsymbol{T} = \boldsymbol{D}^{-1}\boldsymbol{W}$. If the runner keeps moving at the next time $t + 1$, the distribution vector will be updated once as follows:

$$p^{(t+1)} = p^{(t)} \times T. \tag{4.1}$$

So far, a single random walk is completed and it returns a prediction of the indirect relationship from the source user to the target user. For more precise predictions, we can issue multiple random walks from the source user and then aggregate all returned values as the final prediction. We define a new variable s as the total walking length of a single walk, for which we can obtain a distribution vector $p^{(s)}$ by updating Eq. (4.1) recursively. We also denote a column vector $W_{:\mathrm{tar}}$ as the corresponding column in the weighting matrix W for the target user u_{tar}. Clearly, $W_{:\mathrm{tar}}$ represents the weightings of the in-linked edges of the target user. The expectation of the returned value for a single random walk terminated at time s is: $\tilde{w}\left([u_{\mathrm{sou}}, u_{\mathrm{tar}}]\right)|s = p^{(s)}W_{:\mathrm{tar}}$. Aggregating all random walks that start from the source user, the global expectation of the returned values will be:

$$\tilde{w}\left([u_{\mathrm{sou}}, u_{\mathrm{tar}}]\right) = p\left(s=1\right)p^{(1)}W_{:\mathrm{tar}} + p\left(s=2\right)p^{(2)}W_{:\mathrm{tar}} + \ldots. \tag{4.2}$$

The starting distribution would be $q = p^{(0)}$. As all random walks start from the particular source user u_{sou}, q has only one positive element $q(u_{\mathrm{sou}}) = 1$ and all others are zeros. Combining Eq. (4.1) and Eq. (4.2),

$$
\begin{aligned}
\tilde{w}\left([u_{\mathrm{sou}}, u_{\mathrm{tar}}]\right) &= \phi_1 qTW_{:\mathrm{tar}} + (1-\phi_1)\phi_2 qT^2 W_{:\mathrm{tar}} \\
&\quad + (1-\phi_1)(1-\phi_2)\phi_3 qT^3 W_{:\mathrm{tar}} + \ldots \\
&= \sum_{t=1}^{\infty} \phi_t \prod_{i=1}^{t-1}(1-\phi_i)qT^t W_{:\mathrm{tar}} \\
&\triangleq \sum_{t=1}^{\infty} \psi\left(t\right)qT^t W_{:\mathrm{tar}}
\end{aligned} \tag{4.3}
$$

where $\psi\left(t\right)$ denotes the probability of a single random walk terminated at time t,

$$\psi\left(t\right) = P\left(s=t|\phi\right) = \phi_t \prod_{i=1}^{t-1}(1-\phi_i). \tag{4.4}$$

Eq. (4.3) predicts the indirect connections between two users in a social network. From the perspective of the whole network, we obtain an inferred weighting matrix $\tilde{W}$, where $\tilde{W}_{ij}$ is the predicted weighting of the relationship between each pair of users. This matrix can be calculated by:

$$\tilde{W} = \sum_{t=1}^{\infty} \psi\left(t\right)T^t W. \tag{4.5}$$

We can prevent walks that are too long by adjusting the termination parameter ϕ. Based on the idea of "six degrees of separation" [Burke (1999)], most users will be reachable with a walk that is at most six steps in length. If a walk has reached six steps, we force it to terminate, i.e., let $\phi_6 = 1$. Thus Eq. (4.5) can be replaced by:

$$\tilde{W} \approx \sum_{t=1}^{6} \psi\left(t\right) T^t W. \tag{4.6}$$

The termination probability will become higher as random walks go to deeper levels. That is, parameter ϕ increases with time t. Simply, we let ϕ_t increase from 0.5 to 1 in the first six steps, as shown in Table 4.1. Distribution of walking length $\psi = p\left(s = t|\phi_t\right)$ is also computed in this table. We find that most (80%) random walks will stop at the first two steps. Eq. (4.6) is simplified when only the first two steps are considered:

$$\tilde{W} \approx 0.5 TW + 0.3 T^2 W.$$

Table 4.1: An example setting of the termination parameter.

t	1	2	3	4	5	6
ϕ_t	0.5	0.6	0.7	0.8	0.9	1
$\psi_t\colon p(s = t)$	0.5	0.3	0.14	0.048	0.011	0.001
$p(s \leqslant t|\phi_t)$	0.5	0.8	0.94	0.988	0.999	1

Note that we only need to predict the indirect relationships, so the final weighting matrix after propagation will be:

$$\hat{W} = W + \left(J - H\right) \circ \tilde{W}$$

where $\circ$ is entry-wise production, J is a matrix with all elements to be 1 with appropriate size and H is the adjacent matrix of the graph with $H_{ij} = 1$ if there is an edge from the ith user u_i to the j-th user u_j and $H_{ij} = 0$ otherwise.

To summarize, propagation on social network simple graph will be applied to as a pre-processing step to enrich the user relationships. For convenience of expression, we still use the original notations such as W instead of $\hat{W}$, in the remainder of this chapter.

4.2.2 *Single graph ranking*

The graph ranking problem is given by a weighted graph $G = (\mathcal{U}, E, w)$, where $U = \{u_1, \ldots, u_n\}$ is a set of vertices, $E \subseteq \mathcal{U} \times \mathcal{U}$ a set of edges, and $w : E \to [0, 1]$ the weighting function, together with an input query vector $y \in \mathbb{R}^n$, in which the i-th element y_i denotes the initial query score of the node

u_i. The query vector can be seen as an initial ranking function $y : \mathcal{U} \to \mathbb{R}$ on the vertex space such that $y\left(u_i\right) = y_i$. The ranking problem can then be thought of as seeking a new function $f : \mathcal{U} \to \mathbb{R}$ that is smooth and close to the given function y simultaneously. The graph ranking problem is usually formalized to an optimization problem to minimize the following cost function.

$$\min_{f:\mathcal{U}\to\mathbb{R}} Q\left(f\right) = S\left(f\right) + \mu\hat{R}\left(f;y\right) \tag{4.7}$$

where $S\left(f\right)$ measures the smoothness of the ranking function f, $\hat{R}\left(f;y\right)$ measures the empirical error of f compared to y, and $\mu > 0$ is a trade-off parameter. The ranking error is usually measured by the ℓ_2 norm:

$$\hat{R}\left(f;y\right) = \|f - y\|^2 = \left(f - y\right)^T\left(f - y\right).$$

A good ranking function f will not vary greatly across two vertices that are "closely related". By importing the weighting matrix W and the degree matrix D of a simple graph G, the smoothness function is:

$$S\left(f\right) = f^T\left(I - A\right)f$$

where a matrix $A = D^{-1/2}WD^{-1/2}$ is defined. Requiring the gradient of $Q\left(f\right)$ to vanish gives us the following result:

$$\left.\frac{\partial Q}{\partial f}\right|_{f=f^*} = \left(I - A\right)f^* + \mu\left(f^* - y\right) = 0.$$

In defining a decimal parameter $\alpha = 1/\left(\mu + 1\right) \in \left(0, 1\right)$, the optimized ranking result f^* is obtained:

$$f^* = \left(1 - \alpha\right)\left(I - \alpha A\right)^{-1}y := \left(I - \alpha A\right)^{-1}y. \tag{4.8}$$

In the above expression, the positive constant $1 - \alpha$ can be omitted as it does not affect the ranking order.

4.2.3 *Hypergraph ranking*

A simple graph is a representation of a set of vertices in which each edge connects a pair of nodes, while a hypergraph is a generalization of a simple graph with hyperedges, which connects an arbitrary number of vertices [Zhou *et al.* (2007)]. In other words, a hyperedge represents a high-order relationship of two or more vertices. The formal definition of a hypergraph is given as follows:

Definition 4.2 (Hypergraph). A hypergraph $G = \left(\mathcal{U}, E\right)$ is a pair where $\mathcal{U} = \{u_1, u_2, \dots\}$ is the vertex set representing a finite number of objects, and $E = \{e_1, e_2, \dots\}$ is the hyperedge set representing the high-order relationships between vertices. A hyperedge $e \in E$ is represented by the connected nodes, i.e., a non-empty subset of $\mathcal{U}$, to which a weighting function $w : E \to \mathbb{R}$ is also assigned to denote the strength of this connection.

Let $h(u, e) = 1$ denotes that a vertex u is in a hyperedge e and $h(u, e) = 0$ otherwise. We then obtain an incidence matrix $\boldsymbol{H}$ with size $|\mathcal{U}| \times |E|$ in which each element is:

$$H_{ij} = h(u_i, e_j) = \begin{cases} 1, \text{ if } u_i \in e_j \\ 0, \text{ otherwise.} \end{cases} \tag{4.9}$$

The degree of a vertex is defined as $d(u) = \sum_e w(e) h(u, e)$. Unlike the edge in a simple graph, the degree of a hyperedge is defined as the number of connected vertices $\delta(e) = \sum_u h(u, e)$. Thus, a simple graph is a special case of hypergraph in which the edge degrees are two. Throughout the rest of this chapter, we define the following diagonal matrix forms for $w(e)$, $\delta(e)$ and $d(u)$ as $\boldsymbol{W} \in \mathbb{R}^{|E| \times |E|}$, $\boldsymbol{D}_e \in \mathbb{Z}^{|E| \times |E|}$ and $\boldsymbol{D}_u \in \mathbb{R}^{|\mathcal{U}| \times |\mathcal{U}|}$, respectively.

The graph-ranking problem in the hypergraph can be solved in a different way by performing random walks on the graph with appropriate starting points. At the beginning, a starting point is selected randomly from the given labeled vertices according to the input query vector $\boldsymbol{y}$. A runner is supposed to move randomly to adjacent nodes from the starting point following the edges in the graph (hypergraph). Finally, the stationary visiting probabilities are the ranking scores for all vertices.

Usually, the transition probability from one node to an adjacent node is:

$$p(u|u') = \sum\nolimits_{h(u, e) = 1, h(u', e) = 1} {w(e)} \big/ {d(u')\delta(e)} \tag{4.10}$$

and the overall transition matrix for the whole hypergraph is

$$\boldsymbol{T} = \boldsymbol{D}_u^{-1} \boldsymbol{H} \boldsymbol{W} \boldsymbol{D}_e^{-1} \boldsymbol{H}^T.$$

Based on the random walk with restarts theory, the walker will have two options for the next move each time: (1) continually walking to an adjacent node with a certain probability $\alpha \in (0, 1)$; (2) jumping back to the starting point with probability $1 - \alpha$.

Let $\boldsymbol{p}^{(t)}$ be a column vector reporting the visiting probability of every vertex at a certain time t, and $\boldsymbol{q}$ the initial probability of being selected as the starting point. The visiting distribution of the whole vertex set is updated as:

$$\boldsymbol{p}^{(t+1)} = \alpha \boldsymbol{T} \boldsymbol{p}^{(t)} + (1 - \alpha)\boldsymbol{q} \tag{4.11}$$

Finally, the stationary distribution when Eq. (4.11) reaches convergence represents the long-term visiting rate of all vertices. Let $\boldsymbol{p}^{(t+1)} = \boldsymbol{p}^{(t)} = \boldsymbol{p}^{(\infty)}$, then we obtain $\boldsymbol{p}^{(\infty)} = (1 - \alpha)(\boldsymbol{I} - \alpha \boldsymbol{T})^{-1}\boldsymbol{q}$. Because the positive constant $(1 - \alpha)$ does not change the ranking order, the optimal ranking result is:

$$\boldsymbol{f}_{\text{RW}}^* = (\boldsymbol{I} - \alpha \boldsymbol{T})^{-1}\boldsymbol{q}. \tag{4.12}$$

It is easy to find that Eq. (4.12) has the same structure as Eq. (4.8), and the intermediate matrix A is a normalized version of the transition matrix T. However, when the hyperedge degree is in large change scope, the hypergraph ranking method above will produce a bias. Fig. 4.1 gives a numerical example and we use random walks to explain the ranking bias.

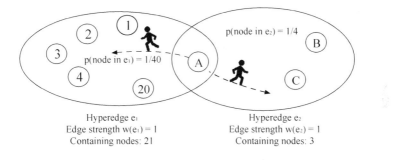

Hyperedge e_1
Edge strength $w(e_1) = 1$
Containing nodes: 21

Hyperedge e_2
Edge strength $w(e_2) = 1$
Containing nodes: 3

Fig. 4.1: Example of ranking bias of traditional hypergraph ranking.

In Fig. 4.1, node A, which is supposed to be the starting point of random walks, is linked by two hyperedges e_1 and e_2. The edge strength indicates that the relationship between the nodes in e_1 is equivalent to the relationship between the nodes in e_2, so the runner shall have equivalent probability to follow any one of the two hyperedges. With the settings of the traditional ranking in the above, however, the runner will strongly prefer to move via edge e_2. Recall the transition formula is Eq. (4.10), the probability of moving to the nodes in the two hyperedge will be $p(n \in e_1) = \frac{1}{2 \times 20} = \frac{1}{40}$ and $p(n \in e_2) = \frac{1}{2 \times 2} = \frac{1}{4}$. The probability of moving to a node in e_2 is heavily overvalued only because the edge degree is much smaller. An improved balanced hypergraph ranking method is presented in Section 4.4.

4.3 Multi-relational Social Recommendation by Multigraph Ranking

In this section, we present a multigraph ranking model that is able to identify nearest neighbor users in multi-relational social networks and help to make recommendations [Mao *et al.* (2017)]. This method contains two main components: (1) a random walk model for single social network propagation to enrich original social data; and (2) a multigraph ranking model to identify the overall closeness between users in multi-relational social networks. The social network propagation model is employed as a preliminary process to enrich the original social data, and the multigraph ranking model undertakes the next step to identify the nearest neighbor users for the purpose of making recommendations.

An example of multi-relational social networks is shown in Fig. 4.2, where four users are connected by relationships: similarity, friendship and tagging, each corresponding to the three types of relationships introduced in Section 4.1. A simple method to handle these high-order relationships is to aggregate the different relationships between each two users into a single relationship (option 1), and then to build a union simple graph connecting all users. As a result, however, the structural information of the original relationships will be lost in this way. Another method is to build a multigraph model (option 2) to retain all the structural information. Unlike union graphs, it allows existence in a multigraph with multiple edges connecting the same nodes. The three types of user relationships shown in Fig. 4.2 can be naturally represented as a multigraph.

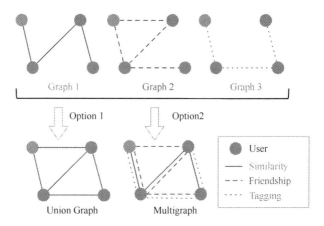

Fig. 4.2: Modeling multi-relational social networks using a union-graph vs. a multigraph.

4.3.1 *Multigraph generation*

Formally, let graphs $G_1 = \{\mathcal{U}, E_1, w_1\}$, $G_2 = \{\mathcal{U}, E_2, w_2\}$, ..., $G_Z = \{\mathcal{U}, E_Z, w_Z\}$ denote the collected and propagated Z types of social networks on a common user set $\mathcal{U}$, which is the population of users in a recommender system, and $E_1, E_2, \ldots, E_Z \subseteq \mathcal{U} \times \mathcal{U}$ are respectively the edge sets of each graph. A graph G_k is associated with a weighting function w_k and correspondingly a weighting matrix W_k as denoted. A simple way to handle multiple social networks is to aggregate different user relationships to build a union graph:

Definition 4.3 (Union graph). A union graph is an ordinary simple graph $G' = \{\mathcal{U}, E', w'\}$ on the vertex set $\mathcal{U}$, in which the edges are given by the union set of all single edge sets, i.e., $E' = \bigcup_{k=1}^{Z} E_k$. Correspondingly, a union weighting function $w' : E' \to [0, 1]$ is associated to aggregate the available edge weightings of single graphs:

$$w'(e) = g(w_1(e), w_2(e), \dots, w_Z(e)), \forall e \in E',$$

where g is an aggregating function such as linear averaging in [Jacob *et al.* (2011)].

In contrast, a multigraph that retains the original structures of all single graphs is defined [Gjoka *et al.* (2011)].

Definition 4.4 (Multigraph). A multigraph $G = \{\mathcal{U}, E\}$ is a special graph on $\mathcal{U}$, where the edge set $E = \biguplus_{k=1}^{Z} E_k$ is given by the multiset of the edge sets of single graphs G_1 to G_2.

As shown in the above definition, a multigraph can be seen as overlapping all single graphs rather than merging them into one simple graph. In the following, we use the subscript symbols i and j to index vertices (users) and k and l to index single graphs.

4.3.2 *Inter-network comparison*

Inter-network comparisons have attracted much study to compare the structural information between different networks. We introduce the average similarity of neighbors [Zhao *et al.* (2014)] as a measurement of the structural similarity of two networks. This metric was not originally proposed for weighted graphs, thus we modify it to the following form:

$$\text{ASN}(A, B) = \frac{\sum_i \text{DEG}_{AB}(i)}{\sum_i \text{DEG}_A(i) + \sum_i \text{DEG}_B(i)}$$

where $\text{DEG}_A(i)$ and $\text{DEG}_B(i)$ are respectively the out degrees of the ith node in graph A and graph B and $\text{DEG}_{AB}(i)$ denotes the summation of the out degrees of this node to the common neighbors in both graphs. Clearly, we have that

$$\text{DEG}_{AB}(i) \leq \text{DEG}_A(i) + \text{DEG}_B(i)$$

and the equation holds only if the node has the exactly same out-linked neighbors in both graphs.

For recommender systems, we put emphasis on the structural "diversity" rather than the "similarity" measurement of different user networks. An inter-network diversity measurement is given as follows:

$$\delta\left(A, B\right) = 1 - \mathrm{ASN}\left(A, B\right).\qquad\qquad(4.13)$$

The proposed inter-network diversity measurement can be used to pre-screen the various input user relationships. For example, we adopt only one if two networks have very small diversity for the following two reasons. First, the two networks have very similar structures such that it is no need to combine them for the data sparse problem. Second, incorporating duplicate networks is equivalent to reusing a same information resource, which is unfair for other input resources.

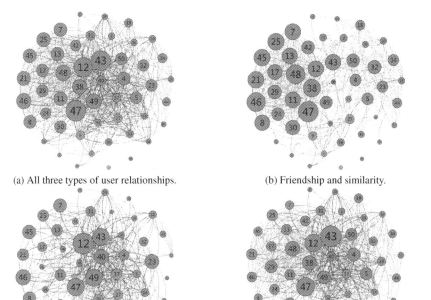

(a) All three types of user relationships.   (b) Friendship and similarity.

(c) Friendship and tagging.   (d) Similarity and tagging.

Fig. 4.3: Inter-network comparisons with Last.fm dataset.

Fig. 4.3 illustrates the network-to-network comparisons in an example data set from Last.fm. We import the complex relationships of the first 50 users in the Last.fm dataset mentioned in the above section. Three relational networks between users are initialized from different resources including the explicit friendships, the preference similarities, and the co-tagging relationships. The overall multigraph structure is presented in Fig. 4.3 (a) by overlapping all three kinds of relationships. We compare each pair from the three single networks to measure their structural diversity in the sub-figures Fig. 4.3 (b), Fig. 4.3 (c) and Fig. 4.3 (d), respectively. Fig. 4.3 (b) shows that the friendship and the similarity networks share a small part of the edges. Fig. 4.3 (c) presents the friendship network and tagging network and illustrates that these two networks are also well distinguished. Fig. 4.3 (d) indicates that similarity and tagging networks have more common edges than is shown in the former two figures. We calculate the inter-network diversity measurement of Eq. (4.13) for each pair of the three networks and obtain the following results.

$$\begin{cases} \delta(\text{friendship}, \text{similarity}) = 0.82, \\ \delta(\text{friendship}, \text{tagging}) = 0.83, \\ \delta(\text{similarity}, \text{tagging}) = 0.42. \end{cases}$$

The result supports the assumption that the friendship and similarity networks differ in structure, and so do the friendship and tagging networks, while the diversity between the similarity and tagging networks is less, i.e., they are more similar in structure. We should note that the proposed inter-network diversity measurement only evaluates the difference in network structure rather than the quantitative weighting of edges. In other words, "high diversity" here indicates that two networks have complementary structures, i.e., they share a small part of the common edges, but it does not mean that the strength of their common edges are inconsistent. Admittedly, it is helpful to alleviate the data sparse problem when utilizing more complementary social networks.

4.3.3 *Multigraph ranking for recommendation*

The three types of user relationships presented in Section 4.1 exist between users which makes it difficult to find user neighbors. Unlike previous methods that only apply to a single type of social relationships, a multigraph ranking model is proposed that can identify user neighbors and provide them recommendations from multiple social networks.

To illustrate the need for multigraph and its advantages, we start this section with a two-moon ranking problem shown in Fig. 4.4. In this example, the users are connected by three types of relationships: similarity, friendship and tagging correlations. User nodes are placed in a geometric figure with regard to the average strength of the three types of relationships with respect to the target user and marked with different circles. Placing all these small groups together, two large partitions are generated by adjacent small user groups. We call this problem a two-moon multi-relational social network ranking problem.

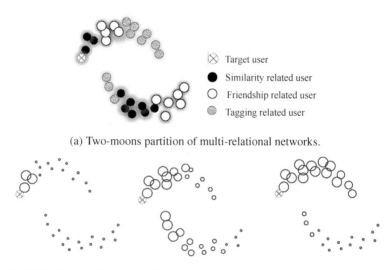

$\boxtimes$ Target user
● Similarity related user
○ Friendship related user
⊚ Tagging related user

(a) Two-moons partition of multi-relational networks.

(b) CF similarity ranking.   (c) Union graph ranking.   (d) Multigraph ranking.

Fig. 4.4: Ranking in a multi-relational network with a two-moon pattern.

The goal is to identify the overall nearest neighbors for the particular target user marked in the figure. In Fig. 4.4 (b-d), three different ranking models are compared. The marker sizes represent the ranking scores predicted by the ranking model. Fig. 4.4 (b) presents the expected ranking result of the CF method using the preference similarity of users. The CF method can only find a small number of neighbors because it is limited to sparse data. Fig. 4.4 (c) presents a union graph-based ranker that uses averaged Euclidean distance. This ranker independently compares the average closeness of the candidate users to the target user, so the connections between the candidates are ignored. As a result, the two-moon pattern cannot be recognized by this kind of ranker. Fig. 4.4 (d) shows the ideal ranking result that we expect to obtain with the proposed multigraph ranking model. This ranker can identify users in the same partition as a result of adjacent small groups with different types of relationships.

A new smoothness function $\mathcal{S}(f)$ for the multigraph ranking problem is proposed. Suppose that a multigraph G has been established from Z types of social networks, the relationship between two users can be represented by a column vector containing the edge weighting in each single network as follows:

$$[u_i, u_j] \leftarrow \begin{pmatrix} w_{ij}^1 \\ w_{ij}^2 \\ \vdots \\ w_{ij}^Z \end{pmatrix}$$

where $w_{ij}^k \in [0, 1]$ is the closeness of the two users in the k-th graph, a simplified expression of $w_k([u_i, u_j])$. Note that $w_{ij}^k = 0$ if there is no connection between u_i and u_j in the k-th single graph.

An edge function is a function that can map a directed pair of vertices to a real value [Jacob *et al.* (2011)]. We import the edge function to multigraphs, which gives an initial estimation of the strength of the overall relationships between two vertices. To utilize both intra-network relationships and inter-network diversities, we define a virtual edge function $\pi : \mathcal{U} \times \mathcal{U} \rightarrow \mathbb{R}$ for the user vertices in a multigraph as follows:

$$\pi([u_i, u_j]; \Delta) = \frac{1}{2} \sum_{k,l}^Z w_{ij}^k w_{ij}^l \Delta_{kl} \qquad (4.14)$$

where Δ_{kl} is the inter-network diversity between the k-th and l-th graphs. Comparing the structural diversity of each pair of single graphs, we obtain a $Z \times Z$ diversity matrix Δ:

$$\Delta_{kl} = \begin{cases} \delta(G_k, G_l), & k \neq l \\ 1, & k = l \end{cases}$$

This setting considers the unique environment in recommender systems. We assume the relationship of two users should be emphasized if they are connected by many and diverse relationships. A matrix Π with $\Pi_{ij} = \pi([u_i, u_j])$ is defined:

$$\Pi = \frac{1}{2} \sum_{k,l=1}^Z \Delta_{kl} \mathbf{W}_k \circ \mathbf{W}_l.$$

Further, we define the virtual out-degree $\eth^+(u_i)$ and in-degree $\eth^-(u_i)$ of a particular user u_i as follows:

$$\eth^+(u_i) = \sum_{j \neq i} \pi([u_i, u_j]), \eth^-(u_i) = \sum_{j \neq i} \pi([u_j, u_i]).$$

Two diagonal matrixes $\mathfrak{D}_+$ and $\mathfrak{D}_-$ are then represented with $(\mathfrak{D}_+)_{ii} = \eth^+(u_i)$ and $(\mathfrak{D}_-)_{ii} = \eth^-(u_i)$ on the diagonals. For a multigraph model, the smoothness of a ranking function consists of the edge derivation crossing every pair of users is defined. For an out-linked virtual edge, the edge derivation is:

$\left.\frac{\partial f}{\partial [u_i, u_j]}\right|_{u_i} = \sqrt{\frac{\pi([u_i, u_j])}{\mathfrak{d}^+(u_i)}} f(u_i) - \sqrt{\frac{\pi([u_i, u_j])}{\mathfrak{d}^-(u_j)}} f(u_j)$. For an in-linked virtual

edge, the edge derivation is: $\left.\frac{\partial f}{\partial [u_j, u_i]}\right|_{u_i} = \sqrt{\frac{\pi([u_j, u_i])}{\mathfrak{d}^-(u_i)}} f(u_i) - \sqrt{\frac{\pi([u_j, u_i])}{\mathfrak{d}^+(u_j)}} f(u_j)$.

t is easy to have that $\left.\frac{\partial f}{\partial [u_i, u_j]}\right|_{u_j} = -\left.\frac{\partial f}{\partial [u_i, u_j]}\right|_{u_i}$. The local variation at each vertex

in a multigraph is:

$$\|\nabla_{u_i} f\| = \sqrt{\frac{1}{2}\left[\sum_{j \neq i} \left(\left.\frac{\partial f}{\partial [u_i, u_j]}\right|_{u_i}\right)^2 + \sum_{j \neq i} \left(\left.\frac{\partial f}{\partial [u_j, u_i]}\right|_{u_i}\right)^2 \right]}.$$

The overall smoothness of the ranking function is the summation of all local variations of all users:

$$
\begin{aligned}
\mathcal{S}(f) &= \frac{1}{2} \sum_{i=1}^{n} \|\nabla_{u_i} f\|^2 \\
&= \frac{1}{4}\left[\sum_{i=1}^{n}\sum_{j=1}^{n} \left(\left.\frac{\partial f}{\partial [u_i, u_j]}\right|_{u_i}\right)^2 + \sum_{i=1}^{n}\sum_{j=1}^{n} \left(\left.\frac{\partial f}{\partial [u_j, u_i]}\right|_{u_i}\right)^2 \right] \\
&= f^T f - f^T \mathfrak{D}_+^{-1/2} \Pi \mathfrak{D}_-^{-1/2} f \\
&= f^T (I - S) f
\end{aligned}
\tag{4.15}
$$

where S is defined: $S = \mathfrak{D}_+^{-1/2} \Pi \mathfrak{D}_-^{-1/2}$. The multigraph ranking problem can thus be formalized to the following optimization:

$$\min_{f:U \to \mathbb{R}} Q(f) = f^T (I - S) f + \mu(f - y)^T (f - y).$$

We can obtain the optimized ranking vector f^* for multigraph ranking following the similar calculations of Eq. (4.8):

$$f^* = (I - \alpha S)^{-1} y \tag{4.16}$$

where $\alpha \in (0, 1)$ is a model parameter balancing the smoothness and consistency of the ranking.

4.3.4 *Recommendation generation*

To generate recommendations for an target user u_a, the closest neighbor users are identified by the proposed multigraph ranking model, which requires a column vector $y \in \mathbb{R}^{|U|}$ given as the input query vector. The edge function defined in Eq. (4.14) can be natively imported to generate an initial query vector, as follows:

$$y(u_i) = \begin{cases} \frac{1}{2} Z^2, & \text{if } u_i = u_a, \\ \pi([u_a, u_i]), & \text{if } u_i \neq u_a. \end{cases}$$

It is easy to find that $\pi \leqslant \frac{1}{2}Z^2$ is from Eq. (4.14). With the query vector $\boldsymbol{y}$, the optimized ranking vector $\boldsymbol{f}$ will be obtained by solving Eq. (4.16). The top-K users who acquire the highest ranking scores are then selected as the nearest neighbors for a specific target user u, denoted as Neib (u).

We now summarize the whole process of the recommendation method by multigraph ranking. First, multiple single social networks are built for users. Next, the proposed random walk-based social network propagation model is employed to enrich the original data of each social network. After this, a multigraph is constructed to represent the multi-relational social networks of users. The proposed multigraph ranking model is then implemented to identify target user's closest neighbor users and the CF rating predictions are made for unseen items.

4.4   Multi-objective Recommendation by Hypergraph Ranking

Except for single objective recommendation in the last section, we also give multi-objective recommendation method by hypergraph ranking. We use restaurant recommendations as an example for e-commerce recommender systems. In this scenario, information such as customer visiting history, restaurant attributes and context information is valuable for recommendation making. We propose a generic user-item-attribute-context (UIAC) data model to summarize four types of information entities and six types of pairwise or high-order relationships, as shown in Fig. 4.5.

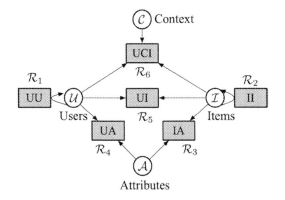

Fig. 4.5: UIAC data model.

4.4.1 *The UIAC data model*

Taking a restaurant recommender system as an example, the four types of information entities are users, items (restaurants), restaurant attributes and context information.

(1) Users (U) are the registered customers and requesters. Users are encouraged to review the restaurants they have visited using numerical ratings, as an explicit means of obtaining user preferences.

(2) Items (I) are the restaurants included in a restaurant recommender system as recommended objects. The ultimate goal of an RSS is to suggest a list of restaurants as alternative options to the users' requests.

(3) Attributes (A) are a set of taxonomy texts describing the conditions of restaurants, such as restaurant types ("breakfast", "lunch", "dinner", *etc.*), restaurant ambiance ("romantic", "intimate", "touristy", *etc.*), noise level ("quite" or "loud") and so on. Usually, an e-commerce platform will provide a standard taxonomy for the items and we can collect them directly. For example, it shows the settings of restaurant taxonomy attributes in Yelp.com in Fig. 4.6.

(4) Context (C) refers to third-party information that may affect user choices [Dey *et al.* (2001)]. Despite environmental information such as time and location, we also treat tags or short comments as context entities because the reviewing behavior also reflects user preference. Thus, we extend the context entities to all third-party resources beyond users and items that may affect or reflect user preferences for items.

Based on the analysis of the literature and real datasets, the possible pairwise or group relationships in a restaurant recommender system are specified in the following six forms.

(1) User-User relationships (UU). This type of relationship refers to the correlations between users. The general considerable relationships could be user social networks, rating similarities, or implicit trust refined from common behaviors.

(2) Item-Item relationships (II). Restaurants may share connections because they are located in the same district or they belong to the same company. It is worth mentioning that some connections are multi-to-multi relationships rather than pairwise relationships.

(3) Item-Attribute association relationships (IA). In e-commerce applications, items usually come with descriptions of various attributes. Thus, we can collect the association relationships between items and attributes.

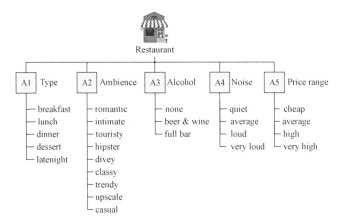

Fig. 4.6: The taxonomy attributes for restaurants in Yelp.com.

(4) User-Attribute preference relationships (UA). Users may prefer some items with particular attributes where the preference relationships between users and item attributes can be collected.

(5) User-Item preference relationships (UI). Personalized ratings of items are the most explicit preferences of users. In addition, if there are no explicit ratings, the visiting or purchasing history can be seen as implicit acceptance of users for items.

(6) User-Context-Item relationship (UCI). We point out that third-party context information is able to affect or reflect user preference. If user acceptance of an item is adjusted by a particular context, we then collect a high-order tripartite relationship for the user, the item and the context entities.

The above elaborates four types of information entities and six types of relationships that may appear in restaurant recommender system. Because some relationships are high-order connections between multiple objects, the conventional pairwise graph models are unable to present them well. We therefore introduce a multipartite hypergraph in the following sub-section.

4.4.2 *Multipartite hypergraph construction*

With the UIAC data model, a hypergraph $G = \{V, E\}$ will be constructed where the vertex set $V = U \cup I \cup A \cup C$ is the union of four types of objects: user nodes, item nodes, attribute nodes and context nodes, and the hyperedge set E consists of six subsets $E^{(1)}$ to $E^{(6)}$ generated from the six types of relationships, UU, II, IA,

UA, UI and UCI. The general initialization of each type of edge is as follows.

The first subset of edges $E^{(1)}$ is initialized from user-user relationships UU. For pairwise social relationships, a pairwise edge will be set to a pair of user nodes. Note that users could be connected by multiple edges if multi-relational connections exist, as in Section 4.3. Hence, a hyperedge will be set to connect multiple user nodes for group social relationships.

The second subset of edges $E^{(2)}$ is initialized from item-item relationships II. Similarly, the items bundled by some relationships are connected with hyperedges. For example, we initialize a hyperedge for restaurants belonging to the same catering company or those that are located in the same district of a city.

The third subset of edges $E^{(3)}$ is initialized from item-attribute associations IA. The item-attribute association relationships are usually represented by pairwise connections between item nodes and attribute nodes. With hypergraphs, in another way, we can instead build an overall hyperedge to include an item node and all its attributes.

The fourth subset of edges $E^{(4)}$ is initialized from user-attribute preferences UA. The same as item-attribute associations, user preference to item attributes can be represented using pairwise edges or hyperedges.

The fifth subset of edges $E^{(5)}$ is initialized from user-item ratings UI. Like most recommendation models, the explicit rating given by a user to an item initializes a pairwise edge between them, together with a scaled number to indicate the preference degrees.

The sixth subset of edges $E^{(6)}$ is initialized from user-context-item relationships UCI. If a user's preference for an item changes in different contexts, a hyperedge will connect the user node, the item node and the related context nodes. As an extension, textual comments or tags are also third-party context entities that reflect user preferences. Hence, the reviewing or tagging behavior of a user will initialize a hyper edge as a connection between the user, the item and several words.

With these settings, a multipartite hypergraph will be formalized with the structural information as shown in Table 4.2.

4.4.3 *Balanced hypergraph ranking*

To overcome the possible ranking bias of traditional ranking for multipartite hypergraphs, we modify the vertex degree $d\left(v\right) = \sum_{v \in e} w(e)$ to an enhanced form:

$$d_{+}\left(v\right) = \sum_{v \in e} w(e)\sqrt{\delta(e)}. \tag{4.17}$$

Table 4.2: Structure of the formalized multipartite hypergraph.

Vertex	$E^{(1)}$	$E^{(2)}$	$E^{(3)}$	$E^{(4)}$	$E^{(5)}$	$E^{(6)}$
U	$UE^{(1)}$			$UE^{(4)}$	$UE^{(5)}$	$UE^{(6)}$
I		$IE^{(2)}$	$IE^{(3)}$		$IE^{(5)}$	$IE^{(6)}$
A			$AE^{(3)}$	$AE^{(4)}$		
C						$CE^{(6)}$
source	UU	II	IA	UA	UI	UCI
relationships						

Different from the traditional vertex degree definition, the enhanced vertex degree of Eq. (4.17) also integrates the degree information of the involved edges. An enhanced node degree matrix D_+ can then be denoted with this new setting. Next, the cost function Eq. (4.7) of the hypergraph ranking model is rewritten to:

$$Q(\boldsymbol{f}) = \frac{1}{2} \sum_{i,j=1}^{|V|} \sum_{e \in E} \frac{w(e)h(v_i,e)h(v_j,e)}{\sqrt{\delta(e)}} \left(\frac{f_i}{\sqrt{d_+(v_i)}} - \frac{f_j}{\sqrt{d_+(v_j)}} \right)^2 + \mu \sum_{i=1}^{|V|} (f_i - y_i)^2.$$

The first part of the right side in the above equation, denoting the smoothness function S (f), can be simplified to matrix-vector form by the following steps:

$$\begin{aligned}
\mathrm{S}(f) &= \frac{1}{2} \sum_{i,j=1}^{|V|} \sum_{e \in E} \frac{w(e)h(v_i,e)h(v_j,e)}{\sqrt{\delta(e)}} \left(\frac{f_i}{\sqrt{d_+(v_i)}} - \frac{f_j}{\sqrt{d_+(v_j)}} \right)^2 \\
&= \boldsymbol{f}^T \boldsymbol{f} - \boldsymbol{f}^T \boldsymbol{D}_+^{-1/2} \boldsymbol{H} \boldsymbol{W} \boldsymbol{D}_e^{-1/2} \boldsymbol{H}^T \boldsymbol{D}_+^{-1/2} \boldsymbol{f} \\
&= \boldsymbol{f}^T (\boldsymbol{I} - \boldsymbol{A}_+) \boldsymbol{f}. \quad (4.18)
\end{aligned}$$

Here, a new intermediate matrix $\boldsymbol{A}_+ = \boldsymbol{D}_+^{-1/2} \boldsymbol{H} \boldsymbol{W} \boldsymbol{D}_e^{-1/2} \boldsymbol{H}^T \boldsymbol{D}_+^{-1/2}$ is introduced to replace the old matrix $\boldsymbol{A}$ in Section 4.2.3. Performing a similar calculation to Eq. (4.8), the optimized ranking order of balanced hypergraph ranking (BHR) is obtained:

$$\boldsymbol{f}_{\mathrm{BHR}} = (\boldsymbol{I} - \alpha \boldsymbol{A}_+)^{-1} \boldsymbol{y}.$$

Correspondingly, the random walk version of BHR will be $\boldsymbol{f}_{\mathrm{BHR(RW)}} = (\boldsymbol{I} - \alpha \boldsymbol{T}_+)^{-1} \boldsymbol{y}$, where $\boldsymbol{T}_+ = \boldsymbol{D}_+^{-1} \boldsymbol{H} \boldsymbol{W} \boldsymbol{D}_e^{-1/2} \boldsymbol{H}^T$. It is easy to find that $\boldsymbol{A}_+$ is the normalized version of $\boldsymbol{T}_+$. With the settings of the proposed BHR, the results of the example in Fig. 4.1 are recalculated as follows:

$$p(B \in e_2)^{\text{new}} = \frac{1 \times \sqrt{2}}{1 \times \sqrt{2} + 1 \times \sqrt{20}} \times \frac{1}{2} \approx 0.12 < p(B)^{\text{old}} = 0.25,$$

$$p(1 \in e_1)^{\text{new}} = \frac{1 \times \sqrt{20}}{1 \times \sqrt{2} + 1 \times \sqrt{20}} \times \frac{1}{20} \approx 0.038 > p(1)^{\text{old}} = 0.025.$$

This indicates that the settings in BHR will alleviate the ranking bias of traditional methods to some extent.

4.4.4 *Multi-objective recommendation*

With the construction of multipartite hypergraphs, we elaborate how to transfer users' multi-objective requests to computable input and propose the multi-objective recommendation framework. In traditional graph ranking-based recommendation models, the current target user is the only query node as input, and the ranking aim is to find the closest (item) nodes to this single node. In this chapter, a multi-objective recommendation request can be seen as multiple requirements to a set of query nodes, and the ranking aim becomes to determine the closest nodes to all members in the query set rather than an individual user. Hence, a multi-objective request can be represented by an input query set containing multiple users, item attributes, context information, *etc.*

Based on this analysis, a multi-objective request can be decomposed to a query set $V_q \subset V$ with a number of vertices in the multipartite hypergraph model. A corresponding input query vector q is then generated with $q_i = 1$ if the i-th hypergraph vertex is included in the query set and zero otherwise. For a single-objective request, as a special case, the input query set contains only the current user so the input query vector will have only one positive element.

Now we can transfer a multi-objective request to a computable query vector q as the input for hypergraph ranking. Generally, the query set is far smaller than the whole vertex set such that the input query vector would be very sparse. Hence, we define a new query vector $y = A_+^T q$ to replace q to enrich the input information.

The overall framework for multi-objective recommendations is proposed in Fig. 4.7 with restaurant recommendations as an example. This framework consists of four steps to complete a multi-objective recommendation task: query generation, hypergraph construction, hypergraph ranking and recommendation generation.

Step 1: Query generation. In this step, the target user sends a multi-objective recommendation request represented by a query set and the system will generate an input query vector.

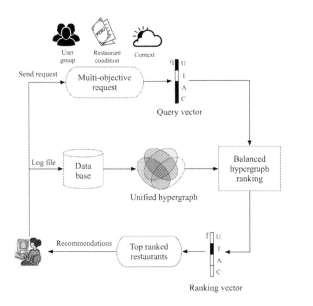

Fig. 4.7: Multi-objective recommendation framework for restaurants.

Step 2: Hypergraph construction. A multipartite hypergraph is constructed from historical data in the background. Different resources in the database will be utilized to generate the diverse relationships between different objects.

Step 3: Balanced hypergraph ranking. In this step, the obtained query vector and a multipartite hypergraph constitute the input of the proposed BHR model. Some intermediate matrixes like D_+ and A_+ are trained in advance. A ranking vector f will be computed using BHR to evaluate the closeness of other vertices to the whole input query set.

Step 4: Recommendation making. This step extracts the ranking order of only item vertices, and suggests the top ranked ones to satisfy the multi-objective recommendation requests of users.

4.5 Summary

To overcome the cold start and data sparsity problem, an increasing number of social network-based recommender systems import user relationships as an additional resource. This chapter presents how social network of users can be used to enhance recommender systems by multigraph and hypergraph ranking. Two methods that handle users connected by multiple relationships simultaneously are proposed: a multi-relational social recommendation method by multigraph ranking of users to help identify nearest neighbors; and a multi-objective recommendation method by hypergraph ranking is, which integrates diverse entities and relationships between users and items in the hypergraph.

Chapter 5

Tag-aware Recommender Systems

User-contributed information, which is also known as folksonomy, is valuable information because it either directly or indirectly expresses user preferences. Users can freely assign items with their own defined words, which are called tags. Tags can be words describing the item's characteristics, which enriches the content information, or they can be subjective judgments, which reflect user preferences. Similar to social networks, tags can help solving cold start and data sparsity problems in user preference prediction, thus improve the accuracy of the recommendation.

In this chapter, we illustrate how tag data can enhance the recommender systems in two ways. One is for recommendation in a single domain and the other is to use tags as a bridge for cross-domain recommendation. In Section 5.1 we provide an introduction to context-aware recommender systems. Tag-aware recommendation methods in single domain are presented in Section 5.2, followed by tag-aware cross-domain recommendation methods in Section 5.3. Finally, Section 5.4 summarizes the chapter.

5.1 Context-aware Recommender Systems

A tag-aware recommender system is a specific context-aware recommender system. In this section, we introduce context-aware recommender systems.

When recommending an item to a user, context information, such as time, place, related companies and mood, may be relevant. Take music for an example, the music recommendation in the afternoon when a person is relaxing can be quite different to the music recommendation before going to sleep; and the music recommendation when at the gym might be different to what would be recommended during a commute or when having a party with friends. Therefore, information that provides context can be more crucial than we think. Moreover, the additional information is very helpful in solving the data sparsity problem. Integrating context information has provided the recommender systems a broader scope on user profiling.

Context is defined as "any information that can be used to characterize the situation of an entity" [Dey *et al.* (2001)]. It is important to incorporate the context information in the recommendation process to be able to recommend items to users in specific circumstances, and so recently the context information, such as time, geometrical information or the company of other people (friends, families or colleagues), has been considered in existing recommender systems. For example, the information obtained with the rapid growth of using mobile handsets. The context information provides additional information for recommendation making, especially for some applications in which it is not sufficient to consider only users and items, such as recommending a vacation package or personalized content on a website.

Context in the recommender system field is a multifaceted concept used across various disciplines, with each discipline adopting a certain angle and adding their own "stamp" on the concept of context. With context awareness, the original two-dimension, user-item adoption relationship becomes a three-dimension relationship. In general, users interact with the system within a particular context and preferences for items within one context may be completely different to those in another context. Context-aware recommender systems take into account contextual factors in generating more relevant recommendations [Ricci *et al.* (2010)].

Three representative methods have been designed to deal with contextual preferences:

(1) Contextual pre-filtering: the context information is used to filter out irrelevant information before applying a traditional recommender system model.

(2) Contextual post-filtering: the recommendation results from traditional recommender system models are further filtered using context information.

(3) Contextual modeling: irrelevant ratings are filtered through context information before the recommendation process begins.

The recommendation processes in methods (1) and (2) are very similar to the traditional recommendation methods. While contextual post-filtering methods are using context information to filter the recommendation results generated, as opposed to contextual pre-filtering which relies on traditional models to generate recommendations, contextual modeling methods model the context information directly in a recommendation function [Hariri *et al.* (2011)], which is the core development of the context-aware recommender system. Based on the utility function of recommender system Eq. (1.1) presented in Chapter 1, the utility function of contextual modeling recommendation methods can be viewed as:

$$f : \mathcal{U} \times \mathcal{V} \times \mathcal{C} \rightarrow \mathcal{D}$$

It defines the utility of a specific item $v \in \mathcal{V}$ to a user $u \in \mathcal{U}$ with context $c \in \mathcal{C}$. $\mathcal{D}$ is the final recommendation list containing a set of items in a ranked order.

The contextual modeling methods integrate various data including tags, reviews, documents, social media information, *etc.* The context information is represented as matrixes, tensors, processed by probabilistic models, and deep learning models as well as integrated into matrix factorizations, factorization machines or other complex models. Many online systems enable users to freely create their own descriptions for items in the form of single words or short phrases, which are called folksonomy tags. In a recommender system, tags provide valuable information and have enriched content information such that other users can better identify items. As well as creating new tags, users also can select existed tags in the systems to classify items.

Users can use any free text, for example "excellent", "fun" and "for kids", as tag to the items. The accumulated tags act as important meta-data, which is recorded with the rating data between users and items in the recommender system. As such, tagged data are widely exploited as an additional data source for enriching user-item interaction data and for improving recommendation performance.

Tag data was first exploited in single-domain recommender systems to exploit user preference. However, the uncontrolled vocabularies employed by users make the tag data noisy and sometimes redundant. At the same time, because there can be so many different user-generated tags, they are generally only found on a small fraction of items as a whole, making the tag data very sparse.

There has been researches that have focused on generating a list of relevant tags for a specific item for recommendation to users, known as tag recommendation. These methods treat the tag as an item so that recommendation methods for implicit feedback, such as CF, can be used to provide a selection of candidate tags for users to choose from. What makes it special to recommend tag compared with other items is tags have semantic meanings.

Tag data also can be an effective way to link two domains, since different users in the two domains may express similar tastes with their tags [Hao *et al.* (2017)]. The goal of cross-domain recommendation is to reuse knowledge from other auxiliary source domains to compensate for data sparsity in the target domain. Overlapping tags are used to profile cross-domain users and items, so that cross-domain user-to-user and item-to-item similarities can be inferred from the tagged data. These similarities can then be exploited as prior knowledge to regularize the joint matrix factorization process.

These methods use the identical tags, which are also called overlapping tags, as bridges to connect two domains. Though the results that have been achieved by utilizing these methods are promising, the overlapping tags take up a very small portion of the total number of tags in each domain. The abundance of information that reflects a domain's unique characteristics is usually embedded within non-overlapping or domain-specific tags. Therefore, neglecting non-overlapping tags when building connections between the domains tends to lead to poorer recommendation performance. Also, since the vocabulary users can use is uncontrolled when they tag items, numerous ambiguous and redundant tags will be produced. In such cases, two non-identical tags in two domains may be semantically related. Exploiting the semantic similarity of tags will greatly strengthen the connection between two domains and enable knowledge transfer from the source domain to the target domain, thereby also improving recommendation accuracy in the sparse target domain.

5.2   Single-domain Tag-aware Recommendation Methods

We give a tag-aware recommendation method in single domain as a representative for integrating tag data in matrix factorization to alleviate the data sparsity and improve the accuracy of recommender systems [Zhen *et al.* (2009)].

Suppose there are M users and N items in one domain, the relationship between users and items is given as $R \in \mathbb{R}^{M \times N}$ (bold letter represents a matrix). If a user's preferences are represented as ratings, then R is a rating matrix where R is subject to $X_{ij} \in \{1, 2, 3, 4, 5, ?\}$ ("?" denotes a missing value). By minimizing its Euclidean distance to the original rating matrix $\boldsymbol{R}$, $\boldsymbol{R}$ is approximated by:

$$\hat{\boldsymbol{R}} = \boldsymbol{U}\boldsymbol{V}^T. \tag{5.1}$$

Thus, $\boldsymbol{U} \in \mathbb{R}^{M \times K}$ is the user feature matrix and $\boldsymbol{V} \in \mathbb{R}^{N \times K}$ is the item feature matrix, two low-rank matrixes for users and items, respectively. The ith user and jth item are represented by the ith and jth row of the two matrixes as U_{i*} and V_{j*}. After matrix factorization, the users and items are mapped to a latent feature space of a lower dimensionality K.

The recommendation task is to predict the missing values in the rating matrix based on historical records of the users' preferences. Since the rating matrix $\boldsymbol{X}$ is usually extremely sparse, the low-rank approximation matrix factorization is easy to overfit. Regularization is usually used on low-rank feature matrixes to avoid this problem. In general, the optimization problem is:

$$\min_{\boldsymbol{U},\boldsymbol{V}} \mathcal{L}(f(\boldsymbol{U},\boldsymbol{V}),\boldsymbol{R}) + \lambda \mathcal{R}(\boldsymbol{U},\boldsymbol{V}) \tag{5.2}$$

where $\mathcal{L}$ is the loss function of the predicted ratings $f(\boldsymbol{U},\boldsymbol{V})$ and the original ratings $\boldsymbol{R}$, $\mathcal{R}(\boldsymbol{U},\boldsymbol{V})$ is the regularization term, and $\lambda \geqslant 0$ is the regularization trade-off parameter. Specifically, the objective function with regularization terms to measure the loss and a Frobenius norm is [Mnih and Salakhutdinov (2008)]:

$$J(\boldsymbol{U},\boldsymbol{V}) = \frac{1}{2}\|\boldsymbol{I} \circ (\boldsymbol{R} - \boldsymbol{U}\boldsymbol{V}^T)\|_F^2 + \frac{\lambda}{2}\|\boldsymbol{U}\|_F^2 + \frac{\lambda}{2}\|\boldsymbol{V}\|_F^2 \tag{5.3}$$

where $\boldsymbol{I}$ is the rating indicator matrix, $I_{ij} \in \{0,1\}$. $I_{ij} = 1$ indicates that the rating is observed, or $I_{ij} = 0$ otherwise. $\circ$ denotes the Hadamard product of the matrixes.

In matrix factorization, the user-item rating matrix is factorized into one user feature matrix and one item feature matrix with regularizations. Based on the assumption "similar users have similar tastes and will thus choose similar items to consume", similarities on users or items can be used to constrain the proposed matrix factorization as prior knowledge. Tags provide extra information about users and items, so that they can provide regularization for matrix factorization. The goal of this method is to use the similarity mined from the tag data to constrain the matrix factorization. The result is to make the user feature vectors similar for those users who give similar tags. The constraints are achieved as:

$$\mathcal{R}(U) = \frac{1}{2} \sum_{u_i=1}^{M} \sum_{u_j=1}^{M} W_{u_i,u_j} \|U_{u_i,*} - U_{u_j,*}\|_F^2 \tag{5.4}$$

$$= \frac{1}{2} \sum_{u_i=1}^{M} \sum_{u_j=1}^{M} \left[W_{u_i,u_j} \sum_{k=1}^{K} (U_{u_i,k} - U_{u_j,k})^2 \right]$$

$$= \sum_{k=1}^{K} U_{*,k}^T L U_{*,k}$$

$$= tr(U^T L U)$$

where tr is the trace of a matrix, L denotes a Laplacian matrix, and $L = D - W$. W is the user similarity matrix, and D is a diagonal matrix defined as $D_{ii} = \sum_j W_{ij}$. As a result the objective function combining Eq. (5.3) and Eq. (5.4) is:

$$J(U, V) = \frac{1}{2} \|I_R \circ (R - UV^T)\|_F^2 \tag{5.5}$$

$$+ \frac{\lambda_1}{2} (\|U\|_F^2 + \|V\|_F^2) + \frac{\lambda_2}{2} tr(U^T L U)$$

where λ_1 and λ_2 are regularization parameters to control the contribution of regularization of the user/item feature matrix and the tag data.

The minimization in Eq. (5.5) can be achieved by gradient decent or other optimization methods. By fixing one variable (U or V) and minimizing the objective function on the other variables iteratively, we can get conditional results under this optimization.

5.3 Cross-domain Tag-aware Recommendation Methods

Data scarcity occurs because most users tend to only rate a small fraction of the items they prefer. To address this problem in CF, prior studies have emphasized the idea of applying transfer learning techniques and have developed cross-domain recommendation methods. Cross-domain recommender systems exploit the shared knowledge of auxiliary domains to assist recommendations in the target domain. Its performance depends on whether an effective domain correlation can be established to connect the domains for knowledge transfer.

Tags can encode both user preferences and item attributes, and tags follow the basic assumption that users with the same tagging behaviors tend to have similar interests. Except for the context information that tags can provide, integrating tags in recommendation is a great solution for the data sparsity problem. In such case, tags and cross-domain recommender systems take the effort together to solve the data sparsity problem. In this section, we will focus on the cross-domain tag-aware recommendation methods. We introduce two methods exploiting structural information and semantic information of tags as bridge for cross-domain recommender systems. More details of cross-domain recommender systems will be given in Chapter 9.

5.3.1 *Structural information of tags as bridge*

As shown in Fig. 5.1, suppose we have a new recommendation application for books. As a result of data sparsity at the outset, the recommender system cannot infer the preferences of a new user, Leo, and fails to make an accurate recommendation. Instead, we take more dense data from an existing movie recommender system, even though the users and items in the two systems are totally different. When we observe the two systems, we find that Rosa rated the movie "Titanic" 3.0 and tagged it #romantic, while Leo tagged the book "Gone with the Wind" as #romantic. The tag #romantic, which is called shared tag, is distributed in both domains and can be used as a link between those two users. It is therefore reasonable to assume that Leo will also remain neutral on the book "Gone with the Wind" since he shares the same tagging behavior as Rosa.

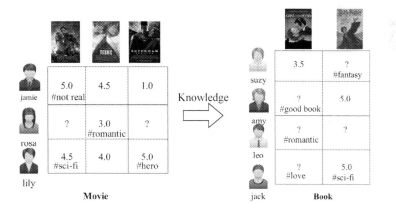

Fig. 5.1: Cross-domain recommendation scenario with tags.

Following the idea explained in the above example, we consider the challenging problem of utilizing tags to connect disjoint domains. To fully explore the knowledge encoded in both shared and domain-specific tags, we first model cross-domain user and item profiles with shared tags, and encode inter-domain correlation with shared tag-based user-to-user and item-to-item similarity matrixes. We then cluster domain-specific tags by using tag co-occurrence pattern and derive new user and item representations based on tag clusters. Therefore, new cross-domain user-to-user and item-to-item similarity matrixes, which are defined from the perspective of domain-specific tags, will be added to previously computed cross- domain similarity matrixes to enhance inter-domain correlation. In addition, we also exploit the tagging information of individual domain to compute similarity of users and items for single domain. This can be likened to building a compact intra-domain correlation. By adopting both inter and intra-domain correlations as structural constraints to regularize joint matrix factorization, we propose a complete tag-induced cross-domain recommendation model, called CTagCDR, to fully explore the contribution of tags in promoting knowledge transfer.

To exploit the full potential of tagging information, the proposed CTagCDR model aims to infer a strong inter-domain correlation and a compact intra-domain correlation from the user and item tagging histories. Specifically, CTagCDR is composed of following four major steps. The work flow of each step within the CTagCDR model is illustrated in Fig. 5.2.

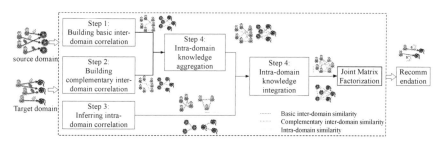

Fig. 5.2: Work flow and components of CTagCDR model.

Step 1: Building basic inter-domain correlations using shared tags.

In traditional CF methods, a user is represented by a vector defined over the entire item space. This reflects a user's preference for items that he/she is interested in. Similarly, an item is represented by a vector defined over the entire user space, which indicates the users that have shown an interest in this item. Due to the heterogeneity of disjoint domains, this way of modeling fails to characterize cross-domain users and items in a unified way. Considering the property that social tags can encode both user preferences and item attributes, Shi et al. proposed breaking {user, item, tag} ternary relationships into {user, tag} and {item, tag} two binary relationships, and built user and item profiles through shared tags, so that cross-domain users and items could be mapped to the same tag space for comparison [Shi *et al.* (2011)].

Nevertheless, when making user and item tagging matrixes, only binary information is taken into account, which may lose the ability to distinguish user tagging behavior or the tag distributions of items. To fully exploit the quantitative information encoded in shared tags T_c, we adopt TF-IDF weighting from text mining to build user tagging matrix X_u^π. In particular, the (i, m)-th element is defined as $tf * idf$ value between user i and shared tag m, as shown below:

$$[X_u^\pi]_{im} = tf_u(i, m) \times log_2 \left(\frac{n_\pi}{df_u(m)} \right) \qquad (5.6)$$

where $tf_u(i, m)$ denotes the normalized frequency of tag m in user i's tagging history on all items, and $df_u(m)$ denotes the number of users who have used tag m. Note that if user i has never used tag m, then $[X_u^\pi]_{im} = 0$.

Similarly, we can model the distribution of the shared tags of the items and represent this relationship in an item tagging matrix X_v^π. The (j, m)-th element is defined as follows,

$$[X_v^\pi]_{jm} = tf_v(j, m) \times log_2 \left(\frac{m_\pi}{df_v(m)} \right) \qquad (5.7)$$

where $tf_v(j, m)$ denotes the normalized occurrence frequency of tag m on item j used by all users, and $df_v(m)$ denotes the number of items that has been attached to the shared tag m. If item j has never been attached by share tag m, then $[X_v^\pi]_{jm} = 0$.

Once user and item profiles are generated by shared tags and vectorized, the cross-domain user and item similarities can be computed with different similarity metrics. For simplicity, we use a cosine similarity to compute the cross-domain user-to-user similarity matrix $S^u \in \mathbb{R}^{n_1 \times n_2}$ and the item-to-item similarity $S^v \in \mathbb{R}^{m_1 \times m_2}$ as:

$$
\begin{aligned}
S_{ip}^u &= \frac{\sum_{d=1}^{l_c} (X_u^1)_{id} \times (X_u^2)_{pd}}{\sqrt{\sum_{d=1}^{l_c} (X_u^1)_{id} \times (X_u^1)_{id}} \sqrt{\sum_{d=1}^{l_c} (X_u^2)_{pd} \times (X_u^2)_{pd}}}, \\
S_{jq}^v &= \frac{\sum_{d=1}^{l_c} (X_v^1)_{jd} \times (X_v^2)_{qd}}{\sqrt{\sum_{d=1}^{l_c} (X_v^1)_{jd} \times (X_v^1)_{jd}} \sqrt{\sum_{d=1}^{l_c} (X_v^2)_{qd} \times (X_v^2)_{qd}}}.
\end{aligned}
\qquad (5.8)
$$

Those similarity matrixes encode the information of shared tags and act as basic inter-domain correlation between source and target domains. We summarize this process in Algorithm 5.1.

Algorithm 5.1: Basic inter-domain correlation construction

Input: Tag assignment triplets $T_{tri}^{\pi}(\pi = 1, 2)$.

Output: Basic cross-domain similarity matrixes S_b^u and S_b^v.

1: Get shared tag set $T_c = T^1 \cap T^2$.

2: Initialize $X_u^{\pi} \in R^{n_{\pi} \times l_c}$ and $X_v^{\pi} \in \mathbb{R}^{m_{\pi} \times l_c}$ with zeros.

3: **for** $\pi = 1, 2$ **do**

4:   **for** $i = 1, 2, \ldots, n_{\pi}$ **do**

5:     **for** $m = 1, 2, \ldots, l_c$ **do**

6:       Given tag assignment triplets T_{tri}^{π}, fill element $[X_u^{\pi}]_{im}$ in X_u^{π} by Eq. (5.6).

7:     **end for**

8:   **end for**

9:   **for** $j = 1, 2, \ldots, m_{\pi}$ **do**

10:     **for** $m = 1, 2, \ldots, l_c$ **do**

11:       Given tag assignment triplets T_{tri}^{π}, fill element $[X_v^{\pi}]_{jm}$ in X_v^{π} by Eq. (5.7).

12:     **end for**

13:   **end for**

14: **end for**

15: Compute S_b^u and S_b^v by Eq. (5.8)

Step 2: Enhancing inter-domain correlations using domain-specific tag clusters.

Shared tags can help to address domain heterogeneity in modeling cross-domain users and items. However, to collect enough shared tags for disjoint domains is usually difficult, the resulting loose coupling between domains leads to inaccurate predictions. Furthermore, it is a waste to abandon such rich domain-specific tags, which are able to reflect the intrinsic properties of the individual domain. By using domain-specific tags to connect the cross-domain users and items, more domain linkages will be established and will enhance the inter-domain correlations.

However, a number of obstacles hinder the application of domain-specific tags. First, it is not trivial to employ heterogeneous domain-specific tags as features to link different domains, even though assembling tags from different domains to construct a pool of tags helps to address domain heterogeneity. In addition, the pairwise interactions between users and tags, resources and tags are sparse due to the power-law phenomenon [Clauset *et al.* (2009)]. This way of modeling poses two more problems: high scalability and heavy computability, when domain involvement increases. Second, tags are arbitrary words generated by users from an uncontrolled vocabulary, as a result ambiguity and redundancy exist in the tagging data. And if this issue is not addressed, final recommendation performance will be inaccurate. In this case, tag clustering provides a natural solution. With the implementation of clustering on domain-specific tags, we can bring domain-specific tags with similar meanings together. The generated tag clusters will also serve as high-level and compact representations for domain-specific tags, making it possible to transfer and share defined and unified user and item profiles between different domains.

Similar to the previous work [Pan *et al.* (2010)], which defines co-occurrence patterns by considering the relationship between pivot and non-pivot features, we devise a tag co-occurrence pattern for the shared and domain-specific tags. In other words, if the domain-specific tags from different domains occur with same shared tag in the user or item tagging histories, they will be grouped into same tag cluster. To avoid focusing on the tag examples that are associated with most users and items, rather than directly selecting the tags with the highest usage frequency, we propose to filter domain-specific tags based on information entropy before the clustering step. Given a shared tag m, the way to measure the importance of domain specific tag n on user side is defined as follows:

$$\theta(m,n) = \begin{cases} -\dfrac{\alpha(m,n)}{\beta(m,n)} \times \log_2 \dfrac{\alpha(m,n)}{\beta(m,n)}, & \text{if } \alpha(m,n) \neq 0, \\ 0, & \text{otherwise,} \end{cases} \tag{5.9}$$

where $\alpha(m,n)$ denotes the number of users who have used both shared tag m and domain-specific tag n in their tagging histories, $\beta(m,n)$ denotes the sum of users who used either the shared tag m or the domain-specific tag n to describe their interests. If $\theta(m,n) > \bar{\theta}(m)$, then we keep the domain-specific tag n, otherwise we abandon it. $\bar{\theta}(m)$ denotes the filtering threshold with regards to the shared tag m, which is set as the average importance over all domain-specific tags. The counterpart filtering on the item side can be obtained in a similar manner.

Filtering on the user-tag relationship, we will result in a tripartite graph $G_u = \{V, E\}$ as shown in Fig. 5.3 to represent the relationship between the domain-specific tags and the shared tags, where V is the set of nodes in this graph, and E denotes the set of undirected edges. Let l_u denote the number of filtered domain-specific tags. Therefore, there are two types of nodes in V: l_u nodes for the domain-specific tags and l_c nodes for the shared tags. Note that an edge in E only exists between different types of nodes, i.e. between the share tag m and the domain-specific tag n, and the edge weight indicates the similarity for the connected nodes. Take the nodes m and n in Fig. 5.3 for example, the edge weight is set as the Jaccard similarity:

$$sim(m, n) = \frac{\alpha(m, n)}{\beta(m, n)}.$$

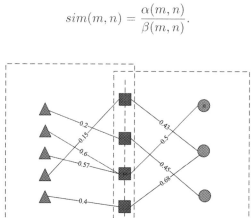

Fig. 5.3: Example of tag tripartite graph with user-tag relationship.

Squares denote shared tags in both domains, while the triangles and circles denote the filtered domain-specific tags from both source and target domains, respectively. The edge weight reflects the similarity between the connected tags.

Then we can define a $(l_u + l_c) \times (l_u + l_c)$ affinity matrix $\boldsymbol{A_u}$ for this graph, which is represented as:

$$A_u = \begin{bmatrix} \boldsymbol{I}_{l_u \times l_u}, & \boldsymbol{B} \\ \boldsymbol{B^{\mathsf{T}}}, & \boldsymbol{I}_{l_c \times l_c} \end{bmatrix}$$

where the connectivity matrix $\boldsymbol{B}$, $l_u \times l_c$, whose elements denote the similarity between the filtered domain-specific tags and shared tags, and $\boldsymbol{I}$ denotes the identity matrix. Similarly, we can derive a tripartite graph G_v and an affinity matrix $\boldsymbol{A_v}$ from the item side.

Once we have affinity matrixes $\boldsymbol{A_u}$ and $\boldsymbol{A_v}$ to represent the tag co-occurrence pattern, any clustering technique that takes a similarity measure as its input can be applied to implement the clustering. Here we adopt affinity propagation [Frey and Dueck (2007)] as our clustering method since it automatically finds the number of clusters based on the data provided, which saves us from tuning this parameter in validation. The generated k_u and k_v tag clusters from user-tag (item-tag) relation will be used as the new features to profile cross-domain users/items, so that users and items from different domains will be mapped to the same space spanned by the domain-specific tag clusters.

Algorithm 5.2: Complementary inter-domain correlation construction

---

Input: Tag assignment triplets T_{tri}^{π} $(\pi = 1, 2)$.

Output: Complementary cross-domain similarity matrixes S_c^u and S_c^v.

1: Combine original domain-specific tags from source and target domains by $T_d = T_d^1 + T_d^2$.

2: Filter T_d by Eq. (5.9) to get l_u domain-specific tags T_d^u based on user-tag relationship. Similarly, filter T_d again to get l_v domain-specific tags T_d^v based on item-tag relationship.

3: Based on filtered domain-specific tags T_d^u and T_d^v, build tagging matrixes Y_u^{π} and Y_v^{π} using Eq. (5.6) and Eq. (5.7), respectively.

4: Construct affinity matrix A_u and A_v as explained in Section 5.3.1.

5: Apply Affinity Propagation on A_u (A_v) to get k_u (k_v) tag clusters, then make tag membership matrix $M_u \in \mathbb{R}^{(l_u + l_c) \times k_u}$ $\left(M_v \in \mathbb{R}^{(l_v + l_c) \times k_v} \right)$, where M_u and M_v only take binary values $\{0, 1\}$, and only one "1" can be in each row of M_u and M_v .

6: **for** $\pi = 1, 2$ **do**

7:     $\hat{Y}_u^{\pi} \leftarrow Y_u^{\pi} \times [M_u]_{[1:l_u, *]}$

    $\hat{Y}_v^{\pi} \leftarrow Y_v^{\pi} \times [M_v]_{[1:l_v, *]}$

8: **end for**

9: Given $\hat{Y}_u^{\pi}$ and $\hat{Y}_v^{\pi}$, compute S_c^u and S_c^v by Eq. (5.8)

In the new subspace, the user and item vectors are aligned and used to compute the new cross-domain user-to-user and item-to-item similarity matrixes, whose construction process takes only the information of the domain-specific tags into account. By doing so, we can separately study the impact of the domain-specific tags in linking different domains, and exploit their encoded information to regularize matrix factorization. We describe this process in Algorithm 5.2.

Step 3: Inferring intra-domain correlations from tags.

Existing tag-based cross-domain recommendation methods mainly focus on using tags directly as aligned features to build a bridge between different domains. This way of modeling helps to build an inter-domain connection for knowledge transfer. However, their models ignore adding constraints to each user or item involved in the domain. The resulting loose coupling of the individual domain will inevitably have side effects for the knowledge transfer. Moreover, the implicit user or item relationships within the individual domain can also be elicited from tagging data and be exploited to add more valuable information to improve the recommendation performance.

Following this thread, we adopt the idea of tag informed collaborative filtering in Section 5.2, which employs user similarities exploited from user tagging histories to regularize the matrix factorization procedure. Specifically, it adds a regularization term $tr(U^T LU)$ to the objective function of the probabilistic matrix factorization [Mnih and Salakhutdinov (2008)], where $tr(\cdot)$ denotes the trace of a matrix, $L = D - W$ is known as the Laplacian matrix, W is the tag-based user similarity matrix, and D is a diagonal matrix whose diagonal elements $D_{ii} = \sum_j W_{ij}$. The tag-based user similarity matrix W can be computed using equations (5-6) in [Zhen *et al.* (2009)].

The regularization term drives the latent factors of the users with similar tagging behaviors to be similar as well. Such an extension can be considered as adding an intra-domain correlation from the perspective of users. Similarly, we can explore the tagging histories of items within individual domain and define another type of intra-domain correlation in the context of items.

Since in our problem we have two disjoint domains, to add an internal control for each domain and keep knowledge flowing among similar users or items, we add regularizations from both user and item perspectives by exploiting intra-domain user and item tagging histories. The inferred intra-domain correlations are added as regularization terms in Eq. (5.11).

Step 4: Aggregation and integration of inter-domain and intra-domain knowledge.

We have studied the role of shared tags and domain-specific tags separately in linking different domains. Both types of tags have their advantages and disadvantages: shared tags serve as aligned features, independent of domain, but fail to satisfy sufficient quantity, while clustering diverse domain-specific tags accurately is nontrivial, which inevitably introduces noise to similarity calculations. As a result, we propose aggregating their contributions to fully explore the complementary role of shared tags and domain-specific tags for transferring knowledge. Therefore, we define cross-domain user-to-user and item-to-item similarities as:

$$W^u = I^{W_b^u} \circ W_b^u + \left[1 - I^{W_b^u}\right] \circ W_c^u$$
$$W^v = I^{W_b^v} \circ W_b^v + \left[1 - I^{W_b^v}\right] \circ W_c^v$$

(5.10)

where $\circ$ denotes element-wise multiplication. By assembling cross-domain similarities generated with shared and domain-specific tags, more user and item connections between domains will be built. In addition, we also need to integrate the intra-domain correlations inferred from both user and item tagging histories from the individual domains, so that the knowledge is not only transferred between domains but also within the domains.

To this end, we propose to extend joint matrix factorization by imposing structural constraints on the inter and intra-domain correlations. Specifically, we minimize following objective function:

$$
\begin{aligned}
&f(\boldsymbol{R}^1, \boldsymbol{R}^2 \mid \boldsymbol{U}^1, \boldsymbol{V}^1, \boldsymbol{U}^2, \boldsymbol{V}^2)\\
&= \frac{1}{2}\sum_{i=1}^{n_1}\sum_{j=1}^{m_1} I_{ij}^{R^1}\left(R_{ij}^1 - g\left(\boldsymbol{U}_{i*}^1 \boldsymbol{V}_{j*}^{1\,T}\right)\right)^2 + \frac{1}{2}\sum_{p=1}^{n_2}\sum_{q=1}^{m_2} I_{pq}^{R^2}\left(R_{pq}^2 - g\left(\boldsymbol{U}_{p*}^2 \boldsymbol{V}_{q*}^{2\,T}\right)\right)^2\\
&+ \frac{\lambda_u}{2}\sum_{i=1}^{n_1}\sum_{p=1}^{n_2} I_{ip}^{W^u}\left(W_{ip}^u - g\left(\boldsymbol{U}_{i*}^1 \boldsymbol{U}_{p*}^{2\,T}\right)\right)^2\\
&+ \frac{\lambda_v}{2}\sum_{j=1}^{m_1}\sum_{q=1}^{m_2} I_{jq}^{W^v}\left(W_{jq}^v - g\left(\boldsymbol{V}_{j*}^1 \boldsymbol{V}_{q*}^{2\,T}\right)\right)^2\\
&+ \frac{\lambda_\alpha}{2}\left(\left[tr(\boldsymbol{U}^{1T}\boldsymbol{L}_u^1 \boldsymbol{U}^1)\right] + \left[tr(\boldsymbol{V}^{1T}\boldsymbol{L}_v^1 \boldsymbol{V}^1)\right] + \left[tr(\boldsymbol{U}^{2T}\boldsymbol{L}_u^2 \boldsymbol{U}^2)\right]\right.\\
&\left. + \left[tr(\boldsymbol{V}^{2T}\boldsymbol{L}_v^2 \boldsymbol{V}^2)\right]\right) + \frac{\lambda_\beta}{2}\left(\|\boldsymbol{U}^1\|^2 + \|\boldsymbol{V}^1\|^2 + \|\boldsymbol{U}^2\|^2 + \|\boldsymbol{V}^2\|^2\right)
\end{aligned}
$$

$$(5.11)$$

where $g(\cdot)$ is a logistic normalization function, which can be set as a sigmoid function, and λ_u, λ_v, λ_α, λ_β are hyper-parameters for controlling inter-domain user similarity, inter-domain item similarity, intra-domain similarity and regularizing latent factors, respectively. The details on how the parameters are tuned and the effects of different values are presented in the following section.

To optimize the proposed model, we apply stochastic gradient descent to update $\boldsymbol{U}^1, \boldsymbol{V}^1, \boldsymbol{U}^2, \boldsymbol{V}^2$ alternately. After updating latent factors of both users and items, we can approximate the target rating matrix $\boldsymbol{R}^1$ by $g(\boldsymbol{U}^1 \boldsymbol{V}^1)$ to verify the performance of our proposed model.

5.3.2 *Semantic information of tags as bridge*

The overlapping tags take up a very small portion of the whole tag set. Abundant information that reflects a domain's unique characteristics is usually embedded in non-overlapping or domain-specific tags. Neglecting non-overlapping tags when building connections between the domains tends to lead to poorer recommendation performance once the users in two domains do not use the same tags. In such cases, two non-identical tags in two domains may be semantically related. Exploiting the semantic similarity of tags will greatly strengthen the connection between two domains and enable knowledge transfer from the source domain to the target domain, thereby also improving recommendation accuracy in the sparse target domain.

In this section, we present a cross-domain recommendation method with semantic correlation in tagging systems. The method aims to constrain the matrix factorization by intra-domain and inter-domain correlation of users and items. The method is in three steps as how to gain the intra-domain similarity, how to gain inter-domain similarity between users and items and how the recommendation is generated.

Step 1: Rating-based user and item intra-domain similarity.

In one domain, it is easy to calculate user and item similarities. Since the rating matrix is very sparse, obviously it will lead to inaccurate results if we calculate the similarities directly from the rating matrixes. We use the latent feature matrixes acquired from matrix factorization to calculate the user and item similarities instead. There are many matrix factorization methods that are suitable to use. Here we use flexible mixture model (FMM) [Si and Jin (2003)] to factorize the user-item rating matrixes in both the source and the target domain as $\hat{R} = USV^T$ where U is the user feature matrix, V is the item feature matrix, S is the user-group to item-group rating pattern.

There are many suitable choices for performing similarity measurement, such as cosine similarity, PCC, Euclidean measurement, or the radial basis function (RBF) measurement. In this problem, we are measuring user similarity from a user vector represented user profile where the feature values are real numbers, so the following RBF measurement is the most appropriate: $W_{ij} = e^{-\frac{\|P_{i*} - P_{j*}\|^2}{\sigma^2}}$, where σ^2 is set to be the median of all the non-zero values calculated by $\|P_{i*} - P_{j*}\|^2$. The user similarity matrix is formulated as follows:

$$W_{\mathcal{U}} = \begin{bmatrix} W_{\mathcal{U}}^{(s,s)}, & W_{\mathcal{U}}^{(s,\tau)} \\ W_{\mathcal{U}}^{(\tau,s)}, & W_{\mathcal{U}}^{(\tau,\tau)} \end{bmatrix} \qquad (5.12)$$

where $W_{\mathcal{U}}^{(s,s)}$ and $W_{\mathcal{U}}^{(\tau,\tau)}$ represent the user similarities in the source and target domains, respectively, and $W_{\mathcal{U}}^{(s,\tau)} = (W_{\mathcal{U}}^{(\tau,s)})^T$ represents the inter-domain user similarities extracted from semantic information of tags.

Step 2: Tag semantic information-based user and item inter-domain similarity.

Inspired by word2vec, which attempts to map words and phrases to a low dimension space to capture semantic and syntactic information in words, the tag data are projected into neutral word embedding space to learn the semantic relationships between the tags [Liu *et al.* (2018)].

There are some similarities in the text data and the tag data. First, the tag data are organized in a similar way as the text data in word2vec. In the tag data, a user-item rating and a list of relevant tags can be collected from each user-item pair. These user-item pairs correspond to documents in word2vec, and the distributed tags associated with the user-item pairs are corresponding to the words in word2vec. Second, the tag data have a similar contextual setting to the words in the text data. Tags are text-based features. A set of tags in the same user-item pair contains context information where relationships between one tag and its surrounding tags are potentially existed.

Since the tag set associated with each user-item pair is usually not very big, we used the skip-gram model with negative sampling. To prepare the input for word2vec, <user-item-tag> triplet data were collected to build the dictionary (corpus). Within the word2vec model, we set the dimensionality to 300 and context window size to 5; the size of the context window size dictates how many tags are considered as context during training. word2vec outputs continuous vector representations for the unique tags in the dictionary, which can be used to calculate which tags are semantically or contextually correlated.

The challenge of our problem is to handle user and item profiles that have various numbers of tags. Hence, each individual tag vector needs to be transformed into a feature space with the same length for both cross-domain users and cross-domain items. One possible way to accomplish this is to use tag clusters as new features to build user and item profiles. The K-means clustering method can then be used to group semantically related tags based on the learned tag vectors. However, other clustering methods could also be applied.

Suppose there are L tag clusters. A function converts the tag-based user profiles into tag-centroids based user profile. A vector with the same length representing user profile on tags is formulated for each user. The function is defined as:

$$f(\mathcal{P}(u)) = (p(c_1|u), \dots, p(c_j|u), \dots, p(c_L|u))$$

$$P(c_j|u) = \frac{|\mathcal{P}(u) \cap \mathcal{P}(c_j)|}{\sum_j^L |\mathcal{P}(c_j)|}, \text{if } \mathcal{P}(u) \cap \mathcal{P}(c_j) \neq \varnothing \qquad (5.13)$$

where $f(\mathcal{P}(u))$ is the user profile we aim to establish, $P(c_j|u)$ measures the probability that user u tends to use tags in cluster c_j based on his/her tagging history, $\mathcal{P}(u)$ denotes the tag set used by user u and $\mathcal{P}(c_j)$ denotes the tag set belonging to the cluster centroid c_j.

Once the user profiles have been projected into the same latent space and refined to the same length, similarity measurements are direct and easy as for intra-domain similarities. As for the items, we can build profiles for cross-domain items and obtain their similarities in the same way as the users. These similarities are used as regulation constrains in our proposed cross-domain recommendation method.

Step 3: Collective matrix factorization with similarity constraints.

With all similarities calculated, we collectively factorize rating matrixes in the source domain and the target domain together. The similarities provide constraints on the factorization. Specifically, the regularization form is [Zhen *et al.* (2009)]:

$$\mathcal{R}_o(U) = tr(U^T L U) \tag{5.14}$$

where L denotes a Laplacian matrix, and $L = D - W$. W is the similarity matrix, and D is a diagonal matrix defined as $D_{ii} = \sum_j W_{ij}$.

With the above regularization, similar users/items tend to have similar latent feature vectors. This way, the knowledge from dense source rating matrix is able to be transferred to the sparse target rating matrix. The final objective function is as follows:

$$
\begin{aligned}
f(&U^s, V^s, U^\tau, V^\tau) \\
&= \frac{1}{2}\|I_{R^s} \circ (R^s - U^s(V^s)^T)\|_F^2 + \frac{1}{2}\|I_{R^\tau} \circ (R^\tau - U^\tau(V^\tau)^T)\|_F^2 \\
&+ \frac{\lambda_u}{2}[tr((U^s)^T L_u^{(s,s)} U^s) + tr((U^s)^T L_u^{(s,\tau)} U^\tau) + tr((U^\tau)^T (L_u^{(s,\tau)})^T U^s) \\
&+ tr((U^\tau)^T L_u^{(\tau,\tau)} U^\tau)] + \frac{\lambda_i}{2}[tr((V^s)^T L_i^{(s,s)} V^s) + tr((V^s)^T L_i^{(s,\tau)} V^\tau) \\
&+ tr((V^\tau)^T (L_i^{(s,\tau)})^T V^s) + tr((V^\tau)^T L_i^{(\tau,\tau)} V^\tau)] \\
&+ \frac{\lambda}{2}(\|U^s\|_F^2 + \|V^s\|_F^2 + \|U^\tau\|_F^2 + \|V^\tau\|_F^2)
\end{aligned}
$$

$$\tag{5.15}$$

where tr is the trace of a matrix, and λ_u, λ_i and λ are the regularization parameters to control the influence of the constraints on the user similarities, item similarities and algorithm complexity. We minimize the objective function using gradient descent. Our method predicts ratings in the target domain by $\hat{R}^\tau = U^\tau(V^\tau)^T$ once optimal parameters have been learned.

A common strategy to increase the computational speed and reduce the redundant constraints is to remove some less important values. This method tends to achieve better performance empirically as it emphasizes local information with high similarity while ignoring information that is likely to be false. In our method, we choose the top 10% similarities in user and item inter-domain similarity matrixes.

5.4 Summary

Context information, in particular tag data, is especially valuable as it enriches the item content and user preference information, which helps alleviate the cold start and data sparsity problems in recommender systems. This chapter introduces the need for and development of tag-aware recommender systems. Two types of tag-aware recommendation methods in both single domain and cross-domain are presented. Both structural information and semantic information of tags are exploited to build a bridge across any two domains to alleviate the data sparsity problem in the recommendation generation.

Chapter 6

Fuzzy Technique-enhanced Recommender Systems

In real-world recommender systems, user preference description, item feature description, item value, and business knowledge often contain various uncertainties, vagueness and imprecision – we generally refer to these as uncertainty issues. The uncertainty issues can appear across the entire recommendation process from data collection to recommendation generation, and involve key recommender system development issues such as the data sparsity problem in a user-item matrix and item similarity and user similarity measure problem. To deal with these uncertainty issues and by doing so improve user preference prediction accuracy, fuzzy techniques have been applied in both content-based, CF-based (including item-based CF and user-based CF) and knowledge-based recommender systems. Fuzzy techniques provide a rich spectrum of methods for the management of uncertainty, vagueness and imprecision in data both in the learning and prediction process and in the recommendation result representation. Particularly, fuzzy techniques are well suited to handling imprecise user preference descriptions (e.g. in linguistic terms), knowledge description, and the gradual accumulation of user preference profiles. This chapter presents how fuzzy techniques can enhance the performance of recommendation methods and recommender systems in practice.

In this chapter, we first introduce in Section 6.1 fuzzy set definitions and related concepts as preliminaries for this chapter and also for Chapters 7, 13 and 14. Main fuzzy set techniques in recommender systems are presented in Section 6.2. Section 6.3 presents a set of fuzzy CF-based recommendation methods. Then Section 6.4 presents a fuzzy content-based recommendation method. Finally, Section 6.5 summarizes the chapter.

6.1 Fuzzy Sets and Fuzzy Relations

In this section, some basic definitions and the properties of fuzzy sets and fuzzy relations from [Zadeh (1965, 1975); Sakawa (2013); Zhang and Lu (2003, 2004, 2009)] are given.

Definition 6.1 (Fuzzy set). A fuzzy set $\widetilde{A}$ in a universe of discourse X is characterized by the membership function $\mu_{\widetilde{A}}(x)$ which associates with each element x in X a real number in the interval $[0, 1]$. The function value $\mu_{\widetilde{A}}(x)$ is termed the grade of membership of x in $\widetilde{A}$.

A fuzzy set $\widetilde{A}$ in a universe of discourse X is convex if and only if for any x_1, $x_2 \in X$, $\mu_{\widetilde{A}}(\lambda x_1 + (1 - \lambda)x_2) \geqslant \min(\mu_{\widetilde{A}}(x_1), \mu_{\widetilde{A}}(x_2))$, where $\lambda \in [0, 1]$.

A fuzzy set $\widetilde{A}$ in a universe of discourse X is called a normal fuzzy set implying that there exists $x_0 \in X$ such that $\mu_{\widetilde{A}}(x_0) = 1$.

Definition 6.2 (Fuzzy number). A fuzzy number $\widetilde{a}$ is a fuzzy subset on the space of real number $\mathbb{R}$ which is both convex and normal.

Definition 6.3 (λ-cut of fuzzy number). The λ-cut of fuzzy number $\widetilde{a}$ is defined as $a_\lambda = \{x;\ \mu_{\widetilde{a}}(x) \geqslant \lambda,\ x \in \mathbb{R}\}$, a_λ is a non-empty bounded closed interval contained in X and it can be denoted by $a_\lambda = [a_\lambda^L,\ a_\lambda^R]$, a_λ^L and a_λ^R are the lower and upper bounds of the closed interval, respectively.

Let $F(\mathbb{R})$ be the set of all fuzzy numbers. By the decomposition theorem of fuzzy set, we have $\widetilde{a} = \bigcup_{\lambda \in (0,1]} \lambda[a_\lambda^L, a_\lambda^R]$ for every $\widetilde{a} \in F(\mathbb{R})$.

Definition 6.4 (Triangular fuzzy number). A triangular fuzzy number $\widetilde{a}$ can be defined by a triplet $(a_0^L,\ a,\ a_0^R)$ and the membership function $\mu_{\widetilde{a}}(x)$ is defined as:

$$\mu_{\widetilde{a}}(x) = \begin{cases} (x - a_0^L)/(a - a_0^L), & a_0^L \leqslant x < a, \\ (a_0^R - x)/(a_0^R - a), & a \leqslant x \leqslant a_0^R, \\ 0, & \text{otherwise.} \end{cases}$$

With the extension principle put forward by Zadeh [Zadeh (1975)], the operational laws of two triangular fuzzy numbers $\widetilde{a}_1 = (b_1, c_1, d_1)$ and $\widetilde{a}_2 = (b_2, c_2, d_2)$ are defined as follows:

- Addition of two fuzzy numbers: $\widetilde{a}_1 \oplus \widetilde{a}_2 = (b_1 + b_2, c_1 + c_2, d_1 + d_2)$
- Subtraction of two fuzzy numbers: $\widetilde{a}_1 \ominus \widetilde{a}_2 = (b_1 - d_2, c_1 - c_2, d_1 - b_2)$

Definition 6.5 (Linguistic variable). A linguistic variable is a variable whose values are words or sentences in a natural or artificial language. A linguistic variable is characterized by a tuple $(\mathcal{X}, T(\mathcal{X}), U, M)$ in which $\mathcal{X}$ is the name of the variable; $T(\mathcal{X})$ is the term-set of $\mathcal{X}$, that is, the collection of its linguistic values X; U is a universe of discourse; and M is a semantic rule which associates linguistic meaning with each linguistic value X, $M(X)$, where $M(X)$ denotes a fuzzy set of U.

Definition 6.6 (Fuzzy relation). Let X and Y be two non-empty sets. A mapping $R : X \times Y \rightarrow [0,1]$ is called a fuzzy relationship on X and Y. For $(x, y) \in X \times Y$, $R(x, y) \in [0,1]$ is referred to as the degree of relationship between x and y. Specifically, a fuzzy relation from X to X is called a fuzzy relation on X.

Fuzzy relational calculus dictates the way information contained in fuzzy relations can be propagated. A t-norm, $\mathscr{T}$ is a commutative, associative, increasing $[0,1]^2 \rightarrow [0,1]$ mapping that satisfies $\mathscr{T}(x,1) = x$ for all x in $[0,1]$. Based on t-norm, we can define an implication operator $\mathscr{I}$ is a $[0,1]^2 \rightarrow [0,1]$ mapping that satisfies the boundary conditions $\mathscr{I}(0,0) = \mathscr{I}(0,1) = \mathscr{I}(1,1) = 1$ and $\mathscr{I}(1,0) = 0$. An implication operator $\mathscr{I}$ is called hybrid monotonous if and only if for any given $x \in [0,1]$, $\mathscr{I}(x,y)$ is increasing with respect to y and for any fixed $y \in [0,1]$ $\mathscr{I}$ is decreasing with respect to x.

6.2 Fuzzy Techniques in Recommender Systems

The uncertainty issues can appear across the entire recommendation process: data input, profile generation, modeling/learning and recommendation generation, as described in Fig. 6.1. The fuzzy recommender system framework takes into consideration the linguistic terms of both users and items and the user-item rating matrix, as shown in the left part of Fig. 6.1. Based on these inputs, fuzzy item representation and fuzzy user preference representation are profiled and fuzzy ratings are generated. The framework will handle user similarity and/or item similarities calculated by fuzzy measure which may involve in a machine learning process and a prediction model. In the right part of Fig. 6.1, fuzzy techniques will assist in the top-K recommendation to users. We discuss the applications of fuzzy techniques in a recommender system: fuzzy item representation, fuzzy user preference/profile and fuzzy user/item similarity.

6.2.1 *Fuzzy item representation*

Item representation is an important aspect in recommender systems since it reflects the characteristics that make the item distinguishable. Item features

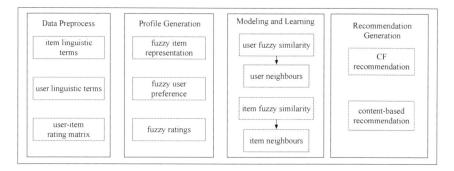

Fig. 6.1: Fuzzy recommender system framework.

are normally defined and rated by domain experts or through feature selection algorithms. This process is usually subjective and often contains some uncertain elements. For example, the description of the phone capacity is described as large, or a package of network service is described as fast rather than numerical speed values.

Fuzzy sets can help dealing with some types of uncertainty in the description of item features in a recommender system. In [Yager (2003)], Yager denotes a set of primitive assertions/statements to describe items, denoted as $A = \{A_1, \ldots, A_n\}$. For one item v, we can view the item v as a fuzzy subset over the space A. If one item v satisfies assertion A_i, the assertion has validity equal to one otherwise zero. The membership degree on A_i in v is $v(A_i)$. Thus, an item in a recommender system can be represented as a fuzzy set over an assertion set. The value of a feature (also called an attribute) for an item is a fuzzy set over the subset of the assertions relevant to the feature.

6.2.2 *Fuzzy user preference/profile*

User preference can be expressed by a user's rating of an item as feedback. In practice, users' ratings for items are often described by linguistic terms, such as "very good" or "very bad"; users' preferences when describing their experiences in linguistic terms could be with words such as "cheap" or "expensive"; users' requirements could be described by linguistic terms such as "close to station" and "close to school"; and user meta-attributes could be described by linguistic terms such as "old people" or "young people". Fuzzy sets can be used to describe the linguistic terms. [Lu *et al.* (2009b)] defined a linguistic term set as a representation of the degree of user's preference of an item. The fuzzy numbers are applied to deal with the linguistic terms.

To represent user preferences, a relation P on user set $\mathcal{U}$ and item set $\mathcal{V}$ is defined: (1) P^+, on $\mathcal{U}$ and $\mathcal{V}$, expresses positive feelings (satisfaction) of a user about an item; and (2) P^-, on $\mathcal{U}$ and $\mathcal{V}$, expresses negative feelings (dissatisfaction) of a user about an item. P^+ and P^- are derived from the actual preference information (e.g., ratings) by a suitable transformation, where $\min(P^+(u, v), P^-(u, v)) = 0$ is imposed for each (u, v) in $\mathcal{U} \times \mathcal{V}$, indicating that a user u is either positively, or negatively, inclined by an item v.

Note that $\min(P^+(u, v), P^-(u, v)) = 0$ splits up users into crisp "pro" and "contra" sides to a given item. But a user cannot feel slightly positive and slightly negative about an item at the same time. This restriction appears unnatural, because generally there is a smooth transition between the two camps, with many users exhibiting both positive and negative attitudes towards (different aspects of) an item. A fuzzy relation P on $\mathcal{U}$ and $\mathcal{V}$ is defined as a fuzzy set in $\mathcal{U} \times \mathcal{V}$, which allows any $(P^+(u, v), P^-(u, v))$ in $[0, 1]^2$ to express a user's feeling to an item. The following special values can be distinguished:

$(1, 0) \rightarrow$ outspoken preference

$(0, 1) \rightarrow$ outspoken dislike

$(0, 0) \rightarrow$ ignorance, the user has not seen or expressed opinion on this item

$(1, 1) \rightarrow$ conflict

It is difficult to have a crisp description about users' preferences, therefore linguistic variable is used to construct the user profile. For example, a linguistic variable is defined as $(\mathcal{X} = \text{"age"}, T(\mathcal{X}) = \{X_1 = \text{"young"}, X_2 = \text{"middle"}, X_3 = \text{"old"}\}, U = [0, 100], M = \{M(X_1) = (10, 20, 30), M(X_2) = (20, 40, 60), M(X_3) = (50, 70, 80)\})$. Each attribute is associated with several fuzzy sets, and a membership vector is obtained for a user. For example in Fig. 6.2, a set of linguistic terms can be represented by fuzzy sets. A man who is described as "normal" in weight and "young" in age (around 60 kg and 28 years old) can be represented by membership degrees on weight and age: $\{0.3/\text{"slim"}, 0.8/\text{"normal"}\}, \{0.1/\text{"young"}, 0.4/\text{"middle"}, 0/\text{"old"}\}$.

6.2.3 *Fuzzy user/item similarity*

Fuzzy similarity has been used for calculating the similarity between items and similarity between users.

(1) Fuzzy item similarity

Computing item content-based similarity with item attribute vectors is a problem well-covered in the literature on fuzzy set theory. The item attribute vector can be

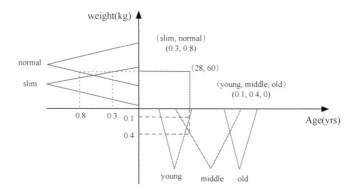

Fig. 6.2: An example with linguistic terms.

represented as a fuzzy item representation, as shown in Example 6.1 below. There are several methods of calculating the similarity between items, including PCC and cosine vector which are two popular methods that are applied widely across the field of recommender systems. The content-based similarity is represented by a fuzzy relation S_{CB} in an item set $\mathscr{I}$.

Example 6.1. Linguistic terms are more suitable to use than numerical values to describe the items. However, we need to establish product relevance degrees that are described by linguistic terms, as shown in Table 6.1. For a target item v, it is easier to acquire domain knowledge about whether it is related to all the business subcategories of one specific category. For example, the category "food and beverage" has subcategories {"liquor and spirits", "wine", "rice and cereals", "meat", "seafood"}. So the item v can be represented by a vector of fuzzy numbers indicating its relevance degree to all the subcategories above. Then the similarities between items can be calculated through a fuzzy similarity measure.

Table 6.1: Linguistic terms express product relevance degree.

Linguistic terms	Triangular fuzzy numbers
Strongly Related (SR)	(4, 5, 5)
More Related (MR)	(3, 4, 5)
Related (R)	(2, 3, 4)
Less Related (LR)	(1, 2, 3)
Not Related (NR)	(1, 1, 2)

To compute item-based CF similarity, the best evaluated is to use PCC. For two items v_i and v_j:

$$S_{\mathrm{CF}}(v_i, v_j) = \frac{\sum_{u \in \mathcal{U}} (P^+(u, v_i) - \bar{P}_{v_i}^+) \cdot (P^+(u, v_j) - \bar{P}_{v_j}^+)}{\sqrt{\sum_{u \in \mathcal{U}} (P^+(u, v_i) - \bar{P}_{v_i}^+)^2 \cdot \sum_{u \in \mathcal{U}} (P^+(u, v_j) - \bar{P}_{v_j}^+)^2}}$$

where $\bar{P}_{v_i}^+$ and $\bar{P}_{v_j}^+$ represent the average rating value of different users on item v_i and v_j, respectively.

Content-based similarity is especially useful for information-rich items, while CF similarity can benefit from statistical features present in the ratings [Cornelis *et al.* (2007)]. To combine and describe the item similarity from these two sides, the fuzzy relation S_v is given by:

$$S_v(v_i, v_j) = \otimes(S_{\mathrm{CB}}(v_i, v_j), S_{\mathrm{CF}}(v_i, v_j)) \qquad (6.1)$$

where $\otimes$ an aggregation operator. In case either S_{CB} or S_{CF} is not available, $\otimes$ can be simply defined by $\otimes(x, y) = x$ or $\otimes(x, y) = y$.

Possible aggregation operator $\otimes$ include:

- Simple weighted average: $\otimes_{i=1}^{n} a_i = \frac{\sum_{i=1}^{n} w_i a_i}{\sum_{i=1}^{n} w_i}$, $w_i > 0$.
- Ordered weighted average [Yager (1988)]: $\otimes_{i=1}^{n} a_i = \sum_{j=1}^{n} w_j b_j$, $w_j \in [0, 1]$, $\sum_{j=1}^{n} w_j = 1$, b_j is the jth largest of the a_i.

(2) Fuzzy user similarity

Fuzzy user similarity is more complicated. It is, however, technically possible to pursue the same approach as with content-based item similarity by comparing user profile vectors. The CF-based user similarity can be calculated through evaluating to what degree everything that user u_i likes, u_j likes too, as follows:

$$S_u(u_i, u_j) = \mathscr{T} \left(\inf_{v \in \mathcal{V}} \mathscr{I}(P^+(u_i, v), P^+(u_j, v)), \inf_{v \in \mathcal{V}} \mathscr{I}(P^-(u_i, v), P^-(u_j, v)) \right)$$
$$(6.2)$$

where $\mathscr{T}$ is a t-norm and $\mathscr{I}$ is an implication operator. The role of inf and $\mathscr{I}$ is to fit the fuzzy relation: for every item v, if user u_i is related to v by $P^+(u_i, v)$, then v is related by $P^+(u_j, v)$ to u_j.

6.3 Fuzzy CF-based Recommendation Method

To deal with the sparsity problem and improve the prediction accuracy, particularly when handling user data uncertainty to fully use business knowledge in recommendation, in this section we introduce a method that integrates item-based CF and user-based CF with fuzzy set techniques and business rules [Zhang *et al.* (2013)]. It first uses item-based CF to produce predictions to form a dense user-item rating matrix, then based on this matrix, user-based CF is developed to generate recommendations. The method takes advantage of both the horizontal and vertical information in the user-item rating matrix, which can reduce the problems caused by the sparsity issue. This method also uses fuzzy techniques to tackle linguistic variables, which are used in describing user preference, and it has the ability to generate recommendations using uncertain information. The method uses the following notations:

Input:

$\mathcal{V}$: the item set containing N products (either services or product bundles) provided.

$\mathcal{U}$: the user set containing M users (existing customers) in the system.

R: the user-item rating matrix where r_{u_i,v_j} is a rating of a customer for a product and could be described in linguistic terms. $(u_i, i = 1, 2, \ldots, M; v_j, j = 1, 2, \ldots, N)$.

Business rules: described as if-then rules and are stored in a knowledge base.

Output:

$p_1, p_2, \ldots, p_K$: K most appropriate products (either services or product bundles) recommended.

The method is described in eight steps as follows.

Step 1: Generate a user-item linguistic term-based rating matrix.

Each user is represented by a set of item-rating pairs and the summary of all the pairs is collected into a user-item rating matrix in which for the user u_i on the item v_i, a rating, r_{u_i,v_i}, is given. These ratings are described in the linguistic terms shown in Table 6.2. There are M users in total in the system and N items are provided. If user u_i has not rated item v_i, then $r_{u_i,v_i} = N/A$.

Table 6.2: Linguistic terms and related fuzzy numbers.

Linguistic terms	Triangular fuzzy numbers
Strongly Interested (SI)	(4, 5, 5)
More Interested (MI)	(3, 4, 5)
Interested (IN)	(2, 3, 4)
Less Interested (LI)	(1, 2, 3)
Not Interested (NI)	(1, 1, 2)
N/A	-

Step 2: Calculate fuzzy item similarity.

In this step, the PCC is selected for measuring the similarities between the two items v_i and v_j. Since the similarity between two items is naturally uncertain, the ratings collected are linguistic terms, and fuzzy numbers are used in the measure. We therefore give the following fuzzy similarity measure, based on the definitions given in Section 6.1:

$$S(v_i, v_j) = \frac{\sum_{u \in U_{v_i, v_j}} \int_0^1 f(\lambda) d\lambda}{\sqrt{\sum_{u \in U_{v_i, v_j}} (\int_0^1 g(\lambda) d\lambda)^2} \sqrt{\sum_{u \in U_{v_i, v_j}} (\int_0^1 h(\lambda) d\lambda)^2}} \tag{6.3}$$

$$f(\lambda) = \frac{1}{2} \Big[([r_{u,v_i}]_\lambda^- - [\bar{r}_{v_i}]_\lambda^-)([r_{u,v_j}]_\lambda^- - [\bar{r}_{v_j}]_\lambda^-)$$
$$+ ([r_{u,v_i}]_\lambda^+ - [\bar{r}_{v_i}]_\lambda^+)([r_{u,v_j}]_\lambda^+ - [\bar{r}_{v_j}]_\lambda^+) \Big]$$

$$g(\lambda) = \frac{1}{2} \Big[([r_{u,v_i}]_\lambda^- - [\bar{r}_{v_i}]_\lambda^-) + ([r_{u,v_i}]_\lambda^+ - [\bar{r}_{v_i}]_\lambda^+) \Big]$$

$$h(\lambda) = \frac{1}{2} \Big[([r_{u,v_j}]_\lambda^- - [\bar{r}_{v_j}]_\lambda^-) + ([r_{u,v_j}]_\lambda^+ - [\bar{r}_{v_j}]_\lambda^+) \Big]$$

where $S(v_i, v_j)$ is the similarity between item v_i and item v_j, U_{v_i, v_j} represents the set of users that both rated items v_i and v_j. $[r_{u,v_i}]_\lambda$ and $[r_{u,v_j}]_\lambda$ represent the ratings of user u on items v_i and v_j under λ-cut respectively, $[r_{u,v_i}]_\lambda^-$ and $[r_{u,v_i}]_\lambda^+$ are the left-end and right-end of λ-cut respectively, and $\bar{r}_{v_i}$ and $\bar{r}_{v_j}$ are the average rating of the users of U_{v_i, v_j} on v_i and v_j respectively. This step aims to obtain similarity between products.

Step 3: Item neighbors selection.

In most CF methods, a number of neighbors will be selected as references when predicting ratings of a target user. According to [Shi *et al.* (2008)], two approaches are possible for this task: the threshold-based selection or the top-K techniques. In this method, we use the top-K technique for neighbor selection. By using this method, a number of most similar items are selected as neighbors. The number of neighbors is predetermined before the item neighbor selection process.

Step 4: Predict empty fuzzy ratings using item-based CF with fuzzy number calculation.

In this step, all the unrated ratings are calculated using the item-based CF method and all the empty cells in the user-item rating matrix $\boldsymbol{R}$ are filled, except the ratings of any new items that have been rated less than two times. The algorithm for prediction is as follows:

$$\hat{r}_{u,v_i} = \frac{\sum_{v_j=v_1}^{v_K} r_{u,v_j} \times S(v_i, v_j)}{\sum_{v_j=v_1}^{v_K} S(v_i, v_j)} \tag{6.4}$$

$$= \bigcup_{\lambda \in [0,1]} \lambda \left[\frac{\sum_{v_j=v_1}^{v_K} [r_{u,v_j}]_\lambda^- \times S(v_i, v_j)}{\sum_{v_j=v_1}^{v_K} S(v_i, v_j)}, \frac{\sum_{v_j=v_1}^{v_K} [r_{u,v_j}]_\lambda^+ \times S(v_i, v_j)}{\sum_{v_j=v_1}^{v_K} S(v_i, v_j)} \right]$$

where $\hat{r}_{u,v_j}$ refers to the predicted rating of user u on item v_j, K is the number of selected neighbors, r_{u,v_i} is the rating of user u on item v_i, and $S(v_i, v_j)$ is the similarity between item v_i and item v_j. This step aims to predict users' ratings to unrated items.

Step 5: Calculate fuzzy user similarity.

Besides predicting the ratings based on the similarities of items, we also predict the ratings by analyzing the similarities between users. Since the similarity between two users is naturally uncertain, fuzzy numbers are used in the similarity measure, similar to Step 2. We use PCC for calculating the user similarity by:

$$S(u_i, u_j) = \frac{\sum_{v \in V_{u_i,u_j}} \int_0^1 f(\lambda)d\lambda}{\sqrt{\sum_{v \in V_{u_i,u_j}} (\int_0^1 g(\lambda)d\lambda)^2} \sqrt{\sum_{v \in V_{u_i,u_j}} (\int_0^1 h(\lambda)d\lambda)^2}} \tag{6.5}$$

$$f(\lambda) = \frac{1}{2} \left[([r_{u_i,v}]_\lambda^- - [\bar{r}_{u_i}]_\lambda^-)([r_{u_j,v}]_\lambda^- - [\bar{r}_{u_j}]_\lambda^-) \right.$$
$$\left. + ([r_{u_i,v}]_\lambda^+ - [\bar{r}_{u_i}]_\lambda^+)([r_{u_j,v}]_\lambda^+ - [\bar{r}_{u_j}]_\lambda^+) \right]$$

$$g(\lambda) = \frac{1}{2} \left[([r_{u_i,v}]_\lambda^- - [\bar{r}_{u_i}]_\lambda^-) + ([r_{u_i,v}]_\lambda^+ - [\bar{r}_{u_i}]_\lambda^+) \right]$$

$$h(\lambda) = \frac{1}{2} \left[([r_{u_j,v}]_\lambda^- - [\bar{r}_{u_j}]_\lambda^-) + ([r_{u_j,v}]_\lambda^+ - [\bar{r}_{u_j}]_\lambda^+) \right]$$

where $S(u_i, u_j)$ is the similarity between user u_i and user u_j, V_{u_i,u_j} is the set of items that rated by both user u_i and user u_j, $[r_{u_i,v}]_\lambda$ and $[r_{u_j,v}]_\lambda$ represent the ratings of user u_i and user u_j on items v under λ-cut respectively, and $[r_{u_i,v}]_\lambda^-$ and $[r_{u_i,v}]_\lambda^+$ are the left-end and right-end of λ-cut respectively, $\bar{r}_{u_i}$ and $\bar{r}_{u_j}$ are the average rating of the users u_i and u_j on V_{u_i,u_j} respectively. This step aims to obtain the similarities between users so that to help predict users' ratings to items.

Step 6: Select top-K similar users.

Similar to Step 3, we need to select a number of neighbor users to predict ratings. The Top-K technique is used in the method.

Step 7: Recommendation generation with fuzzy number calculation.

This step is to predict the ratings of every unrated item for the target users by using user-based CF. The new predicted ratings will replace the ratings predicted in Step 4 and are regarded as the final results. The applied algorithm is as follows:

$$
\begin{aligned}
\hat{r}_{u_i,v} &= \bar{r}_{u_i} + \frac{\sum_{u_j=u_1}^{u_K} r_{u_j,v} \times S(u_i, u_j)}{\sum_{u_i=u_1}^{u_K} S(u_i, u_j)} \\
&= \bigcup_{\lambda \in [0,1]} \lambda \Bigg[[\bar{r}_{u_i}]_\lambda^- + \frac{\sum_{u_j=u_1}^{u_K} ([r_{u_j,v}]_\lambda^- - [\bar{r}_{u_j}]_\lambda^-) \times S(u_i, u_j)}{\sum_{u_j=v_1}^{u_K} S(u_i, u_j)}, \\
&\qquad [\bar{r}_{u_i}]_\lambda^+ + \frac{\sum_{u_j=u_1}^{u_K} ([r_{u_j,v}]_\lambda^+ - [\bar{r}_{u_j}]_\lambda^+) \times S(u_i, u_j)}{\sum_{u_j=v_1}^{u_K} S(u_i, u_j)} \Bigg]
\end{aligned}
\tag{6.6}
$$

where $\hat{r}_{u_i,v}$ is the final predicted rating of item v from user u_i, K is the number of selected neighbors, $r_{u_j,v}$ is the rating of user u_j on item v, and $S(u_i, u_j)$ is the similarity between user u_i and user u_j. This step aims to predict users' rating to unrated items.

Step 8: Final recommendation.

The unrated items for the target user are ranked according to the predicted ratings calculated in Step 7. The top-K items are selected. Each item is checked to establish whether it satisfies the related business rules. Once this happens, a set of most suitable items, $p_1, p_2, \ldots, p_K$, is recommended to the target user.

6.4 Fuzzy Content-based Recommendation Method

To deal with the two challenges: (1) the difficulty of similarity calculation on item hierarchical taxonomy, and (2) the uncertainty of data such as the fuzzy membership of an item and taxonomy features, together with subjective and vague ratings and preferences of users, in this section, we introduce a fuzzy content-based recommendation method that is able to rank the candidate items with fuzzy predictions. This method profiles items with an item descriptor set, which is to discover the possible relationships of different taxonomy features and infer users' preferences on unknown items in the form of fuzzy numbers rather than crisp values [Mao *et al.* (2015)]. The method uses the following notations:

Input:
$\mathcal{V} = \{v_j | j = 1, 2, \ldots, N\}$: the item set containing N products (either services or

product bundles) provided.

$\mathcal{U} = \{u_i | i = 1, 2, \ldots, M\}$: the user set containing M users (existing customers) in the system.

R: the user-item rating matrix where r_{u_i, v_j} is the rating by a customer for a product that may be described in linguistic terms. ($u_i, i = 1, 2, \ldots, M; v_j, j = 1, 2, \ldots, N$).

Item content: The content features of all items are described as a taxonomy tree of the whole item set Θ

Output:

$p_1, p_2, \ldots, p_K$: K most appropriate products (either services or product bundles) recommended.

The method is described in six steps, as follows:

Step 1: Generate triangular rating matrix.

A rating in R is treated as a fuzzy number $\tilde{r}_{u,v}$ since the rating is usually given in the form of graded vague linguistic evaluations. For instance, user ratings on Amazon are in the range of 1 star to 5 stars, where 1 represents "not satisfied at all" and 5 represents "best satisfied". To deal with this vagueness, we use triangle fuzzy numbers to represent ratings. These ratings are described in the linguistic terms shown in Table 6.2.

A fuzzy number closeness/distance calculation method is needed to compare user preference. Similar to [Purba *et al.* (2012)], we compare fuzzy numbers based on the proportion of the overlap area of their membership functions.

Given two triangular fuzzy numbers $\tilde{a}_1$ and $\tilde{a}_2$, whose membership function are $\mu_{\tilde{a}_1}(x)$ and $\mu_{\tilde{a}_2}(x)$ on the same domain of $x \in \mathbb{R}$, the closeness of $\tilde{a}_1$ and $\tilde{a}_2$ is:

$$\ell(\tilde{a}_1, \tilde{a}_2) = \frac{\int \mu_{\tilde{a}_1}(x) \wedge \mu_{\tilde{a}_2}(x) dx}{\int \mu_{\tilde{a}_1}(x) \vee \mu_{\tilde{a}_2}(x) dx} \qquad (6.7)$$

where $\ell(\tilde{a}_1, \tilde{a}_2) \in [0, 1]$, and their distance is $\delta(\tilde{a}_1, \tilde{a}_2) = 1 - \ell(\tilde{a}_1, \tilde{a}_2)$. Note that Eq. (6.7) can be applied to fuzzy numbers with general membership functions. Fig. 6.3 illustrates the calculation of Eq. (6.7): (a), (b) and (c) show three possible situations of the overlapping area of the two triangular fuzzy numbers $\tilde{a}_1$ and $\tilde{a}_2$; (d) shows that for two general fuzzy numbers, their overlapping area is enclosed by the lower bound of the two fuzzy numbers and the x-axis, while their union area is enclosed by their upper bound and the x-axis. Therefore, Eq. (6.7) works for general fuzzy numbers as well as triangular fuzzy numbers.

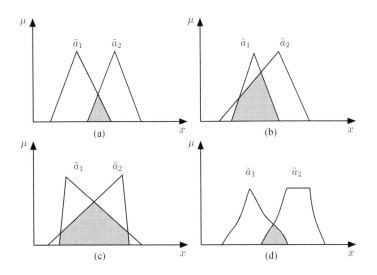

Fig. 6.3: Different situations of area-based closeness calculation for two fuzzy numbers.

(a), (b) and (c) are the three possible overlapping areas of the two triangular fuzzy numbers; and (d) shows the situation of two general fuzzy numbers.

Step 2: Generate the fuzzy item descriptor set.

In e-commerce environments, items are usually described with rich, hierarchical content features. The content features of all items are called the taxonomy tree of the whole item set, denoted as $\Theta = \{C, \hookrightarrow\}$, where $C = \{c_1, c_2, \ldots, c_{|C|}\}$ is a finite set of features of items, and $\hookrightarrow$ is a parent-child relationship. For two nodes $c_i, c_j \in C$, if $c_i \hookrightarrow c_j$, then c_j is a child of c_i. Note that there are no cycles and there is a distinguished root node of Θ, denoted as $c_{\top}$.

Clearly, there is one and only one path from the root to any other nodes in the tree, and we treat a path from the root node $c_{\top}$ to every leaf node $c_{\perp}$ as a descriptor, marked as $d_{\perp}$. Suppose there are in total m leaf nodes in the tree Θ, then a complete descriptor set is constructed as $D = \{d_i\}, i = 1, \ldots, m$, where a single descriptor is denoted as $d_i = \{c_{i1}, c_{i2}, \ldots, c_{i|di|}\}$ satisfying $c_{i1} \hookrightarrow c_{i2} \hookrightarrow \cdots \hookrightarrow c_{i|di|}$. Essentially, the descriptor set D can be seen as the "flat" form of the tree Θ, and inversely, Θ is the hierarchical form of D. An example is given in Fig. 6.4. In the case of Fig. 6.4, the content tree Θ is a three-level tree with eleven nodes denoting the content features. There are in total seven descriptors $d_1, \ldots, d_7$ collected, and the whole set of descriptors represents the flat form of the content tree.

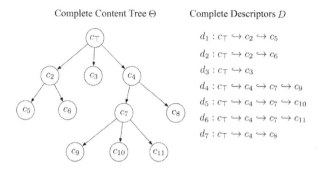

Fig. 6.4: A three-level complete content tree with 11 nodes (features) and the corresponding descriptors set.

    The content information of a specific item $v \in \mathcal{V}$ consists of two parts: the qualitative part and the quantitative part. The qualitative part is the structure of the features associated with an item, and can be seen as a part of the complete content tree, denoted as $\Theta_v = \{C_v, \hookrightarrow\}$, in which $C_v \in C$. The quantitative part indicates the degree of fuzzy membership of an item to each feature (a tree node), denoted by a membership degree $x \in [0, 1]$. The fuzziness of item content information is very common in the real world. For example, a book v is thought to be relevant to a content feature "c_1: computer science" with a degree of $x(v, c_1) = 1$, while it is also considered to relate to "c_2: Management" with a degree of $x(v, c_2) = 0.8$. Consequently, for each item, a fuzzy tree $\Theta_v = \{C_v, \hookrightarrow, X\}$ can be built as a representation of itself, in which, C_v is the nodes set, $\hookrightarrow$ is the hierarchical feature relationships, and $X = \{x(c)\}, c \in C_v$ is an extra set denoting the membership degrees. Fig. 6.5 shows an example item and its content tree Θ_v. We can find that the structure of Θ_v is a part of the complete content tree Θ, but it associates a decimal of each node, announcing the membership degree of the item to the feature.

    For an item v with its fuzzy content tree Θ_v, assuming it has m_v leaf nodes in the tree, we can then find m_v paths from the root node to each leaf node, which are called as descriptors, denoted as $D_v = \{d_1^v, \ldots, d_{m_v}^v\}$. We have known that the qualitative part of an item content tree Θ_v is a part of the complete content tree Θ, but note that the item descriptor set D_v is not guaranteed to be a subset of D, because a leaf node of Θ_v may be not a leaf node in Θ. That is to say, we allowed the incomplete description of items, e.g., we have a three levels taxonomy tree being used to describe books, but for a particular book, it can be detailed only to

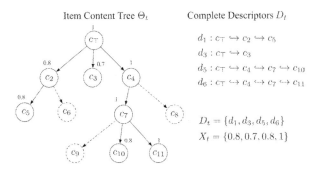

Fig. 6.5: An example of item profile.

For a single item, its content information is a part of the complete content tree Θ, and its descriptor set D_t is a subset of the complete descriptor set D. Additionally, for each node or descriptor, a decimal is associated to represent the membership degree.

two levels. It is easily to obtain the following relationships: $D \subseteq \bigcup_{v \in V} D_v$.

For each single descriptor $d \in D_v$, a membership degree is also allocated, represented by the membership of the last node, that is, $x(v, d) = x(v, c_\perp), c_\perp \in d$. In Fig. 6.5, the descriptor set of the example item contains four descriptors, and a membership set X associating with each descriptor is established. Together, the descriptor and the membership set constitute the fuzzy item profile.

Step 3: Fuzzy user preference on a single descriptor.

For a given user $u \in \mathcal{U}$, the set of items that have been rated by the user is denoted as $\mathcal{V}_u$. For a single descriptor $d \in D$, only if $\exists v \in \mathcal{V}_u: d \in D_v$, the fuzzy preference of this user to the descriptor is calculable as:

$$\tilde{y}(u, d) = \frac{\sum_{v \in \mathcal{V}_u} (\tilde{r}_{u,v} - \bar{r}_v) \cdot x(v, d)}{\sum_{v \in \mathcal{V}_u} x(v, d)} \tag{6.8}$$

where $\bar{r}_v$ is the average rating of item v. Let $\mathcal{U}_v$ denote the users who have rated item v, we have $\bar{r}_v = \frac{\sum_{u \in \mathcal{U}_v} \tilde{r}_{u,v}}{|\mathcal{U}_v|}$.

With our initialization, the value range of a fuzzy rating is $(1, 1, 5) \precsim \tilde{r} \precsim (4, 5, 5)$. According to Eq. (6.8), the value range of a fuzzy preference score is $(-4, -4, 1) \precsim \tilde{y} \precsim (-1, 4, 4)$, so that the definition domain of $\tilde{y}$ is $[-4, 4]$, where a positive score indicates a positive preference to the descriptor, while a negative score indicates a negative preference such as "dislike", "rejecting", *etc.* Comparing to crisp values, the fuzzy preference can preserve the uncertainties derived from fuzzy ratings.

It can be seen that Eq. (6.8) is only practicable for the descriptors that have been reached by the target user. Due to the fact that an individual user commonly reviews only a small part of millions of items in an e-commerce site, the initialized preferences of the user may be only available for a few descriptors. To handle this issue, we infer the missing preference information of the non-reached descriptors by exploring the descriptor-to-descriptor relationships. We use flat descriptor set and propose a cross-dependence relationships between any descriptors, so that we can expand user preference to content features which are not relevant in the taxonomy tree.

We assume the existence of cross-dependence relationships between different descriptors. Two descriptors are compared to evaluate whether they are consistently preferred by users, because descriptors that are always chosen by the same users are considered to have strong dependence relationship.

Step 4: Establish fuzzy user preference profile.

We assume that users' preferences lead to their different ratings (higher or lower) to the same item. The average rating of an item represents the inherent qualities of items. The gap between a user's rating against the average rating can be seen as his/her explicit expression of preference. The user preference is subjective and uncertain, and it connects to the item content. Thus, we establish the user profile by summarizing fuzzy user preference on every single descriptor in the complete descriptor set D, which is defined as follows.

For two descriptors $d_i, d_j \in D$, $d_i \neq d_j$, we define the situation of "a user has similar preferences on the two descriptors" equivalent to:

$$\delta\left(\tilde{y}(u, d_i), \tilde{y}(u, d_j)\right) \leqslant \epsilon \tag{6.9}$$

where ϵ is a small positive threshold. In our experience we suggest $\epsilon = 0.1$. Next, the preference dependence degree of d_j to d_i is:

$$p(d_j|d_i) = \frac{\#\text{users satisfying } Eq.\ (6.9)}{\#\text{users that } \tilde{y}(u, d_i) \text{ is available}}.$$

Now we extend the user preferences by fulfilling the missing preferences to non-reached descriptors. For a user $u \in U$, given a descriptor $d_j \in D$ that has no directed preference information, the preference of this user to this descriptor is estimated by:

$$\tilde{y}(u, d_j) = \frac{\sum_{d_i \neq d_j} \tilde{y}(u, d_i) p(d_j|d_i)}{\sum_{d_i \neq d_j} p(d_j|d_i)}. \tag{6.10}$$

Comparing to semantic similarities, the descriptor preference dependence relationships can discover potential dependencies of two features that are not relevant in the structure of content tree. For a user $u \in U$, there is a vector of triangular fuzzy numbers $\tilde{y}_u = \{\tilde{y}(u, d), d \in D\}^{|D|}$ representing the fuzzy user preference on each descriptor.

Step 5: Fuzzy rating prediction.

For the target user, the goal of recommendation is to identify the top-K from the whole item set. Given a user-item pair as a single prediction task, we predict the fuzzy rating by the inherent quality of the item and the user's preference on the content features of the item. The prediction of the fuzzy rating of user u on item v is:

$$\tilde{r}'_{u,v} = \bar{r}_v + \lambda \frac{\tilde{y}_u x_v^T}{\sum_{x_v \in x_v} x_v} \tag{6.11}$$

where λ is a non-negative parameter of the weight of user personalization. Setting a high level of λ can be understood as the users' ratings are influenced more by their personalized preferences of the content information, and are less impacted by the quality of items.

Step 6: Recommendation generation with fuzzy TOPSIS method.

With fuzzy predictions, a fuzzy TOPSIS ranking method is used to rank the items. For a target user $u \in U$ with n candidate items, the fuzzy ratings are predicted as $\tilde{r}'_{u,v} = (r^a_{u,v}, r^b_{u,v}, r^c_{u,v})$, defining the minimum left bound as $r^{min}_{u,v} = min(r^a_{u,v})$ and the maximum right bound as $r^{max}_{u,v} = max(r^c_{u,v})$. Thus, the worst condition of the rating is $\tilde{r}^-_{u,v} = (r^{min}_{u,v}, r^{min}_{u,v}, r^{max}_{u,v})$ and the best condition is $\tilde{r}^*_{u,v} = (r^{min}_{u,v}, r^{max}_{u,v}, r^{max}_{u,v})$. The distance of the fuzzy rating prediction to the worst condition is $d^-(r_{u,v}) = \delta(\tilde{r}'_{u,v}, \tilde{r}^-_{u,v})$. The distance of the fuzzy rating prediction to the best condition is $d^*(r_{u,v}) = \delta(\tilde{r}'_{u,v}, \tilde{r}^*_{u,v})$.

The ranking score of each user-item pair is calculated by r-score$(u, v) = \frac{d^-(r_{u,v})}{d^-(r_{u,v})+d^*(r_{u,v})}$, the r-score $\in [0, 1]$. Ultimately, the top-K items with highest ranking scores are recommended to the target user and the recommendation is generated.

6.5 Summary

In a recommender system, uncertainties exist within the input data and the learning process and prediction, as well as being associated with the sparsity issue and various different recommendation models. Fuzzy techniques can effectively handle these issues to enhance recommender system performance. This chapter presents a fuzzy recommender system framework that identifies uncertainties that may exist in the item profile, user preference and user-item ratings in recommender systems. It also provides two fuzzy recommendation methods that effectively solve the various uncertainty problems in recommender systems.

Chapter 7

Tree Similarity Measure-based Recommender Systems

In some recommender system applications, item and user profiles are very complex and so they can only be represented as tree structures. For example, a telecom service package that is packaged as a single item, has to be described in a tree structure. Therefore, the item similarity measure and the user similarity measure, as the core technique of the recommendation method, together become a tree similarity measure. To handle the tree-structured data and tree-structured similarity measure, we need to develop related recommendation methods. Moreover, since the information in these tree-structured data is often incomplete and vague, fuzzy techniques are used in the tree structure-based recommendation. This chapter presents a comprehensive similarity measure method to evaluate the semantic similarity between tree-structured items and tree-structured user requirements effectively, and discusses a set of related recommendation methods.

In this chapter, a comprehensive similarity measure on tree-structured data model considering all the information on tree structures, nodes' concepts, weights and values is developed in Section 7.1. The tree-structured items and user requirements are modeled as item trees and user-request trees respectively, and an item tree and user-request tree-based hybrid recommendation method is then developed in Section 7.2. To model users' fuzzy tree-structured preferences, a fuzzy preference tree model and a fuzzy preference tree-based recommendation method are presented in Section 7.3. Finally, Section 7.4 summarizes the chapter.

7.1 Similarity Measure on Tree-structured Data

In this section, a tree-structured data model is defined. A similarity measure method, which considers all the information on the tree structures, nodes' concepts, weights and values, is developed to deal with tree-structured data in recommender systems.

7.1.1 *Tree-structured data model*

The items and user profiles in some recommender system applications can only be described in complicated tree structures. For example, Fig. 7.1 shows two examples of telecom business user account usage. In example 1, the user has three plans: two mobile service plans ("$49 Complete" and "$59 Complete") and a fusion service plan ("$79 Fusion"). In example 2, the user has four plans: two mobile service plans ("$39 Smart" and "$49 Smart"), one land-line service plan ("$45 Lad") and a broadband service plan ("$69 Broadband"). Each plan provides both some services and the relevant usage of the user. Clearly, the user usage data in each case are viewed as tree structures. From the tree structures, it can be seen that each node in the tree represents a specific meaning. Some nodes, such as those that represent the user usage, are assigned values. The numbers in the brackets under the nodes in Fig. 7.1 are the nodes' values. Every node in the tree is assigned a weight to reflect its importance degree to its siblings. When making recommendations of such tree-structured products, whether to find the similar users, to find the similar products, or to search the most matched products to users' requirements, tree-structured data will be compared.

The tree-structured data model is based on the basic mathematical definition of trees, which is given as follows.

Definition 7.1 (Tree). A tree is defined as a directed graph $T = (V, E)$ where the underlying undirected graph has no cycles and there is a distinguished root node in V, denoted by $root$, so that for any node $v \in V$, there is a path in T from $root$ to node v.

However, this definition only defines the hierarchical relations between the nodes. In real applications, the definition is usually extended to represent practical objects. In this book, a tree-structured data model that assigns tree nodes concepts, values and weights is defined.

Definition 7.2 (Tree-structured data model). A tree-structured data model is a tree, in which the following features are added to the tree nodes:

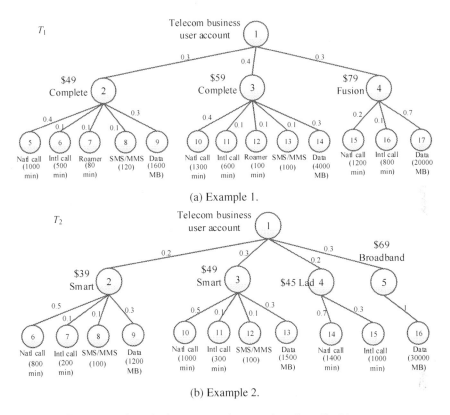

(a) Example 1.

(b) Example 2.

Fig. 7.1: Two examples of telecom users' usage data described in tree-structure.

(1) Node concept.

A set of attributes $A = \{a_1, a_2, \ldots, a_n\}$ to represent the concept of a node are introduced. A range set $D = \{d_1, d_2, \ldots, d_n\}$ is defined accordingly. For each attribute a_i, an attribute assignment function $a_i : V \to d_i$ is defined so that each node can be assigned values for attribute a_i.

(2) Node concept similarity.

Based on the attributes in A, a node concept similarity $sc(\cdot)$ between two nodes is defined as $sc : D \times D \to [0, 1]$.

(3) Node value types.

A set of node value types $VTP = \{tp_1, tp_2, \ldots, tp_m\}$ are defined. For each $tp_i \in VTP$, a node value range $vr_i = vr(tp_i)$ is defined, and the value similarity of type tp_i is defined as $sv_{tp_i} : vr_i \times vr_i \to [0, 1]$. A value type assignment function is defined as $vtp : V \to \{A \cup VTP\}$, where A

represents the *null* set. Therefore, a tree node can be assigned one value type and assigned a value. It is noteworthy that not all nodes are assigned values.

(4) Node value.

If a node n has been assigned a value type tp_i, a value from the value range $vr_i = vr(tp_i)$ can be assigned to the node, which is denoted as $v(n)$.

(5) Node weight.

A weight function $w : V \to [0, 1]$ is defined to assign a weight to each node to represent its importance degree to its siblings.

Two issues should be noticed about the above Definition 7.2. First, for the node concept, a tree node can be assigned several attributes to represent its concept. For example, a node representing a product can be assigned two attributes: a product name and a category, to express the semantic meaning. Second, for node values, a node can only be assigned one type of value. Only the values of the same type can be compared. For a parent node, its children's values can be aggregated only if they are the same value type.

Take the business data in Fig. 7.1 as an example. According to Definition 7.2, the features in the definition are described as follows.

(1) Node concept.

For each tree node, the node concept is defined by a *label* attribute. It is defined as a *label* function $label : V \to L$, where L is a label term set. In this example, the label terms consist of telecom plan names (such as "$49 Complete" and "$45 Lad"); plan family names (such as "Smart", "Complete", and "Fusion"); service item names (such as "Natl call", "Intl call" and "Data"); and so on. Label terms are pre-defined by domain experts.

(2) Node concept similarity.

A conceptual similarity measure within the label set is defined as $sc_L : L \times L \to [0, 1]$. The node concept similarity between two nodes $u, v \in V$ is then defined as $sc(u, v) = sc_L(label(u), label(v))$. Evidently, the node concept similarity meets the commutative law, i.e. $sc(u, v) = sc(v, u)$.

The conceptual similarity between two labels can be given by domain experts or inferred from the domain ontology that describes the relations between the labels. As an example, the conceptual similarity between the labels of T_1 and T_2 in Fig. 7.1 is defined, as shown in Table 7.1. In this table, the conceptual similarity between any two labels l_1 and l_2 is calculated as follows: (1) if $l_1 = l_2$, $sc_L(l_1, l_2) = 1$; (2) if $l_1 \neq l_2$ and they are in Table 7.1, $sc_L(l_1, l_2)$ is defined as the corresponding value in the table; and (3) if $l_1 \neq l_2$ and they are not in Table 7.1, $sc_L(l_1, l_2) = 0$.

Table 7.1: The conceptual similarity between node labels.

Label l_1	Label l_2	Conceptual similarity $sc_L(l_1, l_2)$
$49 Complete	$49 Smart	0.75
$49 Complete	$39 Smart	0.7
$59 Complete	$49 Smart	0.7
$59 Complete	$39 Smart	0.6
$79 Fusion	$45 Lad	0.5
$79 Fusion	$69 Broadband	0.6

(3) Node value types.

Four value types, which are "voice usage", "mobile data usage", "broadband data usage" and "SMS/MMS[1] amount" are defined. Each value type is associated with a value range and a value similarity measure. Every leaf node in the trees, which represents the usage of a service item, is assigned a value type. The nodes, which are labeled with "Natl call", "Intl call" or "Roamer", are assigned the "voice usage" type. The nodes labeled with "Data" for the mobile services are assigned the "mobile data usage" type, and the nodes labeled with "Data" for broadband services are assigned "broadband data usage". The nodes labeled with "SMS/MMS" are assigned the "SMS/MMS amount" type.

(4) Node value.

The leaf nodes in a tree, which represent the usage of service items, are assigned values from the relevant value range. In the example, the node values are shown as the numbers in the bracket under the nodes.

(5) Node weight.

In the example, the number beside an edge represents the weight of the child.

7.1.2 *Similarity measure method on tree-structured data*

Because tree-structured data represent specific concepts and values, the similarity between two tree-structured data is evaluated from both the conceptual and value aspects. The conceptual similarity and value similarity between two tree-structured data are defined respectively. The final similarity measure between them is assessed as the weighted sum of their conceptual and value similarities.

It should be noted that in contrasting application scenarios, the requirements for similarity measures are different. For example, when computing the semantic similarity between two tree-structured items, the weights of both trees should

---

[1] SMS stands for short message service and MMS stands for multimedia messaging service

be considered. Another example is matching a tree-structured item to a user's tree-structured request, where the weights of the user's request tree should be mainly weighted. Therefore, the similarity measure should consider the two situations respectively. In the first example's situation, the similarity measure is symmetric, denoted as S_{sym}. In the second example's situation, the similarity measure is asymmetric, denoted as S_{asym}. The subscript can be omitted if there is no confusion.

Given a tree, it is usually convenient to use a numbering to refer to the nodes of the tree. In this chapter, trees and nodes are represented with the following symbols: Let $t[i]$ be the ith node of the tree T in the given numbering, $T[i]$ be the sub-tree rooted at $t[i]$ and $F[i]$ be the unordered forest obtained by deleting $t[i]$ from $T[i]$. Let $t[i_1], t[i_2], \ldots, t[i_{n_i}]$ represent the children of $t[i]$.

Given two trees $T_1[i]$ and $T_2[j]$ to be compared, let their conceptual similarity be denoted as $sc_T(T_1[i], T_2[j])$, and their value similarity be denoted as $sv_T(T_1[i], T_2[j])$. The final comprehensive similarity measure between $T_1[i]$ and $T_2[j]$ is defined as:

$$S(T_1[i], T_2[j]) = \alpha_1 \cdot sc_T(T_1[i], T_2[j]) + \alpha_2 \cdot sv_T(T_1[i], T_2[j]) \qquad (7.1)$$

where $\alpha_1 + \alpha_2 = 1$. The definitions and computation methods of conceptual similarity $sc_T(T_1[i], T_2[j])$ and the value similarity $sv_T(T_1[i], T_2[j])$ are described in the following sections.

(1) Conceptual similarity between two tree-structured data.

The concept of a tree is derived from the concepts of node attributes and tree structures. Both aspects should be considered when computing the conceptual similarity between two trees. To compare two trees, their concept corresponding parts should be identified first; the corresponding node pairs are then compared separately and finally aggregated into one value. During the conceptual similarity computation, the matched node pairs are recorded, which construct the maximum conceptual similarity tree mapping. The matched node pairs should satisfy both the conceptual and structural constraints. For the conceptual constraints, a node concept similarity measure $sc(\cdot)$ is pre-defined based on the node attributes. Only conceptually similar nodes are to be matched. For the structural constraints, it is required that disjoint sub-trees should be mapped to disjoint sub-trees, because the tree structures represent specific semantic relationships between nodes in a sub-tree. To satisfy the requirements of the structural constraints, the constrained edit distance tree mapping is formally defined as follows:

Definition 7.3 (Constrained edit distance tree mapping). Let V_1 and V_2 be node sets of tree-structured data T_1 and T_2, respectively. A mapping $M \subseteq V_1 \times V_2$ is a constrained edit distance tree mapping if it satisfies the following conditions:

For any pair $(v_1, u_1), (v_2, u_2), (v_3, u_3) \in M$, where $v_1, v_2, v_3 \in V_1$, $u_1, u_2, u_3 \in V_2$,

(1) $v_1 = v_2$ if and only if $u_1 = u_2$;
(2) v_1 is an ancestor of v_2 if and only if u_1 is an ancestor of u_2;
(3) Let $lca(v_1, v_2)$ be the lowest common ancestor of v_1 and v_2. $lca(v_1, v_2) = lca(v_1, v_3)$ if and only if $lca(u_1, u_2) = lca(u_1, u_3)$.

In the above Definition 7.3, the first condition ensures that the mapping is a one-to-one mapping. Condition 2 ensures that the ancestor-descendant relations are preserved in the mapping. Condition 3 ensures that disjoint sub-trees are mapped to disjoint sub-trees.

Given two trees $T_1[i]$ and $T_2[j]$, their conceptual similarity $sc_T(T_1[i], T_2[j])$ is computed as follows considering the constrained edit distance tree mapping constraint.

According to the matching situations of their roots $t_1[i]$ and $t_2[j]$, three cases are considered: (C1) $t_1[i]$ is matched to $t_2[j]$'s child node; (C2) $t_2[j]$ is matched to $t_1[i]$'s child node; (C3) $t_1[i]$ and $t_2[j]$ are matched. The conceptual similarities in the three cases are denoted as $sc_{TC1}(T_1[i], T_2[j])$, $sc_{TC2}(T_1[i], T_2[j])$, and $sc_{TC3}(T_1[i], T_2[j])$, respectively, and $sc_T(T_1[i], T_2[j])$ is computed as:

$$sc_T(T_1[i], T_2[j]) =$$
$$max\{sc_{TC1}(T_1[i], T_2[j]), sc_{TC2}(T_1[i], T_2[j]), sc_{TC3}(T_1[i], T_2[j])\}. \quad (7.2)$$

The matched node pairs in the case with the maximum conceptual similarity value are finally chosen to construct the maximum conceptual similarity tree mapping.

In Case C1, $t_1[i]$ is matched to $t_2[j]$'s child node. In this case, the concept level of $t_1[i]$ is lower than that of $t_2[j]$. $T_1[i]$ is mapped to one sub-tree of $T_2[j]$ which has maximum conceptual similarity with $T_1[i]$. $sc_{TC1}(T_1[i], T_2[j])$, is computed as:

$$sc_{TC1}(T_1[i], T_2[j]) = \max_{1 \leqslant t \leqslant n_j} \{w_t \cdot sc_T(T_1[i], T_2[j_t])\} \quad (7.3)$$

where w_t is the weight of the matched node pair. If the measure is a symmetric measure, both of the corresponding nodes' weights should be considered, $w_t = (1 + w(t_2[j_t]))/2$. If the measure is an asymmetric measure, only the first node's weight is considered, $w_t = 1$.

For example, Fig. 7.2 shows the usage record structures of two business users in the telecom industry. The first customer as shown with T_3 has only mobile services, while the second customer as shown with T_4 has mobile, land-line and broadband services. When comparing the two tree-structured data in Fig. 7.2, node 1 in T_3 is probably matched to node 2 in T_4.

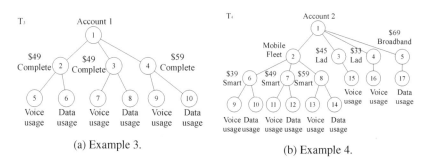

(a) Example 3.

(b) Example 4.

Fig. 7.2: Two examples of tree-structured business data.

Case $C2$ is similar to $C1$. The conceptual similarity between $T_1[i]$ and $T_2[j]$ is calculated as:

$$sc_{TC2}(T_1[i], T_2[j]) = \max_{1 \leqslant t \leq n_i} \{w_t \cdot sc_T(T_1[i_t], T_2[j])\} \qquad (7.4)$$

where w_t is the weight of the matching node pair. If the measure is a symmetric measure, both of the corresponding nodes' weights should be considered, $w_t = (w(t_1[i_t]) + 1)/2$. If the measure is an asymmetric measure, only the first node's weight is considered, $w_t = w(t_1[i_t])$.

In Case $C3$, $t_1[i]$ and $t_2[j]$ are matched. If the node concept similarity between $t_1[i]$ and $t_2[j]$, $sc(t_1[i], t_2[j]) = 0$, $t_1[i]$ and $t_2[j]$ are not similar, so they cannot be matched according to the conceptual constraint, and $sc_{TC3}(T_1[i], T_2[j]) = 0$. If $sc(t_1[i], t_2[j]) > 0$, $t_1[i]$ and $t_2[j]$ are recorded as a matched node pair, and $sc_{TC3}(T_1[i], T_2[j])$ is calculated. The conceptual similarity between $T_1[i]$ and $T_2[j]$ is calculated as:

$$sc_{TC3}(T_1[i], T_2[j]) =$$

$$\begin{cases} 0 & sc = 0 \\ sc & sc > 0, F_1[i] = \emptyset, F_2[j] = \emptyset \\ \alpha \cdot sc + (1 - \alpha) \cdot \sum_{t=1}^{n_j} w_{j_t} \cdot sc_T(T_1[i], T_2[j_t]) & sc > 0, F_1[i] = \emptyset, F_2[j] \neq \emptyset \\ \alpha \cdot sc + (1 - \alpha) \cdot \sum_{t=1}^{n_i} w_{i_t} \cdot sc_T(T_1[i_t], T_2[j]) & sc > 0, F_1[i] \neq \emptyset, F_2[j] = \emptyset \\ \alpha \cdot sc + (1 - \alpha) \cdot sc_F(F_1[i], F_2[j]) & sc > 0, F_1[i] \neq \emptyset, F_2[j] \neq \emptyset \end{cases}$$

$$(7.5)$$

where sc is an abbreviation for $sc(t_1[i], t_2[j])$, w_{j_t} and w_{i_t} are the weights of $t_2[j_t]$ and $t_1[i_t]$ respectively, and α is the influence factor of the parent node. Five situations are listed in Eq. (7.5). When $sc(t_1[i], t_2[j]) = 0$, then $sc_{TC3}(T_1[i], T_2[j]) = 0$, which means the conceptual similarity between $T_1[i]$ and $T_2[j]$ is 0 and these two sub-trees are not matched. When $sc(t_1[i], t_2[j]) > 0$, four other situations are dealt with according to the condition of whether $t_1[i]$ and $t_2[j]$ are leaves. In the second situation, $t_1[i]$ and $t_2[j]$ are both leaves, and their conceptual similarity is equivalent to their node conceptual similarity. In the third and fourth situations, one node is a leaf and the other is an inner node. As the concept of a tree is dependent not only on its root's attribute, but also on its children's attributes, the children of the inner node are also considered in the formula. In the last situation, both $t_1[i]$ and $t_2[j]$ have children. Their children construct two forests $F_1[i] = \{T_1[i_1], T_1[i_2], \ldots, T_1[i_{n_i}]\}$ and $F_2[j] = \{T_2[j_1], T_2[j_2], \ldots, T_2[j_{n_j}]\}$, which are compared with the forest similarity measure $sc_F(F_1[i], F_2[j])$.

Take the two tree-structured data in Fig. 7.1 as examples. Node 12 in T_1 and node 11 in T_2 are both leaves, the conceptual similarity between $T_1[12]$ and $T_2[11]$ is therefore calculated as the node conceptual similarity between $t_1[12]$ and $t_2[11]$, i.e. $sc_{TC3}(T_1[12], T_2[11]) = sc(t_1[12], t_2[11]) = sc_L(\text{"Roamer"}, \text{"Intl call"})$. Node 2 in T_1 and node 3 in T_2 are both inner nodes, the conceptual similarity between $T_1[2]$ and $T_2[3]$ is therefore calculated by aggregating the node conceptual similarity between $t_1[2]$ and $t_2[3]$ and the conceptual similarity between their children:

$$sc_{TC3}(T_1[2], T_2[3])$$
$$= \alpha \cdot sc_L(\text{"\$49 Complete"}, \text{"\$49 Smart"}) + (1 - \alpha) \cdot sc_F(F_1[2], F_2[3]).$$

To calculate the conceptual similarity between two forests $F_1[i]$ and $F_2[j]$, $sc_F(F_1[i], F_2[j])$, the conceptual corresponding sub-trees are first identified based on both their concepts and structures, and are then compared separately. Finally, these local similarities are weight aggregated. To identify the conceptual corresponding node pairs, a bipartite graph $G_{ij} = (V_{1,i} \cup V_{2,j}, E)$ is constructed, in which $V_{1,i} = \{t_1[i_1], t_1[i_2], \ldots, t_1[i_{n_i}]\}$, $V_{2,j} = \{t_2[j_1], t_2[j_2], \ldots, t_2[j_{n_j}]\}$. For any $t_1[i_p] \in V_{1,i}$ and $t_2[j_q] \in V_{2,j}$, a weight is assigned to edge $(t_1[i_p], t_2[j_q])$ as $w_{p,q} = sc_T(T_1[i_p], T_2[j_q])$. A maximum weighted bipartite matching of G_{ij}, denoted as $W_{G_{ij}}$, needs to be constructed. Solving the bipartite graph matching problem in a brute force manner by enumerating all permutations and selecting the one that maximize the objective function leads to an exponential complexity which is unreasonable [Riesen and Bunke (2009)]. Hungarian is one of the best-known and historically most important combinatorial algorithms [Jungnickel

(2007)], which is selected in this chapter. By constructing $W_{G_{ij}}$, the matched corresponding node pairs are identified and recorded. The conceptual similarity between $F_1[i]$ and $F_2[j]$ is calculated as:

$$sc_F(F_1[i], F_2[j]) = \sum_{(t_1[i_p], t_2[j_q]) \in W_{G_{ij}}} w_{i_p, j_q} \cdot sc_T(T_1[i_p], T_2[j_q]) \qquad (7.6)$$

where w_{i_p, j_q} is the weight of the matched node pair $t_1[i_p]$ and $t_2[j_q]$. If the measure is a symmetric measure, $w_{i_p, j_q} = (w(t_1[i_p]) + w(t_2[j_q]))/2$. If the measure is an asymmetric measure, $w_{i_p, j_q} = w(t_1[i_p])$. In Eq. (7.6), the maximum weighted bipartite matching $W_{G_{ij}}$ identifies the most conceptual corresponding node pairs amongst $t_1[i]$ and $t_2[j]$'s children. The contribution of their children can therefore be fully considered when evaluating the conceptual similarity between $T_1[i]$ and $T_2[j]$.

For example, $t_1[1]$ and $t_2[1]$ both have children in Fig. 7.1. To compute $sc_F(F_1[1], F_2[1])$, a bipartite graph $G_{1,1}$ is constructed as shown in Fig. 7.3 (a). Let $\alpha = 0.5$, the conceptual similarities between the sub-trees of $t_1[1]$ and $t_2[1]$ are calculated, which are set as the weights of edges in Fig. 7.3 (a). The maximum weighted bipartite matching of $G_{1,1}$ is then constructed, which is shown in Fig. 7.3 (b). Then, the conceptual similarity between $T_1[1]$ and $T_2[1]$ is calculated by $sc_{TC3}(T_1[1], T_2[1]) = \alpha \cdot sc(t_1[1], t_2[1]) + (1 - \alpha) \cdot (((0.3 + 0.2)/2) \cdot sc_T(T_1[2], T_2[2]) + ((0.4 + 0.3)/2) \cdot sc_T(T_1[3], T_2[3]) + ((0.3 + 0.3)/2) \cdot sc_T(T_1[4], T_2[5])) = 0.856$.

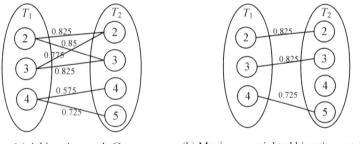

(a) A bipartite graph G_{ij}.   (b) Maximum weighted bipartite matching.

Fig. 7.3: Bipartite graph of two packages.

During the computation process of the conceptual similarity between two trees $T_1[i]$ and $T_2[j]$, the matched conceptual corresponding node pairs are recorded, which construct the maximum conceptual similarity tree mapping between $T_1[i]$ and $T_2[j]$, denoted as M_{S12}. For example, the conceptual similarity between T_1

and T_2 in Fig. 7.1, their maximum conceptual similarity tree mapping M_{S12} is constructed, which is illustrated in Fig. 7.4. In this figure, the matched nodes are connected by dashed lines.

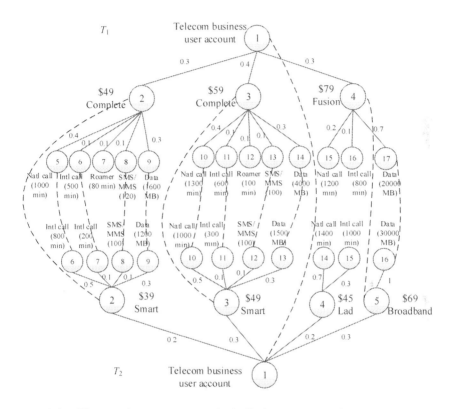

Fig. 7.4: The maximum conceptual similarity tree mapping between tree-structured data T_1 and T_2 in Fig. 7.1.

(2) Value similarity between two tree-structured data

For a specific tree-structured object, some nodes are assigned values to express the quantitative features about the nodes. Because nodes in a branch represent a common concept at different levels, only one node for each branch of a tree is assigned a value. Apart from the concepts, the values of two trees should also be compared to comprehensively evaluate their similarity.

Let $v(t[i])$ represent the value of node $t[i]$, $v(t[i]) = null$ if $t[i]$ is not assigned a value. Let $v(T[i])$ represent the aggregated value of tree $T[i]$. If $v(t[i]) \neq null$ or $t[i]$ is a leaf node, $v(T[i]) = v(t[i])$; Otherwise, if the value types of the $t[i]$'s children are the same, $v(T[i]) = \sum_{t=1}^{n_i} v(T[i_t])$, else $v(T[i]) = null$. Given two trees $T_1[i]$ and $T_2[j]$, a maximum conceptual similarity tree mapping M_{S12} has been constructed. The following two issues must be considered when computing the value similarity between two trees:

(a) The value similarity between two sub-trees can be calculated only if the two sub-trees are matched and they are assigned valid values. Otherwise, their value similarity is zero;

(b) Because the nodes in lower levels represent more specific concepts, the value similarity should be evaluated by comparing the values of levels that are as low as possible.

To deal with the node matching and node values conveniently, a matching tree is constructed by extracting the matched node pairs in M_{S12}. The matching tree between two trees is defined as follows:

Definition 7.4 (Matching tree). Let $T_1[i]$ and $T_2[j]$ be two tree-structured data. The matching tree between $T_1[i]$ and $T_2[j]$ is denoted as T_{M12}. Each node in T_{M12} contains a matched node pair $(t_1[x], t_2[y])$, where $t_1[x]$ and $t_2[y]$ are two nodes in $T_1[i]$ and $T_2[j]$ that are matched.

T_{M12} can be constructed by pre-order traversing $T_1[i]$, selecting the nodes that are in M_{S12}, and adding the relevant matched node pairs into T_{M12} by preserving the ancestor descendant relations of $T_1[i]$. During the construction of T_{M12}, the node values of the matched sub-trees are checked. If the nodes of a sub-tree in $T_1[i]$ or $T_2[j]$ are not assigned values, the matched node pairs in the sub-tree and its matched counterparts will not be added into T_{M12}. As a result, if T_{M12} can be constructed, the matched two nodes contained in each leaf node in T_{M12} both have valid values, either assigned initially or computed by aggregating values of its children.

For example, based on the maximum conceptual similarity mapping between T_1 and T_2, which is shown in Fig. 7.4, the matching tree between T_1 and T_2 can be constructed, as shown in Fig. 7.5. The number pairs beside the nodes in Fig. 7.5 represent the matched node numbers in T_1 and T_2 respectively.

Suppose there is a numbering in T_{M12}. The kth node is represented as $t_{M12}[k]$, which contains a matching pair $(t_1[x_k], t_2[y_k])$. $t_{M12}[k]$'s children are represented as $t_{M12}[k_1], \ldots, t_{M12}[k_{n_k}]$. For two matched nodes $t_1[x_k]$ and $t_2[y_k]$, the value similarity between their sub-trees $T_1[x_k]$ and $T_2[y_k]$,

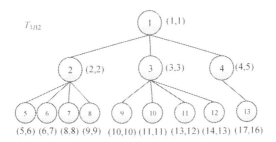

Fig. 7.5: The matching tree between trees T_1 and T_2 in Fig. 7.1.

$sv_T(T_1[x_k], T_2[y_k])$, is calculated by $sv_M(T_{M12}[k])$ as follows:

$$sv_M(T_M[k]) = \begin{cases} 0 & T_M[k] = \emptyset \\ sv_{tp_k}(v(T_1[x_k]), v(T_2[y_k])) & T_M[k] \neq \emptyset, F_M[k] = \emptyset \quad (7.7) \\ \sum_{s=1}^{n_k} w_{k_s} \cdot sv_t(T_M[k_s]) & T_M[k] \neq \emptyset, F_M[k] \neq \emptyset \end{cases}$$

where $sv_{tp_k}(\cdot)$ is the value similarity measure of the value type of $t_1[x_k]$ and $t_2[y_k]$, w_{k_s} is the weight of the matched node pair $t_1[x_{k_s}]$ and $t_2[y_{k_s}]$.

If the measure is a symmetric measure, $w_{k_s} = (w^*(t_1[x_{k_s}]) + w^*(t_2[y_{k_s}]))/2$. If the measure is an asymmetric measure, $w_{k_s} = w^*(t_1[x_{k_s}])$. $w^*(t_1[x_{k_s}])$ is the continued product of the weights of nodes in the branch from $t_1[x_{k_s}]$ to $t_1[x_k]$'s child, and $w^*(t_2[y_{k_s}])$ is the continued product of the weights of nodes in the branch from $t_2[y_{k_s}]$ to $t_2[y_k]$'s child. There are three cases listed in the formula. In the first case, $T_M[k]$ is empty, which means that there are no matched sub-trees or the matched sub-trees do not have comparable values. Thus, the value similarity in this case is 0. In the second case, $t_{M12}[k]$ is a leaf node. The matched nodes $t_1[x_k]$ and $t_2[y_k]$ have no matched descendant nodes, or the matched descendant nodes are not assigned comparable values. The values of $t_1[x_k]$ and $t_2[y_k]$ are compared directly in this case. In the third case, $t_{M12}[k]$ has children. The value similarity between $T_1[x_k]$ and $T_2[y_k]$ is calculated by aggregating their matched sub-trees' value similarities.

To show the computation of the $sv_M(T_{M12}[k])$, nodes $t_{M12}[5]$ and $t_{M12}[2]$ in the matching tree T_{M12} in Fig. 7.5 are taken as examples. The node $t_{M12}[5]$ is a leaf node and it contains the matched node pair $(t_1[5], t_2[6])$. Both $t_1[5]$ and $t_2[6]$ are assigned values of the "voice usage" type, and $v(t_1[5]) = 1000$, $v(t_2[6]) = 800$. According to the discussion above about the calculation of the value of a sub-tree, since $t_1[5]$ and $t_2[6]$ are leaf nodes in T_1 and T_2 respectively, $v(T_1[5]) = v(t_1[5]) = 1000$, $v(T_2[6]) = v(t_2[6]) = 800$. Thus, $sv_M(T_{M12}[5]) =$

$sv_{voiceusage}(1000, 800)$. The value similarity measure of the "voice usage" type $sv_{voiceusage}(\cdot)$ will be discussed in detail in the following sections.

The node $t_{M12}[2]$ is an inner node which contains the matched node pair $(t_1[2], t_2[2])$, and it has four children $t_{M12}[5]$, $t_{M12}[6]$, $t_{M12}[7]$ and $t_{M12}[8]$. Thus, $sv_M(T_{M12}[2]) = \sum_{p=5}^{8} w_p \cdot sv_M(T_{M12}[p])$. w_p is the weight of the matched node pair $t_1[x_p]$ and $t_2[y_p]$ contained in $t_{M12}[p]$, $p = 5, 6, 7, 8$. In this example, the similarity measure is a symmetric measure. Therefore, $w_p = (w^*(t_1[x_p]) + w^*(t_2[y_p]))/2$. For example, $w_5 = (w^*(t_1[5]) + w^*(t_2[6]))/2$. $w^*(t_1[5])$ is calculated as the continued product of the weights of nodes in the branch from $t_1[5]$ to $t_1[2]$'s child, and $w^*(t_1[5]) = w(t_1[5]) = 0.4$. Similarly, $w^*(t_2[6]) = w(t_2[6]) = 0.5$. w_5 is then calculated as 0.45.

Based on Equation Eq. (7.7), the value similarity between $T_1[i]$ and $T_2[j]$, $sv_T(T_1[i], T_2[j])$, is calculated as:

$$sv_T(T_1[i], T_2[j]) = w_r \cdot sv_M(T_{M12}) \qquad (7.8)$$

where w_r is the weight of the matching node pair $(t_1[x_r], t_2[y_r])$ contained in the root of T_{M12}. If the similarity measure is a symmetric measure, $w_r = (w^*(t_1[x_r]) + w^*(t_2[y_r]))/2$. If the measure is an asymmetric measure, $w_r = w^*(t_1[x_r])$. $w^*(t_1[x_r])$ is the continued product of the weights of nodes in the branch from $t_1[x_r]$ to the root of $T_1[i]$, and $w^*(t_2[y_r])$ is the continued product of the weights of nodes in the branch from $t_2[y_r]$ to the root of $T_2[j]$.

For example, given T_1 and T_2 illustrated in Fig. 7.1 and their matching tree T_{M12} illustrated in Fig. 7.5, the value similarity between T_1 and T_2 is calculated by $sv_T(T_1, T_2) = w_r \cdot sv_M(T_{M12}[1])$. Because the roots of T_1 and T_2 are contained in $t_{M12}[1]$, the weight w_r is calculated as 1. After the conceptual similarity $sc_T(T_1[i], T_2[j])$ and value similarity $sv_T(T_1[i], T_2[j])$ are computed, the final similarity measure between $T_1[i]$ and $T_2[j]$ is calculated by Eq. (7.1).

An example is given in this section to show the effectiveness of the proposed similarity measure model on tree-structured data. The similarity between T_1 and T_2 in Fig. 7.1 is computed by the proposed similarity measure model as follows.

(1) The conceptual similarity between T_1 and T_2, $sc_T(T_1[1], T_2[1])$ is computed by use of the Eq. (7.2) to Eq. (7.6) described in Section 7.1.2. Let the coefficient α be 0.5, $sc_T(T_1[1], T_2[1])$ is computed as 0.856. During the computation process, the maximum conceptual similarity tree mapping between T_1 and T_2, M_{S12} is constructed, which is illustrated in Fig. 7.4. The matched nodes in the maximum conceptual similarity tree mapping in Fig. 7.4 are connected by dashed lines.

(2) Based on the maximum conceptual similarity mapping between T_1 and T_2, the matching tree between T_1 and T_2, T_{M12}, is constructed, as shown in Fig. 7.5.

(3) The value similarity between T_1 and T_2, $sv_T(T_1[1], T_2[1])$ is then computed by use of Eqs. (7.7) and (7.8) in Section 7.1.2. Let the value ranges of the four value types be defined in Table 7.2. The value similarity measure for each value type is defined as $sv_{tp_i}(a_1, a_2) = 1 - |a_1 - a_2|/dm_{tp_i}$, where a_1 and a_2 are two values, and dm_{tp_i} is the maximum value in the value range of the value type tp_i. $sv_T(T_1[1], T_2[1])$ is computed as 0.697.

(4) Let the weights α_1 and α_2 be both 0.5. The final similarity measurement between T_1 and T_2, $sim(T_1, T_2)$ is computed by $0.5 \cdot sc_T(T_1[1], T_2[1]) + 0.5 \cdot sv_T(T_1[1], T_2[1]) = 0.776$.

Table 7.2: The value ranges of four value types.

Value type	Voice usage	Mobile data	Broadband data	SMS/MMS
Value range	[0, 2000 min]	[0, 5000 MB]	[0, 100,000 MB]	[0, 1000]

7.2 Item Tree and User-request Tree-based Hybrid Recommendation Method

An item tree and a user-request tree are defined according to the features of items and the requirements of users. The presented similarity measure model is then employed to evaluate the semantic similarity between item trees or between user-request trees. In this section, an item tree and user-request tree-based hybrid recommendation method is presented. This method fully utilizes the semantic information of tree-structured items and users with the requirement matching knowledge and takes advantage of the merits of CF-based recommendation methods.

7.2.1 *Item tree and user-request tree*

Definition 7.5 (Item tree). An item tree is a tree-structured data model to describe the characteristics of tree-structured items in a specific application domain. The features of an item tree are described as follows:

(1) A set of node attributes are defined to assign each node a concept to express one aspect of item features. Nodes at different depths represent concepts with different abstraction levels. The nodes at lower levels represent more specific item features;

(2) A node concept similarity measure is defined on the node attributes to infer the semantic similarity between nodes;

(3) A set of value types and related value ranges are defined for the item tree nodes to express the quantity or quality degrees of the item features. The value similarity of each value type is also defined;

(4) For some specific nodes in an item tree, a value type and a value are assigned;

(5) Each node is assigned a weight to express the importance degree of the item feature represented by the node.

Definition 7.6 (User-request tree). A user-request tree is a tree-structured data model to describe the tree-structured requirements of a user in the application domain. The user-request tree is defined based on the item tree. They have the same node concept definition. The node value represents the quantity or quality degree of the user's requirement for a specific item feature. The node weights represent the user's preferences for different item features.

The semantic similarity between item trees or user-request trees is evaluated by use of the similarity measure on tree-structured data developed in Section 7.1.2. As discussed in Section 7.1.2, there are two types of similarity measures, symmetric (denoted as S_{sym}) and asymmetric (denoted as S_{asym}), for different application situations. When two tree-structured data to be compared are equally treated and the node weights of both trees are considered, the symmetric measure will be applied. Otherwise, when the node weights of one tree are mainly considered, the asymmetric measure will be applied.

7.2.2 *Item tree and user-request tree-based hybrid recommendation method*

As depicted in Fig. 7.6, the proposed method takes three kinds of information resources as inputs: the user-item rating matrix, the item trees and the user-request trees, and produces a user-item prediction matrix as outputs.

In Fig. 7.6, the request matching similarity module considers the semantics of both users and items and computes the matching degree of an item to a user. The item-based semantic similarity module considers the semantic information of items and computes the item-based semantic similarity for any pair of items. Both the request matching similarity module and the item-based semantic similarity module utilize the proposed similarity measure on tree-structured data. The item-based CF similarity module computes the item-based CF similarity between any pair of items. The total weighted similarity module uses the item-item semantic similarity matrix and the item-item CF similarity matrix, to combine

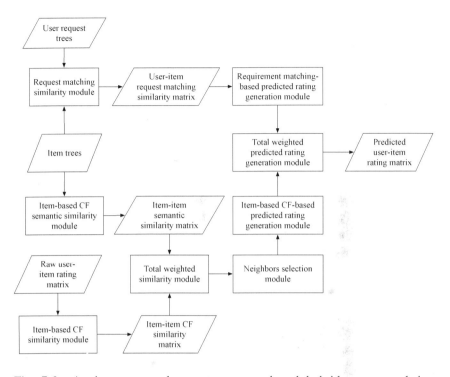

Fig. 7.6: An item tree and user-request tree-based hybrid recommendation method.

both similarity values to obtain the total weighted similarity value for any pair of items. The neighbor selection module selects a set of nearest neighbors of items that are most similar to the target items. The item-based CF-based predicted rating generation module computes the predicted ratings by use of ratings of the selected neighbors. The requirement matching-based predicted rating generation module computes the predicted ratings to unrated items based on the matching degrees of the items to the requirements of users. The total weighted predicted rating generation module hybridizes the above two kinds of prediction values, generates the final predicted user-item rating matrix, and then produces the final ranked recommendations list for the target user.

Let the user-request tree of an active business user u be $T_{\text{req},u}$, and the item tree of a target item v be $T_{\text{item},v}$. The predicted rating of the user u to the item v is calculated by the item tree and user-request tree-based hybrid recommendation method, which consists of six steps and is described as follows:

Input:

    R: the user-item rating matrix

    $T_{\text{req},u}$: the user-request tree of the active business user u

    $T_{\text{item},v}$: the item tree of the target item v

    T_{item,b_i}, $i = 1, 2, \ldots, m$: the item trees of the items rated by u

Output:

    $\hat{r}_{u,v}$: the predicted rating of u to target item v

Step 1: Calculate the request matching degree of item v to user u.

The request matching degree of item v to user u is assessed by calculating the similarity between the user-request tree of u and the item tree of v. The node weights of the user-request tree should be the main consideration. For this reason, the asymmetric (S_{asym}) similarity measure is used in this step.

$$S_m(u, v) = S_{\text{asym}}(T_{\text{req},u}, T_{\text{item},v}). \tag{7.9}$$

Step 2: Calculate the semantic similarity between the target item v and the items rated by user u.

Let user u have rated m items, denoted as $\{b_1, b_2, \ldots, b_m\}$. Let the item tree of b_i be T_{item,b_i}, $i = 1, 2, \ldots, m$. The semantic information of items is expressed by item trees, and the semantic similarity between items is assessed by calculating the similarity between their item trees. To compare two item trees objectively, the node weights of both item trees should be considered. As a consequence, the symmetric (S_{sym}) similarity measure is used in this step. The semantic similarity between v and b_i is calculated as:

$$S_{\text{sem}}(b_i, v) = S_{\text{sym}}(T_{\text{item},b_i}, T_{\text{item},v}). \tag{7.10}$$

Step 3: Calculate the item-based CF similarity between the target item v and the items rated by user u.

Based on the user-item rating matrix, this step computes the item-based CF similarity between item v and the items that have been rated by user u, $b_1, b_2, \ldots, b_m$. The item-based CF similarity between v and b_i is calculated as:

$$S_{\text{CF}}(b_i, v) = \frac{\sum_{k \in U_{b_i,v}} r_{k,b_i} \times r_{k,v}}{\sqrt{\sum_{k \in U_{b_i,v}} r_{k,b_i}^2 \times \sum_{k \in K} r_{k,v}^2}} \tag{7.11}$$

where $U_{b_i,v}$ is the set of users that have rated both items b_i and v, r_{k,b_i} and $r_{k,v}$ are the ratings of user k to items b_i and v respectively.

Step 4: Calculate the total similarity between two items.

The total weighted similarity between two items integrate the item-based CF similarity and the semantic similarity values obtained in the last two steps. In this module, the weighted hybridization method is applied to obtain the total weighted similarity value between the item v and item b_i, $i = 1, 2, \ldots, m$.

$$S(b_i, v) = \beta \times S_{\text{sem}}(b_i, v) + (1 - \beta) \times S_{\text{CF}}(b_i, v) \tag{7.12}$$

where $\beta \in [0, 1]$ represents the relative importance of the item-based semantic similarity, and $1 - \beta$ is the relative importance for the item-based CF similarity. The relative weighting is adopted to adjust the importance of the item-based semantic similarity and the item-based CF similarity. When $\beta = 1$, the item-based semantic similarity value is used as the final similarity value for predictions, while if $\beta = 0$, then only the item-based CF similarity value is used for predictions. β can be determined according to the data provision situations of the specific applications and the application requirements.

Step 5: Select neighbors of items.

The neighbor selection module selects a set of nearest neighbors that contains items that are most similar to the target item. In this module, the items most similar to the target item in terms of the total weighted similarity values are selected for generating the prediction. Currently, two methods have been employed in recommender systems: the Top-N method (e.g., a predefined number of neighbors with greatest similarity are selected), and the similarity threshold (e.g., all neighbors with similarity exceeding a certain threshold are selected). We use the Top-N method [Herlocker *et al.* (2002)].

Step 6: Calculate the predicted rating.

Let the rating of u to b_i be r_{u,b_i}. The predicted rating of u to target item v is calculated as:

$$\hat{r}_{u,tv} = \theta \times S_m(u, v) \times r_{max} + (1 - \theta) \times \frac{\sum_{i=1}^{m} S(b_i, v) \times r_{u,b_i}}{\sum_{i=1}^{m} S(b_i, v)} \tag{7.13}$$

where $\theta \in [0, 1]$, r_{max} represents the maximum value of ratings. The formula contains two parts. $s_m(u, v) \times r_{max}$ is the requirement matching-based predicted rating. If the target item is exactly matched to the user's requirement, the target item should obtain the highest rating. θ represents the relative importance of the requirement matching-based predicted rating, and $1 - \theta$ is the relative importance for the item-based CF-based predicted rating. The relative weighting is adopted to adjust the importance of the two parts. When $\theta = 1$, the requirement matching-based predicted rating is used as the final predicted rating, while if $\theta = 0$, then the item-based CF-based predicted rating is used as the final predicted rating. The predicted ratings for all the potential items are calculated and ranked accordingly. K potential items with the highest predicted ratings are selected as the final recommendations.

The proposed recommendation method draws strength from the content-based, CF-based and knowledge-based recommendation methods. The requirement matching in the predicted rating calculation formula fully utilizes the semantic information of user requirements and item descriptions and the matching knowledge. This makes the recommendation easier to explain. Because it does not require any rating information, the proposed method can deal with the new user and new item problems.

7.3   Fuzzy Preference Tree-based Recommendation Method

This section presents the definition and the construction method of a fuzzy preference tree to model fuzzy tree-structured user preferences. Then an innovative fuzzy preference tree-based recommendation method is introduced based on the fuzzy preference tree model and the similarity measure on tree-structured data in Section 7.1.

7.3.1   *Fuzzy tree-structured preference model*

Users' fuzzy preferences are first modeled by use of fuzzy set techniques; and a fuzzy tree-structured user preference model is then presented by use of the tree-structured data model proposed in Section 7.1.

(1) Users' fuzzy preferences

To express users' preferences, it is assumed that a totally ordered set $R = \{1, 2, \ldots, r\}$ is predefined to represent the crisp values of ratings. Based on the fuzzy set definition, a user u's preference for an item (or feature) j is represented as a fuzzy set over R, $\tilde{p}_{uj} = \{f_{1,uj}/1, f_{2,uj}/2, \ldots, f_{r,uj}/r\}$, where each $f_{i,uj} \in [0, 1]$, $i \in R$, represents the membership degree of the rating i. $\tilde{p}_{uj}$ will be expressed as $\{f_{1,uj}, f_{2,uj}, \ldots, f_{r,uj}\}$ if there is no confusion.

For example, supposing that the crisp ratings are on a scale of 1 to 5, with 1 being the lowest rating and 5 the highest rating, a user's preference for an item is represented as a fuzzy sub-set on$\{1, 2, 3, 4, 5\}$ by membership degree [0,

1]. The preference value (0/1, 0/2, 0/3, 0.9/4, 1/5) indicates that a user likes an item very much by the high membership degree (1) on rating value "5" and also the very high membership degree (0.9) on "4", while the preference value (1/1, 0/2, 0/3, 0/4, 0/5) indicates that the user does not like the item at all by the high membership degree (1) on rating value "1" and the low membership degree (0) on the other rating values.

(2) Fuzzy tree-structured user preference

The items considered in this chapter are presented as tree structures, and the features of items form a hierarchical structure. They are modeled as item trees which are defined in Section 7.2.1. A user's preferences concern a set of products/features, and user preferences are therefore described as a tree structure which has fuzzy preference values.

Definition 7.7 (Fuzzy tree-structured data). A fuzzy tree-structured data model is a tree-structured data whose node features, i.e. the node attributes, node values, node concept similarity and value similarity measures, or node weights, are represented as fuzzy sets.

Definition 7.8 (Fuzzy preference tree). The fuzzy preference tree of a user is a tree-structured data whose node values are the user's fuzzy preferences for the corresponding attributes.

A user's preference is represented as a fuzzy preference tree. Each sub-tree in a user's fuzzy preference tree represents the user's preference for one aspect of the features, and the sub-trees of that aspect represent the user's preferences for the finer features. The leaf nodes represent the preferences for the finest features. The fuzzy preference tree has a similar structure to the item tree except for the node value definition. The value of a node in an item tree represents the quantity or quality degree of the attribute associated with the node, while the value of a node in a fuzzy preference tree represents the user's preference for the attribute represented by the node. The node value of the fuzzy preference tree contains two components. One is the preference $\tilde{p}_u$, which is expressed with a fuzzy set; the other is a count number $count$, which indicates the number of preference sources used to calculate the value. The $count$ is used to incrementally update the user's fuzzy preference tree, as shown below.

The intentionally expressed preference is acquired directly from users. This kind of information is especially important for new users to obtain recommendations. Because the item features present tree structures, the preferences given by

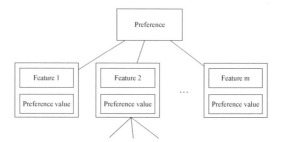

Fig. 7.7: Intentionally expressed user preference.

users are in tree structures, which is shown in Fig. 7.7. To express preferences, a user selects several features. For example, Feature 1, Feature 2, ..., Feature m are selected in Fig. 7.7. For each feature, there are two situations. First, the user can assign a preference value, such as Feature 1 in Fig. 7.7. Second, the user can drill down to detail and express preferences for finer features under the macro feature, as shown for Feature 2. Therefore, users' preference values, which are represented as fuzzy sets, can be expressed at different levels. For different features, the user can also specify various weights to express the different importance degrees of diverse features.

A user's fuzzy preference tree T_u is constructed based on user input preferences. The tree has the same structure as the user preferences shown in Fig. 7.7. The tree node attributes are the relevant features. If the user expresses the preference value for a feature, the value will be assigned to the relevant node accordingly. The node weights are also set according to the user's inputs.

The extensionally expressed preference of a user is constructed from the items experienced by the user. Let the items experienced by a user u be the set $EI_u = \{i_1, i_2, \ldots, i_m\}$. Each item i_j ($j = 1, 2, \ldots, m$) corresponds to an item tree $T_{\text{item},j}$ and a preference value given by the user $\tilde{p}_{uj} = \{f_{1,uj}, f_{2,uj}, \ldots, f_{r,uj}\}$. Let the user's fuzzy preference tree be T_u. The construction process of T_u is presented as follows.

For each item i_j experienced by user u with preference value $\tilde{p}_{uj}$, add the item tree $T_{\text{item},j}$ into the fuzzy preference tree T_u. The add operation integrates the user's preference for an item into T_u. When all the items experienced are added into T_u, the user's fuzzy preference tree T_u will be constructed. The fuzzy preference tree construction algorithm is described in detail in the next section. During the process, the conceptual corresponding parts between two trees considering tree structures, node attributes and weights comprehensively must be identified. Therefore, the conceptual similarity computation algorithm developed in Section 7.1.2 is applied to construct the maximum conceptual similarity tree mapping between two trees.

7.3.2 *Fuzzy preference tree construction algorithm*

Since a user's preference is in a tree structure and has fuzzy values, a fuzzy preference tree is established to cover both the user's intentionally expressed preference and their extensionally expressed preference. As discussed above, the intentionally expressed preference is acquired directly, while the extensionally expressed preference is constructed from the experienced items of the user.

The construction process is an incremental process. The user's preferences for newly-experienced items are integrated into the user's fuzzy preference tree. The integration operation is described in detail as follows. It takes three components as input: the user's fuzzy preference tree T_u, the item tree T_i, and the user's preference value for the item $\tilde{p}_{ui}$, and obtains the merged fuzzy preference tree following the two steps.

Step 1: Generate the maximum conceptual similarity tree mapping between T_u and T_i.

A maximum conceptual similarity tree mapping between T_u and T_i, $M_{u,i}$, is constructed to identify the corresponding parts between two trees and to determine the positions in T_u into which the relevant nodes in T_i can be merged. When constructing the mapping, the node weights of both T_u and T_i should be treated equally, i.e. the symmetric similarity measure computation algorithm should be called. Therefore, $M_{u,i}$ is constructed by the conceptual similarity computation algorithm developed in Section 7.1.2.

Step 2: Merge T_i into T_u.

Based on the maximum conceptual similarity tree mapping between T_u and T_i, $M_{u,i}$, all the features in T_i are merged into T_u. A merge operation is defined which takes the tree mapping $M_{u,i}$, the item tree node n_i, and the user's preference value for the item $\tilde{p}_{ui}$ as input. According to the different mapping situations of n_i, the merge operation is processed in the following five cases:

Case 1: $M_{u,i}$ is empty.

This case emerges when T_u is initially empty or the sub-tree under n_i and T_u represent totally different features. In this case, a new root of T_u is created, and the original T_u is inserted as a sub-tree. The sub-tree under n_i is copied and inserted under the new root of T_u. Each leaf of the copied sub-tree is assigned a value whose preference is $\tilde{p}_{ui}$ and *count* is 1.

Case 2: n_i is mapped to a node n_p in the mapping $M_{u,i}$, but the attributes of n_i and n_p are not identical.

In this case, the sub-tree under n_i is copied and inserted under the parent node of n_p. Each leaf of the copied sub-tree is assigned a value whose preference is $\tilde{p}_{ui}$ and *count* is 1.

Case 3: n_i is mapped to a node n_p in the mapping $M_{u,i}$, and their attributes are identical.

According to the condition of whether or not n_i has children, the operation is processed in the following two cases. In the first case, n_i has no children, i.e. n_i represents the finest feature. The $\tilde{p}_{ui}$ is integrated into the preference value of node n_p which is denoted as $\tilde{p}_{un_p}$ by $f_{k,un_p} = (f_{k,un_p} \cdot count + f_{k,ui})/(count+1), k = 1, 2, \ldots, r$. In the second case, n_i has child nodes. These child nodes are merged recursively.

Case 4: n_i is not in the mapping $M_{u,i}$, but its parent node is mapped to node n_p.

The sub-tree under n_i is copied and inserted under n_p. Each leaf of the copied sub-tree is assigned a value whose preference is $\tilde{p}_{ui}$ and *count* is 1.

Case 5: neither n_i nor its ancestor nodes are in the mapping $M_{u,i}$, but n_i's descendant nodes are in the mapping.

In this case, T_u represents part of the features of the sub-tree under n_i. The root of T_u must be mapped to a node n_t which is the descendant of n_i. The tree under n_i except for the sub-tree under n_t is copied and taken as tree T_u'. Each leaf of the copied sub-tree is assigned a value whose preference is $\tilde{p}_{ui}$ and *count* is 1. Let n_t's parent node be n_p. T_u is inserted into T_u' under the corresponding node of n_p. Replace T_u with T_u', and then merge the node n_t recursively.

7.3.3 *Fuzzy preference tree-based recommendation method*

A fuzzy preference tree-based recommendation method for tree-structured items is presented in this section. This method takes a user's fuzzy preference tree T_u and an item tree T_i as input, and calculates the predicted rating of the user to the target item. The recommendation method contains two steps. In the first step, the corresponding parts of T_u and T_i are matched. In step 2, a predicted rating of the user to the target item is calculated by aggregating the user preferences on the matched part of T_u.

Step 1: Identifying the corresponding parts of T_u and T_i.

A maximum conceptual similarity tree mapping between T_u and T_i, $M_{u,i}$, is constructed to identify the corresponding parts between two trees. The mapping should mainly consider the weights of T_u, i.e., it is an asymmetric mapping. Therefore, $M_{u,i}$ is constructed during calculating $sc_{T\mathrm{asym}}(T_u, T_i)$ by use of the method in Section 7.1.2.

Step 2: A fuzzy preference tree-based recommendation method.

Given a user's fuzzy preference tree T_u and an item tree T_i, the maximum conceptual similarity tree mapping between T_u and T_i, $M_{u,i}$ has been constructed. A function $pr()$, which takes the fuzzy preference tree node and the maximum conceptual similarity tree mapping as input, is developed to calculate the predicted rating of user u to item i.

Let $v(t_u[j])$ represent the fuzzy preference value of node $t_u[j]$ in T_u. $v(t_u[j]) = null$ if $t_u[j]$ is not assigned a value, $mc(t_u[j])$ represent the child nodes of $t_u[j]$ that are in the maximum conceptual similarity tree mapping. According to whether $v(t_u[j])$ and $mc(t_u[j])$ are $null$ or not, $pr(t_u[j], M_{u,i})$ is calculated in the following four cases:

Case 1: $v(t_u[j]) = null$, $mc(t_u[j]) = null$.

In this case, the sub-tree $T_u[j]$ makes no contribution to the predicted rating, $pr(t_u[j], M_{u,i}) = 0$.

Case 2: $v(t_u[j]) \neq null$, $mc(t_u[j]) = null$.

In this case, node $t_u[j]$ is assigned a preference value, which is $\tilde{p}_{uj} = \{f_{1,uj}, f_{2,uj}, \ldots, f_{r,uj}\}$.

$$pr(t_u[j], M_{u,i}) = \begin{cases} 0 & \sum_{k=1}^{r} f_{k,uj} = 0 \\ \sum_{k=1}^{r} k \cdot f_{k,uj} / \sum_{k=1}^{r} f_{k,uj} & \sum_{k=1}^{r} f_{k,uj} \neq 0 \end{cases} \qquad (7.14)$$

Case 3: $v(t_u[j]) = null$, $mc(t_u[j]) \neq null$.

In this case, the predicted rating value of $t_u[j]$ is calculated by aggregating the predicted ratings of its mapped children.

$$pr(t_u[j], M_{u,i}) = \sum_{t_u[j_x] \in mc(t_u[j])} w_x \cdot pr(t_u[j_x], M_{u,i}) \qquad (7.15)$$

where w_x represents the aggregating weight of the node $t_u[j_x]$, $w_x = w(t_u[j_x])/$ $\sum_{t_u[j_s]\in mc(t_u[j])} w(t_u[j_s])$.

Case 4: $v(t_u[j]) \neq null$, $mc(t_u[j]) \neq null$.

This case is a combination of Case 2 and Case 3. Both the values of node $t_u[j]$ and its children should be considered.

$$pr(t_u[j], M_{u,i}) = \beta_j \cdot pr_{uj} + (1-\beta_j) \cdot \sum_{t_u[j_x]\in mc(t_u[j])} w_x \cdot pr(t_u[j_x], M_{u,i}) \quad (7.16)$$

where $pr_{uj} = 0$ if $\sum_{k=1}^{r} f_{k,uj} = 0$; $pr_{uj} = \sum_{k=1}^{r} k \cdot f_{k,uj}/\sum_{k=1}^{r} f_{k,uj}$ if $\sum_{k=1}^{r} f_{k,uj} \neq 0$, $w_x = w(t_u[j_x])/\sum_{t_u[j_s]\in mc(t_u[j])} w(t_u[j_s])$, and β_j is the influence factor of the parent node $t_u[j]$. Let the root node of T_u be $root(T_u)$. The predicted rating of user u to item i is calculated as $pr(root(T_u), M_{u,i})$.

The proposed recommendation method overcomes the cold start issue more efficiently than other methods because a new user's preferences take the form of a tree structure and are intentionally expressed with uncertain values. The method in this chapter handles this issue using fuzzy preference tree and is therefore able to make more accurate recommendations to new users than extant recommendation methods. Similarly, the proposed method can also recommend new items more accurately by constructing new item trees, whereas the CF method cannot. The proposed method also overcomes the sparsity issue more effectively than existing methods, because it does not rely on the user-item rating matrix to calculate the user or item similarity. It therefore does not suffer from the sparsity problem which commonly exists in CF methods. Moreover, the incremental construction of the fuzzy preference tree means that a user's fuzzy preference tree can be updated efficiently, which deals with the scalability problem to some extent.

7.4 Summary

Tree-structured data often appears in item descriptions and user profiles that cannot be dealt with using basic CF-based or content-based recommendation methods. This chapter addresses a tree-structured data issue in recommender systems and proposes a comprehensive similarity measure on tree-structured items and user requirements. Two sets of recommendation methods are presented on the basis of the tree-structured data model. One is an item tree and user-request tree-based hybrid recommendation method. The other is a fuzzy preference tree model and a fuzzy preference tree-based recommendation method, which can model users' tree-structured preferences with subjectivity and uncertainty.

Chapter 8

Group Recommender Systems

The majority of recommender systems provides recommendations to single users (a business or a customer). However, there are some scenarios in which a recommendation is required for a group of people. For example, recommending a TV program to a club or recommending a tour for a group. Group recommender systems are therefore proposed to combine and balance individual expectations of group members to produce satisfying recommendations to the group as a whole. Therefore, in a group environment a group recommender system must respond to all group member's preferences in order to produce recommendations that will be accepted by the whole group, and if not then by the majority of the group. However, the members of a group often have different preferences to items and play different roles/have different weights in the group. Thus the main research issue in group recommender systems is how to generate the "best" group recommendation by taking both individual member's contribution and their importance into account. This chapter will present how a group recommender system generates recommendations in groups.

In this chapter, first we introduce in Section 8.1 the definitions, types, frameworks, and strategies for group recommender systems. Section 8.2 presents in detail a member contribution score (MCS) model and a member contribution score-based group recommendation (MCS-GR) method. A web-based tourism group recommender system prototype, GroTo, is described in Section 8.3. Lastly, a summary of the chapter is given in Section 8.4.

8.1   Group Recommender Systems Framework

This section introduces main concepts, frameworks, strategies and group profile establishment of group recommender systems.

8.1.1   *Groups and group recommender systems*

A group recommender system provides recommendations to a group of users taking into account the preferences of all the users. Below are some concepts related to a group recommender system.

(1) Group

In the group recommender system field, we have three main classifications for the term "group".

(a) Groups can be categorized into two types in terms of their application scenarios:

- Active group
- Passive group

An active group allows users to actively join a specific group. For example, some friends actively form a reading group. The type of groups can obtain recommendations based on the references of all the group members. In a passive group, users are passively allocated to a group. For example, when people attend a music show, in which users passively form a group and the music recommendations cannot be determined by considering all attendees' preferences.

(b) Groups can be categorized into two types regardless of member mobility:

- Stable group
- Random group

In a stable group, members become closely correlated, having been together for a long period, so that group preferences can be centralized over time and items that satisfy all members in the group can be easily found. For instance, a reading group might narrow the range of reading to ultimately focus on realist novels. In contrast, random groups are usually passively formed where members have no opportunity to specify their preferences or negotiate a consensus preference. Therefore, a random group may have highly conflicting group preferences. For example, people at a party form a random group, in which the individual preferences for the type of music to play within the group may be conflicted.

(c) Groups can be categorized into two types based on the way they communicate:

- Off-line groups
- On-line groups

An off-line group is for a group that has already been formed physically (e.g. a family). An online group is for a group that needs to be formed by an online system (e.g. web-based shoppers on a website at a particular time).

(2) Group recommender systems

There are different definitions for group recommender systems. The definition we use is the following one:

Definition 8.1 (Group recommender system). For a group $\mathcal{G}$, which is a collection of Q users (members) gathered actively or passively, stably or randomly, online or off-line from the whole user set $\mathcal{U} = \{u_1, u_2, \ldots, u_M\}, M > Q$, the group recommender system generates a list of recommendations from items $\mathcal{V} = \{v_1, v_2, \ldots, v_N\}$, where N is the number of items, to $\mathcal{G}$ based on group preferences or profile.

The type of a group affects the design of a group recommender system for the group. In principle, generating recommendations for a random group is more difficult than a stable group, because when making recommendations to random groups is the conflict of preferences that arises when members pursue their individual preferences without considering of other members. This problem worsens when a larger and online random group is involved, because finding a compromise for diverse interests is more difficult to model, and consequently recommendations are more difficult to generate. Therefore, it is not enough to only use rating information in modeling group preferences. We need to consider other appropriate solutions to reduce the impact of conflict between group members.

The basic group recommendation methods are developed mainly under two frameworks, as illustrated in Fig. 8.1 (a) and (b).

Framework 1 (Aggregation-Profile): Aggregating individual member's profiles, in which the profile of a pseudo user is modeled by aggregating the individual member's preferences to represent the preferences of the whole group, and the pseudo user's profile is then used to generate the group recommendations.

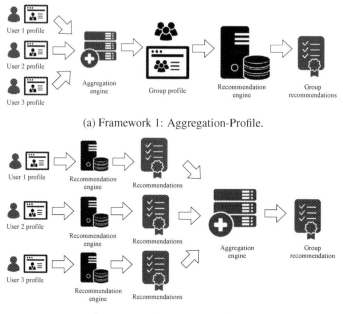

(a) Framework 1: Aggregation-Profile.

(b) Aggregation-Recommendation.

Fig. 8.1: Two frameworks of group recommender systems.

Framework 2 (Aggregation-Recommendation): Aggregating individual recommendations that are generated independently. A group recommendation is produced by aggregating the individual recommendations.

From the two frameworks shown in Fig. 8.1, we can see that in a group recommender system one of the most important procedures is aggregation, be that either aggregating individual profiles or aggregating recommendations.

8.1.2 *Aggregation strategies*

Basically, there are four main aggregation strategies in group recommender systems:

(1) Consensus-based strategy/average-based strategy: on each dimension, to select the average or weighted average of all the observed values. This average value can be different from all the observed values.
(2) Majority-based strategy: the value on each dimension is selected from the most common among the observed values.

(3) Borderline strategy: the extreme value is selected on each dimension.
(4) Dictatorship strategy: only the value from the specific members is selected on every dimension.

Of these four types of strategies, the majority-based strategy is often used to aggregate individual recommendations (Framework 2), while the other three strategies are used to aggregate individual preferences to build a group profile (Framework 1).

For the Framework 1, there are two aspects to consider in modeling a group profile:

(1) The common interest of the group;
(2) The disappointment caused by preference conflicts.

These two aspects drive the basic design principles for generating group recommendations:

(1) Maximizing satisfaction;
(2) Minimizing disappointment.

The consensus-/average-based, majority-based and dictatorship strategies are widely used to maximize satisfaction to aggregate users' rankings. The borderline strategy is often used to minimize the disappointment of a group. A typical example to treat individual members equally is, when a group profile is constructed using the average-based strategy, the system assumes group members equally important, and the group rating for one item is the mean of all the observed ratings specified by members.

For the Framework 2, a group recommender system uses individual recommender methods to generate individual recommendations and then use aggregating methods to generate group recommendations. From this point of view, any individual recommendation method can be adopted in group recommender system to generate individual recommendations. The special aspect that differs from individual recommender systems is the aggregating methods. Another interesting aspect is the modeling of group members communication.

8.1.3   *Group profile and modeling*

Establishing a group profile is an important part of Framework 1. We first give the following definition and explanations.

Definition 8.2 (Group profile). Let $\text{Profile}(\mathcal{G})$ be the profile for a group $\mathcal{G}$:

$$\text{Profile}(\mathcal{G}) = \sum_{u \in \mathcal{G}} w_u \text{Profile}(u) \qquad (8.1)$$

where w_u is the weight vector for u and different w_u leads to different strategies. If $\forall u \in \mathcal{G}, w_u = \frac{1}{|\mathcal{G}|}$, Eq. (8.1) becomes a consensus-based strategy. When only one member's weight vector's elements are equal to 1 and other members are zero vectors, Eq. (8.1) is a dictatorship strategy.

To model a group profile, there are main approaches:

(1) Member social relationship: Social relationship and personalities are used to describe the characteristic and relationships among the group members [Ye *et al.* (2012)] to identify the most representative measures. The basic idea is that users tend to purchase those products that are preferred by the user's social contacts. The group profile combines both the social and content interests of the group members. Moreover, some genetic algorithms are used to obtain the personalities of members and their interactions. The ratings of individual members and subgroups are considered to calculate the weights and individual rating for a target item. The unknown group ratings are computed using the weighted sum of the individual ratings.

(2) Knowledge-based: Domain knowledge is applied in modeling group profiles. For example, user prototypes for tourism activities were predefined to model the pseudo user profile for a random group [Ardissono *et al.* (2005)]. A more complex example is presented for the different preference aspects of TV viewers [Vildjiounaite *et al.* (2009)], in which three support vector machines are trained. The case-based method has been used in modeling group profiles for preference similarity and compatibility computation under the consensus-based strategy. Another example is that [Quijano-Sánchez *et al.* (2012)] used the case-based method to analyze the personalities among the group members, and the raw ratings are transformed into delegation-based rating considering personality.

(3) Interactive functions: Interactive functions are proposed to improve the effectiveness of modeling a group profile. The interactive functions for group members can explicitly specify their preferences [Garcia and Sebastia (2014)]. However, these functions are not always available when a group is formed randomly.

A group profile is often represented as a rating vector or matrix. The group ratings are calculated by an aggregating strategy.

8.2 A Member Contribution Score-based Group Recommendation Method

In this section, the MCS-GR method structure is firstly introduced as in Fig. 8.2, and the two phases of this method are then presented.

Phase 1: A group profile generator;

Phase 2: A group recommendations generator;

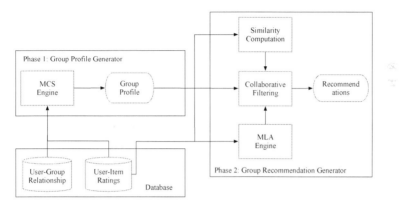

Fig. 8.2: The MCS-GR method structure.

8.2.1 *MCS-GR method structure*

To generate a group recommendation to maximize the satisfaction a group's individual preferences, the group recommendation method requires modeling group profiles and analyzing individual member's ratings (contributions). To model a group profile the representative differences between group members need to be considered. However, this consideration requires introducing prior knowledge about the members, such as social relationships or member behavior patterns. In real-world situations, when a group is formed randomly, the prior knowledge about group members is unavailable for the system to access. Group members can only provide extremely limited information, such as very few ratings comparing to a huge number of available items, and, accordingly for every item in the group profile, a large proportion of members don't specify ratings for it. We consider using the matrix completion techniques to fulfill the rating matrix before modeling the group profile. The performance of pre-processing is highly dependent on whether the used rating distributions match the group members' rating patterns.

To generate a group recommendation that maximizes the satisfaction of the group as a whole, the group recommendation method requires modeling group profiles and analyzing individual member's ratings (contributions) [Wang *et al.* (2016)]. Modeling a group profile is the key to generate better group recommendations. Moreover, it is important to accurately predict and aggregate a group's preference, which can be a challenge when biased and limited information is obtained for group members. It is also quite important to convince members to understand why the specific group recommendations are reasonable. Analyzing individual member's contributions is to numerically measure each group member's importance. Related methods need to address the biased rating problem caused by preference conflicts within a group.

MCS-GR provides a group recommendation effectiveness for handling the biased and sparse information to model and generate predictions of interests for the group. This MCS-GR method is basically under Framework 1 and is suitable for both active and passive groups, and both random and stable groups. The MCS-GR method aims to maximize satisfaction within a random group by modeling preferences through the analysis of contributed member ratings alone. It measures each member's importance in terms of a sub-rating matrix acquired by sampling, which makes it a practical method even when the matrix is highly incomplete and sparse.

8.2.2 *Group profile generator*

In this phase of MCS-GR, we first introduce some notions and concepts to evaluate the representative level of each member and propose a member contribution score (MCS) model to numerically define the representative status of members and generate the group profile.

To build the group profile, especially in a complex random group, the preferences of the most representative members should be considered above others. In practice, these representative members are difficult to identify because of the sparsity in the data. To address this problem, the sampling and aggregating over the item space is employed. The rating vectors of users can be perceived as high-dimensional data, with each dimension representing one item. For example, suppose a movie recommender system consists of N movies.

Let a rating vector of a user u be $\boldsymbol{r}_{u,*} = (r_{u,1}, r_{u,2}, \ldots, r_{u,n})$. Instead of considering the vectors over the whole item space, sampling selects a reduced set of items for which members can provide a rating matrix without missing values, and after which the representative members can be precisely evaluated on this partial rating matrix. After multiple sampling, the representative members across the global item space can be approximated by aggregating the results from all the samplings. A high level of the group profile compromise equation with respect to the MCS model is introduced in Definition 8.2. This phase is illustrated in Fig. 8.3 and its three main steps are described in detail below.

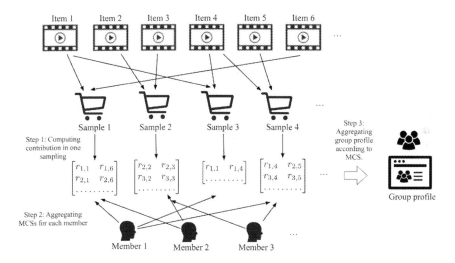

Fig. 8.3: Description of the MCS model.

Step 1: Computing contribution in one sampling.

The contribution of a member to the group profile is highly correlated with the recommendation strategy adopted. The unknown ratings for each item make the generated group profile less reliable. One method of addressing this problem is matrix completion, which predicts missing ratings before building the group profile and introducing new uncertainty to the system. A sampling consists of a projection of a rating matrix and corresponding members who have no missing values. When there are no missing ratings, the representative members can be measured precisely.

Intuitively, a member is not representative when his/her preference is highly correlated with and can be represented by the preferences of others. Taking all the members' profiles as data in high-dimensional vectors, a finite set of vertices can be selected to define a convex hull and all the other data in the convex hull can be linearly represented. These vertices, i.e. preferences, are more representative than the preferences in the convex hull. This is the motivation for proposing the "contribution score" concept to depict the representative degree of a member. Taking this point of view, the representative measuring problem here is converted into the identification of the set of preferences on the hull vertices.

Now we introduce the notations for the rating matrix (mentioned previously): Rating matrix R represents a M by N matrix. M rows represent M users and N columns represent N items. The user set and item set are denoted as $\mathcal{U}$ and $\mathcal{V}$. A sampling on items is noted as $\mathcal{V}^p$, and any item that belongs to it is randomly selected out with equal probability. To select out members, which are denoted $\mathcal{U}^p$, corresponding to $\mathcal{V}^p$, filtering is carried out to exclude members who have missing ratings on $\mathcal{V}^p$. After determined $\mathcal{V}^p$ and $\mathcal{U}^p$, the sub-rating matrix R^p, which has no missing value, can be projected from the original matrix R to items belonging to $\mathcal{V}^p$ and users belonging to $\mathcal{U}^p$. R^p is used as the input of the MCS model to calculate the representative members in $\mathcal{U}^p$.

Since the rating matrix R is incomplete, finding the representative member is divided into several subspaces of R. The representative members are found in the low-dimensional space, which is easier. This is carried out by separable non-negative matrix factorization (SNMF) [Zhou *et al.* (2013)]. It is defined as follows:

Definition 8.3 (Separable non-negative matrix factorization, SNMF). SNMF on a rating matrix can be represented as:

$$u^p := \text{SNMF}(R^p) \tag{8.2}$$

where R^p is the pth sub-matrix from rating matrix R and $R^p \in \mathbb{R}^{K \times L}$, $K < M, L < N$, u^p is the user index that SNMF has found that is a representative member of the sub-matrix R^p. If the user set $\mathcal{U}^p$ of the sub-matrix R^p is a group, then, u^p is the representative member of this group.

SNMF is an appropriate technique to analyze representativeness when only based on ratings. It guarantees a unique and stable solution for a specific matrix, which means the decompositions are not influenced by initial values. SNMF is easy to extend to large groups because of its great scalability and since only the ratings of members need to be analyzed.

With the sub-matrix R^p and its user set $\mathcal{U}^p$ and item set $\mathcal{V}^p$, the contribution score of group member is:

Definition 8.4 (Member Contribution Score, MCS). MCS measures the representative preferences of each member. For each member $u \in U$, the MCS of u on sub-matrix R^p with its user set $\mathcal{U}^p$ and item set $\mathcal{V}^p$ is defined as:

$$\text{MCS}_u^p = \begin{cases} 1, & u = u^p, \\ 0, & \text{others.} \end{cases} \tag{8.3}$$

Here we give a special case of seeking the representative member with a pair of items, i.e. the sub-matrix $\boldsymbol{R}^p \in \mathbb{R}^{M \times 2}$ and $\mathcal{V}^p = \{v1, v2\}$. In such case, the representative member is calculated as:

$$u^p := \arg \max_u \arctan 2(r_{u,v1}, r_{u,v2}) \qquad (8.4)$$

where $r_{u,v1}$ and $r_{u,v2}$ are the rating of user u on item v_1 and v_2, and $\arctan 2$ is calculated as:

$$\arctan 2(y, x) = \begin{cases} \arctan(y/x), & x >; \\ \arctan(y/x) + \pi, & y \geqslant 0, x < 0; \\ \arctan(y/x) - \pi, & y < 0, x < 0; \\ \pi/2, & y > 0, x = 0; \\ -\pi/2, & y < 0, x = 0. \end{cases}$$

Through this step, we can obtain the contribution score of each member on one sampling.

Step 2: Aggregating MCSs for each member.

Note that each sampling selects a portion of items and only selects members who have no missing ratings. Members involved in one sampling may not cover the group. The representative degree of a group member over the whole item space can be approximated by aggregating the MCS results of all the samplings in which he/she is involved.

Theoretically, all the possible samplings should be considered to evaluate each member's contribution accurately. However, in practice, it is impossible to complete all samplings within the time limit, considering the infinite projection probability for a rating matrix of a group. To address this issue, a portion of the projections for any group size are selected out as the samplings, i.e., all the item-pair subspaces to measure MCS. For the whole item space V, the sampling subspaces are producing $d = \binom{n}{2}$ sub-matrixes $\{\boldsymbol{R}^1, \ldots, \boldsymbol{R}^d\}$. As we have introduced, the corresponding user set and item set of the sub-matrix $\boldsymbol{R}^p$ are $\mathcal{U}^p$ and $\mathcal{V}^p$. Here, each item subset contains $l = 2$ items in the following part, but the method can expand to other conditions as long as $l \leqslant n$.

The MCS of user u denoted as MCS_u^p is 1 or 0, depending on whether u can be identified as representative members, and is always 0 when u is not involved. For each group member $u \in \mathcal{G}$, we can aggregate all the MCS of u on all sub-matrixes as the MCS of u on the whole matrix $\boldsymbol{R}$.

$$\text{MCS}_u = \sum_{p=1}^{d} \frac{l}{n} \text{MCS}_u^p. \qquad (8.5)$$

In this step, we obtained each member's aggregated contribution score.

Step 3: Aggregating group profile according to MCS.

Once the MCS for each group member has been obtained, it is normalized for further group profile calculation:

$$w_u = \frac{\text{MCS}_u}{\sum_{u \in \mathcal{G}} \text{MCS}_u}. \tag{8.6}$$

The group profile $\text{Profile}(\mathcal{G})$ is represented as a vector and every dimension represents an item only when it has been rated by group members. Let $\mathcal{V}_\mathcal{G}$ be all the items that have been rated by group members and $\mathcal{V}_\mathcal{G} = \{v_1, \ldots, v_{|\mathcal{V}_\mathcal{G}|}\}$. Then $\text{Profile}(\mathcal{G}) = [r_{\mathcal{G}, v_1}, \ldots, r_{\mathcal{G}, v_{|\mathcal{V}_\mathcal{G}|}}]$. The group rating for each item v is computed as follows:

$$r_{\mathcal{G}, v} = \sum_{u \in \mathcal{G}} w_u r_{u, v}. \tag{8.7}$$

We summarize these three steps to Algorithm 8.1 to show how to compute the group profile with detailed description of the MCS calculation. We give a numerical example to explain the calculation of Algorithm 8.1.

Algorithm 8.1: Group Profile Generator

Input:
    R, the rating matrix
    $\mathcal{V}$, the item set, $\mathcal{G}$, the user group
Output:
    $\text{Profile}(\mathcal{G})$, the group profile

1: initialize $\text{MCS}_u = 0$

2: get $d = \binom{n}{2}$ sub-matrixes $\mathcal{R} = \{R^1, \ldots, R^d\}$

3: **for** each sub-matrix $R^p \in \mathcal{R}$ **do**

4:      get item set $\mathcal{V}^p$

5:      get user set $\mathcal{U}^p$ which contains all the users who have rated $\mathcal{V}^p$

6:      calculate MCS_u^p as in Eq. (8.3)

7: **end**

8: **for** each $u \in \mathcal{G}$ **do**

9:      calculate MCS_u as in Eq. (8.5)

10: **end**

11: normalize MCS_u as in Eq. (8.6)

12: calculate group profile $\text{Profile}(\mathcal{G})$ as in Eq. (8.7)

13: **end**

Table 8.1: Group rating matrix example with four users and four items.

	v_1	v_2	v_3	v_4
u_1	5	4	4	?
u_2	4	4	?	?
u_3	?	?	5	2
u_4	3	1	?	3

Example 8.1. Let $\mathcal{G} = \{u_1, u_2, u_3, u_4\}$, $\mathcal{V} = \{v_1, v_2, v_3, v_4\}$, as shown in Table 8.1.

In step 1, all the item subspaces sampled are: $\{\mathcal{V}_{1,2}, \mathcal{V}_{1,3}, \mathcal{V}_{1,4}, \mathcal{V}_{2,3}, \mathcal{V}_{2,4}, \mathcal{V}_{3,4}\}$. The calculated MCS in the samplings are: $\mathrm{MCS}_{u_4}^{\mathcal{V}_{1,2}} = 1$, $\mathrm{MCS}_{u_1}^{\mathcal{V}_{1,3}} = 1$, $\mathrm{MCS}_{u_4}^{\mathcal{V}_{1,4}} = 1$, $\mathrm{MCS}_{u_1}^{\mathcal{V}_{2,3}} = 1$, $\mathrm{MCS}_{u_4}^{\mathcal{V}_{2,4}} = 1$, $\mathrm{MCS}_{u_3}^{\mathcal{V}_{3,4}} = 1$. In one sampling, only one member is representative.

In step 2, we aggregate MCS from all the samplings.

$$\mathrm{MCS}_{u_1} = \frac{2}{4}(\mathrm{MCS}_{u_1}^{\mathcal{V}_{1,2}} + \mathrm{MCS}_{u_1}^{\mathcal{V}_{1,3}} + \mathrm{MCS}_{u_1}^{\mathcal{V}_{1,4}} + \mathrm{MCS}_{u_1}^{\mathcal{V}_{2,3}} + \mathrm{MCS}_{u_1}^{\mathcal{V}_{2,4}} + \mathrm{MCS}_{u_1}^{\mathcal{V}_{3,4}})$$

$$= \frac{2}{4}(0 + 1 + 0 + 1 + 0 + 0) = 1,$$

$$\mathrm{MCS}_{u_2} = \frac{2}{4}(0 + 0 + 0 + 0 + 0 + 0) = 0,$$

$$\mathrm{MCS}_{u_3} = \frac{2}{4}(0 + 0 + 0 + 0 + 0 + 1) = \frac{1}{2},$$

$$\mathrm{MCS}_{u_4} = \frac{2}{4}(1 + 0 + 1 + 0 + 1 + 0) = \frac{3}{2}.$$

In step 3, contribution scores are normalized and the group profile is then modeled by taking MCS into consideration.

$$w_{u_1} = \frac{\mathrm{MCS}_{u_1}}{\mathrm{MCS}_{u_1} + \mathrm{MCS}_{u_2} + \mathrm{MCS}_{u_3} + \mathrm{MCS}_{u_4}} = \frac{1}{1 + \frac{1}{2} + \frac{3}{2}} = \frac{1}{3},$$

$$w_{u_2} = \frac{0}{1 + \frac{1}{2} + \frac{3}{2}} = \frac{1}{3}, \quad w_{u_3} = \frac{\frac{1}{2}}{1 + \frac{1}{2} + \frac{3}{2}} = \frac{1}{6}, \quad w_{u_4} = \frac{\frac{3}{2}}{1 + \frac{1}{2} + \frac{3}{2}} = \frac{1}{2}.$$

$$r_{\mathcal{G},v_1} = w_{u_1} r_{u_1,v_1} + w_{u_2} r_{u_2,v_1} + w_{u_4} r_{u_4,v_1} = \frac{1}{3} \times 5 + 0 \times 4 + \frac{1}{2} \times 5 = 3.17,$$

$$r_{\mathcal{G},v_2} = \frac{1}{3} \times 4 + 0 \times 4 + \frac{1}{2} \times 1 = 1.83,$$

$$r_{\mathcal{G},v_3} = \frac{1}{3} \times 4 + \frac{1}{6} \times 5 = 2.17, \quad r_{\mathcal{G},v_4} = \frac{1}{6} \times 2 + \frac{1}{2} \times 3 = 0.83.$$

The output group profile is $\mathrm{Profile}(\mathcal{G}) = [3.17, 1.83, 2.17, 0.83]$.

8.2.3   *Group recommendation generator*

In Phase 1, the group profile is generated. It is used in this phase to predict unknown group ratings. The similarity measure, PCC is adopted in to identify neighbors close to the group. To minimize the error caused by the fat tail, a Manhattan distance-based measure is applied to compute local average ratings for the group. By combining PCC similarities and local average ratings, an individual user-based CF method is applied to predict unknown group ratings, and the top-k items are recommended according to the group predictions. This phase contains three steps:

Step 1: Compute profile similarity between group members and non-group members.

The obtained group profile, Profile($\mathcal{G}$) can be seen as a preference of a pseudo user. We can then compute the similarities between the pseudo user and non-group users. PCC is employed for the similarity computation.

Step 2: Compute group local average rating.

Before we adopt user-based CF to predict the unknown group ratings, the fat tail issue should be considered. Neighbor-based CF methods may suffer from the fat tail distribution of user ratings, i.e., many ratings are far away from the pseudo user's mean rating.

The Manhattan distance-based local average rating model aims to search a local approximation considering the target item, and it computes a local average rating that is focused on the target item. The model can alleviate the fat tail problem, because it will not force the approximation by focusing on the dense region. Therefore, the unknown ratings fall on sparse region, mostly the fat tail, and are predicted more accurately. It can estimate the pseudo user's local average ratings with respect to the target items, instead of computing the global average rating on the whole item space. The relevance of a specific target item in relation to other items is ranked by a Manhattan distance-based measure. By locating items with similar distribution using this measure, the local average rating of a member on these items can be seen as a closer estimation of target item than the global measure, therefore the local average rating can be used to predict the unknown group ratings to alleviate the fat tail problem. After computing the item's relevance, we select a portion of the ratings with higher relevance to compute the local average rating.

We use the Manhattan distance-based function to measure the relevance between two items. Item relevance aims to find items that are close to the target item even when fat tail exists. Manhattan distance is sensitive to the fat tail, because it measures relevance according to the absolute rating differences. The Manhattan distance between two items v_i and v_j is:

$$D_{v_i,v_j} = \sum_{u \in \mathcal{U}_{v_i} \cap \mathcal{U}_{v_j}} |r_{u,v_i} - r_{u,v_j}| \tag{8.8}$$

where $\mathcal{U}_{v_i} \cap \mathcal{U}_{v_j}$ is the users who have rated both v_i and v_j.

One limitation of this distance is that it is difficult to achieve a unified threshold for different systems, because one might choose a rating scale of 1 to 5 while another might choose a scale of 1 to 10. Let $\Delta r_u = r_{u,v_i} - r_{u,v_j}$. We first normalize Δr_u before calculating relevance. We divide the possible Δr_u into three relevance levels with respect to the different systems. If the system allows a user to rate an item from $r_{\min}$ to $r_{\max}$, then Δr_u ranges from 0 to $r_{\max}$-$r_{\min}$ and the three levels are $[0, \frac{r_{\max}-r_{\min}}{3})$, $[\frac{r_{\max}-r_{\min}}{3}, \frac{2(r_{\max}-r_{\min})}{3})$ and $[\frac{2(r_{\max}-r_{\min})}{3}, r_{\max} - r_{\min}]$. Clearly, if Δr_u is closer to 0, v_i and v_j are more relevant to user u. We define a subsection function to represent the relevance for each level.

$$\Delta r_u^* = \begin{cases} 1, & 0 \leqslant x < \frac{r_{\max}-r_{\min}}{3}, \\ 0.5, & \frac{r_{\max}-r_{\min}}{3} \leqslant x < \frac{2(r_{\max}-r_{\min})}{3}, \\ 0, & \frac{2(r_{\max}-r_{\min})}{3} \leqslant x < r_{\max} - r_{\min}. \end{cases}$$

The Manhattan distance of item v_i and v_j is $D_{v_i,v_j} = \sum_{u \in \mathcal{U}_{v_i} \cap \mathcal{U}_{v_j}}$. A threshold T is set to determine whether items v_i and v_j are sufficiently close and whether r_{u,v_j} is taken into consideration to compute the average rating of group $\mathcal{G}$ for item v_i. The local average rating of group $\mathcal{G}$ for target item v_j is calculated by averaging all the ratings relevant to v_j, where the relevance is greater than T, which is defined as:

$$\bar{r_{\mathcal{G},v_j}} = \sum_{v_i \in \mathcal{V}_j^{\text{rel}}} (r_{\mathcal{G},v_i}) \tag{8.9}$$

where $\mathcal{V}_j^{\text{rel}}$ is the items that $D_{v_i,v_j} \geqslant T$.

Step 3: Predict group rating for items.

After obtaining the similarities and local average ratings of the pseudo user, we can predict the unknown group ratings. In this step, user-based CF is adopted, and group ratings are calculated by the weighted sum of deviations from the average rating of similar neighbors. The final recommendations are selected as the top-k items with the highest prediction values.

8.3   GroTo: A Web-based Tourist Group Recommender System

Group tourism (GroTo) is a web-based group recommender system prototype that aims to provide personalized recommendation activities for web-based tourist groups taking Australia as an example. In this GroTo system, the activities are classified and labeled in six categories of tourism activity: Nature, Sports, Arts, Aboriginal, Attractions and Social. Each category contains detailed activities for users to rate. For example, going to the beach or visiting state parks and farms, can be rated by users in the Nature category.

The GroTo system has three components: a system interface, a recommender engine and a data server, as shown in Fig. 8.4.

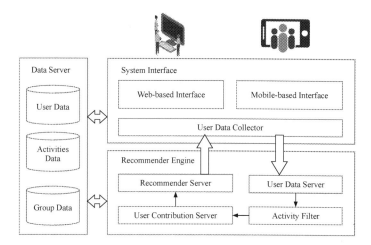

Fig. 8.4: Architecture of the group tourism recommender system - GroTo.

The system interface collects information from users who can actively specify their preferences for various tourist activities via a web-based interface provided by the system. Users' context information can also be passively collected from mobile devices. Note that the preferences and historical visiting information are transformed into structural data. For example, XML in the user data collector module. Users' data are passed to the recommender engine for further processing.

The recommender engine parses structural information of users. User preferences are transformed into rating vectors in the user data server module. Additionally, every historical location, that can be found and labeled in the system, is transformed into ratings in the user data server module. Negative feedback is not transformed into ratings, but will be used as criteria for pre-selection. The activities filter generates available activities by excluding all the activities that clearly do not appeal to members. The user contribution server models a group profile to describe overall group preferences using the MCS model. The group profile and negative list are given to the recommender server to filter appropriate activities to recommend to the group.

The data server is responsible for recording data from the system and individual information, preferences and feedback. It is important to point out that, except for individual information and feedback, the group can be stored as a case for future recommendation. A group can be identified and formed based on varying parameters such as holiday, conference, business or education. Recommendations can be precisely made to future groups by using a group filter that can find similar cases in the database.

We give an example in which only a selection of activities in GroTo is considered as shown in Table 8.2.

Table 8.2: Group rating matrix example with one group and eight non-group members.

users	beach	park	whale watching	botanic garden	farms	fishing	diving	surfing	snow sports	golf	cycling
$u_1 (\in \mathcal{G})$	5				3		4			2	
$u_2 (\in \mathcal{G})$		4			4						3
$u_3 (\in \mathcal{G})$	4						5	2			
$u_4 (\in \mathcal{G})$	4	1					3			5	
$u_5 (\in \mathcal{G})$		5			2				4		
$u_6 (\in \mathcal{G})$	5						1			5	1
u_7	5		4		2	5	4	2			
u_8		3		4							
u_9						5	4			5	
u_{10}		4		4					3		4
u_{11}	2	1									
u_{12}	4	3					4			1	
u_{13}		5		4							
u_{14}									5		3
u_{15}	4		4		1						

A group $\mathcal{G}$ is formed by six members u_1 to u_6 who nominate their own ratings via the system interface. According to MCS-GR method, their weightings are $[0.1216, 0.1622, 0.2162, 0.1622, 0.1622, 0.1757]$. The group profile is $[r_{\mathcal{G},\text{beach}} = 3, r_{\mathcal{G},\text{parks}} = 1.62, r_{\mathcal{G},\text{farms}} = 1.34, r_{\mathcal{G},\text{diving}} = 2.23, r_{\mathcal{G},\text{snow sports}} = 1.96, r_{\mathcal{G},\text{cycling}} = 1.71]$. User-based CF is adopted to predict the unknown group ratings for whale watching, botanic gardens, fishing, surfing and golf, with the results 2.31, 1.73, 1.89, 2.56 and 1 respectively. Based on the results, if we were to recommend the three best activities to the group, they would be surfing, whale watching and fishing. The results of this example show that the group recommendation method MCS-GR can accurately aggregate individual preferences and produce appropriate recommendations for a group.

8.4 Summary

This chapter presents group recommender system concepts, framework, methods and a prototype. In particular, we discussed in this chapter a MCS model to measure the contribution of each group member in which, by partitioning the item space, we can analyze members' opinions using the SNMF technique. In addition, we developed the Manhattan distance-based local average rating model to alleviate the fat tail problem by adaptively calculating the average rating related to the target item when predicting unknown group ratings. The MCS-GR method is proposed to integrate these two models into two phases and to tackle the general group recommendation problem. The group profile is generated according to MCSs, when only the rating information without the need for additional information is considered. A web-based tourism group recommender system prototype, GroTo, is also described.

Chapter 9

Cross-Domain Recommender Systems

A recommender system is usually used for a single domain, which is when items and users' ratings are in the same domain. However, sometimes a recommender system may need to recommend items to users that cross over two or more domains. One reason to exploit multiple domains using the cross-domain recommender systems is to solve the problems of data sparsity or cold start (new user). That is, there may be insufficient data in one domain, but relatively rich data in another domain. The abundance of data in another domain can assist with the recommendation in a target domain with sparse data. Another reason is that cross-domain recommender systems can profile user preferences that cannot be found within single domain data, which benefits each of the single domains. For example, a target user in a movie domain is likely to be interested in books and music related to the movie he/she likes. The demand for rich and diverse recommendation together with the ability to alleviate the data sparsity problem drives the development of the cross-domain recommender systems. This chapter will present related methods and new developments in cross-domain recommender systems.

In this chapter, we first introduce basic concepts and types of cross-domain recommender systems in Section 9.1. In Section 9.2, we present a cross-domain recommendation method with consistent knowledge transfer. In Section 9.3, we present a cross-domain recommendation method with kernel-induced knowledge transfer. Finally, the chapter summary is provided in Section 9.4.

9.1 Concepts and Types

In this section, definition of cross-domain recommender system is formally defined. Then the types of cross-domain recommender systems are presented.

In cross-domain recommender system, domains differ because of different types of users or items [Fernández-Tobías *et al.* (2012)]. A cross-domain recommender system can be built on two domains with different item types such as movies and books, or on two domains with both movies but different categories such as action movies and comedy movies. Also, a cross-domain recommender systems can be built on two domains with the same users and different items, or cross-systems with similar items but different users.

When the rating matrix in the target domain R^τ is very sparse, it raises the question of how to use relatively dense rating matrix R^s in the source domain to assist a recommendation task in the target domain. The recommendation task, as stated in Chapter 2, is to predict a utility score (in this chapter, a rating) of a user on a item to represent his/her preference. In practice, the two rating matrixes may share corresponding entities. The overlapping entity indicator matrix is represented by $W^{(s,\tau)}$, $W_{ij}^{(s,\tau)} \in \{0, 1\}$. $W_{ij}^{(s,\tau)} = 1$ indicates that the ith entity in the source domain is the same as the jth entity in the target domain, and $W_{ij}^{(s,\tau)} = 0$ otherwise. Without loss of generality, let the rating rows of overlapping users be at the top, and the corresponding users be in the same rows in both matrixes. Thus, the form of the entity indicator matrix $W^{(s,\tau)}$ is:

$$W^{(s,\tau)} = \begin{bmatrix} I_o & 0 \\ 0 & 0 \end{bmatrix}$$

where I_o is an identity matrix whose dimension is the number of overlapping entities.

On this basis, we provide a formal definition of the problem formulation of the cross-domain recommender system:

Definition 9.1 (Cross-domain Recommender System). Given a source rating matrix $R^s \in \mathbb{R}^{M^s \times N^s}$ and a target rating matrix $R^\tau \in \mathbb{R}^{M^\tau \times N^\tau}$, a cross-domain recommender system is to assist with recommendation task on R^τ through an auxiliary source rating matrix R^s and an overlapping entity indicator matrix $W^{(s,\tau)}$.

In this chapter, we focus on explicit feedback and rating prediction. Specifically, the cross-domain recommender system is to find a function for user u^τ on item v^τ in the target domain to find a utility function $f(u^\tau, v^\tau)$ to approximate the rating r_{u^τ, v^τ} with the help of rating data in the source domain.

The knowledge extraction and transfer methods used in cross-domain recommender systems differ depending on whether the entities in each domain overlap and how they overlap, as shown in Fig. 9.1. We categorize cross-domain recommender systems using three different scenarios:

(1) Cross-domain recommender systems with fully overlapping entities (Fig. 9.1 (a)-(b)).
(2) Cross-domain recommender systems with partially overlapping entities (Fig. 9.1 (c)-(d)).
(3) Cross-domain recommender systems with non-overlapping entities (Fig. 9.1 (e)).

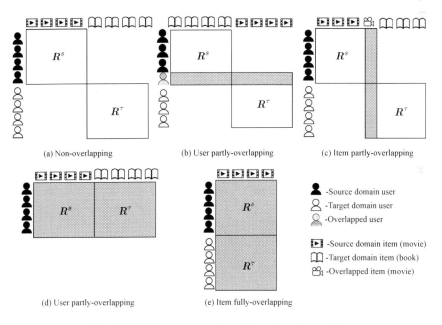

(a) Non-overlapping (b) User partly-overlapping (c) Item partly-overlapping

(d) User partly-overlapping (e) Item fully-overlapping

♟ -Source domain user
♟ -Target domain user
♟ -Overlapped user

▶ -Source domain item (movie)
📖 -Target domain item (book)
📖 -Overlapped item (movie)

Fig. 9.1: Different scenarios of overlapping entities.

Now we explain the three types in detail.

(1) Cross-domain recommender systems with fully overlapping entities.
    The source domain and the target domain share fully overlapping users as shown in Fig. 9.1 (a) or fully overlapping items as in Fig. 9.1 (b). This is an ideal scenario, but it rarely happens in practice. The naïve method to deal with the fully overlapping entities is to match the two matrixes as

one joint matrix and treat it as a recommendation problem in one domain. Since the relationship between two domains is not properly dealt with and the joint matrix is very sparse, the performance of the naïve method is not acceptable. Collective matrix factorization collectively factorizes these two matrixes by sharing the user/item latent factor matrix since the users/items are the same [Singh and Gordon (2008)]. If the data in two domains are heterogeneous, transfer collective factorization is able to use implicit data in the source domain to help predict the explicit feedback i.e., ratings, in the target domain [Pan and Yang (2013)]. The assumption of cross-domain recommender systems with fully overlapping entities is very strict (users and items must have one-by-one mapping in two domains), which limits the scope of its application in practice.

(2) Cross-domain recommender systems with partially overlapping entities.
   Partially overlapping users/items is the most common scenario in cross-domain recommender systems. A real-world example of overlapping users is given as follows: on the Amazon website, some users buy books and some users watch movies, and among these users there will be some overlap and both buy books and watch movies. The overlapping users bridge the source domain and the target domain. Cross-domain recommendation methods take advantages of the overlapping entities as constraints and collectively factorize the two rating matrices of the two domains to predict ratings of users on items. Even though the overlapping entities are only a small portion of the whole entity set, cross-domain recommender systems can still use the information to improve the system performance. However, since the entity correspondence is not always fully available and the identification of the mapping is time-consuming, active-learning strategies are used to identify the most valuable entity correspondences in the source domain.

(3) Cross-domain recommender systems with non-overlapping entities.
   As shown in Fig. 9.1(e), the source domain and the target domain have no requirements on entity overlapping. Therefore, there is no obvious bridge from either the user or the item side for knowledge transfer since the similarities of users/items between the two domains are not easily obtained. The assumption of cross-domain recommender systems with non-overlapping entities is that similar user groups share similar interests on item groups. For example, in the source domain users who like thriller movies are likely to also be interested in sci-fi movies. The same rating pattern for these movies can also be applied to the target domain of books; that is users who like thrillers are likely to prefer detective fictions. There are a number of standard methods in cross-domain recommender systems with

non-overlapping entities. Included among them is codebook transfer, which clusters users and items into groups and extracts group-level knowledge as a "codebook" [Li *et al.* (2009a)]. Another probabilistic model called the rating matrix generated model is developed as an extension of codebook transfer, which relaxes the hard membership (one user belongs to only one group) to soft membership (one user can belong to several groups).

Two challenges remain unsolved in cross-domain recommender systems: (1) Feature inconsistency caused by data sparsity. Typically, there are no explicit features of users or items, only extracted latent features. Additionally the observed sparse interactions do not fully represent a user's preferences, so even features extracted from the same user in two different domains will be inconsistent. Thus, constructing an appropriate way to extract features of users and items is very challenging. (2) Features extracted from different domains are heterogeneous. Extracted latent features from the overlapping entity can be aligned through domain adaptation techniques. But extracted latent features from non-overlapping entities lack direct correlation and their features are heterogeneous. We present two cross-domain recommendation methods in this chapter to tackle the above two challenges.

9.2 Cross-domain Recommendation with Consistent Information Transfer

This section presents a cross-domain recommendation method with consistent information transfer (CIT).

The proposed CIT method uses a domain adaptation technique to ensure that knowledge extracted from the source domain is consistent with that from the target domain. The procedure consists of five steps, as shown in Fig. 9.2: (1) Users/items from the source and target domains are clustered separately into groups; (2) Domain adaptation techniques are used to generate consistent user/item latent groups in the source and target domains; (3) Consistent knowledge is extracted from the latent groups; (4) Group representations in the target domain are adjusted to retain their domain-specific characteristics; (5) A recommender system for the target domain is built. We use a specific algorithm for each step, but substitutions can also be applied [Zhang *et al.* (2018a)].

Step 1: Clustering of users and items in both domains.

This step clusters users and items into groups. Clustering users and items appropriately is a crucial issue. Intuitively, users may have various preferences and items may have diverse content. Therefore, it is usually more appropriate to allow both users and items to fall into multiple groups with different memberships. In this chapter, FMM is used to cluster the users and items separately [Si and Jin (2003)] on both the source domain and the target domain; however, for simplicity, we have only provided the description for one domain.

Suppose users are clustered into K user groups $\{Z_u^{(1)}, \ldots, Z_u^{(K)}\}$, while items are clustered into L item groups $\{Z_v^{(1)}, \ldots, Z_v^{(L)}\}$. Z_u and Z_v are two latent variables that denote the user and item groups respectively. $P(Z_u|u)$ is the conditional probability of a user belonging to a user group, denoting the group membership of the user; $P(Z_v|v)$ is the conditional probability of an item belonging to an item group, denoting its group membership. Each user group has a rating preference for each item group. r is the variable representing the preference of user groups to item groups. $P(r|Z_u, Z_v)$ is the conditional probability of r given user group Z_u and item group Z_v. The rating for a coupled user-item pair is:

$$R(u, v) = \sum_r r \sum_{Z_u, Z_v} P(r|Z_u, Z_v)P(Z_u|u)P(Z_v|v).$$

It can be rewritten into matrix form:

$$\boldsymbol{R} = \boldsymbol{U}\boldsymbol{S}\boldsymbol{V}^T$$

where $\boldsymbol{U} \in \mathbb{R}^{M \times K}$ and $\boldsymbol{V} \in \mathbb{R}^{N \times L}$ are the user and item group membership matrix. U_{ij} represents the membership of user u_i for user group $Z_u^{(j)}$. U_{i*} is the ith row of matrix U representing membership of user u_i to each group. U_{*j} is the jth column of matrix $\boldsymbol{U}$ representing the membership of each user to user group $Z_u^{(j)}$. The same goes for items. $\boldsymbol{S} \in \mathbb{R}^{K \times L}$ is the group-level knowledge matrix. S_{ij} represents the preference of user group $Z_u^{(i)}$ for item group $Z_v^{(j)}$.

After clustering, the user group and item group membership matrixes $\boldsymbol{U}^{(s,0)}$, $\boldsymbol{V}^{(s,0)}$ are acquired for the source domain and $\boldsymbol{U}^{(\tau,0)}$, $\boldsymbol{V}^{(\tau,0)}$ for the target domain:

$$\boldsymbol{U}^{(s,0)} = P(Z_{u^s}|u^s), \; \boldsymbol{V}^{(s,0)} = P(Z_{v^s}|v^s)$$

$$\boldsymbol{U}^{(\tau,0)} = P(Z_{u^\tau}|u^\tau), \; \boldsymbol{V}^{(\tau,0)} = P(Z_{v^\tau}|v^\tau)$$

where $P(Z_u|u) = \frac{P(u|Z_u)P(Z_u)}{\sum_{Z_u} P(u|Z_u)P(Z_u)}$ and $P(Z_v|v) = \frac{P(v|Z_v)P(Z_v)}{\sum_{Z_v} P(v|Z_v)P(Z_v)}$. Five parameters $P(u|Z_u)$, $P(v|Z_v)$,$P(r|Z_u, Z_v)$, $P(Z_u)$ and $P(Z_v)$ are learned from the FMM (for details, see [Si and Jin (2003)]).

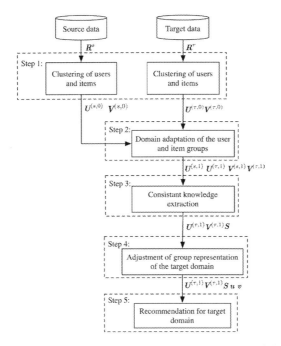

Fig. 9.2: The CIT method procedure.

Step 2: Domain adaptation of the user and item groups.

This step ensures information consistency between the user/item group membership matrixes of two domains. The original user group membership matrixes $U^{(s,0)}$, $U^{(\tau,0)}$ and item group membership matrixes $V^{(s,0)}$, $V^{(\tau,0)}$ from the source and target domains are used as the starting point.

In the source domain, each column $U_{*j}^{(s,0)}$ represents the memberships of all users in a user group j. Thus, it is reasonable to use the marginal probability distribution of column $U_{*j}^{(s,0)}$ to represent the characteristics of the user group information from user group j. This is also applied to the other three matrixes $V^{(s,0)}$, $U^{(\tau,0)}$, $V^{(\tau,0)}$. The disparity of the marginal probability distributions of user/item group membership matrixes in both domains is used to measure the divergence of the user/item group information. If the marginal probability distributions of the memberships of the two user/item groups are the same, these two user/item groups are regarded as having the same characteristics and the same physical meanings - information in the two user/item groups is consistent. This provides a method to measure the similarity between latent user/item groups in both domains. According to the basic assumption of recommender systems, i.e., "similar users like similar items", the preferences of similar user groups to similar item groups can be shared. Therefore, if the user/item group information of two domains is consistent, this group-level knowledge can be shared by both domains. The following formal definition of consistent user/item information and consistent knowledge determines which knowledge is transferable.

Definition 9.2 (Information consistent tri-factorization). Given a source rating matrix $\boldsymbol{R}^s \in \mathbb{R}^{M^s \times N^s}$ and a target rating matrix $\boldsymbol{R}^\tau \in \mathbb{R}^{M^\tau \times N^\tau}$, $\boldsymbol{R}^s$ and $\boldsymbol{R}^\tau$ can be factorized based on non-negative tri-factorization:

$$\boldsymbol{R}^s = \boldsymbol{U}^{(s,0)} \boldsymbol{S}^{(s,0)} (\boldsymbol{V}^{(s,0)})^T,$$

$$\boldsymbol{R}^\tau = \boldsymbol{U}^{(\tau,0)} \boldsymbol{S}^{(\tau,0)} (\boldsymbol{V}^{(\tau,0)})^T.$$

If both tri-factorizations satisfy the following equations, then they are information-consistent tri-factorizations.

$$P(\boldsymbol{U}^{(s,0)}) = P(\boldsymbol{U}^{(\tau,0)})$$

$$P(\boldsymbol{V}^{(s,0)}) = P(\boldsymbol{V}^{(\tau,0)})$$

where $P(\boldsymbol{U}^{(s,0)})$ and $P(\boldsymbol{V}^{(s,0)})$ represent the marginal probability distributions of $\boldsymbol{U}^{(s,0)}$ and $\boldsymbol{V}^{(s,0)}$, respectively. We say that the user group information from $\boldsymbol{U}^{(s,0)}$ and $\boldsymbol{V}^{(s,0)}$ is consistent, and the item group information from $\boldsymbol{V}^{(s,0)}$ and $\boldsymbol{V}^{(\tau,0)}$ is consistent. That is, the user/item groups from source and target domains are consistent. $\boldsymbol{S}^{(s,0)}$ is the "consistent knowledge" of the two matrixes $\boldsymbol{R}^s$ and $\boldsymbol{R}^\tau$.

According to this definition, if the marginal probability distributions of user/item groups from source and target domains are the same, the group-level knowledge matrix can be shared, so that the consistent knowledge $\boldsymbol{S}^{(s,0)}$ can be directly used for the target rating matrix (let $\boldsymbol{S}^{(\tau,0)} = \boldsymbol{S}^{(s,0)}$). If the marginal probability distributions of the user/item group membership matrixes in both domains are not the same, we need to find other tri-factorization results that satisfy the conditions in Definition 9.2. Looking for a solution by trying different kinds of existing matrix factorization techniques is unattainable and time-consuming. Instead, we seek the solution by aligning consistent latent user groups and item groups through domain adaptation techniques. By adjusting the marginal probability distributions of user and item groups from the source and target domains comparatively, the similarities between the latent user and item groups are maximized. Consistent knowledge can then be extracted from the source rating matrix which can be directly used to help predict ratings in the target rating matrix.

To align consistent latent user and item groups, we need to find a projection to adjust the user/item group information of both rating matrixes so that the following equations are achieved:

$$P(\boldsymbol{\Psi}_s(\boldsymbol{U}^{(s,0)}, \boldsymbol{U}^{(\tau,0)})) = P(\boldsymbol{\Psi}_\tau(\boldsymbol{U}^{(s,0)}, \boldsymbol{U}^{(\tau,0)})),$$
$$P(\boldsymbol{\Phi}_s(\boldsymbol{V}^{(s,0)}, \boldsymbol{V}^{(\tau,0)})) = P(\boldsymbol{\Phi}_\tau(\boldsymbol{V}^{(s,0)}, \boldsymbol{V}^{(\tau,0)})).$$

It is apparent that $\boldsymbol{\Psi}_s$, $\boldsymbol{\Psi}_\tau$, $\boldsymbol{\Phi}_s$ and $\boldsymbol{\Phi}_\tau$ are the keys to ensuring that the latent groups remain consistent in both domains. We need to find maps that can force different distributions to become the same after mapping. A geodesic flow kernel (GFK) is a domain adaptation strategy for learning robust features that is flexible against mismatch across domains and can be used to find a space for data in two domains to project into, so that the data distributions of the two domains in the projected space are similar [Gong *et al.* (2014)]. After projecting a GFK, a new representation is learned that satisfies the condition in Definition 9.2. Thus, we use a GFK to map $\boldsymbol{U}^{(s,0)}$, $\boldsymbol{U}^{(\tau,0)}$, $\boldsymbol{V}^{(s,0)}$ and $\boldsymbol{V}^{(\tau,0)}$ to $\boldsymbol{U}^{(s,1)}$, $\boldsymbol{U}^{(\tau,1)}$, $\boldsymbol{V}^{(s,1)}$ and $\boldsymbol{V}^{(\tau,1)}$. Based on the details of GFK, $\boldsymbol{\Psi}_s$, $\boldsymbol{\Psi}_\tau$, $\boldsymbol{\Phi}_s$ and $\boldsymbol{\Phi}_\tau$ can be written as follows:

$$\boldsymbol{\Psi}_s(\boldsymbol{U}^{(s,0)}, \boldsymbol{U}^{(\tau,0)}) = \boldsymbol{\Psi}_G(\boldsymbol{U}^{(s,0)}, \boldsymbol{U}^{(\tau,0)}) \times f_{zs}(\boldsymbol{U}^{(s,0)})$$
$$\boldsymbol{\Psi}_\tau(\boldsymbol{U}^{(s,0)}, \boldsymbol{U}^{(\tau,0)}) = \boldsymbol{\Psi}_G(\boldsymbol{U}^{(s,0)}, \boldsymbol{U}^{(\tau,0)}) \times f_{zs}(\boldsymbol{U}^{(\tau,0)})$$
$$\boldsymbol{\Phi}_s(\boldsymbol{V}^{(s,0)}, \boldsymbol{V}^{(\tau,0)}) = \boldsymbol{\Phi}_G(\boldsymbol{V}^{(s,0)}, \boldsymbol{V}^{(\tau,0)}) \times f_{zs}(\boldsymbol{V}^{(s,0)})$$
$$\boldsymbol{\Phi}_\tau(\boldsymbol{V}^{(s,0)}, \boldsymbol{V}^{(\tau,0)}) = \boldsymbol{\Phi}_G(\boldsymbol{V}^{(s,0)}, \boldsymbol{V}^{(\tau,0)}) \times f_{zs}(\boldsymbol{V}^{(\tau,0)})$$

where $\boldsymbol{\Psi}_s(\boldsymbol{U}^{(s,0)}, \boldsymbol{U}^{(\tau,0)})$ and $\boldsymbol{\Phi}_s(\boldsymbol{V}^{(s,0)}, \boldsymbol{V}^{(\tau,0)})$ are the operators of the GFK method and f_{zs} is the function of Z-score.

Then, the adapted latent user groups of the two rating matrixes can be obtained:

$$\boldsymbol{U}^{(s,1)} = \boldsymbol{\Psi}_s(\boldsymbol{U}^{(s,0)}, \boldsymbol{U}^{(\tau,0)})$$
$$\boldsymbol{U}^{(\tau,1)} = \boldsymbol{\Psi}_\tau(\boldsymbol{U}^{(s,0)}, \boldsymbol{U}^{(\tau,0)})$$

The same goes for the item groups: $\boldsymbol{V}^{(s,1)} = \boldsymbol{\Phi}_s(\boldsymbol{V}^{(s,0)}, \boldsymbol{V}^{(\tau,0)})$, $\boldsymbol{V}^{(s,1)} = \boldsymbol{\Phi}_\tau(\boldsymbol{V}^{(s,0)}, \boldsymbol{V}^{(\tau,0)})$. $\boldsymbol{U}^{(s,1)}$, $\boldsymbol{U}^{(\tau,1)}$ are user group membership matrixes unified to the same domain-invariant feature space for the source and target domains, while $\boldsymbol{V}^{(s,1)}$, $\boldsymbol{V}^{(\tau,1)}$ are unified item group membership matrixes.

Here, an example best illustrates the domain adaptation process of the user and item group information. Consider a source domain and a target domain that both have 1000 non-overlapping users. In each domain, the users are clustered into six user groups, with inconsistent user group information between the source and target domains. The probability distributions of the first user group (the first column of $\boldsymbol{U}^{(s,0)}$ and $\boldsymbol{U}^{(\tau,0)}$) is shown in Fig. 9.3 (a); each is quite different. To force consistency, the information for every user group in each domain is adjusted, after which the user group information of the adapted matrixes $\boldsymbol{U}^{(s,1)}$ and $\boldsymbol{U}^{(\tau,1)}$ are almost the same, as shown in Fig. 9.3 (b).

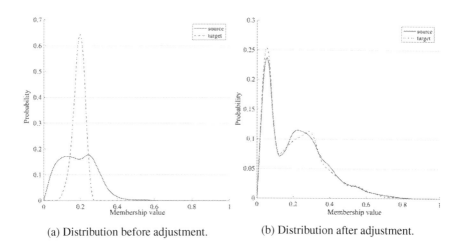

(a) Distribution before adjustment.   (b) Distribution after adjustment.

Fig. 9.3: An example of user group information adjustment.

(a) Marginal probability distribution of the first column in $U^{(s,0)}$ and $U^{(\tau,0)}$.
(b) Marginal probability distribution of the first column in $U^{(s,1)}$ and $U^{(\tau,1)}$.

Step 3: Consistent knowledge extraction.

After the domain adaptation, $U^{(s,1)}$, $U^{(\tau,1)}$ are consistent, and $V^{(s,1)}$, $V^{(\tau,1)}$ are consistent. Once we have obtained consistent group representations that are meaningful across both rating matrixes, the model trained on the source rating matrix and the target rating matrix can be brought together. On this basis, the recommender systems learned from the source and target domains will share the same group-level knowledge matrix S.

Consistent knowledge S is obtained by maximizing the approximation of the available data in both the source rating matrix and the target rating matrix by approximating $R^s \approx U^{(s,1)} S (V^{(s,1)})^T$ together with $R^\tau \approx U^{(\tau,1)} S (V^{(\tau,1)})^T$. To qualify the approximation, one useful and simple measure is to use a Frobenius norm between the original rating matrix and the approximation. We have the following cost function:

$$
\begin{aligned}
J_s(S) = {} & \frac{1}{M^s N^s} \| I^s \circ (R^s - U^{(s,1)} S (V^{(s,1)})^T) \|_F^2 \\
& + \frac{1}{M^\tau N^\tau} \| I^\tau \circ (R^\tau - U^{(\tau,1)} S (V^{(\tau,1)})^T) \|_F^2 + \frac{\lambda}{2KL} \| S \|_F^2
\end{aligned}
\tag{9.1}
$$

where I^s is a binary weighting matrix for R^s, if $(I^s)_{ij} = 1$, then $(R^s)_{ij} \neq 0$ and $(I^s)_{ij} = 0$, otherwise. The same applies to I^τ for R^τ. $\circ$ is an entry-wise product, λ is the parameter for regularization. Since the physical meaning of

S is the preference that the user groups give to the item groups, it should be in range of $(0, 5]$. Regularization to constrain the range of S is added to the cost function. Finally, consistent knowledge is learned through the following optimization problem:

$$\min_{S} J_s(S)$$

$$\text{s.t. } S > 0$$

Gradient descent is a general algorithm for optimization, which leads to the update rule: $s_{ab} \leftarrow s_{ab} + \eta_{ab} \frac{\partial J_s}{\partial S_{ab}}$. For this problem, we need to constrain the non-negativity of S. The partial derivative of the cost function has a special form, so we can use tricks to set the learning rate $\eta_{ab} = \frac{(S)_{ab}}{(A+B+\frac{\lambda S}{2KL})_{ab}}$ to guarantee that S is non-negative, where $A = \frac{1}{M^s N^s}(U^{(s,1)})^T(I^s \circ (U^{(s,1)}S(V^{(s,1)})^T))V^{(s,1)}$, $B = \frac{1}{M^\tau N^\tau}(U^{(\tau,1)})^T(I^\tau \circ (U^{(\tau,1)}S(V^{(\tau,1)})^T))V^{(\tau,1)}$. The objective function is non-increasing under the following update rule:

$$s_{ab} \leftarrow s_{ab} \frac{(\frac{1}{M^s N^s}(U^{(s,1)})^T R^s V^{(s,1)} + \frac{1}{M^\tau N^\tau}(U^{(\tau,1)})^T R^\tau V^{(\tau,1)})_{ab}}{(A + B + \frac{\lambda S}{2KL})_{ab}}.$$

The learning process is summarized in Algorithm 9.1.

Algorithm 9.1: Consistent Knowledge Extraction

Input:

    R^s, the source rating matrix

    R^τ, the target rating matrix

    $U^{(s,1)}$, $V^{(s,1)}$, user and item membership matrix of source domain

    $U^{(\tau,1)}$, $V^{(\tau,1)}$, user and item membership matrix of target domain

    ($U^{(s,1)}$, $V^{(s,1)}$, $U^{(\tau,1)}$, $V^{(\tau,1)}$ are obtained from GFK algorithm)

Output:

    S, the consistent knowledge

1: Initialize $S \in \mathbb{R}^{K \times L}$, $J(S) \leftarrow 0$, $J(S)^{(pre)} \leftarrow 0$

2: **while** $J(S)^{(pre)} - J(S) > \epsilon$ **or** $J(S) = 0$ **do**

3:     $J(S)^{(pre)} = J(u, v)$

4:     **for** each element s_{ab} in S **do**

5:         Update s_{ab} as in Eq.(9.2)

6:     **end for**

7:     Update $J(S)$ as in Eq.(9.1)

8: **end while**

9: **return** S

Step 4: Group representation regulation.

The domain adaptation technique GFK is designed for unsupervised transfer learning where no label is available in the target domain. In this problem setting, some domain-specific characteristics are embedded in the small amount of available data in the target rating matrix. To reveal these idiosyncrasies of the target domain, we amend the group representations of the target rating matrix to make the model fit better to the task in target rating matrix. It is imperative that we find maps $f_u : U^{(\tau,1)} \to \mathbb{R}^{M^\tau \times K}$ and $f_v : V^{(\tau,1)} \to \mathbb{R}^{N^\tau \times L}$ to make $U^{(\tau,1)}$ and $V^{(\tau,1)}$ more suitable for the target rating matrix. At the same time, the adjustment should not impair the consistency of user groups and item groups between two domains. According to Definition 9.2, f_u and f_v should satisfy the following equation:

$$P(S|f_u(U^{(\tau,1)}), f_v(V^{(\tau,1)})) = P(S|U^{(\tau,1)}, V^{(\tau,1)}). \qquad (9.2)$$

Eq.(9.2) ensures that the probability of each element in S will not change after mapping $U^{(\tau,1)}$ and $V^{(\tau,1)}$ using f_u and f_v. Here, we choose $f_u(U^{(\tau,1)}) = U^{(\tau,1)}u$ and $f_v(V^{(\tau,1)}) = V^{(\tau,1)}v$, where $u \geqslant 0$ and $v \geqslant 0$. These two maps satisfy Eq.(9.2), with the following proof:

Proof. When $u \geqslant 0$ and $v \geqslant 0$, $f_u(U^{(\tau,1)}) = U^{(\tau,1)}u$ and $f_v(V^{(\tau,1)}) = V^{(\tau,1)}v$ can satisfy the following equation:

$$P(S|U^{(\tau,1)}u, V^{(\tau,1)}) = P(S|U^{(\tau,1)}I, V^{(\tau,1)}).$$

Then, to fix $f_u(U^{(\tau,1)})$, we use the following equation:

$$P(S|U^{(\tau,1)}u, V^{(\tau,1)}v) = P(S|U^{(\tau,1)}u, V^{(\tau,1)}I).$$

So, we then have

$$P(S|f_u(U^{(\tau,1)}), f_v(V^{(\tau,1)})) = P(S|U^{(\tau,1)}, V^{(\tau,1)}).$$

Based on *Definition B.1*, $f_u(U^{(\tau,1)}) = U^{(\tau,1)}u$ and $f_v(V^{(\tau,1)}) = V^{(\tau,1)}v$ are DCMs. $\qquad \square$

Hence, the linear monotonic map is proven to be a DCM, which means we can let f_u and f_v have the following expressions:

$$f_u(U^{(\tau,1)}) = U^{(\tau,1)}u, \ u \leqslant 0 \qquad (9.3)$$

$$f_v(V^{(\tau,1)}) = V^{(\tau,1)}v, \ v \leqslant 0 \qquad (9.4)$$

where $u \in \mathbb{R}^{K \times K}$ is user tuning factor and $v \in \mathbb{R}^{L \times L}$ is item tuning factor.

Learning f_u and f_v is an optimization problem. The cost function is:

$$J_r(u, v) = \| I^\tau \circ (R^\tau - U^{(\tau,1)}uS(V^{(\tau,1)}v)^T) \|_F^2. \qquad (9.5)$$

Algorithm 9.2: Group representation regulation

Input:

R^τ, the target rating matrix

S, the consistent knowledge

$U^{(\tau,1)}$, $V^{(\tau,1)}$, user and item membership matrix of target domain

($U^{(\tau,1)}$, $V^{(\tau,1)}$ are obtained from GFK algorithm)

Output:

u, user tuning factor

v, item tuning factor

1: Initialize $u \in \mathbb{R}^{K \times K}$, $v \in \mathbb{R}^{L \times L}$, $J(u,v) \leftarrow 0$, $J(u,v)^{(pre)} \leftarrow 0$

2: **while** $J(u,v)^{(pre)} - J(u,v) > \epsilon$ **or** $J(u,v) = 0$ **do**

3:     $J(u,v)^{(pre)} = J(u,v)$

4:     **for** each element u_{ab} in u **do**

5:         Update u_{ab} as in Eq.(9.2)

6:     **end for**

7:     **for** each element v_{cd} in v **do**

8:         Update v_{cd} as in Eq.(9.2)

9:     **end for**

10:     Update $J(u,v)$ as in Eq.(9.5)

11: **end while**

12: **return** u, v

The tuning factors can be learned through optimizing

$$\min_{u,v} J_r(u,v)$$

$$\text{s.t. } u \geqslant 0, v \geqslant 0$$

Similarly, the cost function is non-increasing under the following update rules:

$$u_{ab} \leftarrow u_{ab} \frac{((U^{(\tau,1)})^T R^\tau V^{(\tau,1)} v S^T)_{ab}}{((U^{(\tau,1)})^T (I^\tau \circ (U^{(\tau,1)} u S (V^{(\tau,1)} v)^T)) V^{(\tau,1)} v S^T)_{ab}},$$

$$v_{cd} \leftarrow v_{cd} \frac{((V^{(\tau,1)})^T (R^\tau)^T U^{(\tau,1)} v S^T)_{cd}}{((V^{(\tau,1)})^T (I^{\tau T} \circ (V^{(\tau,1)} v S^T u^T (U^{(\tau,1)})^T)) U^{(\tau,1)} v S)_{cd}}.$$

Finally, the optimization problem is solved by alternatively estimating u, v. How u and v are learned is summarized in Algorithm 9.2.

Step 5: Recommendation in target domain.

The recommendation in target domain is given by:

$$\begin{cases} \hat{\boldsymbol{R}}^\tau = (\boldsymbol{U}^{(\tau,1)}\boldsymbol{u})\boldsymbol{S}(\boldsymbol{V}^{(\tau,1)}\boldsymbol{v})^T, \\ \boldsymbol{U}^{(\tau,1)} = \boldsymbol{\Psi}_G(\boldsymbol{U}^{(s,0)}, \boldsymbol{U}^{(\tau,0)}) \times f_{zs}(\boldsymbol{U}^{(\tau,0)}), \\ \boldsymbol{V}^{(\tau,1)} = \boldsymbol{\Phi}_G(\boldsymbol{V}^{(s,0)}, \boldsymbol{V}^{(\tau,0)}) \times f_{zs}(\boldsymbol{V}^{(\tau,0)}), \end{cases}$$

where $\hat{\boldsymbol{R}}^\tau$ is the reconstructed user-item rating matrix for prediction, $\boldsymbol{u}$, $\boldsymbol{v}$ are user and item tuning factors for target domain, $\boldsymbol{S}$ is the consistent knowledge, $\boldsymbol{U}^{(s,0)}$, $\boldsymbol{U}^{(\tau,0)}$ are user group membership matrixes, and $\boldsymbol{V}^{(s,0)}$, $\boldsymbol{V}^{(\tau,0)}$ are item group membership matrixes for the source domain and the target domain before domain adaptation. $\boldsymbol{U}^{(s,1)}$, $\boldsymbol{U}^{(\tau,1)}$ are user and item group membership matrixes for the target domain after domain adaptation. $\boldsymbol{\Psi}_G$ and $\boldsymbol{\Phi}_G$ are GFK operators to map group membership matrixes to a domain-invariant feature space, and f_{zs} is the Z-score function.

9.3   Cross-domain Recommendation with Kernel-induced Knowledge Transfer

This section introduces another method: cross-domain recommendation method with kernel-induced knowledge transfer (KerKT). The overlapping entities in each domain may be either users or items. For the purposes of this presentation, we have assumed the users overlap. Overlapping items are handled in the same way and have, therefore, been omitted from this book. The section begins with an overview of the entire method, then each of the five steps is explained in detail.

   To share knowledge between the source and target domains with overlapping users, constraints on similarities between the entities in each domain as a bridge for knowledge transfer [Zhang *et al.* (2018b)]. Both the intra-domain and inter-domain entity similarities are important to maintain. It is easy to measure the similarities between entities in the same domain, but inter-domain entity similarities cannot be computed directly. The overlapping entities are mapped to the same feature space through domain adaptation techniques so the similarities can be measured, while the non-overlapping entities are connected by diffusion kernel completion so the similarities between them are also measured. In KerKT, the optimization problem is formalized as:

$$\min_{\boldsymbol{U},\boldsymbol{V}} \; \mathcal{L}(f(\boldsymbol{U},\boldsymbol{V}),\boldsymbol{R}) + \lambda\mathcal{R}(\boldsymbol{U},\boldsymbol{V}) + \lambda_o\mathcal{R}_o(\boldsymbol{U}) \tag{9.6}$$

where $\mathcal{R}_o(\boldsymbol{U})$ is the regularization term for the entity similarity constraints derived from overlapping users, and $\lambda_o \geqslant 0$ is the regularization trade-off parameter.

The KerKT method consists of five steps, as shown in Fig. 9.4. (1) The user features and item features are extracted separately from the source and target domains, and the two sets of user features are aligned to the same feature space through overlapping users. (2) The item features are regulated according to the original rating matrixes and the aligned user feature matrixes. (3) The user and item feature matrixes resulting from the previous two steps are used to measure the user and item similarities in one domain. (4) Kernel-induced completion is conducted to measure the inter-domain user similarities. (5) The user/item features are re-trained based on the constraints of the entity similarities, then recommendations are made. We have selected a specific algorithm to perform each step, but other suitable feature extraction or domain adaptation algorithms could be used as substitutes [Zhang *et al.* (2018c)].

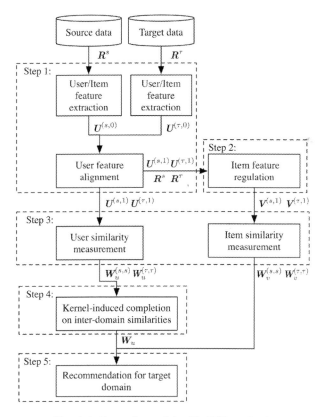

Fig. 9.4: Procedure of the KerKT method.

Step 1: Extracting and aligning user features in both domains.

In this step, the source rating matrix $\boldsymbol{R}^s$ and target rating matrix $\boldsymbol{R}^\tau$ are separately factorized, which results in the user feature matrix $\boldsymbol{U}^s$ for the source domain and $\boldsymbol{U}^\tau$ for the target domain. Recall that the users in the source and target domains partially overlap. Accordingly, each user feature matrix can be divided into two parts: one containing the overlapping users; the other containing non-overlapping users. The overlapping user feature matrix for the source domain is denoted as $\boldsymbol{U}_o^s$ and $\boldsymbol{U}_n^s$ denotes the non-overlapping matrix. The same goes for the target domain i.e., $\boldsymbol{U}_o^\tau$ and $\boldsymbol{U}_n^\tau$.

Assuming the overlapping users have similar tastes or preferences in both domains, we can use them as a bridge to transfer knowledge. However, as mentioned in Section 9.1, even the same user's rating patterns may not be completely the same in two different domains. Data sparsity exacerbates this condition and may lead to two different factorized user feature vectors with different physical meanings. Hence, setting the similarity of the overlapping user entities to 1 may lead to inaccurate similarity measurements, which would eventually negatively impact the effectiveness of the knowledge transfer in the following steps. Therefore, before using the entity correspondences as a strong condition, we need to ensure that distributions of features of overlapping users between two domains should be the same.

The aim is to map the user feature spaces of two overlapping users into a common subspace where distributions of such users are the same. In the source domain, the jth column of the overlapping user feature matrix is the representation of the jth user feature. We use a marginal probabilistic distribution of the jth column to represent the characteristics of the user features in each matrix. Thus, the goal is to minimize the differences between the marginal probabilistic distributions of the user features for the source domain and the target domain. If the marginal probability distributions of one user feature are the same in both domains, then the two user features are considered to have the same physical meaning. In this way, we can align the two user feature spaces. In last section, we provided a definition for information consistent tri-factorization. Here, we give a description for consistent matrix factorization with partially overlapping users.

Given a source rating matrix $\boldsymbol{R}^s \in \mathbb{R}^{M^s \times N^s}$ and a target rating matrix $\boldsymbol{R}^\tau \in \mathbb{R}^{M^\tau \times N^\tau}$, $\boldsymbol{R}^s$ and $\boldsymbol{R}^\tau$ can be factorized as follows:

$$\boldsymbol{R}^s = \begin{bmatrix} \boldsymbol{U}_o^s \\ \boldsymbol{U}_n^s \end{bmatrix} (\boldsymbol{V}^s)^T \tag{9.7}$$

$$\boldsymbol{R}^\tau = \begin{bmatrix} \boldsymbol{U}_o^\tau \\ \boldsymbol{U}_n^\tau \end{bmatrix} (\boldsymbol{V}^\tau)^T \tag{9.8}$$

where U_o^s and U_o^τ are the overlapping user feature matrixes in the source domain and the target domain, and U_n^s and U_n^τ are the non-overlapping user feature matrixes, respectively.

If both factorizations satisfy the following equation, then they are consistent matrix factorizations:

$$P(U_o^s) = P(U_o^\tau) \qquad (9.9)$$

where $P(U_o^s)$ and $P(U_o^\tau)$ represent the marginal probability distribution of U_o^s and U_o^τ. Thus, the user feature spaces in both the source and target domains are aligned.

To solve a matrix factorization optimization problem that satisfies the above constraints is almost impossible. According to Definition 9.2, we can find a mapping function for those two matrixes to achieve the following equation:

$$P(\boldsymbol{\Psi}_s(U_o^{(s,0)}, U_o^{(\tau,0)})) = P(\boldsymbol{\Psi}_\tau(U_o^{(s,0)}, U_o^{(\tau,0)})). \qquad (9.10)$$

A GFK is a domain adaptation strategy to find a space that two different feature spaces can be projected into, thus eliminating the divergence of two distributions. We can use this strategy to find a mapping function to align the two user feature spaces formed by overlapping users. Once the GFK operators $\boldsymbol{\Psi}_s(U^{(s,0)}, U^{(\tau,0)})$ are determined, they can be used through the following mapping functions:

$$\boldsymbol{\Psi}_s(U^{(s,0)}, U^{(\tau,0)}) = U^{(s,0)} \times \boldsymbol{\Psi}_G(U_o^{(s,0)}, U_o^{(\tau,0)}) \qquad (9.11)$$

$$\boldsymbol{\Psi}_\tau(U^{(s,0)}, U^{(\tau,0)}) = U^{(\tau,0)} \times \boldsymbol{\Psi}_G(U_o^{(s,0)}, U_o^{(\tau,0)}) \qquad (9.12)$$

where $\boldsymbol{\Psi}_G(U_o^{(s,0)}, U_o^{(\tau,0)})$ are the GFK operators.

With the divergence eliminated through these mappings, the new representations of the overlapping users will satisfy the conditions in Definition 9.2. Non-overlapping users also need to be projected onto the same feature space. The mapping functions $\boldsymbol{\Psi}_s$ and $\boldsymbol{\Psi}_\tau$ are used for this purpose.

$$U^{(s,1)} = \boldsymbol{\Psi}_s(U^{(s,0)}, U^{(\tau,0)}) \qquad (9.13)$$

$$U^{(\tau,1)} = \boldsymbol{\Psi}_\tau(U^{(s,0)}, U^{(\tau,0)}) \qquad (9.14)$$

where $U^{(s,1)}$ and $U^{(\tau,1)}$ are the aligned user feature matrixes after mapping, and $\boldsymbol{\Psi}_s$ and $\boldsymbol{\Psi}_\tau$ are the mapping functions using GFK.

How the new user feature spaces are derived and how $U^{(s,1)}$ and $U^{(\tau,1)}$ are learned is summarized in Algorithm 9.3.

Algorithm 9.3: Consistent User Feature Extraction

Input:

R^s, the source rating matrix;

R^τ, the target rating matrix;

$W_u^{(s,\tau)}$, the overlapping user indicator matrix;

Output:

$U^{(s,1)}$, the aligned user feature matrix in source domain;

$U^{(\tau,1)}$, the aligned user feature matrix in target domain;

1: Factorize R^s and obtain user feature matrix $\left(\begin{smallmatrix}U_o^{(s,0)}\\U_n^{(s,0)}\end{smallmatrix}\right)$

2: Factorize R^τ and obtain user feature matrix $\left(\begin{smallmatrix}U_o^{(\tau,0)}\\U_n^{(\tau,0)}\end{smallmatrix}\right)$

3: Obtain GFK operator $\Psi_G(U_o^{(s,0)}, U_o^{(\tau,0)})$ as (A.2) in [Zhang *et al.* (2017)]

4: Obtain mapping functions Ψ_s and Ψ_τ as in Eq.(9.11)

5: **return** $U^{(s,1)}$ and $U^{(\tau,1)}$

Step 2: Item feature regulation in both domains.

In matrix factorization, the user feature matrix and the item feature matrix are both low-rank matrixes that map users and items to the same k-dimensional feature space. So, once the distributions of user features are aligned, the item feature matrixes should be regularized to the k-dimensional space to fit the approximations to the original data in the rating matrix. A Frobenius norm is used to measure the distance. The cost function of source domain matrix follows, the target domain matrix has the same form:

$$J_v(V^{(s,1)}) = \frac{1}{2}\|I^s \circ (R^s - U^{(s,1)}(V^{(s,1)})^T)\|_F^2 + \frac{\lambda_{V_s}}{2}\|V^{(s,1)}\|_F^2 \quad (9.15)$$

where λ_{V_s} is the regularization parameter. The item feature matrixes are learned by optimizing:

$$\min_{V^{(s,1)}} J_v(V^{(s,1)})$$

Gradient descent is used for this optimization. The update rule is:

$$V^{(s,1)} \leftarrow V^{(s,1)} - \eta_{V_s}[(U^{(s,1)}(V^{(s,1)})^T - R^s)U^{(s,1)} + \lambda_{V_s}V^{(s,1)}] \quad (9.16)$$

where the learning rate is η_{V_s}. $V^{(\tau,1)}$ can be obtained through the same process. This step is summarized in Algorithm 9.4.

Step 3: Entity similarity measures in one domain.

This step calculates the user and item similarities in one domain. Since the rating matrix is very sparse, making this calculation directly from the rating matrix can

---

Algorithm 9.4: Item Feature Regularization

Input:

  R^s, the source rating matrix $U^{(s,1)}$, the user feature matrix

Output:

  $V^{(s,1)}$, the regularized item feature matrix

1: initialize $V^{(s,1)} \in \mathbb{R}^{N^s \times K}$, Initialize $J_v(V^s)$ and $J_v(V^s)^{(pre)}$

2: **while** $J_v(V^s)^{(pre)} - J_v(V^s) > \epsilon$ **do**

3: $J_v(V^s)^{(pre)} = J_v(V^s)$

4: update V^s as in Eq.(9.16)

5: update $J_v(V^s)$ as in Eq.(9.15)

6: **end while**

7: **return** $V^{(s,1)}$

---

lead to inaccurate results. Hence, using the matrix factorization in Chapter 2, one rating R_{ij} is generated from a user latent feature vector U_{i*} and an item latent feature vector V_{*j}. Thus, the source rating matrix and target rating matrix can be factorized as $R^s = U^s(V^s)^T$ and $R^\tau = U^\tau(V^\tau)^T$. This is a dimensionality reduction and data compression process as users/items are mapped to a lower k-dimensional feature space (usually $k \ll M, k \ll N$). Once complete, users and items are represented as full k-dimensional feature matrixes, and the user/item similarities can be calculated from the user/item feature matrixes.

Similarity measurements are easy with user and item feature spaces in one domain since the feature spaces are homogeneous. And there are many suitable choices for performing these calculations, such as cosine similarity, PCC similarity, Euclidean measurement, or the RBF measurement. The choice depends on the situation and the characteristics of the domain. For example, cosine similarity is very popular and effective for word count and text similarity measurements due to the advantages of using angles rather than distance. PCC measurement tends to be more effective in memory-based CF methods owing to its emphasis on averages. In this chapter, we are measuring user similarity from a user feature matrix where the feature values are real numbers, so the following RBF measurement is the most appropriate: $W_{ij} = e^{-\frac{\|U_{i*} - U_{j*}\|^2}{\sigma^2}}$, where σ^2 is set to be the median of all the non-zero values calculated by $\|U_{i*} - U_{j*}\|^2$.

Step 4: Kernel induced completion of inter-domain user similarity.

In inter-domain user similarity measurement, the user feature spaces are not the same and the user features are heterogeneous, which means their similarities cannot be calculated directly. However, given the first three steps, some user similarities between the source and target domains are now known. The overlapping entity indicator matrix $\boldsymbol{W}^{(s,\tau)}$ contains the observed overlapping user information. Hence, a full user similarity matrix can be constructed as:

$$\boldsymbol{W}_u = \begin{bmatrix} \boldsymbol{W}_u^{(s,s)}, & \boldsymbol{W}_u^{(s,\tau)} \\ \boldsymbol{W}_u^{(\tau,s)}, & \boldsymbol{W}_u^{(\tau,\tau)} \end{bmatrix}$$

where $\boldsymbol{W}_u^{(s,s)}$ and $\boldsymbol{W}_u^{(\tau,\tau)}$ represent the user similarities in the source and target domains, respectively, and $\boldsymbol{W}_u^{(s,\tau)} = (\boldsymbol{W}_u^{(\tau,s)})^T$ represents the inter-domain user similarities.

As in Step 2, the two feature spaces of the overlapping users are aligned to eliminate feature space divergence. Therefore, it is reasonable to set the similarity of observed overlapping users to $(W_u^{(s,\tau)})_{ij} = 1$ in $\boldsymbol{W}^{(s,\tau)}$. For now, the similarities between the overlapping users are the only known entries in the inter-domain similarity matrix. We need to complete $\boldsymbol{W}_u^{(s,\tau)}$ using the information from $\boldsymbol{W}_u$. Note that, here, the non-overlapping users and their features are heterogeneous. Thus, their similarities cannot be computed directly.

This matrix completion problem has a strong connection to a bipartite edge completion problem [He *et al.* (2017a)]. In step 3, the user similarities are all measured within one domain. As a result, we have fully connected nodes in the graph representations of both the source and target domains, as indicated by the different nodes in Fig. 9.5. The overlapping users act as "bridge" to couple the two graphs. To complete the user similarity matrix $\boldsymbol{W}_u$ requires filling in all the edges from the entire graph. The subscript u has been omitted to simplify the notation.

In network propagation, a random walk is a good way to reach to all the nodes. As shown in Fig. 9.5, one user entity denoted as a node x in the source domain has a fully connection with all the other node in the source domain $(W^{(s,s)})_{xp}, p \in \mathcal{U}_s$, so does node y in target domain $W_{yq}^{(\tau,\tau)}, q \in \mathcal{U}_t$. If node p in source domain and node q in target domain are overlapping users, i.e., they are the same user, then $W_{pq}^{(s,\tau)} = 1$. The two nodes x and y are connected and their similarity can be calculated as: $W_{xy}^{(s,\tau)} \leftarrow W_{xp}^{(s,s)} W_{pq}^{(s,\tau)} W_{yq}^{(\tau,\tau)}$. By aggregating all the nodes connected to x in the source domain and y in the target domain, the edge can be completed with: $W_{xy}^{(s,\tau)} \leftarrow \sum\limits_{p \in U^s} \sum\limits_{q \in u^\tau} W_{xp}^{(s,s)} W_{pq}^{(s,\tau)} W_{yq}^{(\tau,\tau)}$. In a matrix form, this is written as:

$$W^{(s,\tau),(1)} = W^{(s,s)} W^{(s,\tau)} W^{(\tau,\tau)}$$

The above equation can be treated as a one-step random walk from both the source domain and the target domain. Generally, M steps of random walk are

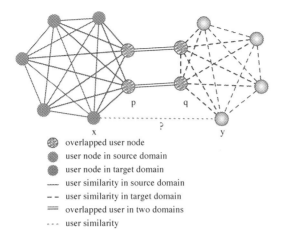

Fig. 9.5: Graphical view of user relationships in source and target domains.

taken in total from the source and target sides, and all the possible steps are added together to complete the final graph:

$$W^{(s,\tau),(K)} = \sum_{K=0}^{M} \binom{M}{K} (W^{(s,s)})^K W^{(s,\tau)} (W^{(\tau,\tau)})^{M-K}.$$

However, the goal in this problem is to find all the similarities between all the users in both domains. Therefore, a finite number of random walk steps may not identify all the possible relationships, but it would be more likely to associate all the indirectly connected users if K was infinite. Hence, we use the diffusion kernel completion method [Chang *et al.* (2017)] to complete the user similarity matrix:

$$W^{(s,\tau)} = e^{(\beta^s W^{(s,s)})} W^{(s,\tau)} e^{(\beta^\tau W^{(\tau,\tau)})}$$

where β^s and β^τ are two positive scalars to regulate the weights of the source and the target domains.

Step 5: Collective matrix factorization with user similarity constraints.

With all similarities measured and all the pairs of nodes connected, a fully connected graph can be constructed. A very common strategy for increasing computational speed is to remove edges, leave a sparse graph. This method tends to achieve better performance empirically as it emphasizes local information with high similarity while ignoring information that is likely to be false. Hence, the

k nearest neighbors of each node are retained in a similar way to the original memory-based CF strategy.

The users have both intra-domain and inter-domain similarities, but the items only have intra-domain similarities. Based on the assumption "similar users have similar tastes and will thus choose similar items to consume", both intra-domain and inter-domain similarities are used to constrain the proposed matrix factorization as prior knowledge. In terms of intra-domain similarities, though the data in the target domain are very sparse, they are still very valuable for measuring the similarities between users/items so as to constrain the matrix factorization. As for inter-domain similarities, users in target domain are not only correlated to users in their own domain but also in the source domain via the overlapping users. As a consequence, users in the source domain with similar preferences to users in the target domain are transferred as knowledge to improve the performance of recommender system.

The constrains result in users who are similar tend to have similar latent factors. Specifically, the regularization form is [Zhen *et al.* (2009)]:

$$\mathcal{R}_o(\boldsymbol{U}) = tr(\boldsymbol{U}^T \boldsymbol{L} \boldsymbol{U})$$

where $\boldsymbol{L}$ denotes a Laplacian matrix, and $\boldsymbol{L} = \boldsymbol{D} - \boldsymbol{W}$. $\boldsymbol{W}$ is the user similarity matrix, and $\boldsymbol{D}$ is a diagonal matrix defined as $D_{ii} = \sum_j W_{ij}$. The proposed constraints are more flexible and reasonable to satisfy in practice. We achieve the goal by minimizing the following objective function:

$$
\begin{aligned}
f(\boldsymbol{U}^s, \boldsymbol{V}^s, \boldsymbol{U}^\tau, \boldsymbol{V}^\tau) = & \frac{\alpha}{2} \|\boldsymbol{I}^s \circ (\boldsymbol{R}^s - \boldsymbol{U}^s (\boldsymbol{V}^s)^T)\|_F^2 + \frac{1}{2}\|\boldsymbol{I}^\tau \circ (\boldsymbol{R}^\tau - \boldsymbol{U}^\tau (\boldsymbol{V}^\tau)^T)\|_F^2 \\
& + \frac{\lambda_u}{2}[tr((\boldsymbol{U}^s)^T \boldsymbol{L}_u^{(s,s)} \boldsymbol{U}^s) + tr((\boldsymbol{U}^s)^T \boldsymbol{L}_u^{(s,\tau)} \boldsymbol{U}^\tau) \\
& + tr((\boldsymbol{U}^\tau)^T (\boldsymbol{L}_u^{(s,\tau)})^T \boldsymbol{U}^s) + tr((\boldsymbol{U}^\tau)^T \boldsymbol{L}_u^{(\tau,\tau)} \boldsymbol{U}^\tau)] \\
& + \frac{\lambda_v}{2}[tr((\boldsymbol{V}^s)^T \boldsymbol{L}_v^{(s,s)} \boldsymbol{V}^s) + tr((\boldsymbol{V}^\tau)^T \boldsymbol{L}_v^{(\tau,\tau)} \boldsymbol{V}^\tau)] \\
& + \frac{\lambda}{2}(\|\boldsymbol{U}^s\|_F^2 + \|\boldsymbol{V}^s\|_F^2 + \|\boldsymbol{U}^\tau\|_F^2 + \|\boldsymbol{V}^\tau\|_F^2)
\end{aligned}
$$

where tr is the trace of a matrix, $\alpha \in (0,1)$ is trade-off parameter to balance the source and target domain data, and λ, λ_u and λ_v are the regularization parameters to control the influence of the constraints on the user similarities, item similarities and algorithm complexity. Using gradient descent, the objective function is minimized with the following update rules:

$$U^s \leftarrow U^s - \eta_{U^s}[\alpha(U^s(V^s)^T - R^s)V^s + \lambda_u L_u^{(s,s)}U^s + \frac{\lambda_u}{2}L_u^{(s,\tau)}U^\tau + \lambda U^s]$$

$$V^s \leftarrow V^s - \eta_{V^s}[\alpha(V^s(U^s)^T - (R^s)^T)U^s + \lambda_v L_v^{(s,s)}V^s + \lambda U_s]$$

$$U^\tau \leftarrow U^\tau - \eta_{U^\tau}[(U^\tau(V^\tau)^T - R^\tau)V^\tau + \lambda_u L_u^{(\tau,\tau)}U^\tau + \frac{\lambda_u}{2}(L_u^{(s,\tau)})^T U^s + \lambda U^\tau]$$

$$V^\tau \leftarrow V^\tau - \eta_{V^\tau}[(V^\tau(U^\tau)^T - (R^\tau)^T)U^\tau + \lambda_v L_v^{(\tau,\tau)}V^\tau + \lambda U_t]$$

By updating U^s, V^s, U^τ and V^τ iteratively, we achieve at a final optimized approximation of $\hat{R}^\tau = U^\tau(V^\tau)^T$. Recommendations are given according to the rating prediction for the target domain.

9.4 Summary

Developing a cross-domain recommender system is an efficient way to deal with the data sparsity and cold start problems in recommender systems. However, using cross-domain recommendation without considering domain shift provide inaccurate and poor quality recommendations. In this chapter, we present the concepts and three main types of cross-domain recommender systems. In particular, we focus on two methods for solving the cross-domain recommendation problems with domain shifts when entities in the source domain are non-overlapping or partly overlapping.

Chapter 10

User Preference Drift-aware Recommender Systems

The rapid change in various environments will directly influence customer's preferences to items, inevitably resulting in changes of data distribution in the data stream of user purchasing history. These changes are known as the user preference drift (in general, called concept drift). To aid accurate recommendation generation, we need to detect user preference drift in a timely manner and adapt the preference change. This cannot be done by simply weighting user contributed data equally, such as ratings, as most recommender systems do. We have to take user preference drift into consideration, by giving different weights to user's ratings in different time slots in order to generate accurate predictions of a user's current preference. In this chapter, we present how user preference drift is identified and how a user preference drift-aware recommender system can provide accurate recommendations in a dynamic environment.

In this chapter, first we introduce related concepts and methods of concept drift and how they are sued in recommender systems in Section 10.1. In Section 10.2, we present a hybrid user preference drift recommendation method and in Section 10.3, we present a fuzzy user preference drift detection recommender system. Finally, the chapter summary is provided in Section 10.4.

10.1   Concept Drift

User preferences are naturally change because of the evolution of their tastes, their personal experiences or because they can be easily influenced by item popularity. This is a phenomenon commonly seen in data streams and widely known as concept drift [Kifer *et al.* (2004)]. This section introduces the definition, and types of concept drift.

Concept drift is a phenomenon in which the statistical properties of a target domain change over time in an arbitrary way. It was first proposed by [Schlimmer and Granger Jr (1986)] whose aim was to point out that noise data may change to non-noise information at different times. These changes might be caused by changes in hidden variables that cannot be measured directly. Formally, concept drift is defined as follows [Gama *et al.* (2014)]:

Definition 10.1 (Concept drift). Given a time period $[0, t]$, a set of samples is denoted as $S_{0,t} = \{d_0, \ldots, d_t\}$, where $d_i = (X_i, y_i)$ is one observation (or a data instance), X_i is the feature vector, y_i is the label, and $S_{0,t}$ follows a certain distribution $F_{0,t}(X, y)$. Concept drift occurs at time stamp $t+1$, if $\exists t: P_t(X, y) \neq P_{t+1}(X, y)$.

Commonly, there are four different types of concept drift as shown in Fig. 10.1. Research into concept drift adaptation in Types 1-3 focuses on how to minimize the drop in accuracy and achieve the fastest recovery rate during the concept drift process. In contrast, the study of Type 4 drift emphasizes the use of historical concepts, that is, how to find the best matched historical concepts with the shortest time. The new concept may suddenly reoccur, incrementally reoccur or gradually reoccur.

To better demonstrate the differences between these types, the term "intermediate concept" was introduced to describe the transformation between concepts [Liu *et al.* (2017a)]. Not only can a concept drift take place at an exact time stamp, but it can also last for a long period of time. As a result, intermediate concepts can appear during the transformation, as one concept (starting concept) changes to another (ending concept). An intermediate concept can be a mixture of the starting concept and the ending concept in the incremental drift.

Handling concept drift is important to real-world applications because streaming data are often ubiquitous. Examples include network traffic, telecommunications, and financial transactions, to name just three. Machine learning and data analysis tasks in these systems will inevitably encounter the concept drift problem. When the environment is very dynamic, the ability to handle concept drift

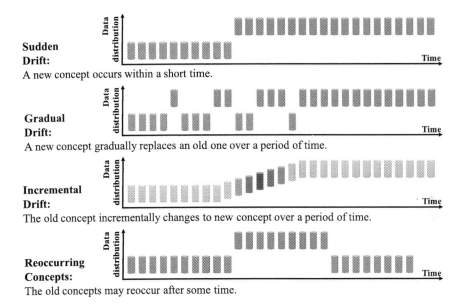

Fig. 10.1: A demonstration of concept drift types.

becomes the key factor in improving system performance. Concept drift detection fulfills the requirement of diagnosing significant changes in the environment of customer preferences [Lu *et al.* (2014)]. For example, drift detection technology is used to diagnose changes in user preferences on the news in [Harel *et al.* (2014)]. Concept drift adaptation concerns the maintenance of a continuously effective evaluation and prediction systems [Lu *et al.* (2016)].

As for a recommender system, user history records, including purchasing data and rating data, are accumulated. Some old history records of a user may be inconsistent with the user's new requests. For example, a user in MovieLens may register in 2010, and continue to rate movies during the next ten years, but his/her preferences may have changed several times during the ten years (all the four types in Fig. 10.1 are possible). As a result, it is not accurate to take all his/her ratings to make an up-to-date recommendation. Traditional recommender systems assume that a user's preferences are relatively static over a period of time, so a user's history records are weighted equally. Using all the data blindly without selectivity, cannot guarantee the accuracy of prediction, and can impair the performance of the recommender system.

A solution to address this problem is to assign larger weights to recent data than older data. Gradual forgetting and time decaying on windows have been applied in recommendation methods [Koren (2010)]. As an alternative to penalizing the old data, some recommendation methods use dynamic matrix factorization where time is considered to be an additional dimension of the data [Chua *et al.* (2013)]. However, this solution is not fully successful because it doesn't detect the change of user preferences and only considers rating changes in a time order. Therefore, the proposed weighting decay can be biased.

In summary, these studies consider time-aware recommendation, but not drift-aware recommendation.

10.2 User Preference Drift-oriented Recommendation Method

In this section, firstly a rating weight model for user preference drift detection, which identifies the ratings that are consistent with the user's current preferences and assigns them high weights, is proposed. The proposed model is then applied and integrated into recommender systems. Hybrid recommendation methods for preference drift environments are developed.

10.2.1 *Rating weight model for user preference drift*

The preference drift of a user can be identified only when current ratings of the user are not consistent with the old ratings of that user. It is reasonable to assume that the latest rating of a user represent the user's latest preference. When preference drift happens, only the user's latest preferences should be utilized to make recommendations. The old ratings, which are not consistent with the latest rating should then be decayed or discarded. To express the consistency degree or the relevance degree of a user's ratings to the user's current preference, a preference weight for a rating is defined. The preference weight of a rating can be used to represent the influence degree of the rating when generating recommendations.

Let $v_u(k)$ be the kth item rated by user u and $r_{u,v_u(k)}$ be the rating. Let n represent the times of rating given by u. n is defined as 1 when u rates the first item, and will increase by 1 when an additional item is rated. Thus, when n items are rated, the preference weight of rating $r_{u,v_u(k)}$ at this point is denoted as $W\left(r_{u,v_u(k)}, n\right)$. This is calculated as:

$$W(r_{u,v_u(k)}, n) =$$
$$\begin{cases} 1, & k = n, \\ F_w\left[S(v_u(k), v_u(n)), D(r_{u,v_u(k)}, r_{u,v_u(n)}), W(r_{u,v_u(k)}, n-1)\right], & k < n, \end{cases}$$

where $F_w(\cdot)$ is a preference weight drift function defined for the old ratings. $F_w(\cdot)$ has three parameters: $S(v_u(k), v_u(n))$ is a semantic similarity measure between two items $v_u(k)$ and $v_u(n)$, $S(\cdot, \cdot) \in [0, 1]$; $D(r_{u,v_u(k)}, r_{u,v_u(n)})$ is the difference degree between two rating values $r_{u,v_u(k)}$ and $r_{u,v_u(n)}$, which can be defined as $d(r_{u,v_u(k)}, r_{u,v_u(n)}) = |r_{u,v_u(k)} - r_{u,v_u(n)}|/(r_{max} - r_{min})$ and $d(\cdot, \cdot) \in [0, 1]$, and $W(r_{u,v_u(k)}, n - 1)$ is the preference weight of $r_{u,v_u(k)}$ at time point $n - 1$. The preference weight drift function $F_w(S, D, W)$ is defined as follows:

$$F_w(S, D, W) = \begin{cases} 1 - \min\{S, D\}, & 1 - \min\{S, D\} < W \\ \min\{S, 1 - D\}, & \min\{S, 1 - D\} > W \\ W, & \text{others} \end{cases} \quad (10.1)$$

In the above definition, the preference weight for the latest (the nth) rating at time n, i.e. $r_{u,v_u(n)}$, and the older ratings are defined separately. It is believed that the latest rating of a user can represent the user's current preference. Therefore, the weight of $r_{u,v_u(n)}$ is set as 1. For the other previous ratings, their consistency with the $r_{u,v_u(n)}$ is evaluated and their weights are determined based on the consistency and calculated by the preference weight drift function defined in Eq. (10.1).

When calculating the preference weight for a previous rating $r_{u,v_u(k)}$, $k < n$, the consistency between the previous rating $r_{u,v_u(k)}$ and the latest rating $r_{u,v_u(n)}$ are assessed form two aspects: the semantic similarity and the rating difference. If $v_u(n)$ is very similar to $v_u(k)$, the preference weight of $r_{u,v_u(k)}$ will be determined according to the rating value difference between $r_{u,v_u(n)}$ and $r_{u,v_u(k)}$. When the value of $r_{u,v_u(n)}$ is quite different from the value of $r_{u,v_u(k)}$, it will be certain that the preference of u to the items that are like $v_u(k)$ and $v_u(n)$ has been changed, and the weight of $r_{u,v_u(k)}$ will be weakened. When the value of $r_{u,v_u(n)}$ is very similar to the value of $r_{u,v_u(k)}$, it will be inferred that the preference of u to the items that are like $v_u(k)$ and $v_u(n)$ is not changed, and the weight of $r_{u,v_u(k)}$ will be strengthened. Otherwise, if $v_u(n)$ is not similar to $v_u(k)$, the consistency between $r_{u,v_u(k)}$ and $r_{u,v_u(n)}$ cannot be inferred. Accordingly, the Eq. (10.1) defines three different cases. In the first case, $1 - \min\{S, D\} < w$, both S and D are relative large, which means that the item $v_u(k)$ is similar to $v_u(n)$ but the ratings are different. In this case, the rating $r_{u,v_u(k)}$ is inconsistent with $r_{u,v_u(n)}$, which results in a low weight of $r_{u,v_u(k)}$. In the second case, $\min\{S, 1 - D\} > w$, S is large and D is small, which means that the item $v_u(k)$ is similar to $v_u(n)$ and their ratings are also similar. In this case, the rating $r_{u,v_u(k)}$ is consistent with $r_{u,v_u(n)}$, which results in a high weight of $r_{u,v_u(k)}$. Otherwise, the consistency cannot be assessed and the weight of $r_{u,v_u(k)}$ remains the same.

The preference weights for ratings defined above can express the preference drift of a user. When a user rates a new item, the current rating is weighted by

1, and the previous ratings are re-weighted according to the current rating, which makes them reflect the user's current preference. When the user rates another new item, the weights of all the ratings are updated the same way. The corresponding preference weights and the ratings together express the user's preference. We give an example to illustrate how to use the proposed preference drift model to describe the preference drift of a user in a movie recommendation scenario. The history of what the user has watched is shown in Table 10.1 in chronological order.

Table 10.1: The movie history records of a user u.

Time	Movie ID	Genre	Rating
1	v_1	Action, Crime	5
2	v_2	Action, Crime, Adventure	4
3	v_3	Romance, Drama	5
4	v_4	Action, Crime	1
5	v_5	Comedy, Romance	5
6	v_6	Action, Crime	4
...	...	...	...

To calculate the preference weights of the ratings, the semantic similarity between movies $S(\cdot, \cdot)$ and the difference degree between two rating values $D(\cdot, \cdot)$ should be defined first. In this example, the semantic of movies mainly depends on the genres. Let the genre set of movies be $\{g_1, \ldots, g_G\}$. The genres of a movie $v_u(k)$ is then represented as a vector $\{\mu_{1,k}, \ldots, \mu_{G,k}\}$, in which $\mu_{t,k} = 1$, $1 \leqslant t \leqslant G$, if $v_u(k)$ belongs to genre g_t; $\mu_{t,k} = 0$ if $v_u(k)$ does not belong to genre g_t. The semantic similarity between two movies $v_u(k)$ and v_j is defined by the use of the cosine similarity between two vectors as follows:

$$S(v_u(k), v_j) = \frac{\sum_{t=1}^{G} \mu_{t,k} \times \mu_{t,j}}{\sqrt{\sum_{t=1}^{G} \mu_{t,k}^2 \times \sum_{t=1}^{G} \mu_{t,j}^2}}.$$

The ratings in the example are made on a 5-star scale, with half-star increments. Therefore, $r_{max} = 5$, $r_{min} = 0.5$. The distance degree between any two rating values r_k and r_j is defined as:

$$D(r_{u,v_u(k)}, r_{u,v_j}) = \frac{|r_{u,v_u(k)} - r_{u,v_j}|}{4.5}.$$

The semantic similarities between movies are calculated and shown in Table 10.2. The preference weights of the ratings at different times are calculated and listed in Table 10.3.

Table 10.2: The semantic similarity between movies.

	v_1	v_2	v_3	v_4	v_5	v_5
v_1	1					
v_2	0.8165	1				
v_3	0	0	1			
v_4	1	0.8165	0	1		
v_5	0	0	0.5	0	1	
v_6	1	0.8165	0	1	0	1

Table 10.3: The preference weight change of the ratings.

Time	Preference weights					
	r_{v_1}	r_{v_2}	r_{v_3}	r_{v_4}	r_{v_5}	r_{v_6}
1	1					
2	0.7778	1				
3	0.7778	1	1			
4	0.1111	0.3333	1	1		
5	0.1111	0.3333	1	1	1	
6	0.7778	0.8165	1	0.3333	1	1

It can be seen from the movie history records that the user's preference in movie genres has changed over time. At the beginning, the user liked "Action" and "Crime" movies and gave high ratings to movies v_1 and v_2. At time 4, the user's preference to this kind of movies changed and the user gave a low rating to the movie v_4. Then, the ratings to v_1 and v_2 are not consistent with the user's preference at time 4. Therefore, the influence of the ratings to v_1 and v_2 must be weakened when making recommendations. This is reflected by the preference weight change shown in Table 10.3. The semantic similarity between movies, where the preference weights of r_{v_1} and r_{v_2} declined sharply at time 4. As time goes on, the user's preference changed again and the user gave a high rating to movie v_6 which is an "Action" and "Crime" movie. The weights of v_1, v_2 and v_4 were then changed. As r_{v_1} and r_{v_2} are consistent with r_{v_6}, their weights increased. By contrast, the weight of r_{v_4} declined as r_{v_4} is not consistent with r_{v_6}. The user also liked "Romance" and "Drama" movies, such as v_3 and v_5. As these ratings do not contradict the others, the preference weights are always high.

10.2.2 *User preference drift recommendation*

By integrating the preference drift model into these recommendation methods, the user's preferences are expressed more precisely, and more accurate recommendations are generated. In the following parts, preference drift model-based CF and content-based recommendation methods are presented. This shows how to utilize the proposed preference drift model in recommender systems.

(1) Preference drift model-based CF recommendation

The conventional CF recommendation takes the user-item rating matrix as input and calculates the predicted ratings to unrated items of users. The predicted rating to item $v_u(k)$ of user u, $r_{u,v_u(k)}$, is calculated by the item-based CF recommendation as follows:

$$\hat{r}_{u,v_j}^{CF} = \bar{r}_{v_j} + \frac{\sum_{v_j \in N_u(v_u(k))} S_{CF}(v_u(k), v_j) \times (r_{u,v_j} - \bar{r}_{v_j})}{\sum_{v_j \in N_u(v_u(k))} |S_{CF}(v_u(k), v_j)|}, \qquad (10.2)$$

where $\bar{r}_{v_u(k)}$ is the average rating of item $v_u(k)$, $N_u(v_u(k))$ is the N most similar items to $v_u(k)$ that are rated by the user u, r_{u,v_j} denotes the rating of a rated item v_j by user u, and $S_{CF}(v_u(k), v_j)$ is the similarity value between items $v_u(k)$ and v_j which is usually defined by the PCC in Chapter 2.

In the item-based CF prediction equation, the average ratings of items and the similarity between items are relatively independent of each user. The user's personalized preferences are reflected by the rated items by the user, i.e. the $N_u(v_u(k))$. By assigning the preference weights to the previous ratings and weakening the ratings that are not consistent with the user's current preferences, the predictions reflect the user's current preference more precisely. Thus, a preference drift model-based CF recommendation method is developed. The preference drift-based CF prediction equation for a rating $r_{u,v_u(k)}$ at time n (when user u has rated n items) is defined as follows:

$$\hat{r}_{u,v_j}^{pdCF} = \bar{r}_{v_j} + \frac{\sum_{v_u(k) \in N_u'(v_j)} W(r_{u,v_u(k)}, t_n) \times S(v_j, v_u(k)) \times (r_{u,v_u(k)} - \bar{r}_{v_u(k)})}{\sum_{v_u(k) \in N_u'(v_j)} |W(r_{u,v_u(k)}, n) \times S(v_j, v_u(k))|}$$

where $N_u'(v_j$ is the N most relevant items that are rated by user u, which are chosen as follows. All the items rated by user u are sorted by $|W(r_{u,v_u(k)}, n) \times S(v_j, v_u(k))|$, and the N highest items are chosen. In the preference drift-based CF prediction equation, the preference weights of the previous ratings of a user change when the user gives a new rating.

(2) Preference drift model and content based recommendation

The items are defined in the space of an attribute $X = \{x_1, x_2, \ldots, x_L\}$. Each item can take multiple values. Thus, a vector $X_j = \{(x_k, \mu_{k,j}), k = 1, \ldots, L\}$ is formed for item I_j, where $\mu_{k,j} = 1$ if the value x_k presents in I_j, and $u_{k,j} = 0$

otherwise. Let the rated items of a user consist of the user's profile. For user u, let the rated items be $\{v(1), v(2), \ldots, v_u(n)\}$, in which $v_u(k)$, $1 \leqslant k \leqslant n$, represents the kth item rated by u. To express the preference drift of a user and model the user profile more precisely, the proposed preference drift model is applied and the preference weight for each rating $r_{u,v_u(k)}, 1 \leqslant k \leqslant n$, $W(r_{u,i(k)}, n)$, is calculated. The preference drift and content based prediction equation for a rating r_{u,v_j} at time n (when user u has rated n items) is defined as follows:

$$\hat{r}^{\mathrm{pdCB}}_{u,v_j} = \frac{\sum_{k=1}^{n} W(r_{u,v_u(k)}, n) \times s(v_j, v_u(k)) \times r_{u,v_u(k)}}{\sum_{k=1}^{n} W(r_{u,v_u(k)}, n) \times s(v_j, v_u(k))}. \tag{10.3}$$

10.3 Fuzzy User Preference Drift Detection-based Recommendation Method

There is uncertainty in item features and user behaviors. On the basis of the method in the last section, we introduce a fuzzy content based recommendation method with user preference drift detection in this section.

10.3.1 *Fuzzy user preference consistency model*

The basis of the Fuzzy user preference consistency model is to detect whether a user interest drift specific to the explicit rating records happened in a user's history records [Zhang *et al.* (2016)]. In recommender systems, the item set $\mathcal{V} = \{v_j | j = 1, 2, \ldots, N\}$ contains all items that are provided to users. $\mathcal{A} = \{a_1, a_2, \ldots, a_{N_A}\}$ is the common item attributes space for item set $\mathcal{V}$. For each item attribute $a_k \in \mathcal{A}, 1 \leqslant k \leqslant n_A$, its value is represented as a vector $Y_k = (y_{k_1}, y_{k_2}, \ldots, y_{k_{N_k}})$, where N_k is the total number of the values for attribute a_k. Based on the item description or document, an item can be represented by its item profile, which is described as follows:

Given an item v_j, its item profile is defined as a vector of its values for each attribute $a_k \in \mathcal{A}$. The item profile is denoted as $A_j = (Y_{1,j}, \ldots, Y_{k,j}, \ldots, Y_{N_A,j})$, where $Y_{k,j}$ is the value of v_j for a_k. $Y_{k,j} = (y_{k_1,j}, \ldots, y_{k_l,j}, \ldots, y_{k_{N_k},j})$, $y_{k_l,j} = 1$ if y_{k_l} is a value of item v_j for attribute a_k and $y_{k_l,j} = 0$ otherwise.

For example, for the movie v_j which belongs to drama and comedy, A_j is the movie's profile, and it contains attributes such as genre (a_1) and cast (a_2). For attribute genre (a_1), say its value set is $Y_k =$ (drama, horror, comedy, sci-fi, action). The value set of m_j for genre (a_1) is $Y_{1,j} = (1, 0, 1, 0, 0)$. Sometimes, the item features are subjective. In that condition, an item cannot be represented by the item profile described above, so the fuzzy item profile is described.

Given an item v_j, its fuzzy item profile is defined as a vector of its membership degree of v_j to each attribute $a_k \in \mathcal{A}$, denoted as $\tilde{A}_j = (\tilde{Y}_{1,j}, \ldots, \tilde{Y}_{k,j}, \ldots, \tilde{Y}_{N_A,j})$, where $\tilde{Y}_{k,j}$ is a fuzzy sub set of Y_k. Let $\mu_{k_l,j}$ be the membership degree of y_{k_l} in $\tilde{Y}_{k,j}$; $\tilde{Y}_{k,j}$ can be represented as $\tilde{Y}_{k,j} = (\mu_{k_1,j}/y_{k_1}, \ldots, \mu_{k_l,j}/y_{k_l}, \ldots, \mu_{k_{N_k},j}/y_{k_{N_k}})$.

For example, Table 10.4 shows the representations of some rated movies by user u. For the movie v_1 and its attribute genre (a_1), say the movie genre is drama, horror, comedy and action, the membership is 1.0, 0.5, 0.1, 0 and 0.1. The fuzzy value set of v_1 for genre (a_1) is $\tilde{Y}_{1,1} = (1.0/\text{drama}, 0.5/\text{horror}, 0.1/\text{comedy}, 0/\text{sci-fi}, 0.1/\text{action})$.

Table 10.4: Movie representation for user u.

Movie	Time	Rating	Genre				
			drama	horror	comedy	sci-fi	action
v_1	t_1	$r_1(5)$	1	0.5	0.1	0	0.1
v_2	t_2	$r_2(1)$	1	0	0.9	0.2	0
v_3	t_3	$r_3(4)$	0.2	0.7	0	0	0.6
v_4	t_4	$r_4(1)$	0.1	0	0.8	1	0
v_5	t_5	$r_5(2)$	0.6	0.1	0.6	0	0

In recommender systems, users' history records are usually explicit ratings assigned to items with timestamps. The rating is usually an integer that ranges from 1 to 5. The time-stamp is usually in a date format like "28-12-2014, 09:45:00". According to the form of the users' history records, the user-rated item and the rated item series are as follows:

A user-rated item is defined to be a 3-tuple containing item, its rating and time-stamp are denoted as $C(v, r, t)$, where v is the item, r is the rating and t is the time-stamp when the rating is assigned to v. Each user u has a rated item series $C_u = \langle C_1(v_1, r_1, t_1), \ldots, C_i(v_i, r_i, t_i), \ldots, C_{N_u}(v_{N_u}, r_{N_u}, t_{N_u}) \rangle$ where N_u is the number of items user u has rated. For $\forall C_i$, C_{i+1} in C_u, it satisfies $t_i < t_{i+1}$.

Users' ratings to items are determined by their preferences at that time. User preferences cannot be obtained explicitly but can be inferred through user rated items implicitly. The user preference is defined as the motivation that determines what item the user will consume and how he/she will like it. Concretely, the user preference at time point (point-UP) is defined as the motivation that determines how user u rates items at time point t denoted as $x_u(t)$. The user preference at time interval (interval-UP) is defined as the motivation that determines how user u

rates items from time point t_i to time point t_j denoted as $x_u(t_i, t_j) = \bigcup_{t=t_i}^{t_j} x_u(t)$. The notation $\bigcup_{t=t_i}^{t_j} x_u(t)$ denotes that interval-UP is a combination of each point-UP from time point t_i to time point t_j. The subscript u will be omitted if there is no confusion.

We now discuss how to estimate the point-UP and interval-UP. Given a rated item $C_i(v_i, r_i, t_i)$, which is determined by $x(t_i)$, $x(t_i)$ can be estimated by:

$$x(t_i) = \operatorname{argmax} P(v_i, r_i | x(t_i)) \tag{10.4}$$

where $P(v_i, r_i | x(t_i))$ is the probability that user u will assign r_i to v_i at time-stamp t_i given point-UP $x(t_i)$.

Corresponding to item series $\langle C_1(v_1, r_1, t_1), \ldots, C_{N_u}(m_{N_u}, r_{N_u}, t_{N_u}) \rangle$, point-UPs in series is represented by $X_u = \langle x(t_1), \ldots, x(t_{N_u}) \rangle$. Every two adjacent point-UPs $x(t_i)$ and $x(t_{i+1})$ in X_u could be either consistent or not consistent. If they are consistent, they can be merged to form interval-UP $x(t_i, t_{i+1}) = \langle x(t_i), x(t_{i+1}) \rangle$. If point-UP from $x(t_i)$ to $x(t_j)$ is consistent, interval-UP is $x(t_i, t_j) = \langle x(t_i), \ldots, x(t_j) \rangle$.

Based on the definitions related to the item profile and user preference, whether the user preference is changing or not, i.e., whether the relation between point-UPs is consistent or not, should be defined. In this part, user preference consistency is defined for preparation of user preference drift detection.

As the latent point-UPs can be estimated by Eq. (10.4), the consistency relation between two point-UPs are correlated with the items that the user rated and the ratings that the user assigned to the rated items. The similarities of the items and ratings are described as:

Fuzzy item similarity is defined as the similarity of the two items v_i and v_j based on their fuzzy item profiles. $S(v_i, v_j)$ is the item profile similarity between item v_i and item v_j, which is calculated as follows:

$$S(v_i, v_j) = \sum_{a_k \in \mathcal{A}} S_{a_k}(v_i, v_j) \times w_{a_k} \tag{10.5}$$

where w_{a_k} is the weight of attribute a_k in attribute set $\mathcal{A}$, and $\sum_{a_k \in \mathcal{A}} w_{a_k} = 1$. The weight can be assigned by domain experts or trained from labeled data. $S_{a_k}(v_i, v_j)$ is the similarity on attribute a_k between item v_i and item v_j, which is calculated by:

$$S_{a_k}(v_i, v_j) = \frac{\sum_{l=1}^{N_k} \mu_{k_l, i} \times \mu_{k_l, j}}{\sqrt{\sum_{l=1}^{N_k} \mu_{k_l, i}^2} \times \sqrt{\sum_{l=1}^{N_k} \mu_{k_l, j}^2}} \tag{10.6}$$

where $\mu_{k_l, i}$ and $\mu_{k_l, j}$ represent the membership degree of y_{k_l} in $\tilde{Y}_{k,i}$ and $\tilde{Y}_{k,j}$ respectively, and N_k is the cardinal number of value domain Y_k of attribute a_k.

$S(v_i, v_j)$ equals 1 when the two items are identical, and equals 0 when they are not. If the item attributes and values are similar, $S(v_i, v_j)$ methods to 1. For example, in Table 10.4 the fuzzy item similarity between v_1 and v_2 is 0.7111, meaning that the fuzzy item similarity between these two movies is 0.7111.

Rating similarity is the similarity measure between two rating values r_i and r_j and it is calculated as follows:

$$S(r_i, r_j) = 1 - \frac{|r_i - r_j|}{r_{\max} - r_{\min}} \tag{10.7}$$

where r_{max} and r_{min} are the highest rating and lowest rating that a user can assign in the recommender system. $S(r_i, r_j)$ equals 1 when the two ratings are identical, and equals 0 when they are not. If the ratings are similar, $R(r_i, r_j)$ methods to 1. For example, in Table 10.4 the rating similarity between r_1 and r_2 is 0, meaning that the two ratings assigned by user u are completely different.

As the latent point-UPs is estimated by Eq. (10.4), the consistency relation between two point-UPs are correlated with the two similarity measures defined above. Since the user preferences are subjective and usually cannot change sharply, therefore the relation between two point-UPs is not a crisp relation but a fuzzy relation, which is defined as fuzzy point-UP consistency relation.

Given point-UPs in series $X_u = \langle x(t_1), \ldots, x(t_i), \ldots, x(t_N) \rangle$, a point-UP set is $I_u = \{x(t_i) | i = 1, 2, \ldots, N_u\}$, where N_u is the number of items user u has rated. Fuzzy point-UP consistency relation is a fuzzy relation on point-UP set I_u and represents the consistency relation between two point-UPs in I_u. The membership function is $P(x(t_i), x(t_j))$. λ-cut of fuzzy point-UP consistency relation is:

$$P_\lambda(x(t_i), x(t_j)) = \begin{cases} 1 & P(x(t_i), x(t_j)) > \lambda \\ 0 & P(x(t_i), x(t_j)) < \lambda \end{cases} \tag{10.8}$$

where λ is a parameter range in $[0, 1]$. After the λ-cut operation, point-UP consistency relation becomes a crisp relation. The point-UP consistency degree is constrained by the following two rules:

Rule 1: IF items are similar AND the ratings assigned to the two items are similar, THEN the point-UPs are consistent.

Rule 2: IF items are similar AND the ratings assigned to the two items are not similar, THEN the point-UPs are inconsistent.

To calculate the point-UP consistency degree by applying the two rules, which contain uncertain linguistic terms, we apply the two fuzzy similar relations on items and ratings to handle these linguistic terms. The fuzzy item similarity relation is defined as a fuzzy relation on item set. The membership degree of the item similarity relation is calculated by the fuzzy item similarity. The fuzzy rating similarity relation is defined as a fuzzy relation on rating set. The membership degree of the rating similarity relation is calculated by the rating similarity. Given an antecedent and the implication relation, the consequent is inferred through fuzzy inference [Gupta and Qi (1991)]. Based on that, we can obtain the degree of positive point-UP consistency and the degree of negative point-UP consistency, denoted by $P^+(x(t_i), x(t_j))$ and $P^-(x(t_i), x(t_j))$ respectively. $P^+(x(t_i), x(t_j))$ and $P^-(x(t_i), x(t_j))$ are inferred, with a t-norm $\mathcal{T}$,

$$P^+(x_i, x_j) = \mathcal{T}(S(v_i, v_j), R(r_i, r_j)), \tag{10.9}$$
$$P^-(x_i, x_j) = \mathcal{T}(S(v_i, v_j), 1 - R(r_i, r_j)). \tag{10.10}$$

To better elaborate the relations defined above, the boundary values of $S(v_i, v_j)$ and $S(r_i, r_j)$ in $[0, 1]^2$ and their corresponding point-UP coherence and incoherence degrees are listed in Table 10.5. The membership function of fuzzy point-UP consistency relation $P(x(t_i), x(t_j))$ is computed by:

$$P(x(t_i), x(t_j)) = (1 - \beta)P^+(x(t_i), x(t_j)) + \beta(1 - P^-(x(t_i), x(t_j))) \tag{10.11}$$

where $\beta \in [0, 1]$ is a weighting parameter.

Table 10.5: Special value for fuzzy point-UP consistency relation.

Item similarity / Rating similarity	Similar $S(r_i, r_j) = 1$	Not similar $S(r_i, r_j) = 0$
Similar $S(v_i, v_j) = 1$	$P^+(x(t_i), x(t_j)) = 1$ $P^-(x(t_i), x(t_j)) = 0$	$P^+(x(t_i), x(t_j)) = 0$ $P^-(x(t_i), x(t_j)) = 1$
Not Similar $S(v_i, v_j) = 0$	$P^+(x(t_i), x(t_j)) = 0$ $P^-(x(t_i), x(t_j)) = 0$	$P^+(x(t_i), x(t_j)) = 0$ $P^-(x(t_i), x(t_j)) = 0$

For example, in Table 10.5 the fuzzy item similarity between v_1 and v_2 is 0.7111. The rating similarity between them is 1. If we use the commonly used minimum t-norm defined as $\mathcal{T}(a, b) = \min(a, b)$, then $P^+(x(t_1), x(t_2)) = 0.7111$, $P^-(x(t_1), x(t_2)) = 0$, meaning that the degree of positive point-UP consistency is 0.7111, and the degree of negative point-UP consistency is 0. Suppose $\beta = 0.5$, then $P(x_1, x_2) = 0.8555$, the degree of point-UP consistency is 0.8555, indicating that relation between point-UPs $x(t_1)$ and $x(t_2)$ is highly consistent. Suppose $\lambda = 0.5$, then $P_{0.5}(x(t_1), x(t_2)) = 1$, indicating that point-UPs $x(t_1)$ and $x(t_2)$ implied by rated items $C_1(v_1, r_1, t_1)$ and $C_2(v_2, r_2, t_2)$ are consistent.

10.3.2 *User-preference drift detection*

To deal with concept drift phenomenon in recommender systems, the drift detection is adopted on the existing data in the database to see whether the user preferences remain unchanged during a period of time. A user preference drift detection method, based on the fuzzy user-preference consistency model, is proposed. First, the test statistic interval-UP density decrement for detection is defined. The statistical guarantee is then discussed. Finally, the overview detection algorithm is presented.

If two adjacent point-UPs are consistent, they can be merged to form an interval-UP. The consistency relation between two interval-UPs should also be evaluated to determine if they are consistent or not. To calculate interval-UP consistency relation, the interval-UP density is defined.

Given an interval-UP $x(t_i, t_j) = \langle x(t_i), \ldots, x(t_j) \rangle$, the corresponding interval-UP graph is $G = (V, E)$, where $V = \{x(t_k)|(i \leqslant k \leqslant j)\}$ and $E = \{(x(t_k), x(t_l))|P_\lambda(x(t_k), x(t_l)) = 1\}$. The interval-UP density is calculated as:

$$\mathcal{D}(x(t_i, t_j)) = \frac{|E|}{\max_E} \qquad (10.12)$$

where $|E|$ is the number of edges contained in G and $\max_E = \binom{j-i+1}{2}$ is the max number of possible edges in G. Specially, to calculate the density decrement between adjacent point-UP and interval-UP, the default density of point-UP is set to 1. It is obvious that the more consistent point-UPs are in one interval-UP, the higher interval-UP density is. An illustrative example is shown in Fig. 10.2. If the point-UPs are all connected in one interval-UP, then the density of the interval-UP is 1, indicating that these point-UPs are all consistent.

If the two interval-UPs are consistent, the density of the combined interval-UP should have a high value. To determine whether two interval-UPs can form a new one, the interval-UP density decrement of two interval-UPs is described as follows:

Given two adjacent interval-UPs $x(t_i, t_k) = \langle x(t_i), \ldots, x(t_k) \rangle$ and $x(t_{k+1}, t_j) = \langle x(t_{k+1}), \ldots, x(t_j) \rangle$, the interval-UP density decrement of $x(t_i, t_k)$ and $x(t_{k+1}, t_j)$ is defined as:

$$d(x(t_i, t_k), x(t_{k+1}, t_j)) = \frac{\mathcal{D}(x(t_i, t_k)) + \mathcal{D}(x(t_{k+1}, t_j))}{2} - \mathcal{D}(x(t_i, t_j)).$$
$$(10.13)$$

Interval-UP density decrement evaluates the consistency between two interval-UPs. As shown in Fig. 10.2, if two interval-UPs are not consistent, the density of new interval-UP will be relatively low compared with the sum of the two interval-

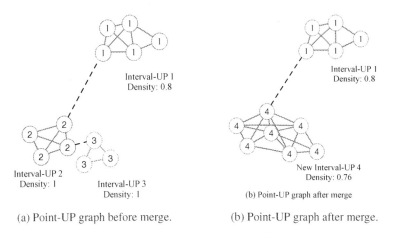

(a) Point-UP graph before merge.　　　　(b) Point-UP graph after merge.

Fig. 10.2: An example of point-UP graph.

UPs before the merge. In Fig. 10.2, interval-UP 2 can be merged with interval-UP 3 but cannot be merged with interval-UP 1. A user-preference drift happens between the two interval-UPs once the decrement is greater than ϵ [Kifer *et al.* (2004)]. If drift happens, the two interval-UPs should not be merged.

There are two aspects to concept drift detection, one is the test statistic and the other is to provide the statistical significance of the detected change. The hypothesis test is to determine whether the decrease of interval-UP density is statistically significance and so you can say the two interval-UPs are inconsistent (i.e., a drift happens). This is the statistical guarantee that we need to determine ϵ. The null hypothesis is "no drift happens (the two interval-UPs can be merged to a new one)". Interval-UP density decrement is the test statistic in the hypothesis test. Here, permutation test is conducted similar to [Lu *et al.* (2014)] to provide statistical guarantee with a significant level α. One calculation of interval-UP density decrement is one observation denoted as $\hat{\theta}$. α is the probability of obtaining an observation as extreme as $\hat{\theta}$. Usually, the significant value is set to be 0.05, suggesting that the false positive of the test is 0.05.

Under the null hypothesis, given two interval-UP $x_1(t_1, t_p)$ containing p point-UPs and $x_2(t_{p+1}, t_{p+q})$ containing q point-UPs, they can be merged and form a new interval-UP $x_{new}(t_1, t_{p+q})$ containing $p + q$ point-UPs. One permutation is to randomly sample p point-UPs to form the interval-UP $x'_1(t_1, t_p)$ without replacement, the remaining q point-UPs are to form the interval-UP $x'_2(t_{p+1}, t_{p+q})$. For the new clique $x'_1(t_1, t_p)$ and $x'_2(t_{p+1}, t_{p+q})$, test statistic $d(x'_1(t_1, t_p), x'_2(t_{p+1}, t_{p+q}))$ is calculated for this permutation. The permutations

---

Algorithm 10.1: User-preference Drift Detection

Input:

$X_u = List(x(t_1), \ldots, x(t_i), \ldots, x(t_N))$, the original point-UP series

Output:

$\mathcal{X}_u$, the final interval-UP series

1: $\mathcal{X}_u = List(C_1, \ldots, C_i, \ldots, C_N)$, $C_i = List(x(t_i))$
2: **while** $ListSize(\mathcal{X}_u) > 1$ **do**
3:     **for** each $i \in ListSize(\mathcal{X}_u)$ **do**
4:        $List(C_i, C_{i+1}) = \text{argmin } d(C_i, C_{i+1})$
5:        $\epsilon = pt(C_i, C_{i+1})$
6:        **if** $d(C_i, C_{i+1}) < \epsilon$ **then**
7:           $\mathcal{X}_u \leftarrow (\mathcal{X}_u - C_i)$
8:           $\mathcal{X}_u \leftarrow (\mathcal{X}_u - C_{i+1})$
9:           $\mathcal{X}_u \leftarrow (\mathcal{X}_u \bigcup List(C_i, C_{i+1})$
10:        **end if**
11:        **if** $i = |\mathcal{X}_u|$ **then**
12:           **break while**
13:        **end if**
14:     **end for**
15: **end while**
16: **return** $\mathcal{X}_u$

---

are repeated for Z times. The larger Z is, the more accurate the Monte Carlo simulation is. Z is suggested to set to 500. The threshold ϵ of the test statistic is calculated by:

$$\alpha \approx \hat{\alpha} = \frac{\#(\epsilon \geqslant \hat{\theta})}{Z}. \qquad (10.14)$$

Given $X_u = \langle x(t_1), \ldots, x(t_i), \ldots, x(t_N) \rangle$, to determine whether point-UP is consistent from $x(t_1)$ to $x(t_N)$, there are two straightforward methods.

One method is called the splitting method, which takes N point-UPs as a whole and checks whether to split it at $N - 1$ positions. Intuitively, we can check the $N - 1$ positions and calculate the difference between the two sub-series. The other method is called the merging method, which takes N point-UPs as N nodes and check whether two or several of them can be merged to be interval-UP. In real-world situations, the drift of user-preference can happen more than once in the series, therefore the splitting method may cause error detection if the user-preference in the sub-series is not consistent. The merging method is used here.

Algorithm 10.1 shows the process of user-preference drift detection. The original point-UP series is represented as $X_u = List(x(t_1), \ldots, x(t_i), \ldots, x(t_N))$ where point-UPs are arranged in time order. Function d is the density decrement measure for two interval-UPs and function pt is the permutation test for two interval-UPs.

In the algorithm, line 1 is to initialize the original point-UP series. Lines 2 to 15 repetitively merge the consistent point-UPs or interval-UPs. Concretely, lines 4 and 5 are calculating the interval-UP decrement and the threshold ϵ for determining whether the two interval-UPs can be merged or not. The function argmin in line 4 is to find the smallest density decrement of all the paired interval-UPs. Lines 6 to 10 are to update the list of user-preferences. Lines 11 to 13 are to judge whether the circulation should be terminated. If all the interval-UPs are detected and any two of them cannot be merged, then the circulation is terminated even though there are more than two interval-UPs in the list.

10.3.3 *Fuzzy user preference drift detection based recommender system*

In this subsection, a fuzzy user-preference drift detection based recommender system is developed. The proposed user-preference drift detection method is applied to prune off the out-of-date user data to acquire the up-to-date user preference. The developed fuzzy user-preference drift detection based recommender system is to understand current user-preference and provide recommendations to meet the current user-preference. Fig. 10.3 shows the framework of the recommender system that adapts to the detected user-preference drift.

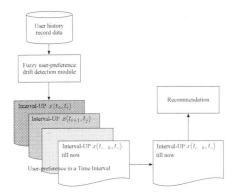

Fig. 10.3: Framework of fuzzy user-preference drift detection-based recommender system.

For each user, based on his/her history rating records, user-preference drift detection is conducted in a user-preference drift detection module. Several interval-UPs will be acquired after the detection which are implied by the rated item series. The most recent interval-UP is the current user-preference. Its corresponding sub-series of the rated item series is acquired for the recommendation. Once a user requests recommendation, the remaining sub-series acquired in the detection module will be used to provide recommendation rather than using the whole user history records. The recommendation method can be content-based, CF-based or any hybrid method.

10.4 Summary

Modeling user-preference drift in recommender systems is a challenge, since the drift of user preferences may occur in different directions for each user and in a distinct time period. Moreover, item features and user behaviors are often uncertain, making the modeling even harder to be accurate. In this chapter, concept drift techniques and their application in recommender systems are introduced. A rating weight model to evaluate the consistency degree of ratings from one user in a period of time is presented takes both the time factor and the semantic factor into consideration. A fuzzy user preference model is proposed to detect the drift and to prune off the out-of-date data. These two models can be applied to any kind of recommendation methods such as content-based, CF-based and hybrid methods.

Chapter 11

Visualization in Recommender Systems

It has been recognized that many recommender systems functioned as black boxes – lack clear explanations and transparency of the recommendation generation process, not providing any additional information to users beyond the recommendations themselves. These are hence resulting in users being distrustful of the recommendations provided, especially in a group recommender system environment. Visualization techniques can be applied in recommender systems to bring users' instinctive understanding and therefore their confidence and trust in accepting the generated recommendations. Visualization can present recommender systems in a human-friendly way and provides users with a more efficient and effective way to interact with the systems. An advanced application of visualization also can explain why the user may be interest an item and why the system recommends the particularly items, that is, "You might like music X because you download same style of music before ...". This chapter carefully explains how visualization enhances users' trust in recommender systems, especially for the group recommender systems.

In this chapter, first we introduce visualization methods and their application in recommender systems in Section 11.1. A novel hierarchical visualization method for group recommender systems is presented in Section 11.2. An illustrative example of visualization is given in 11.3, and then a summary of the chapter is presented 11.4.

11.1   Data Visualization

In this section first we introduce the concept of data visualization and the different types. Then visualization in recommender systems, particularly visualization in group recommender systems, are presented.

11.1.1   *Concept and types*

Data visualization, often referring specifically to information visualization, aims to simplify comprehended and abstract data for easier human understanding. According to the nature of data, information visualization methods are categorized into seven types:

(1) One-dimensional: document lens, code lens and value bars.
(2) Two-dimensional: geographic information systems and images.
(3) Three-dimensional: computer-aided design and architecture.
(4) Multi-dimensional: parallel coordinates.
(5) Tree: folder systems and organization charts.
(6) Network: social networks and topic nets.
(7) Temporal: time-lines and project manager.

One of the most significant problems suffered by recommender systems and their applications is the inadequacy of the explanations about the recommendation generation process, which means the recommendations lack persuasion. In general, most recommender systems are treated as a black box, with only the final recommendation results accessible to the user. Many visualization techniques have been used to provide an instinctive understanding of the system and to reveal deep-level relationships in data. Recommender systems that show results as graphs are known to engender more trust, and therefore more loyalty, from their users.

11.1.2   *Visualization in recommender systems*

Visualization can be applied in recommender systems in the following three ways:

(1) Line and bar charts visualization: Simple methods such as line charts and bar charts can improve user understanding, and are usually used to visualize user profiles. For example, in recommender system for written articles, the user profile is represented in ontological terms that are understandable to the user. When users interact with the recommender system, their behaviors can be presented in line form with varying time to help the user understand

their search and recommendation results. The bar chart is usually used to demonstrate the weight of the item the user has consumed and gives the user a clear visual representation of their consumption composition.

(2) Graph-based visualizations: In graph-based methods, an inherited relationship can be represented easily using a directed edge between two nodes, making them suitable and widely employed in recommender systems. There are many different graph layouts, the simplest being the traditional node-link layout. It computes the position of each node and draws every edge as a curve. Layouts created by tree algorithms and spring algorithms fall within this node-link category. The classic tree is straightforward and provides clear 2D representations. In tree layouts, items are represented as leaves, and the edges between them provide reliable recommendation information. The spring layout is well-known as the force-directed graph, and is also a well-studied graph layout because of its simplicity. Spring layouts are based on a cost function that models graph edges as "springs" with forces between nodes that either pull two nodes together or push them further apart. The graph iteratively changes until it becomes stable. A simple example of a spring layout is a social network graph that moves two nodes either closer together or further apart, depending on the closeness of their relationship.

(3) Map-based visualizations: These are used in many geographic location systems, but this geographic constraint narrows the range of applications. In [Gansner *et al.* (2009)], users can gain a clear image illustrating data of selection for TV shows and music based on canonical maps. In [Gavalas *et al.* (2014)], mobile tourism recommender systems with visualization are introduced. The locations, tours and recommendation lists are visualized to help users gain an intuitive understanding of the system. However, when the geo-information is missing, map-based methods are not feasible.

11.1.3 *Visualization and hierarchical graphs*

Group recommender systems include more complex data, such as group members and group profile, than individual recommender systems. Therefore, group recommender systems visualization typically conveys the overall system. Compared with in individual recommender systems, visualization for group recommender systems place emphasis on the aggregation of the group member's preferences and the relationships between group members.

Hierarchical graphs take the organization of components one step further than each node, and each edge has an indicator to specify a type, thus the hierarchical graph is very suitable for the visualization of group recommender systems. For example, in Fig. 11.1 (a), a spring layout graph of a movie would show the directors, producers and actors as three types of roles. The movie inherits its script from the producer, its visualization from the director, and its performance from the actors. Fig. 11.1 (b) shows the hierarchical graph using different node levels and line types to represent the node and edge types. Obviously, particularly for a hierarchical graph, a multi-level network in which profiles, common friends and recommendations are presented as nodes and are allocated to different levels and depicted using different colors, is needed for a group recommender system [Wang *et al.* (2017a)].

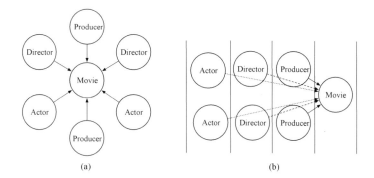

(a)   (b)

Fig. 11.1: A spring layout graph and a hierarchical for multiple relationships.

11.2 Hierarchy Visualization Method for Group Recommender Systems

This section describes a hierarchy visualization method for group recommender systems, as introduced in Chapter 8. We first introduce the structure of the method, then present the components in detail.

11.2.1 *Group recommendation overview*

We give a review on the group recommendation method to show where visualization is needed: Let $\mathcal{U}$ be all the users in the system $\mathcal{U} = \{u_1, u_2 \ldots u_{|\mathcal{U}|}\}$ and $\mathcal{V}$ be all the items $\mathcal{V} = \{v_1, v_2 \ldots v_{|\mathcal{V}|}\}$. Group $\mathcal{G}$ is a sub-set of $\mathcal{U}$ that $\mathcal{G} = \{g_1, g_2 \ldots g_{|\mathcal{G}|}\}$, where group members $g_m \in \mathcal{U}, m = 1, \ldots, |\mathcal{G}|$. The group of users is treated as a pseudo user and the profile is Profile$(\mathcal{G})$, which represents the overall group preference. Profile$(\mathcal{G})$ is defined as a rating vector and every dimension of it is $r_{\mathcal{G},v_i}$ where $v_i \in \mathcal{V}$. After the pseudo user profile is generated, the rating prediction can be given using the individual recommendation methods such as user-based CF in Chapter 2. A neighbor set of user group $\mathcal{G}$ denoted as $\mathcal{N}_{\mathcal{G}}$ is chosen from the whole user set $\mathcal{U}$. The top-K items $P = \{p_1, p_2, \ldots, p_K\}$ are chosen as the recommendation list to the specific group $\mathcal{G}$.

From the above description, four types of entities need visualization to represent their role in the recommendation process: (1) group member, (2) pseudo user profile, (3) neighbors and (4) recommendation. All the entities are represented as four types of nodes and rearranged at four different levels:

(1) Level 1 nodes: the group member nodes (MNs).
    Every node corresponds to a group member.
(2) Level 2 nodes: the pseudo user profile nodes (PNs).
    The pseudo user profile is presented as a rating vector over the items that have been rated by the members and every node in this level corresponds to an item in the profile.
(3) Level 3 nodes: the neighbor user nodes (NNs).
    Every node corresponds to a neighbor which is determined by the similarities calculated with the PCC method.
(4) Level 4 nodes: the recommendation nodes (RNs).
    Every node in this level corresponds to a recommendation.

The three procedures need visualization to help users understand the final recommendations: (1) Pseudo user modeling. The pseudo user profile is represented as a rating vector on items that have been rated by group members. Usually different ratings of group members for one item are aggregated. (2) Neighbor identification. The pseudo user profile then becomes the input of the neighbor identification procedure. This procedure identifies neighbors that have similar preference patterns to the pseudo user, using a similarity calculation method, typically cosine similarity or Pearson's correlation. (3) Recommendation prediction. Top-K items with the highest rating prediction are recommendations. The edges that link two nodes at different levels demonstrate the three main procedures:

(1) MN-PN edges: the edges represent pseudo user modeling.
(2) PN-NN edges: the edges represent neighbor identification.
(3) NN-RN edges: the edges represent recommendation prediction.

With the design, users are given a clear overview of the recommendation they are presented. Although we give visualization of one specific recommendation method below, We need to point out that the visualization method can also support other group recommendation methods. Fig. 11.2 gives an overview of the visualization flowchart of the recommendation, including four types of entities and three procedures with corresponding visual components. We will discuss the components in the rest of this section.

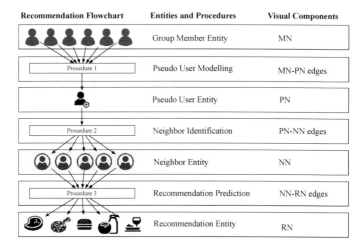

Fig. 11.2: Flowchart of the recommender process including four entities, three procedures and corresponding visual components.

11.2.2 *Recommendation components*

First, we briefly recall the group recommendation method in Chapter 8. Each member has an important attribute, its contribution score, which is a numeric measurement of the representative of group members. This group recommendation method is to maximize group satisfaction for users by modeling group preferences through the analysis of member ratings. The method employs a SNMF to calculate contribution scores in terms of a sub-rating matrix. Then, we give detailed description on how the seven components (four types of nodes and three main procedures) helps in visualize the group recommendation method.

(1) Level 1 MNs: the group member nodes

We use all the item-pair subspaces as sub-rating matrix to measure the contribution score. Let $\mathcal{V}^{sub} = \{\mathcal{V}_1, \ldots, \mathcal{V}_p, \ldots, \mathcal{V}_{|\mathcal{V}^{sub}|}\}$ be the set of all the subspaces. Since we only consider two items to form one subspace, the number of the item subspaces is $|\mathcal{V}^{sub}| = \binom{|\mathcal{V}|}{2}$ and the contribution of group member g_m in subspace $\mathcal{V}_p$ is $\mathrm{MCS}^p_{g_m}$ calculated by Eq. (8.3). The overall contribution score of group member g_m is MCS_{g_m} calculated by Eq. (8.5).

Every group member in $\mathcal{G}$ is visualized as a MN. The MN set is $\{\mathrm{MN}_{g_1}, \mathrm{MN}_{g_2}, \dots, \mathrm{MN}_{g_{|\mathcal{G}|}}\}$ How the MNs are designed mainly depends on two factors: the group member g_m and its corresponding contribution score MCS_{g_m}. The group members are all different and they need to be distinguished in visualization, thus they are shown using different colors. The contribution scores are shown using different radius of nodes, and the radius is determined by Eq. (11.1). The radius of MN_{g_m} is:

$$R_{\mathrm{MN}}(g_m) = R_{\mathrm{MN}}^{\max} \cdot \frac{\mathrm{MCS}_{g_m}}{\max(\mathrm{MCS}_{g_m})} \qquad (11.1)$$

where $R_{\mathrm{MN}}^{\max}$ is the maximum radius of MN. However, the MN level may contain numerous MNs and these unorganized nodes make group members difficult to obtain relation between themselves and others, therefore they are sorted by their contribution scores for clarity of presentation. We will use examples to show details of visualization in each component.

Example 11.1. A two-member group is presented in Table 11.1. The contribution score and MNs calculation are presented. In this and following examples, the maximum radius of nodes $R_{\max}$ is set to 10. The contribution scores of two members are computed according to Eq. (8.3) and Eq. (8.5):

$$
\begin{aligned}
\mathrm{MCS}_{g_1} &= \frac{2}{4}\left(\mathrm{MCS}_{g_1}^{\{v_1,v_2\}} + \mathrm{MCS}_{g_1}^{\{v_1,v_3\}} + \mathrm{MCS}_{g_1}^{\{v_1,v_4\}} \right. \\
&\quad \left. + \mathrm{MCS}_{g_1}^{\{v_2,v_3\}} + \mathrm{MCS}_{g_1}^{\{v_2,v_4\}} + \mathrm{MCS}_{g_1}^{\{v_3,v_4\}} \right) \\
&= \frac{2}{4}\left(0 + 1 + 0 + 1 + 0 + 0 \right) = 1, \\
\mathrm{MCS}_{g_2} &= \frac{2}{4}\left(1 + 0 + 1 + 0 + 1 + 0 \right) = \frac{3}{2}.
\end{aligned}
$$

Table 11.1: Rating matrix of a group example with two users and four items.

	v_1	v_2	v_3	v_4
g_1	5	4	4	?
g_2	3	1	?	3

After normalizing, the contribution scores are:

$$\text{MCS}_{g_1} = \frac{1}{1 + \frac{3}{2}} = \frac{2}{5},$$

$$\text{MCS}_{g_2} = \frac{\frac{3}{2}}{1 + \frac{3}{2}} = \frac{3}{5}.$$

The maximum contribution score is $R_{\text{MN}}^{\max}\text{MCS}_{g_2}$ and we set $R_{\text{MN}}^{\max} = 10$. There are two MNs to represent two members and according to Eq. (11.1), the two radii are:

$$R_{\text{MN}}(g_1) = 10 \times \frac{2/5}{3/5} = 6.67,$$

$$R_{\text{MN}}(g_2) = 10 \times \frac{3/5}{3/5} = 10.$$

(2) Level 2 PNs: the pseudo user profile nodes

Once a group member's contribution score is calculated, the group rating of group member g_m denoted as $r_{g_m,v_i}^{\text{group}}$ is calculated as:

$$r_{g_m,v_i}^{\text{group}} = \text{MCS}_{g_m} \cdot r_{g_m,v_i}.$$

For the group $\mathcal{G}$, we generate a pseudo user profile to represent the preference of this group. The pseudo user profile is represented with the pseudo user rating to each item. As we have acquired the group rating of each group member, the pseudo rating of the group is a weighted sum as:

$$r_{\mathcal{G},v_i} = \sum_{g_m \in \mathcal{G}} r_{g_m,v_i}^{\text{group}}. \tag{11.2}$$

The pseudo user profile of group $\mathcal{G}$ is $\text{Profile}(\mathcal{G}) = [r_{\mathcal{G},v_1}, \ldots, r_{\mathcal{G},v_i}, \ldots, r_{\mathcal{G},v_{|v|}}]$. Each element in $Profile(\mathcal{G})$ is visualized as a PN. Two things are related to the visualization of PN: the pseudo rating of the group on each item and the contribution of each group member. The pseudo rating represents the overall preference of this group to an item and is visualized using the radius of the node. Instead of drawing a node using a solid color, a pie chart is displayed in the node to illustrate the contribution of each group member. All the PNs are sorted and arranged once their radii are calculated. This helps members understand relative relationships within the pseudo user profile. The radius of a PN is determined by:

$$R_{\text{PN}}(\mathcal{G}, v_i) = R_{\text{PN}}^{\max} \times \frac{r_{\mathcal{G},v_i}}{\max(r_{\mathcal{G},v_i})} \tag{11.3}$$

where $R_{\text{PN}}^{\max}$ is the maximum radius of PN. The contribution of each group member is illustrated by slices in a pie chart and the ratio of each slice is calculated by:

$$\text{ratio}_{\text{PN}}(g_m, v_i) = \frac{r_{g_m, v_i}^{\text{group}}}{r_{\mathcal{G}, v_i}} \tag{11.4}$$

Example 11.2. The user group rating calculation using data in Example 11.1 is shown in Table 11.2.

Table 11.2: Group member pseudo rating calculation.

	v_1	v_2	v_3	v_4
g_1	$\frac{2}{5} \times 5 = 2$	$\frac{2}{5} \times 4 = 1.6$	$\frac{2}{5} \times 4 = 1.6$	?
g_2	$\frac{3}{5} \times 3 = 1.8$	$\frac{3}{5} \times 1 = 0.6$	?	$\frac{3}{5} \times 3 = 1.8$

The pseudo user profile is calculated according to Eq. (11.2) as:

$$r_{\mathcal{G}, v_1} = \frac{2}{5} \times 5 + \frac{3}{5} \times 3 = 3.8$$

$$r_{\mathcal{G}, v_2} = \frac{2}{5} \times 4 + \frac{3}{5} \times 1 = 2.2$$

$$r_{\mathcal{G}, v_3} = \frac{2}{5} \times 4 = 1.6$$

$$r_{\mathcal{G}, v_4} = \frac{3}{5} \times 3 = 1.8.$$

The radius of PNs are:

$$R_{\text{PN}}(\mathcal{G}, v_1) = 10 \times \frac{3.8}{3.8} = 10$$

$$R_{\text{PN}}(\mathcal{G}, v_2) = 10 \times \frac{2.2}{3.8} = 5.8$$

$$R_{\text{PN}}(\mathcal{G}, v_3) = 10 \times \frac{1.6}{3.8} = 4.2$$

$$R_{\text{PN}}(\mathcal{G}, v_4) = 10 \times \frac{1.8}{3.8} = 4.7.$$

The ratios of PNs are shown in Table 11.3. From the table, we can see that $\text{ratio}_{\text{PN}}(g_1, v_4)$ and $\text{ratio}_{\text{PN}}(g_2, v_3)$ is zero because there is no historical rating.

(3) MN-PN edges

Similar to the ratios of PNs we introduced above, the MN-PN edges are used to give users a clear illustration on how the user contributes to the group rating.

Table 11.3: Ratio calculation of PNs.

	v_1	v_2	v_3	v_4
g_1	$\frac{2}{2+1.8} = 0.53$	$\frac{1.6}{1.6+0.6} = 0.73$	$\frac{1.6}{1.6+0} = 1$	0
g_2	$\frac{1.8}{2+1.8} = 0.47$	$\frac{0.6}{1.6+0.6} = 0.27$	0	$\frac{1.8}{1.8+0} = 1$

The width of the edge indicates degree of preference, giving the user insight into pseudo user profile. Given a group member may not rate all the items in the group, a MN-PN edge is drawn only when a member g_m has rated item v_i. And the width of edge is used to visualize pseudo rating of the group member. The width of the MN-PN edge is calculated as:

$$D_{\text{MN-PN}}(g_m, v_i) = D_{\text{MN-PN}}^{\max} \cdot \frac{r_{g_m, v_i}^{\text{group}}}{\max(r_{g_p, v_i}^{\text{group}})}. \tag{11.5}$$

Example 11.3. The group member pseudo rating calculation using data in Example 11.1 is shown in Table 11.2. The maximum group rating is $r_{g_1, v_1}^{\text{group}}$, then the widths of all MN-PN edges are shown in Table 11.4.

Table 11.4: MN-PN edge widths.

	v_1	v_2	v_3	v_4
g_1	$5 \times \frac{2}{2} = 5$	$5 \times \frac{1.6}{2} = 4$	$5 \times \frac{1.6}{2} = 4$	0
g_2	$5 \times \frac{1.8}{2} = 4$	$5 \times \frac{0.6}{2} = 1.5$	0	$5 \times \frac{1.8}{2} = 4$

(4) Level 3 NNs: the neighbor user nodes

Based on the pseudo user profile Profile($\mathcal{G}$), we treat the group as a pseudo user and calculate its similarities with other non-group users. Similarity measurements used in Chapter 2 can be applied here, such as PCC similarity or cosine similarity. The similarity between the group $\mathcal{G}$ and a neighbor n_k is denoted as $S(\mathcal{G}, n_k)$. It can be treated as a combination of similarities on the co-rated items $\mathcal{V}_{\mathcal{G}} \cap \mathcal{V}_{n_k}$:

$$S(\mathcal{G}, n_k) = \sum_{v_i \in \mathcal{V}_{\mathcal{G}} \cap \mathcal{V}_{n_k}} S_{v_i}(\mathcal{G}, n_k)$$

where $\mathcal{V}_{\mathcal{G}}$ is the item set that the group $\mathcal{G}$ has rated, $\mathcal{V}_{n_k}$ is the item set that user n_k has rated and $S_{v_i}(\mathcal{G}, n_k)$ is the similarity between the group $\mathcal{G}$ and another user n_k on item v_i.

After all the similarities of non-member users are determined, a collection of neighbors is selected, either according to a predefined number or a similarity threshold, to calculate the predictions. The selected neighbors set is noted as $\mathcal{N}_{\mathcal{G}} = \{n_1, \ldots, n_k, \ldots, n_{|\mathcal{N}_{\mathcal{G}}|}\}$. Every element in $\mathcal{N}_{\mathcal{G}}$ is shown as a NN. The radius of an NN is determined by a mapping function from similarities as:

$$R_{\text{NN}}(n_k) = R_{\text{NN}}^{\max} \times \frac{S(\mathcal{G}, n_k)}{\max(S(\mathcal{G}, n_k))} \qquad (11.6)$$

All the NNs are rearranged according to their similarity value, which provides a clear representation of the neighborhood. A pie chart is used to demonstrate how much a group member influenced a specific neighbor. The contribution of each group member to the group on each item is known as in Eq. (11.4). The contribution of each group member to the neighbor is a combination on all the co-rated items:

$$\text{ratio}_{\text{NN}}(g_m, n_k) = \sum_{v_i \in \mathcal{V}_{\mathcal{G}}} \frac{S_{v_i}(\mathcal{G}, n_k) \times \text{ratio}_{\text{PN}}(g_m, v_i)}{S(\mathcal{G}, n_k)} \qquad (11.7)$$

Example 11.4. Example 11.1 is extended with two non-group members as two neighbors of the group $\mathcal{G}$: n_1 and n_2 and two additional items v_5 and v_6. The new rating matrix is shown in Table 11.5.

Table 11.5: Rating matrix of two non-group neighbors.

	v_1	v_2	v_3	v_4	v_5	v_6
n_1	4	1	?	2	4	3
n_2	4	2	3	?	2	5

PCC similarity measure as follows is used:

$$S_{v_i}(\mathcal{G}, n_k) = \frac{(r_{\mathcal{G}, v_i} - \bar{r}_{\mathcal{G}})(r_{n_k, v_i} - \bar{r}_{n_k})}{\sqrt{\sum_{v_i \in \mathcal{V}_{\mathcal{G}} \cap \mathcal{V}_{n_k}}(r_{\mathcal{G}, v_i} - \bar{r}_{\mathcal{G}})^2 \sum_{v_i \in \mathcal{V}_{\mathcal{G}} \cap \mathcal{V}_{n_k}}(r_{n_k, v_i} - \bar{r}_{n_k})^2}}$$

where $\bar{r}_{\mathcal{G}}$ and $\bar{r}_{n_k}$ are the average rating of user group $\mathcal{G}$ and the user n_k. The similarities are show in Table 11.6. According to this table, we can calculate the similarity of neighbors n_1 and n_2 with pseudo user $\mathcal{G}$ as $S(\mathcal{G}, n_1) = 0.86$ and $S(\mathcal{G}, n_2) = 0.71$. The radius of these two NNs are:

$$R_{\text{NN}}(\mathcal{G}, n_1) = 10 \times \frac{0.86}{0.86} = 10$$

$$R_{\text{NN}}(\mathcal{G}, n_2) = 10 \times \frac{0.71}{0.86} = 8.26.$$

The ratios of NNs are calculated with Eq. (11.7) and shown in Table 11.7.

Table 11.6: Similarities between pseudo user and the non-group member users.

	v_1	v_2	v_3	v_4
$S(\mathcal{G}, n_1, v_i)$	0.62	0.16	–	0.08
$S(\mathcal{G}, n_2, v_i)$	0.56	0.15	0	–

Table 11.7: Ratio calculation of NNs.

	n_1	n_2
g_1	$\frac{0.62}{0.86} \times \frac{2}{2+1.8} + \frac{0.16}{0.86} \times \frac{1.6}{1.6+0.6} =$ 0.51	$\frac{0.56}{0.71} \times \frac{2}{2+1.8} + \frac{0.15}{0.71} \times \frac{1.6}{1.6+0.6} + 0 = 0.57$
g_2	$\frac{0.62}{0.86} \times \frac{1.8}{2+1.8} + \frac{0.16}{0.86} \times \frac{0.6}{1.6+0.6} +$ $\frac{0.08}{0.86} \times \frac{1.8}{1.8} = 0.49$	$\frac{0.56}{0.71} \times \frac{1.8}{2+1.8} + \frac{0.15}{0.71} \times \frac{0.6}{1.6+0.6} = 0.43$

(5) PN-NN edges

It is easy to see that every PN-NN edge represents a historical rating of non-group user on items in pseudo user profile. The width of the edge is calculated as:

$$D_{\text{PN-NN}}(n_k, v_i) = D_{\text{PN-NN}}^{\max} * \frac{S_{v_i}(\mathcal{G}, n_k)}{\max(S_{v_i}(\mathcal{G}, n_k))}. \tag{11.8}$$

Example 11.5. The PN-NN edge calculation continued in Table 11.8.

Table 11.8: PN-NN edge widths.

	v_1	v_2	v_3	v_4
n_1	$5 \times 1 = 5$	$5 \times \frac{0.16}{0.62} = 1.29$		$5 \times \frac{0.08}{0.62} = 0.65$
n_2	$5 \times \frac{0.56}{0.62} = 4.52$	$5 \times \frac{0.15}{0.62} = 1.21$	$5 \times \frac{0}{0.62} = 0$	

(6) Level 4 RNs: the recommendation nodes

Unknown group ratings can be predicted after the neighbors are selected. Here we present user-based CF similar to Chapter 2. The predicted rating of recommended item p_j is calculated by:

$$\hat{r}_{\mathcal{G},p_j} = \bar{r}_{\mathcal{G}} + \frac{\sum_{n_k \in \mathcal{N}_{\mathcal{G}}} (r_{n_k, p_j} - \bar{r}_{n_k}) \times S(\mathcal{G}, n_k)}{\sum_{n_k \in \mathcal{N}_{\mathcal{G}}} |S(\mathcal{G}, n_k)|} \tag{11.9}$$

where $\bar{r}_{\mathcal{G}}$ is the average pseudo user rating of user group $\mathcal{G}$.

Usually, the top-K items with highest predictions are selected as the final recommendations. From the perspective of recommendations, only NN-RN edges those target to final results need to be visualized. The recommendation set is $P = \{p_1, p_2, \ldots, p_K\}$ and each element is shown as a RN. The radius of a RN is determined by:

$$R_{\text{RN}}(p_j) = R_{\text{RN}}^{\max} \frac{\hat{r}_{\mathcal{G},p_j}}{\max(\hat{r}_{\mathcal{G},p_j})}. \tag{11.10}$$

The predicted group rating is derived by aggregating predictions from all neighbors. The contribution of the neighbor n_k for item p_j is $\frac{(r_{n_k,p_j} - \bar{r}_{n_k}) \times S(\mathcal{G}, n_k)}{\sum_{n_k \in \mathcal{N}_{\mathcal{G}}}(r_{n_k,p_j} - \bar{r}_{n_k}) \times S(\mathcal{G}, n_k)}$. The ratio reflected in the pie chart is the contribution ratio of each group member to the final contribution. It reflects the contribution of each neighbor to the group members through $\text{ratio}_{\text{NN}}(g_m, n_k)$:

$$\text{ratio}_{\text{RN}}(n_k, p_j) = \sum_{n_k \in \mathcal{N}_{\mathcal{G}}} \frac{(r_{n_k,p_j} - \bar{r}_{n_k}) \times S(\mathcal{G}, n_k)}{\sum_{n_k \in \mathcal{N}_{\mathcal{G}}}(r_{n_k,p_j} - \bar{r}_{n_k}) \times S(\mathcal{G}, n_k)} \times \text{ratio}_{\text{NN}}(g_m, n_k).$$

A pie chart shows the individual influence of every member in the RN, and becomes a useful tool for members to track the influence they had on each recommendation.

Example 11.6. Consider the two added items in Example 11.4 are two new recommendations for the group $\mathcal{G}$. The average pseudo user rating of user group $\mathcal{G} = \{g_1, g_2\}$ is 2.35. The predicted rating of v_5 and v_6 are:

$$r_{\mathcal{G},v_5} = 2.35 + \frac{0.86 \times (4 - 2.8) + 0.71 \times (2 - 3.2)}{|0.86 + 0.71|} = 2.46,$$

$$r_{\mathcal{G},v_6} = 2.35 + \frac{0.86 \times (3 - 2.8) + 0.71 \times (5 - 3.2)}{|0.86 + 0.71|} = 3.27.$$

The radii of the two RNs are:

$$R_{\text{RN}}(v_5) = 10 \times \frac{2.46}{3.27} = 7.5,$$

$$R_{\text{RN}}(v_6) = 10 \times \frac{3.27}{3.27} = 10.$$

Calculations of ratios of RNs are shown in Table 11.9 and Table 11.10.

(7) NN-RN edges

Every NN-RN edge represents the contribution of a neighborhood user on predicted ratings of items in recommendation set. According to Eq. (11.9), the contribution of each neighbor to the predicted rating is

$$\tilde{r}_{n_k,p_j} = \frac{(r_{n_k,p_j} - \bar{r}_{n_k}) \times S(\mathcal{G}, n_k)}{\sum_{n_k \in \mathcal{N}_{\mathcal{G}}} |S(\mathcal{G}, n_k)|}. \tag{11.11}$$

Table 11.9: Ratio contribution of neighbors for recommendations.

	v_5	v_6
n_1	$\frac{|(4-2.33)\times 0.86|}{|(4-2.33)\times 0.86|+|(2-2.67)\times 0.71|} = 0.75$	$\frac{|(3-2.33)\times 0.86|}{|(3-2.33)\times 0.86|+|(5-2.67)\times 0.71|} = 0.26$
n_2	$\frac{|(2-2.67)\times 0.71|}{|(4-2.33)\times 0.86|+|(2-2.67)\times 0.71|} = 0.25$	$\frac{|(5-2.67)\times 0.71|}{|(3-2.33)\times 0.86|+|(5-2.67)\times 0.71|} = 0.74$

Table 11.10: Ratio calculation of RNs.

	v_5	v_6
g_1	$0.75 \times 0.51 + 0.25 \times 0.57 = 0.53$	$0.26 \times 0.51 + 0.74 \times 0.57 = 0.55$
g_2	$0.75 \times 0.49 + 0.25 \times 0.43 = 0.47$	$0.26 \times 0.49 + 0.74 \times 0.43 = 0.45$

The width of the edge is calculated as:

$$D_{\text{NN-RN}}(n_k, p_j) = D_{\text{NN-RN}}^{\max} * \frac{\tilde{r}_{n_k, p_j}}{\max(\tilde{r}_{n_k, p_j})}. \tag{11.12}$$

Example 11.7. The contribution of neighbor on recommended items v_5 and v_6 are in Table 11.11.

Table 11.11: Calculation of neighbor contribution on predicted rating.

	v_5	v_6
n_1	$\frac{(4-2.33)\times 0.86}{|0.86|+|0.71|} = 0.91$	$\frac{(3-2.33)\times 0.86}{|0.86|+|0.71|} = 0.37$
n_2	$\frac{(2-2.67)\times 0.71}{|0.86|+|0.71|} = 0.30$	$\frac{(5-2.67)\times 0.71}{|0.86|+|0.71|} = 1.05$

From Table 11.11, the maximum contribution is from n_2 on item v_6, $\tilde{r}_{n_2, v_6} = 1.05$. The PN-NN edge calculation continued in Table 11.12.

Table 11.12: NN-RN edges.

	v_5	v_6
n_1	$5 \times \frac{0.91}{1.05} = 4.33$	$5 \times \frac{0.37}{1.05} = 1.76$
n_2	$5 \times \frac{0.30}{1.05} = 1.43$	$5 \times \frac{1.05}{1.05} = 5$

11.3   Hierarchy Visualization Implementation

The method is implemented on a MovieLens 100K dataset to test the feasibility and effectiveness. The implementation includes three procedures to calculate the predictions, and they are summarized as follow:

(1) Contribution score-based group modeling is used to model the pseudo user.
(2) PCC is used to identify the neighbors based on the pseudo user's profile.
(3) CF is used to calculate the unknown group ratings based on the observed ratings of neighbors.

The detail of implementation will be introduced in the first subsection as usability, then interactivity is presented to show the feasibility of users to get explanation on recommendation process. The adaptability of the visualization method is followed to clarify that the visualization method is not limited to the only group recommendation method in this chapter. Finally, evaluation on how the visualization helps when the user interacted with the system.

11.3.1   *Usability*

The result visualization is shown in Fig. 11.3, where the four kinds of nodes, the group member nodes, user profile nodes, neighbor nodes and recommendation nodes, are allocated to different levels. It presents detailed and organized visual information, which will improve group members' confidence in accepting the recommendations.

In Fig. 11.3, a user group consisting of five randomly selecting group members was formed. The overall recommendation procedures are represented using different sized nodes and different width edges. First, the MCS-GR is used to calculate each member's contributions and a pseudo user was modeled from the weighted average. As a result, the five group members are represented with five nodes of different sizes in the MN level. The names of the nodes are displayed to the right side of each node. For example, for Member1 and Member5, their contributions to this group were 0.31 and 0.06. Therefore, the radius of Member1 node is much larger than Member5. Member1 node has three edge sources showing that Member1 rated three items, i.e. P1, P2 and P4, but did not rate P3 and P5.

The width of the edges represents the strength of inheriting information. The MN-PN edge represents the weighted ratings. Since Member1's contribution is constant, the three edges show that Member1 gave her highest rating to P1 and her lowest to P4. Since the group rating is the sum of weighted ratings from all

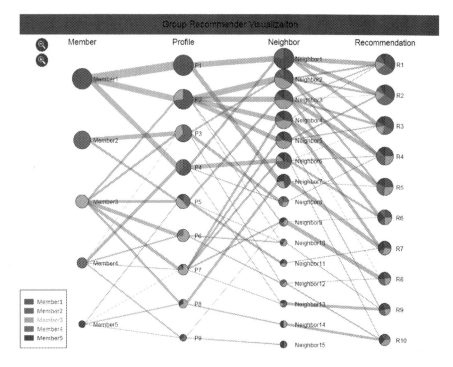

Fig. 11.3: A visualization example on real data set MovieLens 100K.

members, the P1 node which is determined by Member1 becomes the biggest, because of Member1's large contribution. P9's radius is the smallest because the MCSs were small. In this way, all members can easily see what items are in the pseudo user profile and how the group ratings were derived.

The PN-NN edges represent the ratings specified by neighbors for items in the pseudo user profile. Take P1 as an example. Both Neighbor1 and Neighbor7 rated this item. The width of the edge to Neighbor1 is a little wider than Neighbor7. This demonstrates that Neighbor1 preferred P1 more than Neighbor7. Additionally, all the PN-NN edges connected with NN node represent the overall preference of this neighbor. For example, the final similarity of Neighbor7 was 0.65 with the contribution of P1 0.44 and contribution of P4 0.21. It is important to point out that a neighbor is selected by the PCC similarity measure, which means there could be no direct relationships between a group item and a neighbor. For example, Neighbor14 only has direct connections with P8. P8 is only selected because the rating of Neighbor14 on P8 is the only observed one among the items in the pseudo user profile.

The NNs, RNs and NN-RN edges work very similarly to the MNs, PNs and MN-PN edges. The only difference is that the numerical contribution measure for members is their contribution score but for neighbors it is their similarity. Because we employ user-based CF to generate unknown ratings, the recommendations have direct relationships with at least one neighbor. The width of NN-RN edge represents the contribution of a neighborhood user on predicted ratings of items in the recommendation set. Numerically, it equals to rating contribution from this neighbor in the final rating prediction. For example, movie R1 is recommended because Neighbor14 rated it with high preference. The relationship between neighbors and the final recommendation also provides group members with an understanding of why these recommendations were generated.

The connections between group members are shown as pie charts in every level node from the MNs to RNs. This enables members to immediately understand their relationships with others and it makes it easier for members to track their individual influence throughout the recommendation process. For example, tracking Member1 to P2, then Neighbor2 and lastly to R4 shows Member1's individual influence along this path. At P2, she can see his/her dominance in the group rating, because Member3's ratio in this pie chart is much smaller. In Neighbor2 node, Member1 sees his/her ratio has decreased but Member3's ratio has increased, because Member3 has rated both P2 and P3 and Member1 did not rate P3. It indicates that Neighbor2 is more similar to Member3. Lastly, at node R4, Member1's ratio continued to decrease because many other neighbors have influenced the prediction.

11.3.2 *Interactivity*

We give one group visualization and a simple example. In real cases, situations are much more complicated than those described in the previous example. There may be numerous visual components because the group could be larger and relationships between nodes could be sparse. However, the space used to display the visual result is limited, which will definitely lower the readability for users. When this happens, it will be difficult for users to track their path towards recommendation or to focus on the content they are interested in.

The interactivity, zoom and pan, are provided to guarantee the usability of the method when the data is scaled. Zoom and pan techniques allow users to explore the visualization in detail. The interest part of a large graph can be focused, and neighboring parts can be easily viewed. Zoom and pan increases the efficiency of screen usage and guarantees the scalability of the visualization method. Fig. 11.4 gives a demonstration of focusing on the right-top part of the graph using zoom.

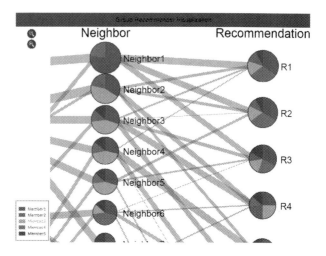

Fig. 11.4: Interactivity zoom and pan to enable usability for large data.

11.3.3 *Adaptability*

We adopt the group recommendation method introduced in Chapter 8 to visualize the recommendation process. However, the proposed visualization method is not limited to the specific group recommendation method, but can be adapted to various group recommendation methods.   The difference between group recommendation methods is how the pseudo user representing the user group is profiled. Many other group recommendation methods use different strategies to combine the group ratings. Take average strategy as an example, the group profile is generated as group rating on an item is the mean of all the ratings the group members rated. In this case, for the pie charts at every PN, the fractions of all the members are same. In Fig. 11.3, at P2 node, the fractions of Member1 and Member3 are 50% and 50%; at P5 node, the fractions of Member2, Member3 and Member5 are all 33.3%. The visualization method is easily adaptable to other group recommendation methods, like plurality voting, least misery, average, *etc.* The meaning of the nodes and edges are the same. Only the radii of PNs and the widths of MN-PN edges need to adjust according to the different strategies to generate the pseudo user profile.

The method could also provide solid explanations in individual CF-based recommendation systems, because an individual recommender process can be seen as a special group recommender process using a group that only contains one member.

Visualization would need to be modified in the first two levels to support individual visualization. The first level would contain a single root node, representing the active user. The radius of the circle would represent their average rating and illustrate their rating pattern. It implies whether the user tends to give higher or lower ratings on average. The pseudo user profile becomes the active user profile, and this profile can still be visualized in the PN level. Each node of PN would represent an item which has been rated by the active user.

11.3.4 *Evaluation*

To evaluate the effectiveness and assess user satisfaction of this visualization method, we use a questionnaire. In total, 30 participants were involved to specify a score for the seven statements listed in Table 11.13.

Table 11.13: The questions used for evaluation.

	Question Description
Q1	Easy to access
Q2	Effective for providing members information
Q3	Effective to illustrate the commonality of the group
Q4	Effective to explore the related uses for the group
Q5	Effective for presenting recommendations
Q6	Instinctive to explain the recommending process
Q7	Easy to obtain relative relationships with other group members

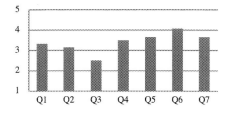

Fig. 11.5: The average score for questionnaire.

The assessment results are summarized in Fig. 11.5. The results show that users feel that the proposed recommendation method provides an instinctive explanation of a recommending process; they therefore can understand why a particular item is recommended and are very likely accept it. Questions 2 to 5 are related to the four types of entities (corresponding to the four types of nodes in visualization) in the recommender process. The results show that, compared with the group members, neighbor users and recommendations, group profile is the most difficult to understand. From Questions 2 to 6, the feedback shows that the key information and process is intuitively presented. Therefore users can trust the recommendations more than before, since the understandability is improved compared to the black box recommendation process. In general, the result of the survey show that the proposed visualization method can improve the transparency of the recommendation process, increase user trust and confidence in the recommended items and the system, and enhance the effectiveness of group recommender systems.

We have also compared this method with existing visualization methods in both individual recommender systems and group recommender systems. Table 11.14 shows the differences between the proposed method and other recommender system visualization methods.

Table 11.14: Main characteristics of different visualization methods on recommender systems.

Method	Group part		Individual part				
	Member	Profile Modeling	Profile	Neighbor Identification	Neighbor	Prediction	Recommendation
Proposed method	✓	✓	✓	✓	✓	✓	✓
[Bogdanov et al. (2013)]		✓					
[Middleton et al. (2004)]		✓					
[Castro et al. (2015)]	✓		✓				
[Hernando et al. (2013)]					✓	✓	✓
[Gotz and Wen (2009)]					✓		✓
[Verbert et al. (2013)]					✓		✓
[Bostandjiev et al. (2012)]	✓	✓	✓		✓	✓	✓
[Heckerman et al. (2000)]			✓		✓	✓	✓
[O'Donovan et al. (2008)]			✓		✓	✓	✓
[Gansner et al. (2009)]					✓	✓	✓
[Gavalas et al. (2014)]							✓
[Hernando et al. (2014)]					✓	✓	✓
[Gretarsson et al. (2010)]	✓	✓	✓		✓	✓	✓

11.4   Summary

An important and practical way to improve user trust in a recommender system is to make the recommendation generation procedure explainable. In this chapter, we introduce visualization methods on recommender systems. In particular, we present a hierarchy visualization method for group recommender systems to provide well-presented information and recommendation explanation. The hierarchy visualization method organizes related recommendation process information using multi-level nodes and edges. The edges connect different level nodes to construct a hierarchical graph in order to illustrate pseudo user modeling and CF procedures. Under this method, users as group members can gain an understanding of their individual influence to the final recommendation and the relative relationships with other members. Therefore, users are able to glean and understand the overall recommendation generation procedure.

PART 3

Recommender Systems: Software and Applications

Chapter 12

Telecom Products/Services Recommender Systems

Telecommunication (telecom) industry provides hundreds of different kinds of telecom products and each product contains several services to its customers. In principle, there are two types of customers: business and consumer. In addition, for each of the two types, a telecom company needs to consider providing product/services not only to existing customers (for customer retention), but also to potential new customers (for customer acquisition). Since it is a challenge for a customer, especially a potential customer or a business customer, to select one or a set of most appropriate telecom products/services, personalized product/service recommender systems become a new way in improving customer relationship management and marketing.

This chapter is primarily focused on, a telecom recommender system that provides personalized products/services recommendations for its existing SMB customers, called SmartAdvisor-SMB. This system can automatically predict the behaviors and requirements of SMB customers through analyzing customer profiles, usage patterns and product/service packages. The recommender system can be used across the business, such as across related sales channels to introduce new prospects to the company binds of products, and therefore can enable the optimization of every customer touch point more effectively.

In this chapter, we first introduce the background of telecom products/services in Section 12.1. The design and development of the recommender system, SmartAdvisor-SMB, is described in Section 12.2. Section 12.3 introduces a fuzzy matching-based method for generating telecom product/service recommendations and a telecom product/service recommendation method for hierarchical item situations. Section 12.4 shows the recommender system implementation. Finally, Section 12.5 gives a summary of the chapter.

12.1 Background

A telecommunication company provides a broad range of telecom products/services including mobile, national and long-distance services, local telephony, business network services, Internet and satellite services, and subscription and Internet television. The company's aim is to provide customers (including both SMBs and individual consumers) the experience of flexible and personalized services anywhere and on any device. Therefore, a series of web-based personalized recommender systems need to be developed to help both business and individual consumers, for both existing and potential customers, respectively, in the selection of the most appropriate telecom products/services. These recommender systems can be used by the company's sales office, call center, customer care department and related marketing channels, and also can be used by the customers themselves to receive personalized recommendations for suitable telecom products/services on the website. They can enable the company to thoroughly understand customer preferences and improve personalized services. The development of the recommender systems is an important part of the telecom business intelligence and customer relationship management, to help predict the company's customer churn and with marketing analytics.

The series of web-based personalized recommender systems developed include (1) a recommender system for existing consumers, (2) a recommender system for potential consumers, (3) a recommender system for existing SMB customers, and (4) a recommender system for potential SMB customers. These developments bring benefits to the company, including improving the customer experience; reducing customer churn, boosting cross-selling, and converting cost-centers into profit centers, particularly by enabling better retention of existing customers and the acquisition of new customers. The personalized recommender systems for potential SMBs and individual customers were developed to support and guide possible new customers in the selection of their first appropriate telecom products/services without any of their usage data history. Additionally, the aim of developing recommender systems was to help the marketing departments conduct real-time marketing analytics to attract new SMBs and individual customers.

The recommender systems initially need to obtain certain requirements from potential new customers through asking specific questions. They then match the obtained answers with existing customers' usage and then finally recommend the most appropriate company's products/services to them. The developments of recommender systems can reduce the sales cycle by minimizing the time-lag between the first appointment and the presentation or negotiation of a solution, providing both additional revenue and costs efficiencies across the business.

Telecom products/services have the following special characteristics:

(1) Multiple attributes.

Table 12.1 shows four telecom services examples. We can see from the table that a telecom service is a specification of the available sub-services with related prices, discounts and rewards. It is represented by a set of attributes such as monthly access fee, call rate, data charging, rewards, *etc.* Different telecom products/services are described by different attribute sets.

(2) Hierarchical tree structure.

Many telecom products/services are available in the form of packages and can only be described by hierarchical tree structures. Fig. 12.1 shows two examples of telecom service packages, which are viewed as tree structures [Wu *et al.* (2010a)]. Taking the first package as an example, the package is composed of three sub-services: fixed line, telecom, and broadband services. Each sub-service is described in greater detail by several aspects. For example, the broadband service is described by four aspects: price, contract duration, allowance, and throttle speed. From the price aspect, we can see that the price of the broadband service is $40 per month. From the tree structure, it also can be seen that every node is assigned a weight to reflect its degree of importance to its siblings.

The two packages' tree structures, nodes' weights, terms and values are all different. This makes it vital to measure the similarity between any two hierarchical tree-structured items. Therefore, a comprehensive similarity measure model to evaluate the semantic similarity was proposed. Chapter 7 introduced the techniques to measure similarity between two trees.

(3) Update frequently.

Telecom products/services are updated frequently. New products/services are introduced very quickly and replace some older.

(4) Service periods are fixed.

When a customer signs a product/service contract, the product/service and costs are normally set for the length of the contract, for example three years. They may change to a competitor after the contract ends. Therefore, the rating information from the customer on the product/service is not sufficient for user-based CF.

These characteristics of telecom products/services should be considered comprehensively when we design and develop recommender systems.

Table 12.1: Business categories in telecom.

Attribute	Mobile services			
	$49 Cap Plan	$49 Yes Plan	Business Plus 500MB	$129 Business Timeless Max
Monthly access fee	$49	$49	$79	$129
Total minimum cost	$1176	$1176	$1896	$3096
Standard national call rate	80c/min	25c/30sec		
Standard national call connection fee	35c	20c		
National video call	$1/min	50c/30sec		
Video call connection fee	35c	35c		
International video call		75c/30sec		
Standard national SMS	25c	25c		
Unlimited standard national SMS Offer			Unlimited	Unlimited
International SMS		50c		
Standard national MMS	25c	50c		
Unlimited standard national MMS offer			Unlimited	Unlimited
International MMS		75c		
Call2Anyone value offer	$330		$330	
On-net call value offer	$350		$350	
Unlimited standard local, national voice calls				Unlimited
Voice mail	Unlimited		Unlimited	Unlimited
Mobile data inclusions			500MB	4GB
Excess data usage			15c/MB	35c/MB
International value offer				$100
Smart voice mail		Optional		
Smart fleet	Optional	Included		
Business time	Optional			
Back to business		Included		
SmartRate		Included		
FleetShare		Included		

12.2   System Design and Development

This section first gives the system design and the methodology of the telecom product/service recommender system: SmartAdvisor-SMB. It then presents the recommendation methodology, which has six steps including the customers' requirement model and the products/services characteristics model.

12.2.1   *System design*

The SmartAdvisor-SMB was developed to automatically predict the behaviors and requirements of existing SMB customers so as to recommend suitable products/services to them, particularly when their service contracts are close to ending. It can be used by SMB customers to select appropriate telecom product/service packages through the internal customer care office or through an external website. The personalized recommendations generated from this system are mainly based on the SMB's product/service purchase history, usage patterns and business rules as well as similar SMB customers' profiles [Wu *et al.* (2010b)].

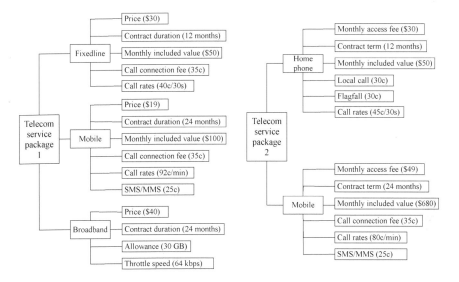

Fig. 12.1: Two examples of telecom product/service package

The development of this recommender system applies fuzzy measure/matching, content-based recommendation methodology and related business rules. In order to develop a prediction model and generate recommendations, classification and clustering are conducted on existing SMB customers through retrieving related customer profile data, attribute determination and feature selection. After that, a SMB customer view from existing SMB customer database is established and the requirements of SMB customer are mined from customer usage data. Also, tree structure presentation of products/services are proposed by analyzing the products/service database. Then, the fuzzy matching algorithms between SMB customer usage/requirements and products/services packages with consideration of marketing strategies are developed. Finally, these models and methods are implemented into the SmartAdvisor-SMB.

The framework of the SmartAdvisor-SMB is shown in Fig. 12.2. It constitutes three main components: data builder, recommendation engine and interface. The data builder component involves the development of three databases: a products/services database, a SMB customer profile database, and a SMB usage database. The recommendation engine generates recommendations by applying the fuzzy matching-based recommendation method. The Interface component communicates with customers and involves the collection of SMB customers' requirements and domain knowledge.

12.2.2 *Development methodology*

The Smartadvisor-SMB development was primarily based on the following methodology, which consists of six main steps:

Step 1: Classifying and clustering existing SMB customer data through retrieving and analyzing the SMB customer profile database.

The existing SMB customer profile database holds rich information such as customer name, customer account(s), current products/services used, contract duration, re-contract time, *etc.* Different from consumers, a SMB customer may have several accounts for taking several services, which makes the process more challenging. In order to identify a SMB customer's requirements and find similar SMB customers in such situations, this step needs to undertake classification, clustering and detailed data analysis in which business size, business location, business types are key features that require particular consideration.

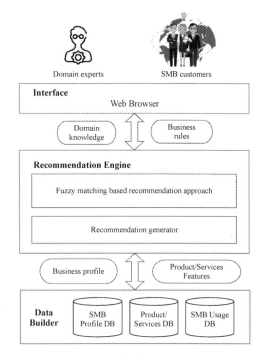

Fig. 12.2: A framework of telecom SMB product/service recommender system: SmartAdvisor-SMB.

Step 2: Classifying and analyzing telecom product/service data, possible packages/binds and business strategies.

To recommend a suitable product/service or package/bind to a SMB customer, we need to classify current products/services data. As seen from Table 12.1, different products/services are described by different attribute sets, and telecom products/services are composed of several sub-services. Different sub-services have different discounts and rewards for different usage situations. For example, some are suitable for a large amount of usage of local voice services while others are more suitable for a large amount of usage of email services. Therefore, these telecom products/services are characterized by the suitable usage amount of the sub-services. As some attributes of telecom products/services are described in linguistic terms, we have to represent the suitable usage amount of sub-services as linguistic terms (e.g. "Large"). This requires mapping between the attributes of the telecom products/services and the suitable amount of usages.

Attributes of all telecom products/services are analyzed and the relevant attribute set for each sub-service is identified. As an example, listed here are seven main sub-services:

S1 Standard local and national calls;
S2 Calls within the same billing account;
S3 International calls;
S4 Standard national SMS/MMS;
S5 International SMS/MMS;
S6 Email services;
S7 Internet browsing services.

Each sub-service contains one or more products/services. For example, the attributes related to "Standard national SMS/MMS (S4)" include "Standard national SMS/MMS rate", "Call2Anyone Value Offer", "On-net Call Value Offer" and "Unlimited Standard National SMS/MMS Offer" (see Table 12.1). For each sub-service, a business rule is defined to identify the suitable usage amount, based on the attribute set. For example, the rule for measuring the suitable usage amount of "Standard national SMS/MMS service" can be defined as:

if "Unlimited Standard National SMS/MMS Offer" is included, it is "Absolute Large";
else if "Call2Anyone Value Offer" and "On-net Call Value Offer" is included,
   if the sum of the two offers is larger than $1000, it is "Very Large";
   else it is "Large";
else it is "Small".

Through this approach, linguistic terms are used to more accurately describe the attributes of products/services. To support the recommendations, we also collected a set of business strategies, such as discount strategies, through data analysis.

Step 3: Modeling SMB customer product/service usage and requirements.

In this step, the feature selection is conducted for measuring the similarity between SMB customers. Some important features are identified, such as business size, business location, business types and received product/service type, which provide a basis to build up the recommendation framework for existing SMB customers. For each sub-service, a customer's requirements contain two aspects: the usage amount and the priority on the sub-service.

We can obtain information about SMBs' usage from their accounts and purchase database, such as how many hours every month are used by a SMB for international calls and how much data a SMB downloads every month. The usage information can reflect the characteristics of telecom products/services and be used to match with customers' requirements. The view structure of customers' usage records is usually constructed according to the sub-services. Table 12.2 is an example to list three different customer's usage records in one month. We also obtain similar customer's usages and the products/services they used. One difficulty, however, is that the customers' usage records are often described in tree structure. This will be discussed in the following sections.

Table 12.2: Usage record of three customers.

	Customer 1	Customer 2	Customer 3
Mobile service	$49 Yes Plan	Business Plus 500MB	Business Plus 500MB
Standard local and national calls	40min	620min	610min
Calls within the same billing account	680min	220min	270min
International calls	25min	20 min	
Standard national SMS/MMS	390	760	590
International SMS/MMS	24		
Email		450MB	410MB
Internet browsing		60MB	120MB

Another aspect of the requirements is the priority on the sub-service. In many situations, there may not by an existing telecom product/service that fully matches the customer's requirements. Therefore, we need to find out which requirement (such as international call) is the most important to the customer. This can be obtained through direct feedback from the customer and the customer's neighbors (i.e., similar SMBs). To do this we use similar SMBs' products/services usage data. Finally, by combining the SMB's usage analysis we form the SMB's requirements for the new contract period.

Step 4: Developing a linguistic term-based presentation for SMB customer usage/requirements.

In most real-world situations, it is hard to describe the usage/requirements precisely with exact numbers. We thus measure their usage/requirements by linguistic terms, such as "large amount", "small amount", *etc.* To describe the SMB usage/requirements, we define the linguistic terms. These are designed based on the analysis of the usage record database and the knowledge of domain experts, as well as SMB customer input. Table 12.3 is an example for mapping real SMB usage data to linguistic terms.

Table 12.3: Mapping from usage to linguistic description

Amount of usage (min)	Linguistic description
0	*Absolutely Small (AS)*
(0, 200]	*Very Small (VS)*
(200, 400]	*Small (S)*
(400, 600]	*Medium (M)*
(600, 800]	*Large (L)*
(800, 1000]	*Very Large (VL)*
> 1000	*Absolutely Large (AL)*

Step 5: Developing a fuzzy matching algorithm between SMB customer requirements and the company's products/services.

The matching algorithm to handling linguistic terms in the SMB requirements and product/service packages is based on fuzzy measure. Since it is almost impossible to find a telecom product/service that can fully match a customer's requirements, a fuzzy matching algorithm needs to be developed to find the best match. The customer's requirement priority needs to be fully considered in the matching process. This step uses user-based CF recommendation methods to help SMB customers making a choice and an item-based CF algorithm which is concerned with suggesting available new products/services since telecom company updated and replaced previously available products. The fuzzy matching algorithm details are described in the following section.

Step 6: Implementation of the proposed models and methods into a web-based telecom product/service recommendation system (SmartAdvisor-SMB).

12.3 Fuzzy Matching and Tree Matching-based Recommendation Method

We first introduce some notations, which are used to describe the fuzzy matching algorithm-based recommendation method.

- Let $U = \{u_1, u_2, \ldots, u_M\}$ be a user/customer set, M is the number of customers.
- Let $P = \{p_1, p_2, \ldots, p_N\}$ be a telecom product/service set, N is the number of products/services.
- Let $S = \{s_1, s_2, \ldots, s_T\}$ be a set of sub-services abstracted for describing the telecom products/service, T is the number of sub-services. In practical situations, the sub-services should be identified by domain experts. They can be updated as new products are continuously introduced. As described in the last section, seven main sub-services were selected: $\{S1, S2, \ldots, S7\}$.
- A linguistic term set R=$\{AS, VS, S, M, L, VL, AL\}$, which is to describe the products' service levels and users' requirements on a sub-service.
- A linguistic term set W= $\{Very\ Low\ (VL),\ Low\ (L),\ Medium\ Low\ (ML),\ Medium\ (M),\ Medium\ High\ (MH),\ High\ (H),\ Very\ High\ (VH)\}$, which is to describe users' priority on a sub-service.
- A product's linguistic characteristic vector LCV= $(c_1, c_2, \ldots, c_T)$, $c_i \in R$. c_i represents the service level on sub-service s_i. Here, $T = 7$. An example of four products' LCV is shown in Table 12.4.
- A linguistic customer requirement vector LRV= $(r_1, r_2, \ldots, r_T)$, $r_i \in R$, where r_i represents the a customer's requirements on sub-service s_i.
- A linguistic customer usage vector, LUV= $(u_1, u_2, \ldots, u_T)$, $u_i \in R$, where u_i represents the usage amount of a customer on sub-service s_i. Here, $T = 7$. As an example, the usage records of the three customers can be described as the following: $\text{LUV}_{u_1} = (VS, L, VS, S, VS, AS, AS)$, $\text{LUV}_{u_2} = (L, S, AS, VL, AS, M, VS)$, and $\text{LUV}_{u_3} = (L, S, AS, L, AS, M, S)$.
- A customer's linguistic weight vector LWV= $(w_1, w_2, \ldots, w_T)$, $w_i \in$

W, where w_i represents the customer's priority on sub-service s_i.

- Fuzzy numbers are applied to describe linguistic terms in R and W, which is shown in the Table 12.5.

Table 12.4: Four products' service levels by linguistic terms.

Services	Levels
$49 Cap Plan	(L, AL, VS, L, VS, VS, VS)
$49 Yes Plan	(S, AL, S, S, S, VS, VS)
Business Plus 500MB	(L, L, VS, AL, VS, M, M)
$129 Business Timeless Max	(AL, AL, L, AL, L, VL, VL)

Table 12.5: Linguistic terms and related fuzzy numbers.

R		W	
AS	$(0, 0, 0.1)$	VL	$(0, 0, 0.1)$
VS	$(0, 0.1, 0.3)$	VL	$(0, 0.1, 0.3)$
S	$(0.1, 0.3, 0.5)$	ML	$(0.1, 0.3, 0.5)$
M	$(0.3, 0.5, 0.7)$	M	$(0.3, 0.5, 0.7)$
L	$(0.5, 0.7, 0.6)$	MH	$(0.5, 0.7, 0.6)$
VL	$(0.7, 0.9, 1.0)$	H	$(0.7, 0.9, 1.0)$
AL	$(0.9, 1.0, 1.0)$	VH	$(0.9, 1.0, 1.0)$

There are N telecom products/services in the market: $\{p_1, p_2, \ldots, p_N\}$. Each telecom product/service p_i is described by a linguistic characteristic vector $\text{LCV}_i = (c_{i1}, c_{i2}, \ldots, c_{i7})$. For p_i, its users form a set $\mathcal{U}_i = \{u_{i,1}, u_{i,2}, \ldots, u_{i,m_i}\}$. For a SMB customer $u_{i,j}$, its usage record is described by a linguistic vector $\text{LUV}_{ij} = (u_{ij,1}, u_{ij,2}, \ldots, u_{ij,7})$. With the notations, a fuzzy matching-based recommendation method is presented with the following four steps.

Step 1: Capturing the requirements of a customer.

Customer requirements are described by a linguistic requirement vector $\text{LRV} = (r_1, r_2, \ldots, r_7)$ and a linguistic weight vector $\text{LWV} = (w_1, w_2, \ldots, w_7)$.

Step 2: Weights normalization.

Normalized weights on the sub-services are calculated based on $\text{LWV} = (w_1, w_2, \ldots, w_7)$, and are denoted as:

$$\widetilde{w}_k^* = \frac{\widetilde{w}_k}{\sum_{i=1}^7 w_{i,0}^R} \text{ for } k = 1, 2, \ldots, 7 \qquad (12.1)$$

where $w_{i,0}^R$ is the normalized weight of node p_i.

Step 3: Computing the products' matching degrees to the customer's requirements.

A fuzzy matching optimization problem needs to be solved here to find the best matched products. A matching degree, which is a fuzzy concept, is computed.

For a telecom product/service p_i, its matching degree to the customer's requirements is evaluated based on both LCV_i and all LUV_{ij}. The matching degree of p_i to a customer's requirements based on p_i's linguistic characteristic vector is calculated by the following equation:

$$\widetilde{m}_{c,i} = \sum_{j=1}^7 \widetilde{w}_j^* \cdot (1 - d\,(r_j, c_{ij})) \qquad (12.2)$$

where $d(\cdot)$ is the quasi-distance of two finite fuzzy numbers. $\widetilde{m}_{c,i}$ is normalized to be a positive fuzzy number, and its range belongs to closed interval $[0, 1]$. We define fuzzy positive-ideal solution (FPIS, m^*) and fuzzy negative-ideal solution (FNIS, m^-) as: $m^* = 1$ and $m^- = 0$ for item ranking.

The distance between $\widetilde{m}_{c,i}$ and m^* is called positive distance, and the distance between $\widetilde{m}_{c,i}$ and m^- is called negative distance. The two kinds of distances are calculated by $d_{c,i}^* = d\,(\widetilde{m}_{c,i}, m^*)$ and $d_{c,i}^- = d\,(\widetilde{m}_{c,i}, m^-)$ respectively, where $d(\cdot)$ is the quasi-distance of two finite fuzzy numbers. Then, to determine the ranking order of all telecom products/services, a closeness coefficient of p_i is defined based on its $d_{c,i}^*$ and $d_{c,i}^-$ as:

$$CC_{c,i} = \frac{1}{2}\left(d_{c,i}^- + \left(1 - d_{c,i}^*\right)\right) \qquad (12.3)$$

Considering p_i's customer usage records, the matching degree of $u_{i,j}$ to the potential customer's requirements is calculated by:

$$\widetilde{m}_{u,ij} = \sum_{k=1}^7 \widetilde{w}_k^* \cdot (1 - d\,(r_k, u_{ij,k})). \qquad (12.4)$$

Then a closeness coefficient of $u_{i,j}$ is defined as:

$$CC_{u,ij} = \frac{1}{2}\left(d_{u,ij}^- + \left(1 - d_{u,ij}^*\right)\right) \qquad (12.5)$$

where $d_{u,ij}^* = d\,(\widetilde{m}_{u,ij}, m^*)$ and $d_{u,ij}^- = d\,(\widetilde{m}_{u,ij}, m^-)$.

Considering all the customers using product p_i, $\mathcal{U}_i$, the closeness coefficient of p_i based on its customers $CC_{u,i}$, is defined as:

$$CC_{u,i} = \frac{1}{n_i} \sum_{j=1}^{n_i} CC_{u,ij}. \tag{12.6}$$

Finally, the closeness coefficient of the product pi is defined as:

$$CC_i = \alpha_1 \cdot CC_{c,i} + \alpha_2 \cdot CC_{u,i} \tag{12.7}$$

where α_1 and α_2 are weights of the two parts satisfying $\alpha_1 + \alpha_2 = 1$. If p_i is a new product, $\alpha_2 = 0$. Otherwise, α_1 and α_2 are defined depending on the analysis of the data and the knowledge of the domain experts.

Step 4: Generating recommendations.

Based on Eq. (12.7), the closeness coefficient of all the telecom products/services can be computed. k telecom products/services with the largest closeness coefficient are chosen to be recommended.

Although the proposed method can solve most of the recommendation requests, it is worth mentioning that sometimes the packages and user requirements are very complex and are described as tree structures. In Chapter 7, we had introduced tree structure matching techniques, including node matching and tree matching. These techniques have been used in related telecom product/service recommendation systems. In principle, the tree structure matching techniques have been used in the following two situations:

(1) Considering a telecom product package is an "item", it is used to find similar items as similar trees. As the case shown in Fig. 12.3, we constructed a matching algorithm to maximize correspondence tree mapping between two telecom product packages T_{p1} and T_{p2}, which is used for finding similar items.
(2) Matching customer usage/requirement (in tree structure) with the most suitable telecom product (also in tree structure). Fig. 12.3 and Fig. 12.4 are examples of matching customer (consumer) usage and telecom product packages.

The tree matching techniques are used to find the most suitable products/services for a customer based on their usage/requirement [Wu *et al.* (2013a)]. The products are represented as product trees and are shown in Fig. 12.3. The values in the leaf nodes are assigned as the linguistic terms discussed in last section and represent the service level of the specific sub-service that is represented by the

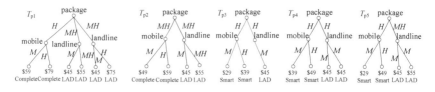

Fig. 12.3: Telecom product packages.

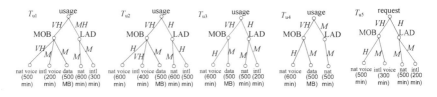

Fig. 12.4: User usage profiles or requests.

node. Customers' usage/requirement are described as usage/requirement trees, as shown in Fig. 12.4. The values in the leaf nodes represent the usage/requirement of the specific sub-service that is represented by the node. The conceptual similarity between the product tree and the user usage/requirement tree can be calculated by use of the tree similarity measure algorithm presented in Chapter 7. The maximum correspondence tree mapping between the product tree and the user usage/requirement can be constructed.

The value similarity between the linguistic terms of the product tree and the user usage/requirement tree can be calculated by the fuzzy matching measure in Chapter 7. The final matching degree between product tree and the user requirement tree is calculated as the weighted average of their conceptual and value similarities. The most suitable products for the customer are then obtained based on the matching degrees.

12.4   System Implementation

Consider the situation where a SMB customer's contract will expire in four weeks' time and the telecom sales office will automatically run the recommender system to recommend a new package based on the prediction of the SMB's requirements in the coming re-contracting period, which includes handsets, plans and extra telecom services. The SMB customer will log into the system homepage to see the generated recommendations.

The system will firstly get settings from the configuration file, which include parameters such as the number of neighbors and the number of items (telecom product/service packages) to be recommended. The system will then return a list of recommended packages to the customer for re-contracting.

Fig. 12.5 is a re-contracting page of the recommender system, which shows two telecom product/service contracts that contain a set of products/services with prices. If the SMB prefers recommendation 1, Fig. 12.6 presents some details of each telecom product/service. The recommendation will be highly based on the SMB's usage/requirements. If the customer would like to know more about of each service or to sign the contract, a draft contract in PDF is generated as well.

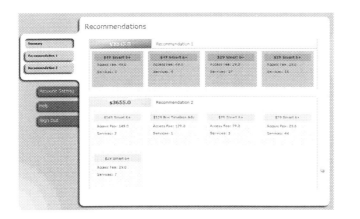

Fig. 12.5: Telecom product packages.

To generate recommendations, both the products' attributes and related customers' usage records are considered and learned comprehensively, which makes the recommendations more accurate and reliable. The system can be used in shops to conduct the customer "conversation" and across all customer touch points.

In recommender system development for new SMB or individual customers, since we have very limited data about them, in particular their usage data, the recommender systems need initially to ask the SMB or consumer customer some questions. The recommender systems will obtain their requirements through matching the answers with similar existing customers. The system will then match their requirements to the telecom products/services. The set of questions are designed to relate to the sub-services of telecom products/services.

Fig. 12.6: User usage profiles or requests.

12.5 Summary

A set of personalized telecom product/service recommendation systems for existing and potential SMB and individual customer have been developed respectively. These systems aim to support the telecom company guiding existing and potential SMB and individual customers in their selection of the most appropriate telecom products/services. This chapter mainly describes a recommender system, SmartAdvisor-SMB, which focuses on existing SMB customers. The development applied fuzzy measure, fuzzy matching tree similarity and content-based/CF recommendation methods. It can automatically predict the requirements of SMB customers and allows related SMB and consumer channels to use actual data about business customers' telecom usage to match against their existing product profile. Generating personalized recommendations and outlining relevant products/services to customers via the right channel, can support businesses by offering a real-time decision solution.

Chapter 13

Recommender System for Small and Medium-sized Businesses Finding Business Partners

Finding qualified business partners, both buyers and suppliers, is important for companies that are expanding their business, especially for new small and medium-sized businesses (SMBs). Providing SMBs suitable partners through a web system is also a core task of e-government services. The increasing online business development is creating information overload, which is makes businesses providing online e-services finding partners difficult. Personalized recommender system can assist the e-service. However, the differences in business models, market size and product categories can lead to both various and complex requirements for the SMB. This in turn makes it difficult for a recommender system to generate the right personalized recommendations about business partners. This chapter presents how a recommender system, called SmartBizSeeker, an advanced version of BizSeeker, is built for assisting SMBs to find personalized business partners.

In this chapter, first we introduce the background of recommender systems in e-government for SMBs in Section 13.1. The system design of the Smart-BizSeeker recommender system for SMBs is Section 13.2. In Section 13.3, we present a fuzzy tree-based recommendation method, which is implemented in the SmartBizSeeker system. This is followed by the system implementation and a case study of the proposed methods in Section 13.4. Finally, the chapter summary is provided in Section 13.5.

13.1 Background

E-government has become a global phenomenon with governments across the world using information technology to enhance their government's management and service processes. Adopting e-government offers not only benefits to governments and citizens, but also to businesses, particularly to SMBs. The service is called G2B e-service.

Businesses often use the web to search for business partners, buyers and providers, and to build new partnerships. Meanwhile, as the amount of information available on the web is overwhelming, searching for qualified business partners requires excessive amounts of time and effort, which sometimes turns out to be too costly, unreliable and risky [Lu *et al.* (2010)]. But searching for and selecting qualified business partners is one of the most vital services offered by e-government to SMBs, and is a core task. For example, The Australian Trade and Investment Commission (Austrade[1]), and Australian government agency, supports Australian export companies in buyer/partner identification and selection by searching overseas markets for relevant buyers/partners. However, due to its simplicity, low recall and imprecision, keyword query is not efficient and cannot satisfy the personalized needs of businesses [Lu *et al.* (2013)]. Recommender systems, as an effective method for the implementation of e-service personalization, are required to assist SMBs to find business partners [Wu *et al.* (2014b)].

Compared with other applications, the user profiles and items in the SMB recommender systems for finding business partners have very specific characteristics, which involve special recommendation methods and similarity measure requirements.

(1) The item descriptions and user preferences in recommender systems for the SMB are usually very complex, containing abundant semantic information. To make effective and accurate recommendations, methods to calculate semantic similarities between users and items need to be developed.
(2) The information of items or user profiles is often presented in tree structures, where nodes concepts, nodes values and nodes weights need to be defined and measured.
(3) In a real-world situation, the preferences of business users are usually vague and uncertain
(4) When making business partner recommendations to a business user, both supplier partners and buyer partners need to be considered.

---

[1] www.austrade.gov.au

To fulfill these special characteristics, a recommender system called BizSeeker has been developed to generate recommendations and assist the SMB to find business partners [Lu *et al.* (2010)]. In this system, products are represented as taxonomy trees and the similarities between items are calculated by a product semantic relevance model with the help of the relevance degree provided by domain experts. Based on the recommender system BizSeeker, an advanced version called SmartBizSeeker has been developed. This uses the tree similarity measure-based recommendation methods to represent the tree-structured products and to calculate similarities between them. In this chapter, we focus on SmartBizSeeker, since it is an advanced version.

In the BizSeeker/SmartBizSeeker, the "items" can be either potential supplier partners who supply products or potential buyer partners with specific buying requests; the "users" are businesses searching for partners. For example, business A needs to find product material providers; business B may supply related materials, and, business C may have interests in purchasing A's products. Now, the SmartBizSeeker aims to assist business A to find B and then C to find A among the many potential business candidates.

13.2   System Design and Development

In this section, the system architecture of SmartBizSeeker is presented. As a web-based online system, the SmartBizSeeker recommender system has a standard multi-tier architecture, which includes a web browser, a web server and a database server. The web browser is the user interface for users to actively access the system. When a user visits the website of SmartBizSeeker, the web browser sends requests to the web server every time the user performs an action such as logging in or visiting a new page. When the web server receives the requests, it retrieves the requested resources and sends them back to the web browser. The web site and application are hosted in the web server, which provides business partner recommendation services and other relevant services. The SmartBizSeeker system can be divided into three layers: the presentation layer, the business logic layer and the data access layer. The databases of the system are maintained in the database server.

This business partner recommender system, as depicted in Fig. 13.1, is designed to be used by business users, with a system administrator in charge of the system maintaining the product categories and business categories and managing the recommendation algorithms and related parameters. Business users can register a business into the system; manage the profile of the business and input into the system its products and buying requests; seek and search for potential business partners (buyers and suppliers) and receive recommendations on their suitability; and give feedback and rate the recommended partners.

The main components of the SmartBizSeeker recommender system are described in detail as follows.

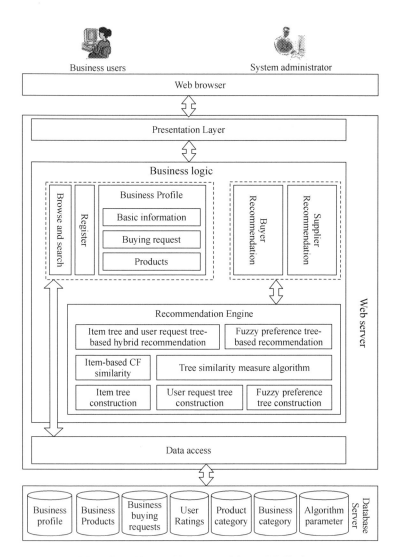

Fig. 13.1: The architecture of SmartBizSeeker.

13.2.1 *Databases*

The database stores all the data of the recommender system, which includes the following main components:

(1) Business profiles: stores the basic information of businesses registered in the recommender system, such as business name, business category, scale and contact information.
(2) Business products: stores the products and their detailed features provided by each business.
(3) Business buying requests: stores the product categories and products required by each business.
(4) User ratings: stores the two types of business user ratings to their business partners – the ratings to buyer partners and the ratings to supplier partners.
(5) Product category: maintains the hierarchical structured product categories.
(6) Business category: maintains the hierarchical structured business categories.
(7) Algorithm parameter: maintains the parameters used in the recommendation algorithms.

13.2.2 *Web application component*

The application in the web server contains three layers: the presentation layer, the business logic layer and the data access layer.

(1) Presentation layer. This layer is responsible for generating the requested web pages and handling the user interface logics and events. When a user requests to view a new page, the presentation layer will invoke corresponding methods in the business logic layer, extract the request data, transform the data into an HTML page and send it back to the client.
(2) Business logic layer. The business logic layer defines the business processes and functions of the application, and serves as a mediator between the presentation layer and the recommendation engine and the data access layer. It provides the following main functionalities:

   (a) Browse and search: This function concerns the user's ability to browse the potential business partners' profiles and their products/buying requests, or search potential business partners and products/buying requests based on the keyword-based search engine, and then to view the matching results.
   (b) Register: This function supports new business users to register on the system.
   (c) Business profile management: The business profile management module

collects the basic information, the supplied product information, and the buying request information of the business user. Users can modify, add and delete collected information through this module.

(d) Buyer recommendation: This module calls the recommendation engine to generate buyer partner recommendations to the business user and passes the recommendation list to the user. Users' comments and ratings of the buyer partner recommendation results are also collected through the module.

(e) Supplier recommendation: This module calls the recommendation engine to generate supplier partner recommendations to the business user and passes the recommendation list to the user. Users' comments and ratings to the supplier partner recommendation results are also collected.

(f) Recommendation engine: The recommendation engine implements the proposed item tree and user-request tree-based hybrid recommendation method and the fuzzy preference tree-based recommendation method introduced in Chapter 5. It generates a recommendation list of potential business partners, buyers or suppliers, according to the user's requirement.

(3) Data access layer. The data access layer provides the interfaces to access the data in the database. It deals with the data operations of the database and transfers data with the business logic layer.

13.3 Tree-based Recommendation Methods in SmartBizSeeker

As we mentioned before, items and users are often described in complicated tree structures and contain various uncertainties. Therefore, it requests tree-based and fuzzy hybrid recommendation method. The recommendation engine in SmartBizSeeker implements the proposed item tree and user-request tree-based hybrid recommendation method and the fuzzy preference tree-based recommendation method in Chapter 7. A recommendation list of potential business partners (buyers or suppliers) is generated according to the user's requirement. The main components in the recommendation engine are described as follows:

(1) Tree similarity measure algorithm.
   This component implements the tree similarity measure computation algorithms. It provides not only the interface to calculate the similarity measure between two tree-structured data, but also the interface to generate the maximum conceptual similarity tree mapping between tree-structured data.
(2) Item-based CF similarity.

This component computes the item-based CF similarity between two items based on the user-item rating matrix, which is used in the item tree and user-request tree-based hybrid recommendation method in Section 7.2.

(3) Item tree construction.

This component constructs products or buying requests of a business in tree structures, as shown in Fig. 13.2. The tree node attributes and values are assigned according to the user-request tree definitions in Chapter 7. The potential suppliers' product and the potential buyers' buying request will be constructed as the item trees.

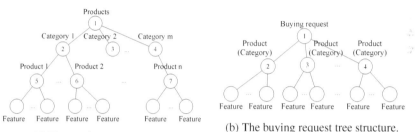

(a) The product tree structure.

(b) The buying request tree structure.

Fig. 13.2: Tree structures in SmartBizSeeker.

(4) User-request tree construction.

This component constructs user-request trees, as shown in Fig. 13.2. The tree node attributes and values are assigned according to the user-request tree definitions in Chapter 7. The business buying request and their product will be constructed as the user-request trees.

(5) Fuzzy preference tree construction.

This component implements the fuzzy preference tree construction algorithm and constructs the fuzzy preference tree for the user. When recommending suppliers, the user's fuzzy preference tree is constructed by merging the user's buying request and the product trees of businesses rated by the user. When recommending buyers, the user's fuzzy preference tree is constructed by merging the user's product tree and the buying requirement trees of businesses rated by the user.

(6) Item tree and user-request tree-based hybrid recommendation.

This method uses the semantic information of tree-structured items and users with the requirement matching knowledge, and takes advantage of the merits of CF-based recommendation methods as introduced in Section 7.2.

(7) Fuzzy preference tree-based recommendation.

This method takes a user's fuzzy preference tree and an item tree as input, and calculates the predicted rating as introduced in Section 7.3.

13.4 Implementation and Prototype

We introduce the system implementation in two parts: system implementation and visualization implementation.

(1) Implementation of the system

The system is developed and implemented using the Netbeans development platform. JSF, EJB and JPA frameworks are used in the implementation of the presentation layer, business logic layer and data access layer respectively. The site map of SmartBizSeeker is shown in Fig. 13.3.

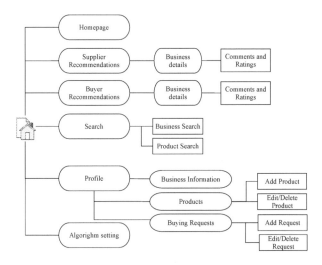

Fig. 13.3: The SmartBizSeeker site map.

The database is designed and implemented in the PostgreSQL database server. Tables are designed and created to store the entities described as requirements in Section 13.1. To evaluate the semantic similarity between products effectively, the product category must be maintained in the system. To infer the semantic relations between businesses, the business category must be provided. In the SmartBizSeeker recommender system, the business category follows the existing categorization used by Austrade. A two-level product category is also constructed according to the classification of industry classes by Austrade. Part of the product category is shown in Table 13.1.

Table 13.1: Product categories in SmartBizSeeker.

Product Category	Product sub-category	Product Category	Product sub-category
Food	Pastry	Drink	Wine
	Roll		Beer
	Sandwich		Spirit
	Pizza		Cider
	Quiche		Soft drink
	Muffin		Juice
	Cake		Coffee
	Tart		Milk
	Cookie	Fruit&Veg	Apple
	Noodles		Pear
	Bread		Grape
	Pie		Vegetable
Meat	Beef		Orange
	Chicken		Banana
	Lamb		Avocado
	Sausage		Watermelon
	Pork	...	...

To test the recommender system, it is deployed in the Glassfish web server. We give an example to illustrate how the SmartBizSeeker works: a wine company called "Laurance Wines Company" would like to find buyer partners and material suppliers by use of the SmartBizSeeker recommender system.

After logging onto the system, the company can manage its business profile through the profile management module, as shown in Fig. 13.4 (a). The company produces ciders and red wines, and needs apples, grapes and some other fruits as materials. The product and buying request are in tree-structured data. The products of the company can be enter into the system through the product management page, as shown in Fig. 13.4 (b). The company can specify its buying requests for particular products or product categories if it is looking for suitable supplier partners, as shown in Fig. 13.4 (c). At the same time, the information is also used so that the company can be recommended to other companies, which is very helpful to expand businesses. In the supplier recommendation page, a list of fruit providers is recommended. At the same time, in the buyer recommendation page, a list of bottle shops and hotels that might want to buy products from this company are recommended to "Laurance Wines Company", as shown in Fig. 13.5.

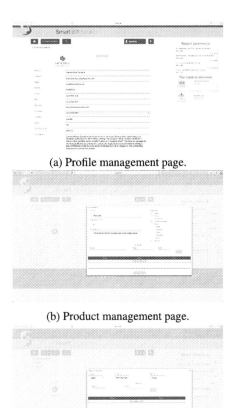

(a) Profile management page.

(b) Product management page.

(c) Buying request management page.

Fig. 13.4: Management pages in SmartBizseeker.

(2) Implementation of visualization

It is quite important to point that most recommendation methods implemented in SmartBizSeeker are neighbor-based methods containing two main procedures. The first procedure, for a specific active user (business), is to identify similar businesses. The second procedure is to predict the unknown ratings according to similarity results and select top-N recommendations. The module constructs two sub-modules: a traceable hierarchical visualization module to illustrate the predicting procedure and a similarity visualization module to show the similarity evaluating procedure.

Fig. 13.5: The supplier and buyer recommendation page.

(a) Hierarchical visualization module

This module consists of two levels: profile level and recommendation level. Every node in the profile level represents a preferred business and every node in recommendation level represents a recommended supplier/buyer business. Similar to the group visualization in Chapter 11, PN level and RN level construct a two-level hierarchical graph. A profile rating for a business is represented as a PN where the radius of the node represents the mean of all the specified ratings on that business; a recommendation is represented as a RN where the radius of the node represents the prediction for it. The two levels are represented as two lines. The recommendation line is at the top and the profile line is at the bottom. An example of traceable hierarchical visualization is shown in Fig. 13.6 (a). The recommendations are generated for North Strathfield Cellars. In this example, the user has rated three businesses and obtain four recommendations.

More information including business information and corresponding rating is designed to displayed when the cursor is moving over the business nodes as shown in Fig. 13.6 (a). The historical rating of rated businesses or predictions of the recommendation are also shown in floating information. Because the radius of business node is determined by the rating, node for recommendation "IronBark Hill Vineyard" is little larger than "Sopranos Gourmet Pizza and Pasta". It is important to note that the distance between two points does not represent the similarity between them.

PN-NN edges and NN-RN edges are combined as PN-RN edges to describe the entire recommender process. Links for PN-RN edges are utilized to illustrate

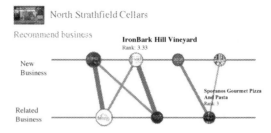

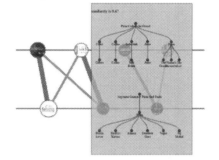

(a) An example on traceable hierarchical visualization.

(b) An example for tree similarity visualization.

Fig. 13.6: Example on data visualization.

the degree of similar between recommendations and profile businesses. A link is wider when the similarity is higher. Using these links, users can have an intuitive understanding of how the recommendation provided is connected with their historical records.

(b) Similarity visualization module

To calculate recommendations, relations between businesses, i.e. similarity measures, play an important role. The similarity visualization module is designed for demonstrating the relevance between two businesses. In SmartBizSeeker, many similarity measures are implemented including PCC, cosine, trust and their variations. There are great differences in the calculations that cause no uniform design for explanation. Hence, similarity visualization designs different layouts for them and an example for fuzzy product tree similarity is given.

In Fig. 13.6 (b), when the mouse is moved over an edge, a floating layer is displayed. In this layer, the similarity calculation result is shown at top left corner. The user preference tree of North Strathfield Cellars and the recommended business are all presented to give an intuitive comparison between the two companies.

13.5 Summary

This chapter presents a business finding partner recommender system, called SmartBizSeeker, which aims to assist SMB users to effectively select the right business partners (both buyers and suppliers, e.g. international buyers, distributors, and retailers) that match their business needs. The aim of the BizSeeker recommender system, as the first version, is to effectively recommend the business partners based on their requirements and business product categories. The proposed SmartBizSeeker utilizes the item tree and user-request tree-based hybrid recommendation method developed in Chapter 7 to deal with the tree-structured data and users' fuzzy preferences in business partner recommendation applications. Recommendation visualization is also implemented in the SmartBizSeeker.

Chapter 14

Recommender System for Personalized E-learning

The rapid growth of e-learning systems has changed traditional learning behaviors and provided new opportunities to both learners (students) and teachers. Due to the increasing learning activities caused by e-learning market expansion, the e-learning recommender systems have been developed to deliver personalized learning services to learners. The learners' needs may vary depending on their educational background and occupation, while the learning activities may include individual subjects or topics, whole courses; accessing learning materials and resources; *etc*. In an e-learning recommender system, learners are the "users" and learning activities are the "items". Both learner profiles and learning activities have complex structures and contain various uncertainties. Also, the e-learning recommender systems need to deal with precedence relations between various learning activities. Therefore, fuzzy tree-based models are used in the e-learning recommender system. This chapter will present how an e-learning recommender system, called LESS, is built for personalized services to learners.

In this chapter, first we introduce the background of e-learning recommender system in Section 14.1. The system design of LESS is presented in Section 14.2. In Section 14.3, we present the fuzzy tree-based recommendation method, which is implemented in the LESS system, followed by the system implementation and a case study in Section 14.4. Finally, a summary of the chapter is provided in Section 14.5.

14.1 Background

E-learning systems fit into the ever-changing and challenging situations, where learners need new knowledge to stay competitive or achieve success. The e-learning market had expanded to $107 Billion in 2015 and according to Forbes[1] will expand to $325 by 2025. The rapid growth of e-learning systems has greatly supported and enhanced learning practices online. Due to the emergence of numerous kinds of learning activities in the e-learning environment, learners find it difficult to select the learning activities that best meet their criteria. Therefore, it is imperative for an e-learning system to automatically generate personalized recommendations to guide the learners through the selection process. A personalized recommender system can assist online learners to choose the most suitable courses/subjects and learning materials as well as other learning activities in an e-learning environment [Lu (2004)].

E-learning systems can be divided into two types according to their application environments: a formal setting and an informal setting [Salehi and Kamalabadi (2013)]. A formal setting e-learning system includes learning offers from educational institutions (e.g. universities, schools) within a curriculum or syllabus. An informal setting is described as a learning phase of so-called lifelong learners who are responsible for their own learning pace and whose learning are often self-directed.

E-learning recommender systems have been proposed and applied in practice to support various e-learners. For example, a personalized e-learning material recommender system framework is proposed in [Lu (2004)]. In this framework, a multi-criteria student requirement analysis model is developed to identify a student's requirements; and a fuzzy matching method is used to deal with the uncertain criteria values in real-life situations. The CF recommendation method was adapted to be used in an e-learning context by considering the learners' knowledge levels. Also, attributes of materials are considered in content-based and hybrid recommendation methods.

In comparison with other application domains, e-learning activities have their own special characteristics [Drachsler *et al.* (2008)], which involve special requirements for recommendation methods and similarity measures as listed below:

(1) Both learning activities and learner profiles are presented as tree-structured data. Learning activities contain several aspects of information, such as the subject content description, lecture information and prerequisite information,

---

[1] www.forbes.com

while a learner profile contains the learner's background, learning goals, prior knowledge, learner characteristics and so on. Each aspect of information can be described in detail with several sub-aspects.

(2) Learning activities and learner profiles always contain vague and uncertain data. A learning activity may fall into several categories. For example, the subject "Business Intelligence" is mainly used in the information technology area, but also used in the business area. A learner's requirements are usually described in linguistic terms such as "highly required".

(3) The precedence relations between learning activities need to be considered. Some learning activities require prerequisite subjects/courses. For example, studying the subject "Data Mining" requires the prerequisite subject "Database".

To fulfill the above characteristics, we will present a personalized e-LEarning recommender SyStem (LESS) by using fuzzy tree-structure based recommendation techniques [Wu *et al.* (2015)].

14.2   System Design and Development

The architecture of the e-learning recommender system is shown in Fig. 14.1. Students/learners are the users of the LESS system. They search appropriate learning activities and receive personalized recommendations. They may provide related background information and learning requirements when registering in the system. Teachers are responsible for managing the learning activities, and it is the teachers who input the learning activities with detailed descriptions and categories into the system. A system administrator maintains the learning activity categories and the possible career list of learners, which are used to support the operation of the system.

As a web-based online system, LESS has a standard multi-tier architecture that includes a web browser, web server, and database server. The main components of the system are described as follows.

14.2.1   *Databases*

The database stores all the data of the system, which includes the following main components:

(1) Learning activities: the information of each learning activity, which is used to construct the learning activity tree.

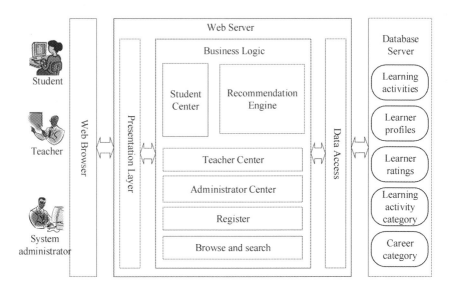

Fig. 14.1: The architecture of the e-learning recommender system LESS.

(2) Learner profiles: the profile of each learner, which is used to construct the learner profile tree.
(3) Learner ratings: the learners' ratings to their learned learning activities.
(4) Learner activity category: maintains the tree-structured learning activity categories.
(5) Career category: maintains the career list of learners.

14.2.2 *Web application component*

The application in the web server contains three layers: the presentation layer, the business logic layer and the data access layer.

(1) Presentation layer: is responsible for generating the requested web pages and handling the user interface logic and events for the three kinds of users.
(2) Business logic layer: realizes the learning services and the core recommendation algorithm. It provides the following main functionalities:

    (a) Browse and search: based on a keyword-based search engine, supports learners both browse to find appropriate learning activities and search the learning activities, and then to view the matching results.

    (b) Register: supports new users during the registration process in LESS.

    (c) Administrator center: used by administrators to manage the users and common data.

(d) Teacher center: supports teachers when inputing and managing the learning activities.

(e) Student center: collects the learner's profiles and requirements; tracks the user's learning behavior; and calls the recommendation engine to generate learning activity recommendations. Learners' ratings to the recommendation results are also collected.

(f) Recommendation engine: implements the proposed recommendation method and generates recommendations for student users.

(3) Data access layer: deals with the data operations of the database.

14.3   Tree-based Recommendation Method for E-learning

In this section, we firstly introduce the definition and similarity calculation for the learning activity tree and the learning profile tree. Then, based on both these models, we present a tree-based recommendation method for learning activities.

14.3.1   *Learning activity tree*

A learning activity tree is defined based on the fuzzy tree-structured data model (introduced in Section 7.3) to describe the learning activities in LESS. The structure of a learning activity tree is illustrated in Fig. 14.2. A learning activity is composed of multiple definitions, such as the prerequisite subjects/courses, its categories, and the content and the lecturer; and some features may be several sub-features, which form a tree structure.

(1) Node concept of the learning activity tree

In the learning activity tree, each node is assigned a label attribute, as shown in Fig. 14.2 (a). Some nodes are assigned a category attribute. The node concept similarity is calculated based on the two attributes. If two nodes are both assigned category, the category similarity is taken as the node concept similarity. Otherwise, their labels are compared. In a real-world situation, one learning activity may belong to several categories with different degrees. Therefore, the value of a category is a fuzzy category tree in the system.

The learning activity category, as shown in Fig. 14.2 (b), has three levels. Level 1 is the root node. On level 2, there are six general categories, which are "IT/Computer Science", "Nature Science", "Humanities/Social Sciences", "Business", "Engineering/Technology", and "Medicine/Health". Each category on level 2 is divided into several sub-categories at level 3. For example, the "IT/Computer Science" category is divided into four sub-categories, which are "Internet", "Software", "Hardware", and "Business Intelligence".

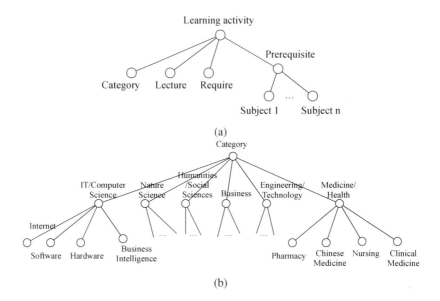

Fig. 14.2: The structures of a learning activity tree and a learning activity category tree.

(2) Fuzzy category tree

In a real-life situation, one learning activity may belong to several categories with different degrees. Therefore, the value of a category is a fuzzy category tree in the system, which is defined as:

Definition 14.1 (Fuzzy category tree). A fuzzy category tree of a learning activity represents the categories the learning activity belongs to, which is a sub-tree of the learning activity category tree. The nodes of the fuzzy category tree are assigned category values, which represent the membership degrees of the learning activity belonging to the relevant sub-categories.

Two examples of fuzzy category tree are shown in Fig. 14.3. The subject "Business Intelligence" is under the categories "Business Intelligence", "Software", "Marketing", and "Management" with different membership degrees, as shown in Fig. 14.3 (a). The number under each sub-category represents the membership degree of the subject that belongs to the sub-category. The sub-categories and corresponding membership degrees are specified by the learning activity providers when they insert the learning activities into the system.

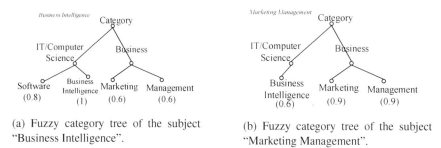

(a) Fuzzy category tree of the subject "Business Intelligence".

(b) Fuzzy category tree of the subject "Marketing Management".

Fig. 14.3: Two examples of fuzzy category tree.

Recall that trees and nodes are represented with the following symbols. Let $t[i]$ be the ith node of the tree T in the given numbering, $T[i]$ is the sub-tree rooted at $t[i]$ and $F[i]$ be the unordered forest obtained by deleting $t[i]$ from $T[i]$. Let $t[i_1], t[i_2], \ldots, t[i_{n_i}]$ represent the children of $t[i]$.

Let $v_c(t[i])$ represents the category value of node $t[i]$. If a learning activity does not belong to the sub-category represented by node $t[i]$, then $v_c(t[i]) = 0$. The category value of $T[i]$, the sub-tree under the node $t[i]$ can be inferred from the category values of nodes in the sub-tree $T[i]$, which is calculated by:

$$v_c(T[i]) = \begin{cases} v_c(t[i]), & F[i] = \emptyset, \\ (\bigvee_{j=1}^{n_i} v_c(T[i_j])) \vee v_c(t[i]), & F[i] \neq \emptyset. \end{cases} \tag{14.1}$$

Similarly, the category value of the forest $F[i]$ can be defined, and calculated by:

$$v_c(F[i]) = \begin{cases} 0, & F[i] = \emptyset, \\ \bigvee_{j=1}^{n_i} v_c(T[i_j]), & F[i] \neq \emptyset. \end{cases} \tag{14.2}$$

The category value of the sub-tree $T[i]$ or the forest $F[i]$ will be 0, if the learning activity is not relevant to the categories under the sub-tree $T[i]$ or the forest $F[i]$.

(3) Fuzzy category similarity

To measure the similarity between categories, which are represented as fuzzy category trees, is a necessary step in order to generate recommendations.

To evaluate the similarity between two fuzzy category trees, the values of all nodes must be taken into account. Let $T_1[i]$ and $T_2[i]$ represent two fuzzy category trees of two learning activities a_1 and a_2, respectively. According to Definition 14.1, four properties of the fuzzy category trees must be considered for similarity calculation: (1) the structures of $T_1[i]$ and $T_2[i]$ are the same as they are based on the same category tree; (2) only the sub-trees with positive category values need to be considered when calculating the similarity as the sub-trees with zero category values are not relevant; (3) the category values may be assigned to nodes at different levels; (4) category values in different levels present different weights. According to the conditions whether the children of $t_1[i]$ and $t_2[i]$ are assigned positive values or zero, four situations are considered in the similarity measure formula. The fuzzy category similarity between $T_1[i]$ and $T_2[i]$ is calculated as:

$$S_{\text{fc}}(T_1[i], T_2[i]) = \begin{cases} v_c(t_1[i]) \wedge v_c(t_2[i]), \ v_c(F_1[i]) = 0, v_c(F_2[i]) = 0, \\ v_c(t_1[i]) \wedge v_c(T_2[i]), \ v_c(F_1[i]) = 0, v_c(F_2[i]) \neq 0, \\ v_c(T_1[i]) \wedge v_c(t_2[i]), \ v_c(F_1[i]) \neq 0, v_c(F_2[i]) = 0, \\ (\alpha^{h-d_i} - \alpha^h) \cdot v_c(T_1[i]) \wedge v_c(T_2[i]) \\ + (1 - \alpha^{h-d_i} + \alpha^h) \cdot (\bigvee_{j=1}^{n_i} S_{\text{fc}}(T_1[i], T_2[i])), \\ \qquad\qquad v_c(F_1[i]) \neq 0, v_c(F_2[i]) \neq 0. \end{cases}$$
(14.3)

where α is the influence factor of the parent node, h is the height of the learning category tree, and d_i is the depth of node i in the category tree. In the first situation, $v_c(F_1[i]) = 0$ and $v_c(F_2[i]) = 0$ which means that $t_1[i]$ and $t_2[i]$ have no children nodes or their children nodes are not assigned positive values. Therefore, only the values of $t_1[i]$ and $t_2[i]$ are considered. In the second situation, $t_1[i]$ has no children or its children nodes are not assigned positive values. Thus, the two trees $T_1[i]$ and $T_2[i]$ can only be compared at the level of $t_1[i]$. The third situation is similar to the second one. In the fourth situation, the children of both $t_1[i]$ and $t_2[i]$ are assigned positive values. Therefore, the lower levels of $t_1[i]$ and $t_2[i]$ should also be compared. As the categories in the lower level are more specific, the lower level should gain more weight in the similarity measure. The coefficient α^{h-d_i} in Eq. (14.3) reflects the point. To guarantee that the similarity between different general categories be 0, α^h is subtracted from α^{h-d_i}.

Take two subjects, "Business Intelligence" and "Marketing Management" illustrated in Fig. 14.3, as examples. Let α be 0.5. In the example, $h = 2$. $s_{\text{fc}}(T_a[4], T_b[4]) = 0$, $s_{\text{fc}}(T_a[5], T_b[5]) = 0.6$, $v_c(T_a[2]) = v_c(T_a[4]) \vee v_c(T_a[5]) = 1$, $v_c(T_b[2]) = 0.6$, $s_{\text{fc}}(T_a[2], T_b[2]) = (\alpha^{h-1} - \alpha^h) \cdot (v_c(T_a[2]) \wedge v_c(T_b[2])) + (1 - \alpha^{h-1} + \alpha^h)(s_{\text{fc}}(T_a[4], T_b[4]) \vee s_{\text{fc}}(T_a[5], T_b[5])) = 0.6$. Similarly, $s_{\text{fc}}(T_a[3], T_b[3]) = 0.6$. The fuzzy category similarity between these two subjects is calculated as $s_{\text{fc}}(T_a[1], T_b[1]) = s_{\text{fc}}(T_a[2], T_b[2]) \vee s_{\text{fc}}(T_a[3], T_b[3]) = 0.6$.

In practice, there are times when the fuzzy category trees need to be combined.

For example, a learner has completed several learning activities. To examine the categories learned by the learner comprehensively, the categories of all the learning activities learned by the user should be combined. A fuzzy category tree combination procedure $combine(\cdot)$ is presented. Fig. 14.4 is the combination tree of two fuzzy category trees in Fig. 14.3. Let $S_{T_c} = \{T_1[i], T_2[i], \ldots, T_m[i]\}$ represent a set of fuzzy category trees. The combination of the fuzzy category trees in S_{T_c} is denoted as $combine(S_{T_c})$. For each node $t_c[j]$ in $T_c[i]$, $v_c(t_c[j]) = \bigvee_{k=1}^{m} v_c(t_k[j])$.

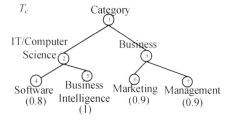

Fig. 14.4: The combination of two fuzzy category trees in Fig. 14.3.

(4) The pedagogical relations between learning activities

In the learning activity recommendation, the learning process, which is concerned with repeatability, periodicity and some dependency relations, must be considered [Salehi and Kamalabadi (2013)]. Recommended learning activities must be new or have a level slightly above the learner's current competence level. For some learning activities with similar contents, or under the similar categories, it is not reasonable to recommend the elementary activities to a learner if he/she has already learned some advanced activities.

The LESS considers two kinds of precedence relations between learning activities. The first kind of precedence relations are derived from the prerequisites of learning activities. These prerequisite learning activities are specified for the learning activity and described in the learning activity trees. The second kind of precedence relations are derived from learning sequences in learner's learning history. These learning sequences can be used to infer the advanced levels of learning activities, which are difficult to identify due to the open environment in the informal learning setting. Some sequential feature factors are defined as follows to identify the sequential relations between learning activities from the learning sequences.

For a learning activity a learned by a learner u, there is a starting time t_s

and a finishing time t_f. Obviously, $t_s(a) < t_f(a)$. Let a_1 and a_2 be two learning activities which are both learned by a learner. According to Allen's interval algebra [Allen (1983)], there are thirteen temporal relations between a_1 and a_2. Here, only the precedence relations are concerned. The following three sequential relations are considered: (1) a_1 is prior to a_2, denoted as $a_1 \rightarrow a_2$, if $t_f(a_1) \leq t_s(a_2)$; (2) a_2 is prior to a_1, denoted as $a_2 \rightarrow a_1$, if $t_f(a_2) \leq t_s(a_1)$; (3) a_1 and a_2 are concurrent, if $t_s(a_1) < t_f(a_2)$ and $t_s(a_2) < t_f(a_1)$. In the learning history, the relevant learning times of the learning activities for each learner are recorded.

To analyze the sequential relations between learning activities from the whole learner's learning histories, the following coefficients are defined. Let the support of a learning activity set L, $support(L)$, be defined as the percentage of the learners who learned all the activities in L in all learners. $support(a_1, a_2)$ represents the proportion of learners who learned both a_1 and a_2. $support(a_1 \rightarrow a_2)$ represents the proportion of learners who learned a_1 before a_2. A prior relation confidence coefficient is defined as:

$$\mathrm{priorc}(a_1 \rightarrow a_2) = \frac{support(a_1 \rightarrow a_2)}{support(a_1, a_2)}. \tag{14.4}$$

When learning activities a_1 and a_2 satisfy a minimum prior relation confidence and a minimum support threshold, i.e. $\mathrm{priorc}(a_1 \rightarrow a_2) > \mathrm{priorc}_{\mathrm{thre}}$ and $support(a_1, a_2) > support_{\mathrm{thre}}$, it indicates that there is a dependency relation between a_1 and a_2, and a_1 is usually learned before a_2. If a learner has learned a_2, it is not suitable to recommend a_1 to him/her. A sequence set S_{prior} is used to record these relations. S_{prior} is constructed offline periodically.

14.3.2 *Learner profile tree*

In the learner profile, the learned activities are recorded by the system during the learning process. Other information, such as the learner's background, planned career and required learning categories, are specified by the learner when the learner registers. In particular, the planned career is selected from a predefined career list, such as software engineer, developer programmer, *etc.* The requirements are usually uncertain and described in linguistic terms, therefore they are represented as fuzzy required category trees as shown in Fig. 14.5.

(1) Node concept of the learner profile tree

Similar to the learning activity tree, the learner profile tree nodes are assigned a label attribute and a category attribute, which are used to calculate the node concept similarity.

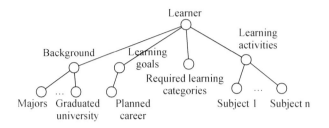

Fig. 14.5: The structure of a learner profile tree.

A linguistic term set $R = \{$*Very Low Required (VLR), Low Required (LR), Medium Required (MR), High Required (HR), Very High Required (VHR)*$\}$ is defined for learners to express their requirements for a specific learning category. To handle these linguistic terms in the recommendation calculation process, fuzzy numbers are applied as shown in Table 14.1.

Table 14.1: Linguistic terms and related fuzzy numbers for learner requirements.

Linguistic terms	Triangular fuzzy numbers
Very Low Required (VLR)	(0, 0, 0.25)
Low Required (LR)	(0, 0.25, 0.5)
Medium Required (MR)	(0.25, 0.5, 0.75)
High Required (HR)	(0.5, 0.75, 1)
Very High Required (VHR)	(0.75, 1, 1)

Two examples of fuzzy required category trees are shown in Fig. 14.6. The linguistic terms under the nodes represent the learner's requirement. It can be seen from the examples that learners' requirements can be specified at different levels. For each branch of the tree, only one node is assigned to the user's requirement.

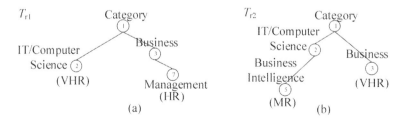

Fig. 14.6: Two fuzzy required category trees.

(2) Similarity measure for fuzzy required category tree

We introduce two similarity calculations for fuzzy required category tree. One is the similarity between two learners' fuzzy required category trees, which is to assist to compare the two learners. The other is the matching similarity of a learning activity's fuzzy category tree to a learner's fuzzy required category tree, which is to help select proper learning activities.

Let T_{r1} and T_{r2} be two fuzzy required category trees. Because learners' fuzzy required category trees are based on the learning activity category tree, T_{r1} and T_{r2} have the same base structure and labels. We use the numbering of the learning activity category tree to represent the nodes in T_{r1} and T_{r2}. The fuzzy required category similarity between T_{r1} and T_{r2} is calculated by:

$$S_{\text{frc}}(T_{r1}[i], T_{r2}[i]) = \begin{cases} S_v(v_r(t_{r1}[i]), v_r(t_{r2}[i])), & v_r(F_{r1}[i]) = 0, v_r(F_{r2}[i]) = 0, \\ S_v(v_r(t_{r1}[i]), v_r(T_{r2}[i])), & v_r(F_{r1}[i]) = 0, v_r(F_{r2}[i]) \neq 0, \\ S_v(v_r(T_{r1}[i]), v_r(t_{r2}[i])), & v_r(F_{r1}[i]) \neq 0, v_r(F_{r2}[i]) = 0, \\ (\alpha^{h-d_i} - \alpha^h) \cdot S_v(v_r(T_{r1}[i]), v_r(T_{r2}[i])) \\ + (1 - \alpha^{h-d_i} + \alpha^h) \cdot (\sum_{j=1}^{n_i} w_j \cdot S_{\text{frc}}(T_{r1}[i], T_{r2}[i])), \\ \qquad\qquad v_c(F_1[i]) \neq 0, v_c(F_2[i]) \neq 0. \end{cases}$$

$$(14.5)$$

where α is the influence factor of the parent node, h is the height of the learning category tree, and d_i is the depth of node i in the category tree; w_j is the weight of $T_{r1}[i_j]$ and $T_{r2}[i_j]$, which is calculated as $w_j = \frac{w(t_{r1}[i_j]) + w(t_{r1}[i_j])}{2}$; $v_r(t_{r1}[i])$ represents the value of node $t_{r1}[i]$, which is a fuzzy number; $v_r(F_{r1}[i])$ represents the value of forest $F_{r1}[i]$, which is 0 if $F_{r1}[i]$ is null or none of its nodes are assigned values; $v_r(T_{r1}[i])$ represents the value of the sub-tree $T_{r1}[i]$, which is calculated by:

$$v_r(T_r[i]) = \begin{cases} v_r(t_r[i]), & v_r(F[i]) - 0, \\ \sum_{j=1}^{n_i} w(t_r[i_j]) \cdot v_r(T_r[i_j]), & v_r(F[i]) \neq 0. \end{cases} \qquad (14.6)$$

$S_v(\cdot)$ is the similarity measure for two fuzzy numbers and is calculated by:

$$S_v(\tilde{a}, \tilde{b}) = 1 - d(\tilde{a}, \tilde{b})/d_{\max}. \qquad (14.7)$$

where $d(\tilde{a}, \tilde{b})$ is the distance between two fuzzy numbers and $d_{\max}$ is the maximum distance between fuzzy numbers in the domain.

Let $\alpha = 0.5$, taking the two learner requirement trees in Fig. 14.6 as an example, the fuzzy required category similarity between them is computed by $S_{\text{frc}}(T_{r1}[1], T_{r2}[1]) = w_2 \cdot S_v(v_r(t_{r1}[2]), v_r(t_{r2}[2])) + w_3 \cdot S_v(v_r(T_{r1}[3]), v_r(t_{r2}[3]))$, and the result is 0.675.

Let T_r be a learner's fuzzy required category tree, and T_c represent the fuzzy category tree of a learning activity. The fuzzy category matching similarity measure of T_c to T_r is calculated by Eq. (14.8).

$$S_{\text{fcm}}(T_r[i], T_c[i]) = \begin{cases} S_v(v_r(t_r[i]), v_c(t_c[i])), v_r(F_r[i]) = 0, v_c(F_c[i]) = 0, \\ S_v(v_r(t_r[i]), v_c(T_c[i])), v_r(F_r[i]) = 0, v_c(F_c[i]) \neq 0, \\ S_v(v_r(T_r[i]), v_c(t_c[i])), v_r(F_r[i]) \neq 0, v_c(F_c[i]) = 0, \\ (\alpha^{h-d_i} - \alpha^h) \cdot S_v(v_r(T_r[i]), v_c(T_c[i])) \\ + (1 - \alpha^{h-d_i} + \alpha^h) \cdot (\sum_{j=1}^{n_i} w(t_r[i_j]) \cdot S_{\text{fcm}}(T_r[i_j], T_c[i_j])), \\ \qquad v_c(F_1[i]) \neq 0, v_c(F_2[i]) \neq 0. \end{cases}$$

(14.8)

In respect of the fuzzy category matching similarity measure, first, the category values of nodes in T_c are real numbers, which are seen as special fuzzy numbers in the similarity measure $S_v(\cdot)$. Second, the similarity between T_r and T_c is asymmetric, and only the weights of T_r are considered.

Taking the fuzzy required category tree T_{r1} in Fig. 14.6 and the two fuzzy category trees in Fig. 14.3 as examples, the matching similarity of "Business Intelligence" to T_{r1} is computed by $S_{\text{fcm}}(T_{r1}[1], T_a[1]) = w_2 \cdot S_v(v_r(t_{r1}[2]), v_c(T_a[2])) + w_3 \cdot S_{\text{fcm}}(T_{r1}[3], T_a[3])$, and calculated as 0.845. Similarly, the matching similarity of "Marketing Management" to T_{r1} is calculated as 0.722. Because T_{r1} expresses very high requirement on "IT" category, and the degree of Business Intelligence belonging to "IT" is higher than that of Marketing Management, the calculated matching similarity degrees reflect the requirement.

14.3.3 *Recommendation method for learning activities*

To effectively recommend new learning activities to learners, the user-based CF method is employed in the LESS system. For a target learner u_t, the recommendation process is described in seven steps, as follows.

Step 1: Determine the recommendation alternatives.

There are numerous learning activities under various categories in an e-learning system, but for a specific target learner, only the learning activities under certain relevant categories are suitable for recommendation. The relevant categories of the target learner are first identified, and the learning activities under the categories are then selected.

The relevant learning categories of the target learner u_t are identified in two ways: the learning activities that have been learned by u_t and other learners with the same learning goals; and the fuzzy required category tree T_{frc} of u_t. Let the learning goal of u_t be g_t. The learners whose learning goal is g_t are selected to constitute a set U_{g_t}. For each learner $u_i \in U_{g_t}$, the learned

activities are $\{a_{i,1}, a_{i,2}, \ldots, a_{i,n_i}\}$, and the corresponding fuzzy category trees
are $\{T_{i,1}, T_{i,2}, \ldots, T_{i,n_i}\}$. The learned category tree of u_i denoted as T_i, can be
calculated as $T_i = combine(\{T_{i,1}, T_{i,2}, \ldots, T_{i,n_i}\})$. The learned category trees
of all the users in U_{g_t} are combined, and the learned category tree for the learning
goal g_t is obtained and denoted as T_{g_t}. A fuzzy category tree T_{cr} is derived from
the learner's fuzzy required category tree by setting the membership degrees of
leaf nodes in T_{frc} as 1. The relevant learning category tree is obtained by combing
U_{g_t} and T_{cr}, as $T_{cr} = combine(T_{cr}, T_{g_t})$. For any learning activity a with fuzzy
category tree T_{ca}, if $S_{\text{fc}}(T_{ca}, T_{cr})$, it is preselected.

The pedagogical constraints are considered when preselecting the learning
activities. Let the profile tree of the target learner u_t be denoted as T_t. The
sub-tree of T_t which represents the learned learning activities, is denoted as
$T_{t,l}$. The learned activities are $\{a_{t,1}, a_{t,2}, \ldots, a_{t,n_t}\}$. For a learning activity
a, the sequential and prerequisite constraints are verified separately. For the
sequential constraints, if $\exists(a \rightarrow a_{t,i}) \in S_{\text{prior}}, 1 \leqslant i \leqslant n_t$, a will not be
suitable for recommendation. For the prerequisite constraints, let the learning
activity's prerequisite sub-tree be denoted as $T_{a,p}$. The proposed tree matching
method is used to check if a learning activity is suitable for the learner. A sub-tree
matching is calculated by the conceptual similarity introduced in Chapter 7, as
$S_a = SC_{T_{\text{asym}}}(T_{a,p}, T_{t,l})$. A matching similarity threshold S_{thre} is predefined.
If $S_a > S_{\text{thre}}$, then learning activity a can be selected as a recommendation
alternative.

*Step 2: Calculate the matching degree of the learning activity a to the
learner's requirement.*

The learner u_t's fuzzy required category tree is T_{req}, and the learning activity a's
fuzzy category tree is T_{ca}. The matching degree of a to u_t is calculated by:

$$S_m(u_t, a) = S_{\text{fcm}}(T_{req}, T_{ca}).$$

Step 3: Calculate the semantic similarity between users.

The users who have rated a are selected, denoted as $U_a = \{u_1, u_2, \ldots, u_m\}$. For
each user $u_i \in U_a$, let the profile tree be T_i. The semantic similarity between
u_t and u_i is calculated by use of the conceptual similarity between two tree-
structured data proposed in Chapter 7 as:

$$S_{\text{sem}}(u_t, u_i) = SC_{T_{\text{sym}}}(T_t, T_i, M_{t,i}).$$

During the calculation process of $S_{\text{sem}}(u_t, u_i)$, a maximum conceptual similarity tree mapping between the profile trees of u_t and u_i is constructed. Their

most similar learned activities can be matched. Let the matched learning activities be recorded in $M_{t,i}$. For any $(p,q) \in M_{t,i}$, p and q are the learning activities rated by u_t and u_i respectively.

Step 4: Calculate the CF similarity between users.

A learning activity similarity threshold $S_{a,\text{thre}}$ is predefined. For any learning activity pair (p,q), T_p and T_q are their learning activity trees respectively. p and q will be shown to be irrelevant if the similarity between T_p and T_q, $S_{\text{sem}}(p,q) = sc_{T_{\text{sym}}}(T_p, T_q)$ is less than $S_{a,\text{thre}}$. Given the matched learning activity set $M_{t,i}$ of u_t and u_i, a sub-set $M'_{t,i} = \{(p,q) : p,q \in M_{t,i}, S_{\text{sem}}(p,q) > S_{a,\text{thre}}\}$ is selected. Based on $M'_{t,i}$, the CF similarity between u_t and u_i is calculated as:

$$S_{\text{CF}}(u_t, u_i) = \frac{\sum_{(p,q) \in M'_{t,i}} r_{t,p} \cdot r_{i,q}}{\sqrt{\sum_{(p,q) \in M'_{t,i}} r^2_{t,p}} \sqrt{\sum_{(p,q) \in M'_{t,i}} r^2_{i,q}}}$$

where $r_{t,p}$ is the rating of item p from user u_t.

Step 5: Select top-K similar users.

The total similarity between learners u_t and u_i is computed by integrating the two similarity measures computed in the last two steps.

$$S_u(u_t, u_i) = \beta \times S_{\text{sem}}(u_t, u_i) + (1 - \beta) \times S_{\text{CF}}(u_t, u_i) \qquad (14.9)$$

where $\beta \in [0,1]$ is a semantic combination parameter specifying the weight of similarity in the integrating measure. The users in U_a are sorted according to the total similarity. The top-K most similar users are selected as neighbors to predict ratings.

Step 6: Calculate the predicted rating.

The predicted rating to learning activity a of learner u_t is calculated as:

$$\hat{r}_{u_t,a} = \theta \times S_m(u_t, a) \times r_{\max} + (1 - \theta) \times \frac{\sum_{u_i=1}^{N} r_{u_i,a} \times S_u(u_t, u_i)}{\sum_{u_i=1}^{N} S_u(u_t, u_i)}$$

where $\theta \in [0,1]$, $r_{\max}$ represents the maximum value of ratings. The formula contains two parts. $S_m(u_t, a) \times r_{\max}$ is the requirement matching-based predicted rating. If the target learning activity is exactly matched to the user's requirement, the target item should achieve the highest rating. $\frac{\sum_{u_i=1}^{N} r_{u_i,a} \times S_u(u_t, u_i)}{\sum_{u_i=1}^{N} S_u(u_t, u_i)}$ is the traditional user-based CF-based predicted rating. θ is a parameter that combines the two parts.

Step 7: Generate recommendations.

The predicted ratings of all the alternative learning activities of learner u_t are calculated. The alternatives are ranked according to the predicted rating, and the top-K of them are recommended to the learner.

14.4 Implementation and Prototype

The LESS is implemented using the Netbeans development platform. JSF, EJB and JPA frameworks are used in the implementation of the presentation layer, business logic layer and data access layer respectively. The database is designed in the PostgreSQL database server. To test the recommender system, it is deployed in the Glassfish web server. Fig. 14.7 shows the home page of the LESS.

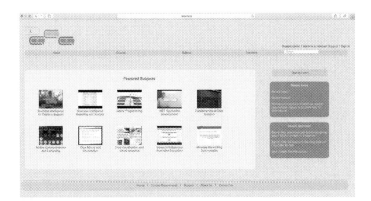

Fig. 14.7: The homepage of the LESS.

A case study including five learners $\{L_1, \ldots, L_5\}$ and eight subjects $\{$S1-Business Intelligence, $\ldots$, S8-Business Process Design$\}$ is given to better explain how LESS works, specifically when new learner and new subjects are involved. Each of these entities contain tree-structured data. The learner-subject rating matrix in the case study is depicted in Table 14.2. For example, the study room of L_4 is shown in Fig. 14.8. It can be seen that L_5 is a new registered learner, and the subject S8 (Business Process Design) is a new item. In this case study, subjects recommended to L_4 and L_5 will be generated. The recommendation process is:

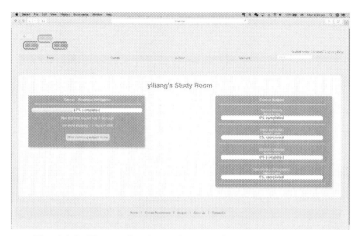

Fig. 14.8: The student's study room home page in LESS.

(1) The recommendation alternatives are selected for L_4 and L_5 according to Step 1 in Section 14.3. The potential learning activities for L_4 are $\{S2, S3, S4, S5, S8\}$, and for L_5 are $\{S1, S2, S3, S4, S5, S6, S7, S8\}$.

(2) The matching degrees of the alternative learning activities to the learners are calculated. The semantic similarity degrees between learners are calculated.

(3) The total similarity degrees between learners are calculated

(4) The predicted ratings of the alternative learning activities by the learners are calculated, as shown in Table 14.3.

(5) The alternative learning activities are ranked according to their predicted ratings. The learning activities with the highest ratings are recommended to the learners.

Table 14.2: Learner-subject rating matrix.

	L_1	L_2	L_3	L_4	L_5
S1: Business Intelligence		4	4	5	
S2: BI Modeling and Analysis	3		2		
S3: BI for Decision Support		3	3		
S4: Database	3	4			
S5: Fundamentals of Data Analytics	4		3		
S6: Data Visualization and Analytics	5			2	
S7: Data Mining and Visualization		2		4	
S8: Business Process Design					

Table 14.3: The predicted ratings.

	S1	S2	S3	S4	S5	S6	S7	S8
L_4		2.91	3.05	2.48	2.59			4.26
L_5	3.92	2.56	2.57	3.54	3.04	3.47	3.16	1.53

We give the recommendation result for L_4 in the system as shown in Fig. 14.9. In the case study, L_4 expresses very high requirement on "Business" category and medium requirement on "IT" category, while L_5 requires very high on "IT" category. Even though L_5 is a new learner, his/her similar learners can also be identified with the semantic similarity. The new subject "Business Process Design" can also be recommended through the requirement matching knowledge.

Fig. 14.9: Learning activity recommendation results for L_4.

14.5 Summary

The E-learning system increasingly attracts learners to participate in online learning activities in today's fast-paced society, which has prompted the development of personalized e-learning recommender systems. This chapter has outlined the e-learning recommender system LESS, which assists learners to effectively select appropriate learning activities. In LESS, to deal with the uncertain tree-structured data the learning activities and learner profiles are modeled as fuzzy category trees and fuzzy required category trees. The user-based CF recommendation method, which combines both the semantic and CF similarities to find similar users, is used in this system to effectively recommend existing or new learning activities to learners. A case study shows the effectiveness of the developed, in which both a new learner and a new learning activity can be recommended.

Chapter 15

Recommender System for Real Estate Property Investment

People purchase real estate properties for two purposes: one is as an investor expecting to generate rental income and profits through price appreciation, the other is as a primary residence. In this chapter, we call both types of people as property buyers. The growth of web-based real estate information has prompted various e-services, but it has also caused information overload, that is, it can be difficult for buyers to efficiently find the property they want.

To help buyers retrieve the most relevant information from a massive amount of online information, thereby providing personalized property suggestions, recommender systems are proposed. For the real estate market, it is crucial to recommend suitable properties to buyers at an early stage since, in most situations, a property is on the market for less than one month before it is sold, and buyers spend a long time searching before making their decisions. Also, unlike many other purchases a property is not repetitively consumed by other buyers and is not consumed twice in a short period of time. Particularly, the recommendation on new properties need to be provided to buyers, and the buyer's short-term and long-term interests need to be taken into consideration. This chapter will present how recommender system called NewHome is built for real estate property investment.

In this chapter, we first introduce the background of recommender systems in real estate in Section 15.1. The system design of NewHome is presented in Section 15.2. In Section 15.3 we present a two stage content-based recommendation method for new properties which is implemented in NewHome. This is followed by a case study of the proposed methods with real-world data in Section 15.4. Finally, the summary is provided in Section 15.5.

15.1 Background

The real estate marketplace is a very active and dynamic marketplace. Keeping the loyalty of both the real estate buyers, who are going to buy a house, and the agents who are selling and renting the houses, has become highly competitive in this market. Therefore, optimizing the search results for both the buyers and the sellers, is the target of the recommendation. The search and recommendation algorithm can vary depend on the platform and application scenarios.

Unlike widely studied e-commerce recommender systems, property recommendation has its own unique characteristics, such as longer decision time when properties generally have a short-shelf life for properties, data sparsity, and locality. For example, properties in metro area in Australia last between thirty to forty days on the market before it is sold. And users usually spend more than six months searching before they came into the final decision on buying a property. It is better if new properties for sale can be recommended to buyers as soon as they enter the market or in the early stage of a property sale circle. This long-time decision making and short-time property availability is contradictory, therefore delivering the information to property buyers at an early stage of their search helps real estate companies win the edge in the dynamic market.

Collaborative Filtering (CF) is typically used in mature websites or platforms such as Netflix. However, the buyer-property interactions are not always abundant in real estate scenarios. When recommending a new property that has just landed in the market, CF suffers the cold start problem and the recommendation results are either inaccurate or cannot be generated. Moreover, unlike recommendation on movies, rich information about buyers and properties is available.

Content-based recommender systems may be more suitable for real estate recommendations [Gu *et al.* (2016)]. However, there are three challenges when building content-based recommender systems: (1) The content information is heterogeneous, therefore it is difficult to build profiles for buyers and properties. The content information usually contains categorical features, numerical features, free-text features or even images. How to do the data engineering and fuse all these features into the buyer/property profile remains one problem to be solved; (2) The interactions between buyers and properties are in multiple types, such as view, click, subscribe or enquiry. How to define the level of preference these behaviors represent is not easy and will affect the accuracy of recommendations; and (3) In the real estate business, the spam of recommendation is taken very seriously. When pushing email/App notifications, buyers will quickly lose interests if they receive irrelevant information. This greatly damages a brand's image and may quickly lose buyers' trust.

15.2   System Design and Development

In this section, the system architecture of the NewHome system for real estate is presented.

Buyers are users of the system and system administrators are in charge of maintain the system. The buyers search for the appropriate properties and wish to receive recommendations. When a new property that is of potential interest to buyers enters the market, the system will recommender other related properties that may also be of interest. The different behaviors of home buyers will be recorded, such as view, click and enquiry. The role of the system administrator is to maintain both the buyer profiles and the property profiles, which are used to support the operation of the system.

The architecture of NewHome is depicted in Fig. 15.1. As a web-based online system, the recommender system has a standard multi-tier architecture, which includes web browser, web server and database server. The main components of the system are described as follows.

15.2.1   *Databases*

The database contains the following main components:

(1) Buyer profiles: the information about the buyers.
(2) Property attributes: the attributes of the properties, which are used to construct the property profiles.
(3) Buyer history records: the buyers' historical behaviors to properties.
(4) New properties: the new properties that just landed in the market and their attributes.
(5) Trained model: the parameters of the trained models.

15.2.2   *Web application component*

The application in the web server contains three layers: the presentation layer, the business logic layer and the data access layer.

(1) Web browser layer: for generating the requested web pages and handling the user interface logic and events for the two different kinds of user.
(2) Email notifications layer: for generating and sending emails to buyers who may be interested in the new properties.
(3) Business logic layer: for business services and the core recommendation algorithm. It provides the following main functionalities:

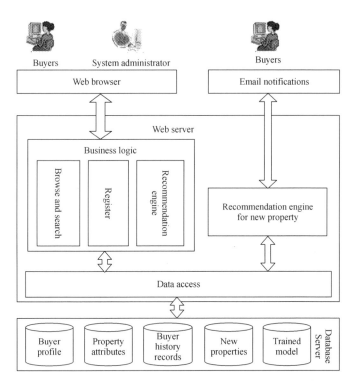

Fig. 15.1: The architecture of recommender system for real estate.

(a) Browse and search: supports buyers to browse the properties, or search the properties based on a keyword-based search engine, and to view the matching results.

(b) Register: supports new buyers enabling them to register on the system.

(c) Recommendation engine: implements the existing recommendation method, including CF methods, to recommend existing properties to buyers.

(d) Recommendation engine for new properties: implements the proposed recommendation method and generates the top-K buyers who may be interested in the new property.

(4) Data access layer: deals with the data operations of the database.

15.3   Two Stage Content-based Recommendation Method

In the NewHome system, recommending new property to buyers is the primary purpose, therefore a content-based recommender system is used since the interactions on new properties are not sufficient. A data processing and feature engineering method is proposed for dealing with the heterogeneous property content information. Moreover, a boosting tree model is applied to predict the relevance of properties to buyers to prevent potential spam when we push email notifications to buyers. The two stage content-based recommendation method, which is to solve the new property recommendation in real estate, shown in Fig. 15.2, contain two stages:

Stage 1. We build a content-based recommendation method that can select the top fifty buyers for each property. This can be used as a final recommendation list or as a set of candidate buyers, much smaller than the whole buyer set.

Stage 2. For each pair (candidate buyer, property), the probability that candidate buyer will interact with this item is learned, and this information is used for preventing potential spam when we push email notifications to buyers.

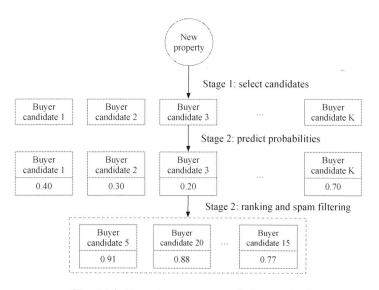

Fig. 15.2: Two stage recommendation method.

Let X denote a matrix. The i-th row and the j-th column in the matrix are denoted as X_{i*} and X_{*j}, respectively. The (i, j)-th element of matrix X is denoted as $X_{i,j}$. Suppose we have M buyers and N properties, $X \in \mathbb{R}^{M \times N}$. One buyer i may have interacted with one property j in different behaviors. These behaviors are represented by a set $B = \{b_1, \ldots, b_p, \ldots, b_P\}$, in which each of the element represents one kind of interaction behavior such as view, click or enquiry. The types of buyer behaviors are listed in Table 15.1. And the interaction matrix on buyer behavior b_p is represented as $\boldsymbol{X}^{b_p}$. The interaction between buyer i and property j is represented as $X_{i,j}^{b_p}$. If the buyer i has interacted with property j on the behavior type b_p, $X_{i,j}^{b_p}$ is 1, otherwise 0.

Table 15.1: Types of buyer behaviors.

Level	Buyer Behavior Type	Buyer Behavior
1	Click	AdvertView
2	Detailed View	FloorPlanView
		InteractiveFloorPlanView
3	Bookmarked	Shortlisted
		AutoShortlist
4	Enquiry	EmailEnquiry
		SMSEnquiry

Given a property j, it has L features on the feature set $F = \{f_1, \ldots, f_l, \ldots, f_L\}$ according to its content, where L is the number of features in the property profile. The features are extracted from property attributes which are in different values. Some attributes are categorical value; some are numerical values. We will talk more about how to do feature extraction in the next section. All the M items feature vectors are composed as property profile matrix, represented as $\boldsymbol{V} \in \mathbb{R}^{N \times L}$. The jth row $\boldsymbol{V}_{j*}$ represents the content vector of property j.

The problem solved in this section is based on the assumption that buyer-property interactions are very sparse and the interaction behavior are in multiple types. Given buyer-property interaction matrixes on multiple buyer behaviors: $\{\boldsymbol{X}^{b_1}, \ldots, \boldsymbol{X}^{b_p}, \ldots, \boldsymbol{X}^{b_P}\}$ and property profile matrix $\boldsymbol{V}$, the content recommender system is to use the property content information to assist with the recommendation of new properties where have been no interactions with buyers in the system.

(1) Stage 1: Content-based recommendation.

Different attributes are processed and then features are extracted to represent the property. We extract these features and process the values to numerical value 0 and 1. As a result, a property profile encoded with $\{0, 1\}$ has been obtained. For the categorical values and numerical values in property attributes, we use one-hot encoding to encode the features as categorical. For H property attributes, we extract L features. Note that L and H are different since each of the attributes contains various feature dimensions because of the one-hot encoding. The H attributes $\{a_1, \ldots, a_h, \ldots, a_H\}$ are corresponding to L feature dimensions $\{d_1, \ldots, d_h, \ldots, d_H\}$ where $\sum_{h=1}^{H} d_h = L$. For $\forall V_{j,l}$ in property profile V, $V_{j,l} \in \{0, 1\}$. For example, one attribute for properties is the property type. Suppose that there are five property types: {house, unit, apartment, townhouse, villa}. Property j is an apartment, then the one-hot encoding vector is $[0, 0, 1, 0, 0]$. This one attribute will be encoded into a five-dimension feature.

The buyer's preference is profiled from properties in a his/her consumption records. For each buyer, their historical data contain various behaviors and are represented in several interaction matrixes X^{b_v}. We firstly consider one buyer behavior denoted as X, and buyer profile is generated as follows:

$$U = X \cdot V. \tag{15.1}$$

For buyer profile U, it has the same structure as property profile V. The difference is that the buyer profile is an aggregated result where for the entry $U_{i,l}$ in U, $U_{i,l} \in \mathbb{N}^+$. To normalize values in U to $[0, 1]$, U can be divided according to H attributes $\{a_1, \ldots, a_h, \ldots, a_H\}$. As a result, U is divided to $\{U_1, \ldots, U_h, \ldots, U_H\}$ where $U_h \in \mathbb{R}^{M \times d_h}$. The normalization of buyer profile is:

$$(U_h)_{i,l} = \frac{(U_h)_{i,l}}{\sum_{l=1}^{d_h} (U_h)_{i,l}}. \tag{15.2}$$

To take each type of buyer behavior X^{b_v} into consideration, we assign weights to indicate the importance of the behaviors. These weights can be trained by the data, or they can be assigned by experienced domain experts. For each type of buyer behavior, we have a buyer profile U^{b_v}, and assign the weight W^{b_v}. We introduce one possible weight-learning strategy through logistic regression. The probability of whether the buyer i will apply the property j is given by:

$$p_{ij} = p(y_{ij} = 1) = \sigma[\boldsymbol{\theta}(W_i^{b_v} U_i^{b_v} + V_j) + b] \tag{15.3}$$

where $\boldsymbol{\theta}$ and b are parameters of the logistic regression.

Property profiles and buyer profiles are constructed in the same feature space and prepared for distance measurement. There are many suitable choices for performing these calculations such as cosine similarity, Pearson's similarity, Euclidean measurement or the RBF measurement. In this problem, we are measuring buyer-property similarity from two vectors containing weights on each features, which is very similar to the situation of measuring the weight between two documents with weights on words. Therefore, cosine similarity is used to measure the distance between buyer i and property j as follows:

$$W^{cos}_{(i,j)} = \frac{\sum_{l=1}^{L} U_{i,l} \times V_{j,l}}{\sqrt{\sum_{l=1}^{L} U_{i,l}^2} \times \sqrt{\sum_{l=1}^{L} V_{j,l}^2}} \qquad (15.4)$$

where $U_{i,l}$ is the lth dimension in the profile of buyer i, $V_{j,l}$ is the lth dimension in the profile of property j; L is the total number of dimension in for both profiles.

After calculating the cosine similarities, the buyers are ranked by cosine similarity scores. Top-K buyers will be recommended to send notification for the new properties.

(2) Stage 2: Boosting tree-based spam filtering.

Pushing email notifications to buyers can be risky, since buyers could be overwhelmed or harassed by the irrelevant information. The second stage of the method is to compute the probability that a buyer will interact with a property for a given buyer-property pair (i, j). In order to estimate the probability, we use XGBoost[1] to implement boosting tree (also known as GBDT, GBM) and rank the candidates chosen by stage 1 in order to filter the possible spam notifications.

For training the model, we take buyers and properties from the training set as positive examples. Meanwhile, we sampled negative buyer-property pairs. Specifically, to be consistent to the cold start scenario on properties, we take an item-oriented random sampling strategy for each property from the entire buyer set (excluding buyers who already interacted with the property in the training set). Random negative sampling is appropriate, since both buyer and property sets are large enough to ensure the randomness of the selection.

The top-K candidate buyers from stage 1 content-based recommendation are ranked in stage 2. The candidate buyers that have lower probability to interact with the property are filtered out. In this way, possible spam notification is limited.

15.4   Real-world Case Study

In this section, how to do feature engineering and feature selection with a dataset descriptions are introduced. Finally the experimental results on these dataset and comparison results are presented.

---

[1] github.com/dmlc/xgboost

15.4.1 *Feature selection and feature engineering*

The case study is conducted on real estate data in Australia. The attributes of properties vary in different areas. For example, the price of properties from Sydney and Melbourne can be quite different. And the preferences of buyers who are renting a house are quite different from those who are buying a house. We divide the data according to geographic information and the property market purpose information (sale/rent/invest). We suggest that recommendation engines should be built separately for different areas and based on different market purposes.

We made subsets of the dataset on several different settings. For pre-processing, we filter out the properties that have less than two interactions with buyers. This is because the dataset will be randomly split into a training set and a test set, partitioned as 80% training set and 20% test set using an item-oriented method. If the property is checked by the buyer less than two times, it will be allocated either to the training set or the test set. Thus, it is meaningless to retain the property in the dataset. data1 in Table 15.2 contains one-week of data while data2 contains two weeks of data. These two subsets are made for testing the stage 1 and we test the performance of stage 2 on data3.

Table 15.2: Data description of different settings.

	User No.	Item No.	Train No.	Test No.
data1	88818	50972	1024823	280587
data2	77053	31902	946678	237456
data3	76583	24907	935748	226782

The purpose of choosing different data settings are as follows: Firstly, feature selection and feature engineering are processed to extract related attributes that are important to making recommendations. This work is mainly focused on data1 and also verified on data2. Secondly, the length of the time period of the dataset is another interesting factor that we need to take into consideration. Here, we presented results on one week and two weeks of data.

We designed three scenarios for case study on data2. Scenario 1 is randomly splitting the data to 80% and 20% to the training set and the test set, respectively. Scenario 2 is to split the training set and the test set according to the time window so that it is close to a real situation. Scenario 3 is to predict the new property, which has never seen by any buyer in the training set. This scenario is to simulate the cold start item scenario when a new property comes freshly on the market.

We use three evaluation metrics: precision, recall and MAP (mean average precision, is the average of AP on all buyers) for evaluation. They are defined as follows:

$$\text{Precison@K} = \frac{\text{\# of recommended items @K that are relevant}}{\text{\# of recommended items @K}}$$

$$\text{Recall@K} = \frac{\text{\# of recommended items @K that are relevant}}{\text{total \# of relevant items}}$$

$$\text{AP@K} = \frac{1}{|\text{itemset}|} \sum_{k=1}^{K} (P(j) \text{ if item } j \text{ is relevant})$$

The baseline used in this chapter is an existing query-based recommendation method used in the real estate company. Specifically, in this baseline buyer profiles are firstly built with aggregated property attributes in their historical records. They use the median number for the numerical attributes such as bedroom number, bathroom number, car space number and price, and they use the most frequently appeared value for the categorical attributes such as suburb and property type as their profile. The query-based recommendation method uses the user profile to match with the property attributes and chose properties by query rules to generate the recommendation list. The query rules are as follows:

Rule 1. The attributes of the property on bedroom number, bathroom number and car space number should be within a range of less than one of the of the attributes on the buyer's profile;

Rule 2. The property suburb should be in the same suburb as the buyer's profile;

Rule 3. The property type should be in the same property type as the buyer's profile;

Rule 4. The property price should be within the range of less than 15K of the price on the buyer's profile.

We have tried different combinations of features and found that geographical features and price are especially important. In this case study, we fix features to the following: property type, property area, property region, property suburb, number of bedroom, number of bathroom, number of car spaces, property price, and train station information.

For all these features, we use one-hot encoding to align them to a vector where values are in $\{0, 1\}$. For the property price, we use two methods to encode it in one-hot vectors. One is to uniformly divide it according to its distribution. The other is to divide the price in the following range: {10K, 100K, 200K, 300K,

400K, 500K, 600K, 700K, 800K, 900K, 1M, 2M, 3M, 4M, 5M}. There is no significant difference between the two methods, so we have chosen to use the second strategy. Where there is a missing property price, the price used is the average price of properties in the suburb where the property is located. The price of a property which is either below $10K$ and above $5M$ are set to be $10K$ and $5M$, because a price that is either high or lower is not realistic. The train station information is collected from the NSW train station open dataset. This feature is created based on whether the property is within 1.5 km to the train station or not and whether the train station has an express train service or not.

The attributes used in stage 2 are different from those in stage 1. Both buyer and property attributes are encoded using one-hot encoding in stage 2. The final set of buyer attributes at the end of stage 1 and stage 2 are: persona, engagement level, value segmentation, average price, median bathroom, median bedroom, median car space, favorite property type. The three-month data set is comprised of these attributes, with the attributes for persona, engagement level and value segmentation set according to the real estate company's business rules.

15.4.2 Comparison results and analysis

To compare the performance of the proposed method with the existing query-based recommendation method, we evaluate them with the same evaluation metrics on the same dataset. The results on data1 are in Table 15.3. We compare these two methods on two different scenarios on data2 in Table 15.4.

Table 15.3: Comparison results with query based method on data1.

Method	K	Precision	Recall	MAP
Proposed method	5	0.0165	0.0296	0.0172
	10	0.0090	0.0321	0.0176
	50	0.0018	0.0321	0.0177
Query-based	5	0.0103	0.0098	0.0065
	10	0.0068	0.0120	0.0070
	50	0.0019	0.0146	0.0072

We have tested the proposed method on the three scenarios in Table 15.5. The results suggest that our proposed method can recommend the properties to users even for cold start properties (scenario 3) while the query-based method failed on the recommendation.

Finally, and importantly, the stage 2 of the proposed method is tested on data3. By using the stage 2 spam filter the precision and recall can be improved, as shown in Table 15.5. This indicates that stage 2 can help filter any possible spam when pushing email notifications to buyers.

Table 15.4: Comparison results with query based method on data2.

Scenario	Method	K	Precision	Recall	MAP
Scenario 1	Proposed method	5	0.0275	0.0211	0.0093
		10	0.0250	0.0398	0.0121
		50	0.0066	0.0592	0.0138
	Query-based	5	0.0003	0.0002	0.0001
		10	0.0002	0.0003	0.0001
		50	0.0001	0.0004	0.0001
Scenario 2	Proposed method	5	0.0375	0.0082	0.0040
		10	0.0381	0.0159	0.0053
		50	0.0219	0.0471	0.0080
	Query-based	5	0.0228	0.0087	0.0055
		10	0.0161	0.0117	0.0061
		50	0.0053	0.0175	0.0067

Table 15.5: Recommendation results of the proposed method in three scenarios.

Scenario	K	Precision	Recall	MAP
Scenario 1	5	0.0103	0.0141	0.0069
	10	0.0109	0.0286	0.0088
	50	0.0078	0.0995	0.0124
Scenario 2	5	0.0110	0.0037	0.0016
	10	0.0116	0.0081	0.0022
	50	0.0098	0.0345	0.0037
Scenario 3	5	0.0229	0.0052	0.0021
	10	0.0252	0.0112	0.0030
	50	0.0275	0.0576	0.0064
stage 1	5	0.0154	0.0146	0.0067
	10	0.0155	0.0276	0.0085
	50	0.0139	0.0971	0.0124
stage 1	5	0.0171	0.0154	0.0072
+ stage 2	10	0.0174	0.0304	0.0094
	50	0.0156	0.0906	0.0130

15.5 Summary

Since purchasing property, either as your primary residence or as an investment, is an important decision for buyers, the demand for personalized services prompts the development of recommender systems for real estate properties. This chapter proposes a recommender system NewHome to assist buyers in property investment, especially for new properties that come on the market. A two stage content-based recommendation method is implemented in the NewHome system. The stage 1 of the method is able to generate the recommendations for buyers. Then we add a boosting tree model as stage 2 to effectively reduce the potential spam when we push email notifications to buyers. The case study results show that the two stage content-based recommendation method can better perform the baseline for property recommendations and can properly handle the cold start properties.

The Future Direction of Recommender System

Recommender systems are designed to identify the items that a user will be interested in, with the recommendations put forward primarily based on the user's prior preferences and activities. Though the developments in recommender system methods, algorithms and applications have been significant during recent years, as we present in this monograph, there are still some issues that require further study, particularly with the emerging AI techniques.

In general, the future direction of recommender systems will be to continue the original task: the delivery of "the right item to the right user". However, there are still some challenging problems when it comes to understanding and finding the "right users" and what their desired "'right items" are. The expectation of recommender systems is that they operate in the background, identifying recommendations when the user may not know or is not sure what they want or like, and they are passive. By learning the user's tastes, despite there being very little user history data, the recommender system can find personalized items that the user prefers or, at least, are useful to them. This capacity mainly comes from the power of AI. In the next stage of recommender system development, AI, particularly machine learning, is the key to personalization; to ensuring a better understanding of the user's preferences; to accurately predicting the user's unknown favorites; and ultimately providing recommendations beyond a matching-based simple search.

In detail, there are some issues which are not well-addressed concerning recommender systems and there is room for improvement. Here we list just six future directions for recommender system research and development:

1. **Recommender systems cross multi-source and multi-target domains:** Cross-domain recommender systems, with one source and one target domain, have been developed recently to deal with the data sparsity issue in the target domain, as presented in Chapter 9. In the current big data situation, user

data are often accumulated from a vast number of domains and we may require data from any one of them to generate recommendations as a target domain (which may not have enough data for training a prediction model). Recommender systems are needed to find the most suitable source domain(s) and obtain the desired pattern that can be applied to the target domain. The key difficulty is to autonomously select the most-suitable source domain(s) for the target domain(s) from the massive domains without manual human-nomination. Therefore to improve user's satisfaction in recommendation, there is the need to develop a recommender system with the capacity to identify either one or a set of the most suitable source domains and then effectively transfer the desired and effective knowledge to one or more target domains.

2. **Federated recommender systems:** When collecting data from multiple sources, it can lead to serious privacy and security risks that go against laws on data privacy protection (e.g. the General Data Protection Regulation[1])). Federated learning, which was proposed by Google [Konečný *et al.* (2016)], is a promising way to achieve privacy preserving by learning a centered model with data locally on each user's mobile phone without transmit to a central server. A federate recommender system works by computing the gradients locally and then transmitting the gradients to the centered recommendation model instead of the user's raw data. Federated recommender systems are required to secure the user raw data while maintaining accuracy.

3. **From deep learning to deep understanding:** Deep learning methods are the superior method for effective feature learning, especially when there is no known effective feature, as in many recommender systems. However, the outcome of deep learning in recommender systems are sometimes surprisingly unexpected, in particular when there is no supervised true label in the learning process. In fact, deep learning, which is mainly used in building the user profiles, does little to solve an understanding of what users really need. Therefore, new recommendation methods are required to develop not only using data-driven deep learning but also knowledge-driven techniques for recommender systems, where we can have a deep understanding of why the recommendation is generated and how the user requirements and needs are fulfilled.

4. **Explanation in recommender systems:** It has been recognized that many recommender systems functions are as black boxes, neither providing trans-

---

[1] https://eur-lex.europa.eu/legal-content/EN/TXT/?uri=CELEX:32016R0679R(02)

parency about how a recommendation is generated, nor offering any additional explanation to help users understand why the specific recommendation(s) was generated. Explanation in recommender systems contains two aspects: explaining how the recommendation engine works (transparency) and explaining why the user may prefer an item (effectiveness) [Gedikli *et al.* (2014)]. The visualization in the recommender system mentioned in Chapter 11, which gives explanations such as "Movie R1 is recommended because...", is a possible solution for the second aspect. More research into the development of explanations in recommender systems is required for both recommendation process transparency and the reasoning behind a generated list of recommendations. When a recommender system is explicable, it can better help the e-service providers to increase user trust and loyalty; make the system easier for users to find what they need; and to persuade users to purchase recommended items with confidence.

5. **Healthcare as a significant application area of recommender systems:** Considering existing applications, as mentioned in Chapter 3, e-commence was the first domain to implement recommender systems. Later on the development of e-business, e-government, e-learning, e-tourism, *etc.* also prompted the application of recommender systems. Looking forwards, healthcare is an important emerging domain of e-services that will have a significant impact on our society. Healthcare domain requires advanced personalized recommendation methods to help clinicians take next-step action for patients. In a healthcare recommender system, the items recommended could be a test, prescription, the risk level of a disease, or a treatment plan. High precision of recommendation is required, and domain knowledge in medicine must be included. These unique requirement characteristics will trigger significant developments of advanced recommender systems in the area of healthcare.

6. **Mobile-based recommender systems:** When considering application platforms, offering more personalized and context-aware mobile-based recommender systems as Apps are required because of the ever increasing usage of Internet-accessing smart phones. Mobile data are dynamic, noisy, structure-complex, and context-sensitive, therefore advanced recommender systems are needed. This direction should focus on investigating the potential use and effect of mobile technology on recommender systems.

When studying these future directions, you should feel that the development of recommender systems in these fields is still rich in challenges and opportunities.

List of Abbreviations

AI   artificial intelligence
AUC   area under the curve
BHR   balanced hypergraph ranking
BPR   Bayesian personalized ranking
CBR   case-based reasoning
CF   collaborative filtering
CIT   consistent information transfer
DCG   discounted cumulative gain
FMM   flexible mixture model
GFK   geodesic flow kernel
interval-UP user preference at time interval
KerKT   kernel-induced knowledge transfer
MAE   mean absolute error
MCS   member contribution score
MCS-GR   member contribution score-based group recommendation
NDCG   normalized discounted cumulative gain
PCC   Pearson correlation coefficient
pLSA   probabilistic latent semantic analysis
point-UP user preference at time point
RBF   radial basis function
RMSE   root mean square error
ROC   receiver operating characteristic
SMB   small and medium-size business
SNMF   separable non-negative matrix factorization
SVD   singular value decomposition
TF-IDF   term frequency-inverse document frequency
UIAC   user-item-attribute-context

Bibliography

Aamodt, A. and Plaza, E. (1994). Case-based reasoning: foundational issues, methodological variations, and system approaches, *AI Communications* **7**, 1, pp. 39–59.

Abel, F., Herder, E., Houben, G.-J., Henze, N., and Krause, D. (2013). Cross-system user modeling and personalization on the social web, *User Modeling and User-Adapted Interaction*, pp. 1–41.

Abreu, J., Almeida, P., Velhinho, A., Fernandes, S., and Guedes, R. (2018). An itv prototype for content unification, in *International Conference on Entertainment Computing*, pp. 293–296.

Adadi, A., Berrada, M., Chenouni, D., and Bounabat, B. (2015). Ontology based composition of e-government services using ai planning, in *The 10th International Conference on Intelligent Systems: Theories and Applications*, pp. 1–8.

Adomavicius, G. and Tuzhilin, A. (2005). Toward the next generation of recommender systems: a survey of the state-of-the-art and possible extensions, *IEEE Transactions on Knowledge and Data Engineering* **17**, 6, pp. 734–749.

Agarwal, D., Chen, B.-C., He, Q., Hua, Z., Lebanon, G., Ma, Y., Shivaswamy, P., Tseng, H.-P., Yang, J., and Zhang, L. (2015). Personalizing linkedin feed, in *Proceedings of the 21th ACM SIGKDD International Conference on Knowledge Discovery and Data Mining*, pp. 1651–1660.

Agarwal, S. (2006). Ranking on graph data, in *Proceedings of the 23rd International Conference on Machine Learning*, pp. 25–32.

*Al-Hassan, M., Lu, H., and Lu, J. (2009). A framework for delivering personalized e-government services from a citizen-centric approach, in *Proceedings of the 11th International Conference on Information Integration and Web-based Applications & Services*, pp. 436–440.

*Al-hassan, M., Lu, H., and Lu, J. (2010). Personalized e-government services: tourism recommender system framework, in *The 6th International Conference on Web Information Systems and Technologies*, pp. 173–187.

*Al-Hassan, M., Lu, H., and Lu, J. (2015). A semantic enhanced hybrid recommendation approach: a case study of e-government tourism service recommendation system, *Decision Support Systems* **72**, pp. 97–109.

Al-Shamri, M. Y. H. and Bharadwaj, K. K. (2008). Fuzzy-genetic approach to recommender systems based on a novel hybrid user model, *Expert Systems with Applications* **35**, 3, pp. 1386–1399.

Albadvi, A. and Shahbazi, M. (2009). A hybrid recommendation technique based on product category attributes, *Expert Systems with Applications* **36**, 9, pp. 11480–11488.

Ali, K. and Van Stam, W. (2004). Tivo: making show recommendations using a distributed collaborative filtering architecture, in *Proceedings of the 10th ACM SIGKDD International Conference on Knowledge Discovery and Data Mining*, pp. 394–401.

Allen, J. F. (1983). Maintaining knowledge about temporal intervals, *Communications of the ACM* **26**, 11, pp. 832–843.

Amer-Yahia, S., Roy, S. B., Chawlat, A., Das, G., and Yu, C. (2009). Group recommendation: semantics and efficiency, *Proceedings of the VLDB Endowment* **2**, 1, pp. 754–765.

Amoroso, D. L. and Reinig, B. A. (2004). Personalization management systems: minitrack introduction, in *Proceedings of the Proceedings of the 37th Annual Hawaii International Conference on System Sciences*, p. 70201.

Anderson, M., Ball, M., Boley, H., Greene, S., Howse, N., Lemire, D., and McGrath, S. (2003). Racofi: a rule-applying collaborative filtering system, in *WIC International Conference on Web Intelligence/Intelligent Agent Technology*, pp. 430–434.

Andjelkovic, I., Parra, D., and O'Donovan, J. (2016). Moodplay: interactive mood-based music discovery and recommendation, in *Proceedings of the 2016 Conference on User Modeling Adaptation and Personalization*, pp. 275–279.

Ardissono, L., Goy, A., Petrone, G., and Segnan, M. (2005). A multi-agent infrastructure for developing personalized web-based systems, *ACM Transactions on Internet Technology* **5**, 1, pp. 47–69.

Ardissono, L., Goy, A., Petrone, G., Segnan, M., and Torasso, P. (2003). Intrigue: personalized recommendation of tourist attractions for desktop and hand held devices, *Applied Artificial Intelligence* **17**, 8-9, pp. 687–714.

Arnold, A., Nallapati, R., and Cohen, W. W. (2007). A comparative study of methods for transductive transfer learning, in *The 7th IEEE International Conference on Data Mining Workshops*, pp. 77–82.

Asnicar, F. A. and Tasso, C. (1997). ifweb: a prototype of user model-based intelligent agent for document filtering and navigation in the world wide web, in *The 6th International Conference on User Modeling*, pp. 2–5.

Athreya, K. B., Doss, H., and Sethuraman, J. (1996). On the convergence of the markov chain simulation method, *The Annals of Statistics* **24**, 1, pp. 69–100.

Avesani, P., Massa, P., and Tiella, R. (2005). Moleskiing. it: a trust-aware recommender system for ski mountaineering, *International Journal for Infonomics* **20**, 35, pp. 1–10.

Balabanović, M. and Shoham, Y. (1997). Fab: content-based, collaborative recommendation, *Communications of the ACM* **40**, 3, pp. 66–72.

Baltrunas, L. and Amatriain, X. (2009). Towards time-dependant recommendation based on implicit feedback, in *Workshop on Context-aware Recommender Systems*.

Baltrunas, L., Makcinskas, T., and Ricci, F. (2010). Group recommendations with rank aggregation and collaborative filtering, in *Proceedings of the 4th ACM Conference on Recommender systems*, pp. 119–126.

Bao, T., Ge, Y., Chen, E., Xiong, H., and Tian, J. (2012). Collaborative filtering with user ratings and tags, in *Proceedings of the 1st International Workshop on Context Discovery and Data Mining*, p. 1.

Barragáns-Martínez, A. B., Costa-Montenegro, E., Burguillo, J. C., Rey-López, M., Mikic-Fonte, F. A., and Peleteiro, A. (2010). A hybrid content-based and item-based collaborative filtering approach to recommend tv programs enhanced with singular value decomposition, *Information Sciences* **180**, 22, pp. 4290–4311.

Basu, C., Hirsh, H., and Cohen, W. (1998). Recommendation as classification: using social and content-based information in recommendation, in *The 15th National Conference on Artificial Intelligence*, pp. 714–720.

Basu Roy, S., Amer-Yahia, S., Chawla, A., Das, G., and Yu, C. (2010). Space efficiency in group recommendation, *The International Journal on Very Large Data Bases* **19**, 6, pp. 877–900.

Bedi, P. and Vashisth, P. (2014). Empowering recommender systems using trust and argumentation, *Information Sciences* **279**, pp. 569–586.

Belkin, M., Matveeva, I., and Niyogi, P. (2004). Regularization and semi-supervised learning on large graphs, in *International Conference on Computational Learning Theory*, pp. 624–638.

Bellogín, A., Cantador, I., Díez, F., Castells, P., and Chavarriaga, E. (2013). An empirical comparison of social, collaborative filtering, and hybrid recommenders, *ACM Transactions on Intelligent Systems and Technology* **4**, 1, p. 14.

Ben-Shimon, D., Tsikinovsky, A., Rokach, L., Meisles, A., Shani, G., and Naamani, L. (2007). Recommender system from personal social networks, in *Advances in Intelligent Web Mastering* (Springer), pp. 47–55.

Bennett, J. and Lanning, S. (2007). The netflix prize, in *Proceedings of KDD Cup and Workshop*, Vol. 2007, p. 35.

Beutel, A., Covington, P., Jain, S., Xu, C., Li, J., Gatto, V., and Chi, E. H. (2018). Latent cross: making use of context in recurrent recommender systems, in *Proceedings of the 11th ACM International Conference on Web Search and Data Mining*, pp. 46–54.

Biletskiy, Y., Baghi, H., Keleberda, I., and Fleming, M. (2009). An adjustable personalization of search and delivery of learning objects to learners, *Expert Systems with Applications* **36**, 5, pp. 9113–9120.

Bille, P. (2005). A survey on tree edit distance and related problems, *Theoretical Computer Science* **337**, 1-3, pp. 217–239.

Billsus, D. and Pazzani, M. J. (1998). Learning collaborative information filters, in *The 15th International Conference on Machine Learning*, Vol. 98, pp. 46–54.

Billsus, D. and Pazzani, M. J. (2000). User modeling for adaptive news access, *User Modeling and User-Adapted Interaction* **10**, 2-3, pp. 147–180.

Bivainis, J. (2006). Development of business partner selection, *Ekonomika* **73**, pp. 7–18.

Bjelica, M. (2010). Towards tv recommender system: experiments with user modeling, *IEEE Transactions on Consumer Electronics* **56**, 3, pp. 1763–1769.

Bobadilla, J., Ortega, F., Hernando, A., and Gutiérrez, A. (2013). Recommender systems survey, *Knowledge-Based Systems* **46**, pp. 109–132.

Bobadilla, J., Serradilla, F., and Hernando, A. (2009). Collaborative filtering adapted to recommender systems of e-learning, *Knowledge-Based Systems* **22**, 4, pp. 261–265.

Bogdanov, D., Haro, M., Fuhrmann, F., Xambó, A., Gómez, E., and Herrera, P. (2013).

Semantic audio content-based music recommendation and visualization based on user preference examples, *Information Processing & Management* **49**, 1, pp. 13–33.

Bogers, T. (2010). Movie recommendation using random walks over the contextual graph, in *Proceeding of the 2nd Workshop on Context-Aware Recommender Systems*.

Bostandjiev, S., O'Donovan, J., and Höllerer, T. (2012). Tasteweights: a visual interactive hybrid recommender system, in *Proceedings of the 6th ACM Conference on Recommender Systems*, pp. 35–42.

Boutemedjet, S. and Ziou, D. (2012). Predictive approach for user long-term needs in content-based image suggestion, *IEEE Transactions on Neural Networks and Learning Systems* **23**, 8, pp. 1242–1253.

Braunhofer, M., Elahi, M., Ge, M., and Ricci, F. (2013). Sts: design of weather-aware mobile recommender systems in tourism, in *In Proceedings of the 1st Workshop on AI*HCI: Intelligent User Interfaces*.

Breese, J. S., Heckerman, D., and Kadie, C. (1998). Empirical analysis of predictive algorithms for collaborative filtering, in *Proceedings of the 14th Conference on Uncertainty in Artificial Intelligence*, pp. 43–52.

Brin, S. and Page, L. (1998). The anatomy of a large-scale hypertextual web search engine, *Computer networks and ISDN systems* **30**, 1-7, pp. 107–117.

Brusilovski, P., Kobsa, A., and Nejdl, W. (2007). *The adaptive web: methods and strategies of web personalization*, Vol. 4321 (Springer Science & Business Media).

Burke, R. (1999). The wasabi personal shopper: a case-based recommender system, in *Proceedings of the 16th National Conference on Artificial Intelligence and the Eleventh Innovative Applications of Artificial Intelligence Conference Innovative Applications of Artificial Intelligence*, p. 844–849.

Burke, R. (2002). Hybrid recommender systems: survey and experiments, *User Modeling and User-Adapted Interaction* **12**, 4, pp. 331–370.

Burke, R. D., Hammond, K. J., and Young, B. C. (1996). Knowledge-based navigation of complex information spaces, in *Proceedings of the National Conference on Artificial Intelligence*, Vol. 462, p. 468.

Cabrerizo, F. J., Morente-Molinera, J. A., Pérez, I. J., López-Gijón, J., and Herrera-Viedma, E. (2015). A decision support system to develop a quality management in academic digital libraries, *Information Sciences* **323**, pp. 48–58.

Cai, Y., Leung, H.-f., Li, Q., Min, H., Tang, J., and Li, J. (2014). Typicality-based collaborative filtering recommendation, *IEEE Transactions on Knowledge and Data Engineering* **26**, 3, pp. 766–779.

Campos, P. G., Díez, F., and Cantador, I. (2014). Time-aware recommender systems: a comprehensive survey and analysis of existing evaluation protocols, *User Modeling and User-Adapted Interaction* **24**, 1-2, pp. 67–119.

Cao, H., Chen, E., Yang, J., and Xiong, H. (2009). Enhancing recommender systems under volatile user interest drifts, in *Proceedings of the 18th ACM Conference on Information and Knowledge Management*, pp. 1257–1266.

Cao, Y. and Li, Y. (2007). An intelligent fuzzy-based recommendation system for consumer electronic products, *Expert Systems with Applications* **33**, 1, pp. 230–240.

Capuano, N., Gaeta, M., Ritrovato, P., and Salerno, S. (2014). Elicitation of latent learning needs through learning goals recommendation, *Computers in Human Behavior* **30**, pp. 663–673.

Carter, L., Schaupp, L. C., Hobbs, J., and Campbell, R. (2012). E-government utilization: understanding the impact of reputation and risk, *International Journal of Electronic Government Research* **8**, 1, pp. 83–97.

*Castro, J., Lu, J., Zhang, G., Dong, Y., and Martínez, L. (2017). Opinion dynamics-based group recommender systems, *IEEE Transactions on Systems, Man, and Cybernetics: Systems* **48**, 12, pp. 2394–2406.

Castro, J., Quesada, F. J., Palomares, I., and Martínez, L. (2015). A consensus-driven group recommender system, *International Journal of Intelligent Systems* **30**, 8, pp. 887–906.

Celma, Ò. and Serra, X. (2008). Foafing the music: bridging the semantic gap in music recommendation, *Web Semantics: Science, Services and Agents on the World Wide Web* **6**, 4, pp. 250–256.

Chai, D., Wang, L., Chen, K., and Yang, Q. (2019). Secure federated matrix factorization, *arXiv preprint arXiv:1906.05108* .

Chang, W.-C., Wu, Y., Liu, H., and Yang, Y. (2017). Cross-domain kernel induction for transfer learning, in *The 31st AAAI Conference on Artificial Intelligence*, pp. 1763–1769.

Chao, D. L. and Forrest, S. (2003). Information immune systems, *Genetic Programming and Evolvable Machines* **4**, 4, pp. 311–331.

Chen, C., Zheng, X., Wang, Y., Hong, F., and Lin, Z. (2014). Context-aware collaborative topic regression with social matrix factorization for recommender systems, in *Proceedings of the 28th AAAI Conference on Artificial Intelligence*, pp. 9–15.

Chen, C.-M. and Duh, L.-J. (2008). Personalized web-based tutoring system based on fuzzy item response theory, *Expert Systems with Applications* **34**, 4, pp. 2298–2315.

Chen, C.-M., Duh, L.-J., and Liu, C.-Y. (2004). A personalized courseware recommendation system based on fuzzy item response theory, in *IEEE International Conference on e-Technology, e-Commerce and e-Service*, pp. 305–308.

Chen, L. and Pu, P. (2012). Critiquing-based recommenders: survey and emerging trends, *User Modeling and User-Adapted Interaction* **22**, 1-2, pp. 125–150.

Chen, W., Hsu, W., and Lee, M. L. (2013). Making recommendations from multiple domains, in *Proceedings of the 19th ACM SIGKDD International Conference on Knowledge Discovery and Data Mining*, pp. 892–900.

Cheng, H., Koc, L., Harmsen, J., Shaked, T., Chandra, T., Aradhye, H., Anderson, G., Corrado, G., Chai, W., Ispir, M., Anil, R., Haque, Z., Hong, L., Jain, V., Liu, X., and Shah, H. (2016). Wide & deep learning for recommender systems, in *Proceedings of the 1st Workshop on Deep Learning for Recommender Systems*, pp. 7–10.

Cheng, H., Tan, P.-N., Sticklen, J., and Punch, W. F. (2007). Recommendation via query centered random walk on k-partite graph, in *The 7th IEEE International Conference on Data Mining*, pp. 457–462.

Chesnevar, C. I. and Maguitman, A. G. (2004). Arguenet: an argument-based recommender system for solving web search queries, in *The 2nd International IEEE Conference on Intelligent Systems*, Vol. 1, pp. 282–287.

Cho, Y. H. and Kim, J. K. (2004). Application of web usage mining and product taxonomy to collaborative recommendations in e-commerce, *Expert Systems with Applications* **26**, 2, pp. 233–246.

Chua, F. C. T., Oentaryo, R. J., and Lim, E.-P. (2013). Modeling temporal adoptions using dynamic matrix factorization, in *2013 IEEE 13th International Conference on Data Mining*, pp. 91–100.

Clauset, A., Shalizi, C. R., and Newman, M. E. (2009). Power-law distributions in empirical data, *SIAM Review* **51**, 4, pp. 661–703.

Codina, V., Ricci, F., and Ceccaroni, L. (2013). Exploiting the semantic similarity of contextual situations for pre-filtering recommendation, in *International Conference on User Modeling, Adaptation and Personalization*, pp. 165–177.

Console, L., Torre, I., Lombardi, I., Gioria, S., and Surano, V. (2003). Personalized and adaptive services on board a car: an application for tourist information, *Journal of Intelligent Information Systems* **21**, 3, pp. 249–284.

Contreras, D., Salamo, M., Rodriguez, I., and Puig, A. (2018). Shopping decisions made in a virtual world: defining a state-based model of collaborative and conversational user-recommender interactions, *IEEE Consumer Electronics Magazine* **7**, 4, pp. 26–35.

*Cornelis, C., Guo, X., Lu, J., and Zhang, G. (2005). A fuzzy relational approach to event recommendation, in *Proceedings of the 2nd Indian International Conference on Artificial Intelligence*, Vol. 5, pp. 2231–2242.

*Cornelis, C., Lu, J., Guo, X., and Zhang, G. (2007). One-and-only item recommendation with fuzzy logic techniques, *Information Sciences* **177**, 22, pp. 4906–4921.

Cremonesi, P. and Quadrana, M. (2014). Cross-domain recommendations without overlapping data: myth or reality? in *Proceedings of the 8th ACM Conference on Recommender Systems*, pp. 297–300.

Crossen, A., Budzik, J., and Hammond, K. J. (2002). Flytrap: intelligent group music recommendation, in *Proceedings of the 7th International Conference on Intelligent User Interfaces*, pp. 184–185.

Dai, H., Wang, Y., Trivedi, R., and Song, L. (2016). Recurrent coevolutionary latent feature processes for continuous-time recommendation, in *Proceedings of the 1st Workshop on Deep Learning for Recommender Systems*, pp. 29–34.

Das, A. S., Datar, M., Garg, A., and Rajaram, S. (2007). Google news personalization: scalable online collaborative filtering, in *Proceedings of the 16th International Conference on World Wide Web*, p. 271–280.

Davidson, J., Liebald, B., Liu, J., Nandy, P., Van Vleet, T., Gargi, U., Gupta, S., He, Y., Lambert, M., Livingston, B., and et al. (2010). The youtube video recommendation system, in *Proceedings of the 4th ACM Conference on Recommender Systems*, p. 293–296.

Davidson, R. and Harel, D. (1996). Drawing graphs nicely using simulated annealing, *ACM Transactions on Graphics* **15**, 4, pp. 301–331.

De Meo, P., Quattrone, G., and Ursino, D. (2008). A decision support system for designing new services tailored to citizen profiles in a complex and distributed e-government scenario, *Data & Knowledge Engineering* **67**, 1, pp. 161–184.

DeHon, A. (2000). Compact, multilayer layout for butterfly fat-tree, in *Proceedings of the 12th Annual ACM Symposium on Parallel Algorithms and Architectures*, pp. 206–215.

Deng, Z., Choi, K.-S., Jiang, Y., and Wang, S. (2014). Generalized hidden-mapping ridge regression, knowledge-leveraged inductive transfer learning for neural networks, fuzzy systems and kernel methods, *IEEE Transactions on Cybernetics* **44**, 12, pp. 2585–2599.

Deshpande, M. and Karypis, G. (2004). Item-based top-n recommendation algorithms, *ACM Transactions on Information Systems* **22**, 1, pp. 143–177.

Dey, A. K., Abowd, G. D., and Salber, D. (2001). A conceptual framework and a toolkit for supporting the rapid prototyping of context-aware applications, *Human-Computer Interaction* **16**, 2-4, pp. 97–166.

Diao, Q., Qiu, M., Wu, C.-Y., Smola, A. J., Jiang, J., and Wang, C. (2014). Jointly modeling aspects, ratings and sentiments for movie recommendation, in *Proceedings of the 20th ACM SIGKDD International Conference on Knowledge Discovery and Data Mining*, pp. 193–202.

Ding, C., Li, T., Peng, W., and Park, H. (2006). Orthogonal nonnegative matrix t-factorizations for clustering, in *Proceedings of the 19th ACM SIGKDD International Conference on Knowledge Discovery and Data Mining*, pp. 126–135.

Ding, Y. and Li, X. (2005). Time weight collaborative filtering, in *Proceedings of the 14th ACM International Conference on Information and Knowledge Management*, pp. 485–492.

Drachsler, H., Hummel, H. G., and Koper, R. (2008). Personal recommender systems for learners in lifelong learning networks: the requirements, techniques and model, *International Journal of Learning Technology* **3**, 4, pp. 404–423.

Du, N., Wang, Y., He, N., Sun, J., and Song, L. (2015). Time-sensitive recommendation from recurrent user activities, in *Advances in Neural Information Processing Systems*, pp. 3492–3500.

Eades, P. (1984). A heuristic for graph drawing, *Congressus Numerantium* **42**, pp. 149–160.

Eades, P. (1991). *Drawing free trees* (International Institute for Advanced Study of Social Information Science).

Eirinaki, M., Louta, M. D., and Varlamis, I. (2013). A trust-aware system for personalized user recommendations in social networks, *IEEE Transactions on Systems, Man, and Cybernetics: Systems* **44**, 4, pp. 409–421.

Elkahky, A. M., Song, Y., and He, X. (2015). A multi-view deep learning approach for cross domain user modeling in recommendation systems, in *Proceedings of the 24th International Conference on World Wide Web*, p. 278–288.

Eriksson, M., Fleischer, R., Johansson, A., Snickars, P., and Vonderau, P. (2019). *Spotify teardown: Inside the black box of streaming music* (MIT Press).

Esteban, B., Tejeda-Lorente, Á., Porcel, C., Arroyo, M., and Herrera-Viedma, E. (2014). Tplufib-web: a fuzzy linguistic web system to help in the treatment of low back pain problems, *Knowledge-Based Systems* **67**, pp. 429–438.

Fan, B., Liu, L., Li, M., and Wu, Y. (2008). Knowledge recommendation based on social network theory, in *2008 IEEE Symposium on Advanced Management of Information for Globalized Enterprises*, pp. 1–3.

Fankhauser, S., Riesen, K., and Bunke, H. (2011). Speeding up graph edit distance computation through fast bipartite matching, in *International Workshop on Graph-Based Representations in Pattern Recognition*, pp. 102–111.

Farzan, R. and Brusilovsky, P. (2006). Social navigation support in a course recommendation system, in *International Conference on Adaptive Hypermedia and Adaptive Web-Based Systems*, pp. 91–100.

Felfernig, A. and Burke, R. (2008). Constraint-based recommender systems: technologies and research issues, in *Proceedings of the 10th International Conference on Electronic Commerce*, p. 3.

Felfernig, A., Friedrich, G., Jannach, D., and Zanker, M. (2006). An integrated environment for the development of knowledge-based recommender applications, *International Journal of Electronic Commerce* **11**, 2, pp. 11–34.

Felfernig, A., Gula, B., Leitner, G., Maier, M., Melcher, R., and Teppan, E. (2008). Persuasion in knowledge-based recommendation, in *International Conference on Persuasive Technology*, pp. 71–82.

Fernández, Y. B., Arias, J. J. P., Nores, M. L., Solla, A. G., and Cabrer, M. R. (2006). Avatar: an improved solution for personalized tv based on semantic inference, *IEEE Transactions on Consumer Electronics* **52**, 1, pp. 223–231.

Fernández-Tobías, I., Cantador, I., Kaminskas, M., and Ricci, F. (2012). Cross-domain recommender systems: a survey of the state of the art, in *Spanish Conference on Information Retrieval*, pp. 1–12.

Fesenmaier, D. R., Ricci, F., Schaumlechner, E., Wöber, K., and Zanella, C. (2003). Dietorecs: travel advisory for multiple decision styles, in *Proceedings of the International Conference on Information and Communication Technologies in Tourism*, pp. 232–241.

Foote, J. T. (1997). Content-based retrieval of music and audio, in *Multimedia Storage and Archiving Systems II*, Vol. 3229, pp. 138–148.

Fouss, F., Pirotte, A., Renders, J.-M., and Saerens, M. (2007). Random-walk computation of similarities between nodes of a graph with application to collaborative recommendation, *IEEE Transactions on Knowledge and Data Engineering* **19**, 3, pp. 355–369.

Frey, B. J. and Dueck, D. (2007). Clustering by passing messages between data points, *Science* **315**, 5814, pp. 972–976.

Freyne, J., Smyth, B., Coyle, M., Balfe, E., and Briggs, P. (2004). Further experiments on collaborative ranking in community-based web search, *Artificial Intelligence Review* **21**, 3-4, pp. 229–252.

Gama, J., Žliobaitė, I., Bifet, A., Pechenizkiy, M., and Bouchachia, A. (2014). A survey on concept drift adaptation, *ACM Computing Surveys* **46**, 4, p. 44.

Gansner, E., Hu, Y., Kobourov, S., and Volinsky, C. (2009). Putting recommendations on the map: visualizing clusters and relations, in *Proceedings of the 3rd ACM Conference on Recommender Systems*, pp. 345–348.

Gao, S., Luo, H., Chen, D., Li, S., Gallinari, P., and Guo, J. (2013). Cross-domain recommendation via cluster-level latent factor model, in *Joint European Conference on Machine Learning and Knowledge Discovery in Databases*, pp. 161–176.

Garcia, I. and Sebastia, L. (2014). A negotiation framework for heterogeneous group recommendation, *Expert Systems with Applications* **41**, 4, pp. 1245–1261.

Garcia, I., Sebastia, L., and Onaindia, E. (2011). On the design of individual and group recommender systems for tourism, *Expert Systems with Applications* **38**, 6, pp. 7683–7692.

Garcia, I., Sebastia, L., Onaindia, E., and Guzman, C. (2009). A group recommender system for tourist activities, in *International Conference on Electronic Commerce and Web Technologies*, pp. 26–37.

García-Crespo, A., Chamizo, J., Rivera, I., Mencke, M., Colomo-Palacios, R., and Gómez-Berbís, J. M. (2009). Speta: social pervasive e-tourism advisor, *Telematics and Informatics* **26**, 3, pp. 306–315.

Garfinkel, R., Gopal, R., Tripathi, A., and Yin, F. (2006). Design of a shopbot and recommender system for bundle purchases, *Decision Support Systems* **42**, 3, pp. 1974–1986.

Gartrell, M., Xing, X., Lv, Q., Beach, A., Han, R., Mishra, S., and Seada, K. (2010). Enhancing group recommendation by incorporating social relationship interactions, in *Proceedings of the 16th ACM International Conference on Supporting Group Work*, pp. 97–106.

Gavalas, D., Konstantopoulos, C., Mastakas, K., and Pantziou, G. (2014). Mobile recommender systems in tourism, *Journal of Network and Computer Applications* **39**, pp. 319–333.

Gedikli, F., Jannach, D., and Ge, M. (2014). How should i explain? a comparison of different explanation types for recommender systems, *International Journal of Human-Computer Studies* **72**, 4, pp. 367 – 382.

Gemmell, J., Ramezani, M., Schimoler, T., Christiansen, L., and Mobasher, B. (2009). The impact of ambiguity and redundancy on tag recommendation in folksonomies, in *Proceedings of the 3rd ACM Conference on Recommender Systems*, pp. 45–52.

Gjoka, M., Butts, C. T., Kurant, M., and Markopoulou, A. (2011). Multigraph sampling of online social networks, *IEEE Journal on Selected Areas in Communications* **29**, 9, pp. 1893–1905.

Golbeck, J. and Hendler, J. (2006). Filmtrust: movie recommendations using trust in web-based social networks, in *Proceedings of the IEEE Consumer Communications and Networking Conference*, Vol. 96, pp. 282–286.

Golbeck, J. A. (2005). *Computing and applying trust in web-based social networks*, Ph.D. thesis.

Goldberg, D., Nichols, D., Oki, B. M., and Terry, D. (1992). Using collaborative filtering to weave an information tapestry, *Communications of the ACM* **35**, 12, pp. 61–70.

Goldberg, K., Roeder, T., Gupta, D., and Perkins, C. (2001). Eigentaste: a constant time collaborative filtering algorithm, *Information Retrieval* **4**, 2, pp. 133–151.

Gong, B., Grauman, K., and Sha, F. (2014). Learning kernels for unsupervised domain adaptation with applications to visual object recognition, *International Journal of Computer Vision* **109**, 1-2, pp. 3–27.

Gong, Y. and Zhang, Q. (2016). Hashtag recommendation using attention-based convolutional neural network. in *Proceedings of the 25th International Joint Conference on Artificial Intelligence*, pp. 2782–2788.

Gonzalez-Carrasco, I., Colomo-Palacios, R., Lopez-Cuadrado, J. L., Garcı, Á., and Ruiz-Mezcua, B. (2012). Pb-advisor: a private banking multi-investment portfolio advisor, *Information Sciences* **206**, pp. 63–82.

Gope, J. and Jain, S. K. (2017). A learning styles based recommender system prototype for edx courses, in *International Conference on Smart Technologies for Smart Nation*, pp. 414–419.

Goren-Bar, D. and Glinansky, O. (2004). Fit-recommending tv programs to family members, *Computers & Graphics* **28**, 2, pp. 149–156.

Gori, M. and Pucci, A. (2007). ItemRank: a random-walk based scoring algorithm for recommender engines, in *Proceedings of the 20th International Joint Conference on Artificial Intelligence*, Vol. 7, pp. 2766–2771.

Gorla, J., Lathia, N., Robertson, S., and Wang, J. (2013). Probabilistic group recommendation via information matching, in *Proceedings of the 22nd International Conference on World Wide Web*, pp. 495–504.

Gotz, D. and Wen, Z. (2009). Behavior-driven visualization recommendation, in *Proceedings of the 14th International Conference on Intelligent User Interfaces*, pp. 315–324.

Gretarsson, B., O'Donovan, J., Bostandjiev, S., Hall, C., and Höllerer, T. (2010). Smallworlds: visualizing social recommendations, in *Computer Graphics Forum*, Vol. 29, pp. 833–842.

Gu, Y., Zhao, B., Hardtke, D., and Sun, Y. (2016). Learning global term weights for content-based recommender systems, in *Proceedings of the 25th International Conference on World Wide Web*, pp. 391–400.

Guan, B., Hu, L., Liu, P., Xu, H., Fu, Z., and Wang, Q. (2019). Dpsmart: a flexible group based recommendation framework for digital repository systems, in *IEEE International Congress on Big Data*, pp. 111–120.

Guo, H., Tang, R., Ye, Y., Li, Z., and He, X. (2017). DeepFM: a factorization-machine based neural network for CTR prediction, *Proceedings of the 26th International Joint Conference on Artificial Intelligence*, pp. 1725–1731.

*Guo, X. and Lu, J. (2005a). Recommending trade exhibitions by integrating semantic information with collaborative filtering, in *The 2005 IEEE/WIC/ACM International Conference on Web Intelligence* (IEEE), pp. 747–750.

*Guo, X. and Lu, J. (2005b). Stef: Personalized trade exhibition recommendation, in *1st International Workshop on E-Service Intelligence in conjunction with the 8th Joint Conference on Information Sciences* (Joint Conference on Information Sciences).

*Guo, X. and Lu, J. (2007). Intelligent e-government services with personalized recommendation techniques, *International Journal of Intelligent Systems* **22**, 5, pp. 401–417.

*Guo, X., Lu, J., and Zhang, G. (2004). A recommender system by two-level collaborative filtering. in *Proceedings of the 8th IASTED Information Conference on Software Engineering and Applications*, pp. 65–69.

Gupta, M. M. and Qi, J. (1991). Theory of t-norms and fuzzy inference methods, *Fuzzy Sets and Systems* **40**, 3, pp. 431–450.

*Hao, P., Zhang, G., and Lu, J. (2016). Enhancing cross domain recommendation with domain dependent tags, in *Proceedings of the 2016 IEEE International Conference on Fuzzy Systems*, pp. 1266–1273.

*Hao, P., Zhang, G., Martinez, L., and Lu, J. (2017). Regularizing knowledge transfer in recommendation with tag-inferred correlation, *IEEE Transactions on Cybernetics* **49**, 1, pp. 83–96.

Harel, M., Mannor, S., El-Yaniv, R., and Crammer, K. (2014). Concept drift detection through resampling, in *Proceedings of the 31st International Conference on Machine Learning*, pp. 1009–1017.

Hariri, N., Mobasher, B., Burke, R., and Zheng, Y. (2011). Context-aware recommendation based on review mining, in *Proceedings of the 9th Workshop on Intelligent Techniques for Web Personalization and Recommender Systems*, pp. 30–68.

Harries, M. and Horn, K. (1995). Detecting concept drift in financial time series prediction using symbolic machine learning, in *The 8th Australian Joint Conference on Artificial Intelligence*, pp. 91–98.

Hauver, D. B. and French, J. C. (2001). Flycasting: using collaborative filtering to generate a playlist for online radio, in *Proceedings 1st International Conference on WEB Delivering of Music*, pp. 123–130.

Hayes, C. and Cunningham, P. (2001). Smart radio—community based music radio, *Knowledge-Based Systems* **14**, 3-4, pp. 197–201.

He, R. and McAuley, J. (2016). Ups and downs: Modeling the visual evolution of fashion trends with one-class collaborative filtering, in *Proceedings of the 25th International Conference on World Wide Web*, pp. 507–517.

He, T., Yin, H., Chen, Z., Zhou, X., Sadiq, S., and Luo, B. (2016). A spatial-temporal topic model for the semantic annotation of pois in lbsns, *ACM Transactions on Intelligent Systems and Technology* **8**, 1, p. 12.

He, X., Gao, M., Kan, M.-Y., and Wang, D. (2017a). Birank: towards ranking on bipartite graphs, *IEEE Transactions on Knowledge and Data Engineering* **29**, 1, pp. 57–71.

He, X., Liao, L., Zhang, H., Nie, L., Hu, X., and Chua, T.-S. (2017b). Neural collaborative filtering, in *Proceedings of the 26th International Conference on World Wide Web*, pp. 173–182.

He, X., Pan, J., Jin, O., Xu, T., Liu, B., Xu, T., Shi, Y., Atallah, A., Herbrich, R., Bowers, S., and Candela, J. Q. n. (2014). Practical lessons from predicting clicks on ads at facebook, in *Proceedings of the 8th International Workshop on Data Mining for Online Advertising*, pp. 1–9.

Heckerman, D., Chickering, D. M., Meek, C., Rounthwaite, R., and Kadie, C. (2000). Dependency networks for inference, collaborative filtering, and data visualization, *Journal of Machine Learning Research* **1**, Oct, pp. 49–75.

Herlocker, J., Konstan, J. A., and Riedl, J. (2002). An empirical analysis of design choices in neighborhood-based collaborative filtering algorithms, *Information Retrieval* **5**, 4, pp. 287–310.

Herlocker, J. L., Konstan, J. A., Terveen, L. G., and Riedl, J. T. (2004). Evaluating collaborative filtering recommender systems, *ACM Transactions on Information Systems* **22**, 1, pp. 5–53.

Hernando, A., Bobadilla, J., Ortega, F., and GutiéRrez, A. (2013). Trees for explaining recommendations made through collaborative filtering, *Information Sciences* **239**, pp. 1–17.

Hernando, A., Moya, R., Ortega, F., and Bobadilla, J. (2014). Hierarchical graph maps for visualization of collaborative recommender systems, *Journal of Information Science* **40**, 1, pp. 97–106.

Herrera, F. and Martínez, L. (2001). A model based on linguistic 2-tuples for dealing with multigranular hierarchical linguistic contexts in multi-expert decision-making, *IEEE Transactions on Systems, Man, and Cybernetics, Part B Cybernetics* **31**, 2, pp. 227–234.

Herzog, D. and Wörndl, W. (2019). User-centered evaluation of strategies for recommending sequences of points of interest to groups, in *Proceedings of the 13th ACM Conference on Recommender Systems*, pp. 96–100.

Hidasi, B. and Tikk, D. (2012). Fast als-based tensor factorization for context-aware recommendation from implicit feedback, in *Joint European Conference on Machine Learning and Knowledge Discovery in Databases*, pp. 67–82.

Hofmann, T. (2004). Latent semantic models for collaborative filtering, *ACM Transactions on Information Systems* **22**, 1, pp. 89–115.

Homburg, V. M. and Dijkshoorn, A. (2013). Diffusion of personalized e-government services among dutch municipalities: an empirical investigation and explanation, in *E-Government Services Design, Adoption, and Evaluation* (IGI Global), pp. 221–237.

Hong, W., Li, L., and Li, T. (2012). Product recommendation with temporal dynamics, *Expert Systems with Applications* **39**, 16, pp. 12398–12406.

Hotho, A., Jäschke, R., Schmitz, C., and Stumme, G. (2006). Information retrieval in folksonomies: Search and ranking, in *European Semantic Web Conference*, pp. 411–426.

Hu, G., Pan, W., Lin, H., Kang, K., and Best, M. L. (2014). Study on the framework of e-government services capability: an empirical investigation, *Social Science Computer Review* **32**, 1, pp. 56–73.

Hu, L., Cao, J., Xu, G., Cao, L., Gu, Z., and Zhu, C. (2013a). Personalized recommendation via cross-domain triadic factorization, in *Proceedings of the 22nd International Conference on World Wide Web*, pp. 595–606.

Hu, Y., Zhang, D., Ye, J., Li, X., and He, X. (2013b). Fast and accurate matrix completion via truncated nuclear norm regularization, *IEEE Transactions on Pattern Analysis and Machine Intelligence* **35**, 9, pp. 2117–2130.

Huang, C.-L., Yeh, P.-H., Lin, C.-W., and Wu, D.-C. (2014). Utilizing user tag-based interests in recommender systems for social resource sharing websites, *Knowledge-Based Systems* **56**, pp. 86–96.

Huang, J., Smola, A. J., Gretton, A., Borgwardt, K. M., and Scholkopf, B. (2006). Correcting sample selection bias by unlabeled data, in *Proceedings of the 19th International Conference on Neural Information Processing Systems*, pp. 601–608.

Huang, Z., Chung, W., and Chen, H. (2004). A graph model for e-commerce recommender systems, *Journal of the American Society for Information Science and Technology* **55**, 3, pp. 259–274.

Hung, L.-p. (2005). A personalized recommendation system based on product taxonomy for one-to-one marketing online, *Expert Systems with Applications* **29**, 2, pp. 383–392.

Hwang, C.-S. and Chen, Y.-P. (2007). Using trust in collaborative filtering recommendation, in *International Conference on Industrial, Engineering and Other Applications of Applied Intelligent Systems*, pp. 1052–1060.

Jacob, Y., Denoyer, L., and Gallinari, P. (2011). Classification and annotation in social corpora using multiple relations, in *Proceedings of the 20th ACM International Conference on Information and Knowledge Management*, pp. 1215–1220.

Jalali, M., Mustapha, N., Sulaiman, M. N., and Mamat, A. (2010). Webpum: a web-based recommendation system to predict user future movements, *Expert Systems with Applications* **37**, 9, pp. 6201–6212.

Jamali, M. and Ester, M. (2009). Trustwalker: a random walk model for combining trust-based and item-based recommendation, in *Proceedings of the 15th ACM SIGKDD International Conference on Knowledge Discovery and Data Mining*, pp. 397–406.

Jameson, A. (2004). More than the sum of its members: challenges for group recommender systems, in *Proceedings of the Working Conference on Advanced Visual Interfaces*, pp. 48–54.

Jameson, A., Baldes, S., and Kleinbauer, T. (2004). Two methods for enhancing mutual awareness in a group recommender system, in *Proceedings of the Working Conference on Advanced Visual Interfaces*, pp. 447–449.

Jäschke, R., Marinho, L., Hotho, A., Schmidt-Thieme, L., and Stumme, G. (2007). Tag recommendations in folksonomies, in *European Conference on Principles of Data Mining and Knowledge Discovery*, pp. 506–514.

Jiang, M., Cui, P., Chen, X., Wang, F., Zhu, W., and Yang, S. (2015). Social recommendation with cross-domain transferable knowledge, *IEEE Transactions on Knowledge and Data Engineering* **27**, 11, pp. 3084–3097.

Jiang, M., Cui, P., Liu, R., Yang, Q., Wang, F., Zhu, W., and Yang, S. (2012a). Social contextual recommendation, in *21st ACM International Conference on Information and Knowledge Management*, pp. 45–54.

Jiang, M., Cui, P., Wang, F., Yang, Q., Zhu, W., and Yang, S. (2012b). Social recommendation across multiple relational domains, in *Proceedings of the 21st ACM International Conference on Information and Knowledge Management*, pp. 1422–1431.

Jiang, M., Cui, P., Wang, F., Yang, Q., Zhu, W., and Yang, S. (2012c). Social recommendation across multiple relational domains, in *21st ACM International Conference on Information and Knowledge Management* (ACM), pp. 1422–1431.

Jing, H., Liang, A.-C., Lin, S.-D., and Tsao, Y. (2014). A transfer probabilistic collective factorization model to handle sparse data in collaborative filtering, in *IEEE International Conference on Data Mining*, pp. 250–259.

Jing, H. and Smola, A. J. (2017). Neural survival recommender, in *Proceedings of the 10th ACM International Conference on Web Search and Data Mining*, pp. 515–524.

Jonker, R. and Volgenant, A. (1987). A shortest augmenting path algorithm for dense and sparse linear assignment problems, *Computing* **38**, 4, pp. 325–340.

Jungnickel, D. (2007). *Graphs, networks and algorithms*, Vol. 5 (Springer Science & Business Media).

Kapoor, K., Subbian, K., Srivastava, J., and Schrater, P. (2015). Just in time recommendations: Modeling the dynamics of boredom in activity streams, in *Proceedings of the 8th ACM International Conference on Web Search and Data Mining*, pp. 233–242.

Kaššák, O., Kompan, M., and Bieliková, M. (2016). Personalized hybrid recommendation for group of users: top-n multimedia recommender, *Information Processing & Management* **52**, 3, pp. 459–477.

Katakis, I., Tsapatsoulis, N., Mendez, F., Triga, V., and Djouvas, C. (2013). Social voting advice applications — definitions, challenges, datasets and evaluation, *IEEE Transactions on Cybernetics* **44**, 7, pp. 1039–1052.

Kazai, G., Yusof, I., and Clarke, D. (2016). Personalised news and blog recommendations based on user location, facebook and twitter user profiling, in *Proceedings of the 39th International ACM SIGIR Conference on Research and Development in Information Retrieval*, pp. 1129–1132.

Kazienko, P., Musial, K., and Kajdanowicz, T. (2011). Multidimensional social network in the social recommender system, *IEEE Transactions on Systems, Man, and Cybernetics, Part A: Systems and Humans* **41**, 4, pp. 746–759.

Kifer, D., Ben-David, S., and Gehrke, J. (2004). Detecting change in data streams, in *Proceedings of the 30th International Conference on Very Large Data Bases*, pp. 180–191.

Kim, D., Park, C., Oh, J., Lee, S., and Yu, H. (2016). Convolutional matrix factorization for document context-aware recommendation, in *Proceedings of the 10th ACM Conference on Recommender Systems*, pp. 233–240.

Kim, H.-N., El-Saddik, A., and Jo, G.-S. (2011). Collaborative error-reflected models for cold-start recommender systems, *Decision Support Systems* **51**, 3, pp. 519–531.

Kim, J. K., Kim, H. K., Oh, H. Y., and Ryu, Y. U. (2010). A group recommendation system for online communities, *International Journal of Information Management* **30**, 3, pp. 212–219.

Kim, K.-R. and Moon, N. (2012). Recommender system design using movie genre similarity and preferred genres in smart phone, *Multimedia Tools and Applications* **61**, 1, pp. 87–104.

Knijnenburg, B. P., Willemsen, M. C., Gantner, Z., Soncu, H., and Newell, C. (2012). Explaining the user experience of recommender systems, *User Modeling and User-Adapted Interaction* **22**, 4-5, pp. 441–504.

*Komkhao, M., Li, Z., Halang, W. A., and Lu, J. (2012). An incremental collaborative filtering algorithm for recommender systems, in *Uncertainty Modeling in Knowledge Engineering and Decision Making* (World Scientific), pp. 327–332.

*Komkhao, M., Lu, J., Li, Z., and Halang, W. A. (2013). Incremental collaborative filtering based on mahalanobis distance and fuzzy membership for recommender systems, *International Journal of General Systems* **42**, 1, pp. 41–66.

*Komkhao, M., Lu, J., Li, Z., and Halang, W. A. (2014). Improving group recommendations by identifying homogenous subgroups, in *The 7th International Conference on Intelligent System and Knowledge Engineering* (Springer), pp. 453–462.

Konečný, J., McMahan, H. B., Yu, F. X., Richtárik, P., Suresh, A. T., and Bacon, D. (2016). Federated learning: Strategies for improving communication efficiency, *arXiv preprint arXiv:1610.05492* .

Konstan, J. A., Miller, B. N., Maltz, D., Herlocker, J. L., Gordon, L. R., and Riedl, J. (1997). Grouplens: applying collaborative filtering to usenet news, *Communications of the ACM* **40**, 3, pp. 77–87.

Konstas, I., Stathopoulos, V., and Jose, J. M. (2009). On social networks and collaborative recommendation, in *Proceedings of the 32nd International ACM SIGIR Conference on Research and Development in Information Retrieval*, pp. 195–202.

Koren, Y. (2008). Factorization meets the neighborhood: a multifaceted collaborative filtering model, in *Proceedings of the 14th ACM SIGKDD International Conference on Knowledge Discovery and Data Mining*, pp. 426–434.

Koren, Y. (2010). Collaborative filtering with temporal dynamics, *Communications of the ACM* **53**, 4, pp. 89–97.

Koren, Y., Bell, R., and Volinsky, C. (2009). Matrix factorization techniques for recommender systems, *Computer* **42**, 8, pp. 30–37.

Krestel, R., Fankhauser, P., and Nejdl, W. (2009). Latent dirichlet allocation for tag recommendation, in *Proceedings of the 3rd ACM conference on Recommender Systems*, pp. 61–68.

Krulwich, B. (1997). Lifestyle finder: intelligent user profiling using large-scale demographic data, *AI Magazine* **18**, 2, pp. 37–37.

Kuhn, H. W. (1955). The hungarian method for the assignment problem, *Naval Research Logistics Quarterly* **2**, 1-2, pp. 83–97.

Kumar, A., Kumar, N., Hussain, M., Chaudhury, S., and Agarwal, S. (2014). Semantic clustering-based cross-domain recommendation, in *IEEE Symposium on Computational Intelligence and Data Mining*, pp. 137–141.

Kwon, H.-J. and Hong, K.-S. (2011). Personalized smart tv program recommender based on collaborative filtering and a novel similarity method, *IEEE Transactions on Consumer Electronics* **57**, 3, pp. 1416–1423.

Lampropoulos, A. S., Lampropoulou, P. S., and Tsihrintzis, G. A. (2012). A cascade-hybrid music recommender system for mobile services based on musical genre classification and personality diagnosis, *Multimedia Tools and Applications* **59**, 1, pp. 241–258.

Lang, K. (1995). Newsweeder: learning to filter netnews, in *Machine Learning Proceedings* (Elsevier), pp. 331–339.

Lathia, N., Hailes, S., and Capra, L. (2009). Temporal collaborative filtering with adaptive neighbourhoods, in *Proceedings of the 32nd International ACM SIGIR Conference on Research and Development in Information Retrieval*, pp. 796–797.

Lawrence, R. D., Almasi, G. S., Kotlyar, V., Viveros, M., and Duri, S. S. (2001). Personalization of supermarket product recommendations, in *Applications of Data Mining to Electronic Commerce* (Springer), pp. 11–32.

LeCun, Y., Bengio, Y., and Hinton, G. (2015). Deep learning, *Nature* **521**, 7553, p. 436.

Lee, D. D. and Seung, H. S. (2001). Algorithms for non-negative matrix factorization, in *Advances in Neural Information Processing Systems*, pp. 556–562.

Lee, S. K., Cho, Y. H., and Kim, S. H. (2010). Collaborative filtering with ordinal scale-based implicit ratings for mobile music recommendations, *Information Sciences* **180**, 11, pp. 2142–2155.

Lee, T., Chun, J., Shim, J., and Lee, S.-g. (2006). An ontology-based product recommender system for b2b marketplaces, *International Journal of Electronic Commerce* **11**, 2, pp. 125–155.

Lee, W.-P., Kaoli, C., and Huang, J.-Y. (2014). A smart tv system with body-gesture control, tag-based rating and context-aware recommendation, *Knowledge-Based Systems* **56**, pp. 167–178.

Leung, C. W.-k., Chan, S. C.-f., and Chung, F.-l. (2006). A collaborative filtering framework based on fuzzy association rules and multiple-level similarity, *Knowledge and Information Systems* **10**, 3, pp. 357–381.

Leung, W. K. C. (2009). *Enriching user and item profiles for collaborative filtering: from concept hierarchies to user-generated reviews* (Hong Kong Polytechnic University).

Li, B., Yang, Q., and Xue, X. (2009a). Can movies and books collaborate? cross-domain collaborative filtering for sparsity reduction, in *The 21st International Joint Conference on Artificial Intelligence*, Vol. 9, pp. 2052–2057.

Li, B., Yang, Q., and Xue, X. (2009b). Transfer learning for collaborative filtering via a rating-matrix generative model, in *Proceedings of the 26th Annual International Conference on Machine Learning*, pp. 617–624.

Li, B., Zhu, X., Li, R., and Zhang, C. (2015). Rating knowledge sharing in cross-domain collaborative filtering, *IEEE Transactions on Cybernetics* **45**, 5, pp. 1068–1082.

Li, C.-Y. and Lin, S.-D. (2014). Matching users and items across domains to improve the recommendation quality, in *Proceedings of the 20th ACM SIGKDD International Conference on Knowledge Discovery and Data Mining*, pp. 801–810.

Li, X., Wang, M., and Liang, T.-P. (2014). A multi-theoretical kernel-based approach to social network-based recommendation, *Decision Support Systems* **65**, pp. 95–104.

Li, Y.-M., Wu, C.-T., and Lai, C.-Y. (2013). A social recommender mechanism for e-commerce: combining similarity, trust, and relationship, *Decision Support Systems* **55**, 3, pp. 740–752.

Liang, H., Xu, Y., Li, Y., and Nayak, R. (2010a). Personalized recommender system based on item taxonomy and folksonomy, in *Proceedings of the 19th ACM International Conference on Information and Knowledge Management*, pp. 1641–1644.

Liang, H., Xu, Y., Li, Y., Nayak, R., and Tao, X. (2010b). Connecting users and items with weighted tags for personalized item recommendations, in *Proceedings of the 21st ACM Conference on Hypertext and Hypermedia*, pp. 51–60.

Linden, G., Smith, B., and York, J. (2003). Amazon.com recommendations: item-to-item collaborative filtering, *IEEE Internet Computing* **7**, 1, pp. 76–80.

*Liu, A., Song, Y., Zhang, G., and Lu, J. (2017a). Regional concept drift detection and density synchronized drift adaptation, in *Proceedings of the 26th International Joint Conference on Artificial Intelligence*, pp. 2280–2286.

Liu, B., Wei, Y., Zhang, Y., Yan, Z., and Yang, Q. (2018). Transferable contextual bandit for cross-domain recommendation, in *Proceedings of the 32nd AAAI Conference on Artificial Intelligence* (AAAI Press), pp. 3619–3626.

Liu, B., Xiong, H., Papadimitriou, S., Fu, Y., and Yao, Z. (2015). A general geographical probabilistic factor model for point of interest recommendation, *IEEE Transactions on Knowledge and Data Engineering* **27**, 5, pp. 1167–1179.

Liu, D., Hua, X.-S., Yang, L., Wang, M., and Zhang, H.-J. (2009). Tag ranking, in *Proceedings of the 18th International Conference on World Wide Web*, pp. 351–360.

*Liu, D., Lin, L., and Lu, J. (2004). Cbr-based recommender systems for research topic finding, p. 47.

*Liu, F., Zhang, G., Lu, H., and Lu, J. (2017b). Heterogeneous unsupervised cross-domain transfer learning, *arXiv preprint arXiv:1701.02511* .

Liu, H., Hu, Z., Mian, A., Tian, H., and Zhu, X. (2014). A new user similarity model to improve the accuracy of collaborative filtering, *Knowledge-Based Systems* **56**, pp. 156–166.

Liu, J., Jiang, Y., Li, Z., Zhang, X., and Lu, H. (2016). Domain-sensitive recommendation with user-item subgroup analysis, *IEEE Transactions on Knowledge and Data Engineering* **28**, 4, pp. 939–950.

Liu, J., Wu, C., and Liu, W. (2013). Bayesian probabilistic matrix factorization with social relations and item contents for recommendation, *Decision Support Systems* **55**, 3, pp. 838–850.

Liu, N. N., Meng, X., Liu, C., and Yang, Q. (2011). Wisdom of the better few: cold start recommendation via representative based rating elicitation, in *Proceedings of the 2011 ACM Conference on Recommender Systems* (ACM), pp. 37–44.

*Liu, Q., Huang, H., Zhang, G., Gao, Y., Xuan, J., and Lu, J. (2018). Semantic structure-based word embedding by incorporating concept convergence and word divergence, in *32nd AAAI Conference on Artificial Intelligence*.

Logesh, R., Subramaniyaswamy, V., Vijayakumar, V., and Li, X. (2019). Efficient user profiling based intelligent travel recommender system for individual and group of users, *Mobile Networks and Applications* **24**, 3, pp. 1018–1033.

Long, M., Wang, J., Ding, G., Pan, S. J., and Philip, S. Y. (2014a). Adaptation regularization: a general framework for transfer learning, *IEEE Transactions on Knowledge and Data Engineering* **26**, 5, pp. 1076–1089.

Long, M., Wang, J., Ding, G., Shen, D., and Yang, Q. (2014b). Transfer learning with graph co-regularization, *IEEE Transactions on Knowledge and Data Engineering* **26**, 7, pp. 1805–1818.

Lopes, G. R., Moro, M. M., Wives, L. K., and De Oliveira, J. P. M. (2010). Collaboration recommendation on academic social networks, in *International Conference on Conceptual Modeling*, pp. 190–199.

Lorenzi, F., dos Santos, F., Ferreira, P. R., and Bazzan, A. L. (2008). Optimizing preferences within groups: a case study on travel recommendation, in *Brazilian Symposium on Artificial Intelligence*, pp. 103–112.

Losing, V., Hammer, B., and Wersing, H. (2016). Knn classifier with self adjusting memory for heterogeneous concept drift, in *Proceedings of the 16th IEEE International Conference on Data Mining*, pp. 291–300.

*Lu, J. (2004). A personalized e-learning material recommender system, in *International Conference on Information Technology and Applications*.

*Lu, J., Behbood, V., Hao, P., Zuo, H., Xue, S., and Zhang, G. (2015a). Transfer learning using computational intelligence: a survey, *Knowledge-Based Systems* **80**, pp. 14–23.

*Lu, J., Guo, X., Huynh, A., and Benkovich, L. (2004). Srs: a subject recommender system to enhance e-learning personalisation, in *International Conference on Information* (International Information Institute).

*Lu, J., Shambour, Q., Xu, Y., Lin, Q., and Zhang, G. (2010). Bizseeker: a hybrid semantic recommendation system for personalized government-to-business e-services, *Internet Research* **20**, 3, pp. 342–365.

*Lu, J., Shambour, Q., Xu, Y., Lin, Q., and Zhang, G. (2013). A web-based personalized business partner recommendation system using fuzzy semantic techniques, *Computational Intelligence* **29**, 1, pp. 37–69.

*Lu, J., Shambour, Q., and Zhang, G. (2009a). Recommendation technique-based government-to-business personalized e-services, in *NAFIPS Annual Meeting of the North American Fuzzy Information Processing Society*, pp. 1–6.

*Lu, J., Wu, D., Mao, M., Wang, W., and Zhang, G. (2015b). Recommender system application developments: a survey, *Decision Support Systems* **74**, pp. 12–32.

*Lu, J., Zhu, Y., Zeng, X., Koehl, L., Ma, J., and Zhang, G. (2009b). A linguistic multi-criteria group decision support system for fabric hand evaluation, *Fuzzy Optimization and Decision Making* **8**, 4, p. 395.

*Lu, N., Lu, J., Zhang, G., and De Mantaras, R. L. (2016). A concept drift-tolerant case-base editing technique, *Artificial Intelligence* **230**, pp. 108–133.

*Lu, N., Zhang, G., and Lu, J. (2014). Concept drift detection via competence models, *Artificial Intelligence* **209**, pp. 11–28.

Lu, Z., Dou, Z., Lian, J., Xie, X., and Yang, Q. (2015). Content-based collaborative filtering for news topic recommendation, in *Proceedings of the 29th AAAI Conference on Artificial Intelligence*.

Lu, Z., Pan, S. J., Li, Y., Jiang, J., and Yang, Q. (2016). Collaborative evolution for user profiling in recommender systems. in *Proceedings of the 25th International Joint Conference on Artificial Intelligence*, pp. 3804–3810.

Lu, Z., Pan, W., Xiang, E. W., Yang, Q., Zhao, L., and Zhong, E. (2013a). Selective transfer learning for cross domain recommendation, in *Proceedings of the 13th SIAM International Conference on Data Mining*, pp. 641–649.

Lu, Z., Zhong, E., Zhao, L., Xiang, E. W., Pan, W., and Yang, Q. (2013b). Selective transfer learning for cross domain recommendation, in *Proceedings of the 2013 SIAM International Conference on Data Mining*, pp. 641–649.

Lucas, J. P., Luz, N., Moreno, M. N., Anacleto, R., Figueiredo, A. A., and Martins, C. (2013). A hybrid recommendation approach for a tourism system, *Expert Systems with Applications* **40**, 9, pp. 3532–3550.

Luo, X., Zhou, M., Li, S., You, Z., Xia, Y., and Zhu, Q. (2016). A nonnegative latent factor model for large-scale sparse matrices in recommender systems via alternating direction method, *IEEE Transactions on Neural Networks and Learning Systems* **27**, 3, pp. 579–592.

Ma, H., Yang, H., Lyu, M. R., and King, I. (2008). Sorec: social recommendation using probabilistic matrix factorization, in *Proceedings of the 17th ACM Conference on Information and Knowledge Management*, pp. 931–940.

Maâtallah, M. and Seridi, H. (2012). Enhanced collaborative filtering to recommender systems of technology enhanced learning, *ICWIT* **2012**, pp. 129–138.

Mao, K., Fan, J., Shou, L., Chen, G., and Kankanhalli, M. (2014). Song recommendation for social singing community, in *Proceedings of the 22nd ACM International Conference on Multimedia*, pp. 127–136.

*Mao, M., Lu, J., Han, J., and Zhang, G. (2019). Multiobjective e-commerce recommendations based on hypergraph ranking, *Information Sciences* **471**, pp. 269–287.

*Mao, M., Lu, J., Zhang, G., and Zhang, J. (2015). A fuzzy content matching-based e-commerce recommendation approach, in *2015 IEEE International Conference on Fuzzy Systems*, pp. 1–8.

*Mao, M., Lu, J., Zhang, G., and Zhang, J. (2017). Multi-relational social recommendations via multigraph ranking, *IEEE Transactions on Cybernetics* **47**, 12, pp. 4049–4061.

*Mao, M., Zhang, G., Lu, J., and Zhang, J. (2014). A signed trust-based recommender approach for personalized government-to-business e-services, in *The 7th International Conference on Intelligent System and Knowledge Engineering* (Springer), pp. 91–101.

Marceau, V., Noël, P.-A., Hébert-Dufresne, L., Allard, A., and Dubé, L. J. (2011). Modeling the dynamical interaction between epidemics on overlay networks, *Physical Review E* **84**, 2, p. 026105.

Marinho, L. B. and Schmidt-Thieme, L. (2008). Collaborative tag recommendations, in *Data Analysis, Machine Learning and Applications* (Springer), pp. 533–540.

Martinez, L., Rodriguez, R. M., and Espinilla, M. (2009). Reja: a georeferenced hybrid recommender system for restaurants, in *Proceedings of the 2009 IEEE/WIC/ACM International Joint Conference on Web Intelligence and Intelligent Agent Technology*, pp. 187–190.

Massa, P. and Avesani, P. (2007). Trust-aware recommender systems, in *Proceedings of the 2007 ACM Conference on Recommender Systems*, pp. 17–24.

Massa, P. and Avesani, P. (2009). Trust metrics in recommender systems, in *Computing with social trust* (Springer), pp. 259–285.

Mbipom, B., Massie, S., and Craw, S. (2018). An e-learning recommender that helps learners find the right materials, in *The 32nd AAAI Conference on Artificial Intelligence*, pp. 7928–7933.

McAuley, J. and Leskovec, J. (2013a). Hidden factors and hidden topics: understanding rating dimensions with review text, in *Proceedings of the 7th ACM Conference on Recommender Systems*, pp. 165–172.

McAuley, J., Targett, C., Shi, Q., and Van Den Hengel, A. (2015). Image-based recommendations on styles and substitutes, in *Proceedings of the 38th International ACM SIGIR Conference on Research and Development in Information Retrieval*, pp. 43–52.

McAuley, J. and Yang, A. (2016). Addressing complex and subjective product-related queries with customer reviews, in *Proceedings of the 25th International Conference on World Wide Web*, pp. 625–635.

McAuley, J. J. and Leskovec, J. (2013b). From amateurs to connoisseurs: modeling the evolution of user expertise through online reviews, in *Proceedings of the 22nd International Conference on World Wide Web*, pp. 897–908.

McCarthy, J. F. (2002). Pocket restaurant finder: a situated recommender system for groups, in *Workshop on Mobile Ad-Hoc Communication at the 2002 ACM Conference on Human Factors in Computer Systems*, pp. 1–8.

McCarthy, J. F. and Anagnost, T. (1998). Musicfx: an arbiter of group preferences for computer-supported cooperative workouts, in *ACM Conference on Computer-Supported Cooperative Work*, pp. 96–102.

McCarthy, K., Reilly, J., McGinty, L., and Smyth, B. (2004). Thinking positively-explanatory feedback for conversational recommender systems, in *Proceedings of the European Conference on Case-Based Reasoning Explanation Workshop*, pp. 115–124.

McCarthy, K., Salamó, M., Coyle, L., McGinty, L., Smyth, B., and Nixon, P. (2006). Cats: a synchronous approach to collaborative group recommendation, in *Florida Artificial Intelligence Research Society Conference*, pp. 86–91.

McFee, B., Barrington, L., and Lanckriet, G. (2012). Learning content similarity for music recommendation, *IEEE Transactions on Audio, Speech, and Language Processing* **20**, 8, pp. 2207–2218.

Melville, P., Mooney, R. J., and Nagarajan, R. (2002). Content-boosted collaborative filtering for improved recommendations, *The 18th National Conference on Artificial Intelligence* **23**, pp. 187–192.

Middleton, S. E., Shadbolt, N. R., and De Roure, D. C. (2004). Ontological user profiling in recommender systems, *ACM Transactions on Information Systems* **22**, 1, pp. 54–88.

Mikolov, T., Sutskever, I., Chen, K., Corrado, G. S., and Dean, J. (2013). Distributed representations of words and phrases and their compositionality, in *Advances in Neural Information Processing Systems*, pp. 3111–3119.

Milicevic, A. K., Nanopoulos, A., and Ivanovic, M. (2010). Social tagging in recommender systems: a survey of the state-of-the-art and possible extensions, *Artificial Intelligence Review* **33**, 3, pp. 187–209.

Miller, B. N., Konstan, J. A., and Riedl, J. (2004). Pocketlens: toward a personal recommender system, *ACM Transactions on Information Systems* **22**, 3, pp. 437–476.

Milton, A., Green, M., Keener, A., Ames, J., Ekstrand, M. D., and Pera, M. S. (2019). Storytime: eliciting preferences from children for book recommendations, in *Proceedings of the 13th ACM Conference on Recommender Systems*, pp. 544–545.

Miranda, T., Claypool, M., Gokhale, A., Mir, T., Murnikov, P., Netes, D., and Sartin, M. (1999). Combining content-based and collaborative filters in an online newspaper, in *In Proceedings of ACM SIGIR Workshop on Recommender Systems*.

Mirbakhsh, N. and Ling, C. X. (2015). Improving top-n recommendation for cold-start users via cross-domain information, *ACM Transactions on Knowledge Discovery from Data* **9**, 4, pp. 1–19.

Misue, K., Eades, P., Lai, W., and Sugiyama, K. (1995). Layout adjustment and the mental map, *Journal of Visual Languages & Computing* **6**, 2, pp. 183–210.

Mnih, A. and Salakhutdinov, R. R. (2008). Probabilistic matrix factorization, in *Advances in Neural Information Processing Systems*, pp. 1257–1264.

Mobasher, B., Cooley, R., and Srivastava, J. (2000). Automatic personalization based on web usage mining, *Communications of the ACM* **43**, 8, pp. 142–151.

Mooney, R. J. and Roy, L. (2000). Content-based book recommending using learning for text categorization, in *Proceedings of the 5th ACM Conference on Digital Libraries*, pp. 195–204.

Morales, G. D. F., Bifet, A., Khan, L., Gama, J., and Fan, W. (2016). Iot big data stream mining, in *Proceedings of the 22nd ACM International Conference on Knowledge Discovery and Data Mining*, pp. 2119–2120.

Moreno, A., Valls, A., Isern, D., Marin, L., and Borràs, J. (2013). Sigtur/e-destination: ontology-based personalized recommendation of tourism and leisure activities, *Engineering Applications of Artificial Intelligence* **26**, 1, pp. 633–651.

Moukas, A. (1997). Amalthaea information discovery and filtering using a multiagent evolving ecosystem, *Applied Artificial Intelligence* **11**, 5, pp. 437–457.

Moukas, A. and Maes, P. (1998). Amalthaea: an evolving multi-agent information filtering and discovery system for the www, *Autonomous Agents and Multi-agent Systems* **1**, 1, pp. 59–88.

Munkres, J. (1957). Algorithms for the assignment and transportation problems, *Journal of the Society for Industrial and Applied Mathematics* **5**, 1, pp. 32–38.

Nanopoulos, A., Rafailidis, D., Symeonidis, P., and Manolopoulos, Y. (2009). Musicbox:

personalized music recommendation based on cubic analysis of social tags, *IEEE Transactions on Audio, Speech, and Language Processing* **18**, 2, pp. 407–412.

Ndou, V. (2004). E-government for developing countries: opportunities and challenges, *The Electronic Journal of Information Systems in Developing Countries* **18**, 1, pp. 1–24.

Nguyen, Q. V. and Huang, M. L. (2003). Space-optimized tree: a connection+ enclosure approach for the visualization of large hierarchies, *Information Visualization* **2**, 1, pp. 3–15.

*Nguyen, T. T. S., Lu, H. Y., and Lu, J. (2013). Web-page recommendation based on web usage and domain knowledge, *IEEE Transactions on Knowledge and Data Engineering* **26**, 10, pp. 2574–2587.

Nilashi, M., bin Ibrahim, O., and Ithnin, N. (2014a). Multi-criteria collaborative filtering with high accuracy using higher order singular value decomposition and neuro-fuzzy system, *Knowledge-Based Systems* **60**, pp. 82–101.

Nilashi, M., Ibrahim, O. B., and Ithnin, N. (2014b). Hybrid recommendation approaches for multi-criteria collaborative filtering, *Expert Systems with Applications* **41**, 8, pp. 3879–3900.

O'connor, M., Cosley, D., Konstan, J. A., and Riedl, J. (2001). Polylens: a recommender system for groups of users, in *Proceedings of the 7th European Conference on Computer Supported Cooperative Work*, pp. 199–218.

O'Donovan, J. (2009). Capturing trust in social web applications, in *Computing with Social Trust* (Springer), pp. 213–257.

O'Donovan, J. and Smyth, B. (2005). Trust in recommender systems, in *Proceedings of the 10th International Conference on Intelligent User Interfaces*, pp. 167–174.

O'Donovan, J., Smyth, B., Gretarsson, B., Bostandjiev, S., and Höllerer, T. (2008). Peerchooser: visual interactive recommendation, in *Proceedings of the SIGCHI Conference on Human Factors in Computing Systems*, pp. 1085–1088.

Page, L., Brin, S., Motwani, R., and Winograd, T. (1999). The pagerank citation ranking: bringing order to the web, Tech. rep., Stanford InfoLab.

Palau, J., Montaner, M., López, B., and De La Rosa, J. L. (2004). Collaboration analysis in recommender systems using social networks, in *International Workshop on Cooperative Information Agents*, pp. 137–151.

Pan, R., Zhou, Y., Cao, B., Liu, N. N., Lukose, R., Scholz, M., and Yang, Q. (2008). One-class collaborative filtering, in *The 8th IEEE International Conference on Data Mining*, pp. 502–511.

Pan, S. J., Ni, X., Sun, J.-T., Yang, Q., and Chen, Z. (2010). Cross-domain sentiment classification via spectral feature alignment, in *Proceedings of the 19th International Conference on World Wide Web*, pp. 751–760.

Pan, S. J., Tsang, I. W., Kwok, J. T., and Yang, Q. (2011). Domain adaptation via transfer component analysis, *IEEE Transactions on Neural Networks* **22**, 2, pp. 199–210.

Pan, S. J. and Yang, Q. (2010). A survey on transfer learning, *IEEE Transactions on Knowledge and Data Engineering* **22**, 10, pp. 1345–1359.

Pan, W. (2016). A survey of transfer learning for collaborative recommendation with auxiliary data, *Neurocomputing* **177**, pp. 447–453.

Pan, W. and Yang, Q. (2013). Transfer learning in heterogeneous collaborative filtering domains, *Artificial Intelligence* **197**, pp. 39–55.

Pan, W., Yang, Q., Duan, Y., and Ming, Z. (2016). Transfer learning for semisupervised collaborative recommendation, *ACM Transactions on Interactive Intelligent Systems* **6**, 2, pp. 1–21.

Panniello, U., Tuzhilin, A., Gorgoglione, M., Palmisano, C., and Pedone, A. (2009). Experimental comparison of pre-vs. post-filtering approaches in context-aware recommender systems, in *Proceedings of the 3rd ACM Conference on Recommender Systems*, pp. 265–268.

Pashtan, A., Blattler, R., Andi, A. H., and Scheuermann, P. (2003). Catis: a context-aware tourist information system, in *Proceedings of the 4th International Workshop of Mobile Computing* (Citeseer).

Paterek, A. (2007). Improving regularized singular value decomposition for collaborative filtering, in *Proceedings of KDD Cup and Workshop*, pp. 5–8.

Pazzani, M. J. (1999). A framework for collaborative, content-based and demographic filtering, *Artificial Intelligence Review* **13**, 5-6, pp. 393–408.

Popescu, G. (2013). Group recommender systems as a voting problem, in *International Conference on Online Communities and Social Computing*, pp. 412–421.

Porcel, C. and Herrera-Viedma, E. (2010). Dealing with incomplete information in a fuzzy linguistic recommender system to disseminate information in university digital libraries, *Knowledge-Based Systems* **23**, 1, pp. 32–39.

Porcel, C., López-Herrera, A. G., and Herrera-Viedma, E. (2009a). A recommender system for research resources based on fuzzy linguistic modeling, *Expert Systems with Applications* **36**, 3, pp. 5173–5183.

Porcel, C., Moreno, J. M., and Herrera-Viedma, E. (2009b). A multi-disciplinar recommender system to advice research resources in university digital libraries, *Expert Systems with Applications* **36**, 10, pp. 12520–12528.

Pourgholamali, F., Kahani, M., Bagheri, E., and Noorian, Z. (2017). Embedding unstructured side information in product recommendation, *Electronic Commerce Research and Applications* **25**, pp. 70–85.

*Purba, J. H., Lu, J., Zhang, G., and Ruan, D. (2012). An area defuzzification technique to assess nuclear event reliability data from failure possibilities, *International Journal of Computational Intelligence and Applications* **11**, 4, pp. 125–22.

Qian, X., Feng, H., Zhao, G., and Mei, T. (2014). Personalized recommendation combining user interest and social circle, *IEEE Transactions on Knowledge and Data Engineering* **26**, 7, pp. 1763–1777.

Quijano-Sánchez, L., Bridge, D., Díaz-Agudo, B., and Recio-García, J. A. (2012). A case-based solution to the cold-start problem in group recommenders, in *International Conference on Case-Based Reasoning*, pp. 342–356.

Quijano-Sanchez, L., Recio-Garcia, J. A., Diaz-Agudo, B., and Jimenez-Diaz, G. (2013). Social factors in group recommender systems, *ACM Transactions on Intelligent Systems and Technology* **4**, 1, p. 8.

Rae, A., Sigurbjörnsson, B., and van Zwol, R. (2010). Improving tag recommendation using social networks, in *Adaptivity, Personalization and Fusion of Heterogeneous Information*, pp. 92–99.

Ramirez-Garcia, X. and García-Valdez, M. (2014). Post-filtering for a restaurant context-aware recommender system, in *Recent Advances on Hybrid Approaches for Designing Intelligent Systems* (Springer), pp. 695–707.

Recio-Garcia, J. A., Jimenez-Diaz, G., Sanchez-Ruiz, A. A., and Diaz-Agudo, B. (2009). Personality aware recommendations to groups, in *Proceedings of the 3rd ACM Conference on Recommender Systems*, pp. 325–328.

Reingold, E. M. and Tilford, J. S. (1981). Tidier drawings of trees, *IEEE Transactions on Software Engineering*, 2, pp. 223–228.

Renda, M. E. and Straccia, U. (2005). A personalized collaborative digital library environment: a model and an application, *Information Processing & Management* **41**, 1, pp. 5–21.

Rendle, S. (2012). Factorization machines with libfm, *ACM Transactions on Intelligent Systems and Technology* **3**, 3, p. 57.

Rendle, S., Freudenthaler, C., Gantner, Z., and Schmidt-Thieme, L. (2009). BPR: Bayesian personalized ranking from implicit feedback, in *Proceedings of the 25th Conference on Uncertainty in Artificial Intelligence*, pp. 452–461.

Rendle, S., Gantner, Z., Freudenthaler, C., and Schmidt-Thieme, L. (2011). Fast context-aware recommendations with factorization machines, in *Proceedings of the 34th international ACM SIGIR Conference on Research and Development in Information Retrieval*, pp. 635–644.

Rendle, S. and Schmidt-Thieme, L. (2010). Pairwise interaction tensor factorization for personalized tag recommendation, in *Proceedings of the 3rd ACM international Conference on Web Search and Data Mining*, pp. 81–90.

Resnick, P., Iacovou, N., Suchak, M., Bergstrom, P., and Riedl, J. (1994). Grouplens: an open architecture for collaborative filtering of netnews, in *Proceedings of the 1994 ACM Conference on Computer Supported Cooperative Work*, pp. 175–186.

Resnik, P. (1995). Using information content to evaluate semantic similarity in a taxonomy, in *Proceedings of the 14th International Joint Conference on Artificial Intelligence*, pp. 448–453.

Ricci, F., Rokach, L., Shapira, B., and Kantor, P. B. (2010). *Recommender systems handbook*, 1st edn. (Springer-Verlag, Berlin, Heidelberg).

Riesen, K. and Bunke, H. (2009). Approximate graph edit distance computation by means of bipartite graph matching, *Image and Vision Computing* **27**, 7, pp. 950–959.

Romero, C., Ventura, S., Zafra, A., and De Bra, P. (2009). Applying web usage mining for personalizing hyperlinks in web-based adaptive educational systems, *Computers & Education* **53**, 3, pp. 828–840.

Ruiz-Montiel, M. and Aldana-Montes, J. F. (2009). Semantically enhanced recommender systems, in *OTM Confederated International Conferences on the Move to Meaningful Internet Systems*, pp. 604–609.

Ruotsalo, T., Haav, K., Stoyanov, A., Roche, S., Fani, E., Deliai, R., Mäkelä, E., Kauppinen, T., and Hyvönen, E. (2013). Smartmuseum: a mobile recommender system for the web of data, *Web Semantics: Science, Services and Agents on the World Wide Web* **20**, pp. 50–67.

Russo, C., Ghezzi, C. M., Fiamengo, G., and Benedetti, M. (2014). Benefits sought by citizens in multichannel e-government payment services: evidence from italy, *Procedia-Social and Behavioral Sciences* **109**, pp. 1261–1276.

Sakawa, M. (2013). *Fuzzy sets and interactive multiobjective optimization* (Springer Science & Business Media).

Salakhutdinov, R., Mnih, A., and Hinton, G. (2007). Restricted Boltzmann machines for collaborative filtering, in *Proceedings of the 24th International Conference on Machine Learning*, pp. 791–798.

Salamó, M., McCarthy, K., and Smyth, B. (2012). Generating recommendations for consensus negotiation in group personalization services, *Personal and Ubiquitous Computing* **16**, 5, pp. 597–610.

Salehi, M. and Kamalabadi, I. N. (2013). Hybrid recommendation approach for learning material based on sequential pattern of the accessed material and the learner's preference tree, *Knowledge-Based Systems* **48**, pp. 57–69.

Salehi, M. and Kmalabadi, I. N. (2012). A hybrid attribute-based recommender system for e-learning material recommendation, *Ieri Procedia* **2**, pp. 565–570.

Salter, J. and Antonopoulos, N. (2006). Cinemascreen recommender agent: combining collaborative and content-based filtering, *IEEE Intelligent Systems* **21**, 1, pp. 35–41.

Salton, G. and Buckley, C. (1988). Term-weighting approaches in automatic text retrieval, *Information Processing & Management* **24**, 5, pp. 513–523.

Salton, G., Wong, A., and Yang, C.-S. (1975). A vector space model for automatic indexing, *Communications of the ACM* **18**, 11, pp. 613–620.

Santos, O. C., Boticario, J. G., and Pérez-Marín, D. (2014). Extending web-based educational systems with personalised support through user centred designed recommendations along the e-learning life cycle, *Science of Computer Programming* **88**, pp. 92–109.

Sarwar, B., Karypis, G., Konstan, J., and Riedl, J. (2001). Item-based collaborative filtering recommendation algorithms, in *Proceedings of the 10th International Conference on World Wide Web*, pp. 285–295.

Sarwar, B. M. (2001). *Sparsity, scalability, and distribution in recommender systems* (University of Minnesota).

Schafer, J. B., Konstan, J., and Riedl, J. (1999). Recommender systems in e-commerce, in *Proceedings of the 1st ACM Conference on Electronic Commerce*, pp. 158–166.

Schafer, J. B., Konstan, J. A., and Riedl, J. (2001). E-commerce recommendation applications, *Data Mining and Knowledge Discovery* **5**, 1-2, pp. 115–153.

Schiaffino, S. and Amandi, A. (2009). Building an expert travel agent as a software agent, *Expert Systems with Applications* **36**, 2, pp. 1291–1299.

Schlimmer, J. C. and Granger Jr, R. H. (1986). Incremental learning from noisy data, *Machine Learning* **1**, 3, pp. 317–354.

Schmitz, C., Hotho, A., Jäschke, R., and Stumme, G. (2006). Mining association rules in folksonomies, in *Data science and classification* (Springer), pp. 261–270.

Schröder, G., Thiele, M., and Lehner, W. (2011). Setting goals and choosing metrics for recommender system evaluations, in *UCERSTI2 Workshop at the 5th ACM Conference on Recommender Systems*, Vol. 23, pp. 78–85.

Sebastiani, F. (2002). Machine learning in automated text categorization, *ACM Computing Surveys* **34**, 1, pp. 1–47.

Sedhain, S., Menon, A. K., Sanner, S., and Xie, L. (2015). Autorec: autoencoders meet collaborative filtering, in *Proceedings of the 24th International Conference on World Wide Web*, pp. 111–112.

Semerci, O., Gruson, A., Edwards, C., Lacker, B., Gibson, C., and Radosavljevic, V. (2019). Homepage personalization at spotify, in *Proceedings of the 13th ACM Conference on Recommender Systems*, p. 527.

Sen, S., Vig, J., and Riedl, J. (2009). Tagommenders: connecting users to items through tags, in *Proceedings of the 18th International Conference on World Wide Web*, pp. 671–680.

Serrano-Guerrero, J., Herrera-Viedma, E., Olivas, J. A., Cerezo, A., and Romero, F. P. (2011). A google wave-based fuzzy recommender system to disseminate information in university digital libraries 2.0, *Information Sciences* **181**, 9, pp. 1503–1516.

*Shambour, Q. and Lu, J. (2010). A recommender system for personalized g2b e-services using metadata-based ontology and focused web crawler, in *Intelligent Decision Making Systems-Proceeding of 2009 International Conference on Intelligent Systems and Knowledge Engineering* (World Scientific), pp. 332–337.

*Shambour, Q. and Lu, J. (2011a). Government-to-business personalized e-services using semantic-enhanced recommender system, in *International Conference on Electronic Government and the Information Systems Perspective* (Springer), pp. 197–211.

*Shambour, Q. and Lu, J. (2011b). A hybrid multi-criteria semantic-enhanced collaborative filtering approach for personalized recommendations, in *2011 IEEE/WIC/ACM International Conferences on Web Intelligence and Intelligent Agent Technology*, Vol. 1 (IEEE), pp. 71–78.

*Shambour, Q. and Lu, J. (2011c). A hybrid trust-enhanced collaborative filtering recommendation approach for personalized government-to-business e-services, *International Journal of Intelligent Systems* **26**, 9, pp. 814–843.

*Shambour, Q. and Lu, J. (2011d). Integrating multi-criteria collaborative filtering and trust filtering for personalized recommender systems, in *Proceedings of the 2011 IEEE Symposium on Computational Intelligence in Multi-criteria Decision-Making* (IEEE), pp. 44–51.

*Shambour, Q. and Lu, J. (2012). A trust-semantic fusion-based recommendation approach for e-business applications, *Decision Support Systems* **54**, 1, pp. 768–780.

*Shambour, Q. and Lu, J. (2015). An effective recommender system by unifying user and item trust information for b2b applications, *Journal of Computer and System Sciences* **81**, 7, pp. 1110–1126.

Shambour, Q. Y. (2012). *Hybrid recommender systems for personalized government-to-business e-services*, Ph.D. thesis.

Shardanand, U. and Maes, P. (1995). Social information filtering: algorithms for automating "word of mouth", in *Proceedings of the SIGCHI Conference on Human Factors in Computing Systems*, pp. 210–217.

Sharon, T., Lieberman, H., and Selker, T. (2003). A zero-input interface for leveraging group experience in web browsing, in *Proceedings of the 8th International Conference on Intelligent User Interfaces*, pp. 290–292.

Shi, X., Ye, H., and Gong, S. (2008). A personalized recommender integrating item-based and user-based collaborative filtering, in *International Seminar on Business and Information Management*, Vol. 1, pp. 264–267.

Shi, Y., Larson, M., and Hanjalic, A. (2011). Tags as bridges between domains: improving recommendation with tag-induced cross-domain collaborative filtering, *User Modeling, Adaption and Personalization*, pp. 305–316.

Shi, Y., Larson, M., and Hanjalic, A. (2014). Collaborative filtering beyond the user-item matrix: a survey of the state of the art and future challenges, *ACM Computing Surveys* **47**, 1, pp. 1–45.

Shiratsuchi, K., Yoshii, S., and Furukawa, M. (2006). Finding unknown interests utilizing the wisdom of crowds in a social bookmark service, in *Proceedings of the 2006 IEEE/WIC/ACM International Conference on Web Intelligence and Intelligent Agent Technology*, pp. 421–424.

Si, L. and Jin, R. (2003). Flexible mixture model for collaborative filtering, in *Proceedings of the 20th International Conference on Machine Learning*, pp. 704–711.

Singh, A. P. and Gordon, G. J. (2008). Relational learning via collective matrix factorization, in *Proceedings of the 14th ACM SIGKDD International Conference on Knowledge Discovery and Data Mining*, pp. 650–658.

Siskos, E., Askounis, D., and Psarras, J. (2014). Multicriteria decision support for global e-government evaluation, *Omega* **46**, pp. 51–63.

Smyth, B. and Balfe, E. (2006). Anonymous personalization in collaborative web search, *Information Retrieval* **9**, 2, pp. 165–190.

Smyth, B., Balfe, E., Freyne, J., Briggs, P., Coyle, M., and Boydell, O. (2004). Exploiting query repetition and regularity in an adaptive community-based web search engine, *User Modeling and User-Adapted Interaction* **14**, 5, pp. 383–423.

Smyth, B. and Cotter, P. (2000a). A personalised TV listings service for the digital TV age, *Knowledge-Based Systems* **13**, 2-3, pp. 53–59.

Smyth, B. and Cotter, P. (2000b). A personalized television listings service, *Communications of the ACM* **43**, 8, pp. 107–111.

Snead, J. T. and Wright, E. (2014). E-government research in the united states, *Government Information Quarterly* **31**, 1, pp. 129–136.

Son, L. H. and Thong, N. T. (2015). Intuitionistic fuzzy recommender systems: an effective tool for medical diagnosis, *Knowledge-Based Systems* **74**, pp. 133–150.

Sousa, M. R., Gama, J., and Brandão, E. (2016). A new dynamic modeling framework for credit risk assessment, *Expert Systems with Applications* **45**, pp. 341–351.

Strub, F., Gaudel, R., and Mary, J. (2016). Hybrid recommender system based on autoencoders, in *Proceedings of the 1st Workshop on Deep Learning for Recommender Systems*, pp. 1–5.

Su, X. and Khoshgoftaar, T. M. (2009). A survey of collaborative filtering techniques, *Advances in Artificial Intelligence* **2009**, pp. 1–19.

Sugiyama, M., Nakajima, S., Kashima, H., Buenau, P. V., and Kawanabe, M. (2008). Direct importance estimation with model selection and its application to covariate shift adaptation, in *Advances in Neural Information Processing Systems*, pp. 1433–1440.

Suykens, J. A. K. and Vandewalle, J. (1999). Least squares support vector machine classifiers, *Neural Processing Letters* **9**, 3, pp. 293–300.

Tan, S., Bu, J., Chen, C., Xu, B., Wang, C., and He, X. (2011). Using rich social media information for music recommendation via hypergraph model, *ACM Transactions on Multimedia Computing, Communications, and Applications* **7**, 1, pp. 1–22.

Terán, L. and Meier, A. (2010). A fuzzy recommender system for e-elections, in *International Conference on Electronic Government and the Information Systems Perspective*, pp. 62–76.

Treerattanapitak, K. and Jaruskulchai, C. (2012). Exponential fuzzy C-means for collaborative filtering, *Journal of Computer Science and Technology* **27**, 3, pp. 567–576.

Tso-Sutter, K. H. L., Marinho, L. B., and Schmidt-Thieme, L. (2008). Tag-aware recommender systems by fusion of collaborative filtering algorithms, in *Proceedings of the 2008 ACM Symposium on Applied Computing*, pp. 1995–1999.

Tsymbal, A. (2004). The problem of concept drift: definitions and related work, *Computer Science Department, Trinity College Dublin* **106**, 2.

Tung, H.-W. and Soo, V.-W. (2004). A personalized restaurant recommender agent for mobile e-service, in *IEEE International Conference on e-Technology, e-Commerce and e-Service*, pp. 259–262.

Tyler, S. K. and Zhang, Y. (2008). Open domain recommendation: social networks and collaborative filtering, in *International Conference on Advanced Data Mining and Applications*, pp. 330–341.

Verbert, K., Parra, D., Brusilovsky, P., and Duval, E. (2013). Visualizing recommendations to support exploration, transparency and controllability, in *Proceedings of the International Conference on Intelligent User Interfaces*, pp. 351–362.

Vildjiounaite, E., Kyllönen, V., Hannula, T., and Alahuhta, P. (2009). Unobtrusive dynamic modelling of tv programme preferences in a finnish household, *Multimedia Systems* **15**, 3, pp. 143–157.

Wang, C. and Blei, D. M. (2011). Collaborative topic modeling for recommending scientific articles, in *Proceedings of the 17th ACM SIGKDD International Conference on Knowledge Discovery and Data Mining*, pp. 448–456.

Wang, H., Wang, N., and Yeung, D.-Y. (2015). Collaborative deep learning for recommender systems, in *Proceedings of the 21th ACM SIGKDD International Conference on Knowledge Discovery and Data Mining*, pp. 1235–1244.

Wang, J., Huang, P., Zhao, H., Zhang, Z., Zhao, B., and Lee, D. L. (2018a). Billion-scale commodity embedding for e-commerce recommendation in alibaba, in *Proceedings of the 24th ACM SIGKDD International Conference on Knowledge Discovery & Data Mining*, pp. 839–848.

Wang, J., Yu, L., Zhang, W., Gong, Y., Xu, Y., Wang, B., Zhang, P., and Zhang, D. (2017). IRGAN: a minimax game for unifying generative and discriminative information retrieval models, in *Proceedings of the 40th International ACM SIGIR Conference on Research and Development in Information Retrieval*, pp. 515–524.

Wang, J.-C. and Chiu, C.-C. (2008). Recommending trusted online auction sellers using social network analysis, *Expert Systems with Applications* **34**, 3, pp. 1666–1679.

Wang, S., Lo, D., Vasilescu, B., and Serebrenik, A. (2018b). Entagrec++: an enhanced tag recommendation system for software information sites, *Empirical Software Engineering* **23**, 2, pp. 800–832.

Wang, W., Chen, Z., Liu, J., Qi, Q., and Zhao, Z. (2012). User-based collaborative filtering on cross domain by tag transfer learning, in *Proceedings of the 1st International Workshop on Cross Domain Knowledge Discovery in Web and Social Network Mining*, pp. 10–17.

*Wang, W., Zhang, G., and Lu, J. (2016). Member contribution-based group recommender system, *Decision Support Systems* **87**, pp. 80–93.

*Wang, W., Zhang, G., and Lu, J. (2017a). Hierarchy visualization for group recommender systems, *IEEE Transactions on Systems, Man, and Cybernetics: Systems* **49**, 6, pp. 1152–1163.

Wang, X., Donaldson, R., Nell, C., Gorniak, P., Ester, M., and Bu, J. (2016). Recommending groups to users using user-group engagement and time-dependent matrix factorization, in *Proceedings of the 30th AAAI Conference on Artificial Intelligence*, pp. 1331–1337.

*Wang, X., Liu, Y., Lu, J., Xiong, F., and Zhang, G. (2019). Trugrc: Trust-aware group recommendation with virtual coordinators, *Future Generation Computer Systems* **94**, pp. 224–236.

*Wang, X., Liu, Y., Zhang, G., Xiong, F., and Lu, J. (2017b). Diffusion-based recommendation with trust relations on tripartite graphs, *Journal of Statistical Mechanics: Theory and Experiment* **2017**, 8, p. 083405.

*Wang, X., Liu, Y., Zhang, G., Zhang, Y., Chen, H., and Lu, J. (2017c). Mixed similarity diffusion for recommendation on bipartite networks, *IEEE Access* **5**, pp. 21029–21038.

Wei, K., Huang, J., and Fu, S. (2007). A survey of e-commerce recommender systems, in *International Conference on Service Systems and Service Management*, pp. 1–5.

Widmer, G. and Kubat, M. (1996). Learning in the presence of concept drift and hidden contexts, *Machine Learning* **23**, 1, pp. 69–101.

Wiesner, M. and Pfeifer, D. (2010). Adapting recommender systems to the requirements of personal health record systems, in *Proceedings of the 1st ACM International Health Informatics Symposium*, pp. 410–414.

Woerndl, W., Brocco, M., and Eigner, R. (2009). Context-aware recommender systems in mobile scenarios, *International Journal of Information Technology and Web Engineering* **4**, 1, pp. 67–85.

Woerndl, W. and Groh, G. (2007). Utilizing physical and social context to improve recommender systems, in *Proceedings of the 2007 IEEE/WIC/ACM International Conferences on Web Intelligence and Intelligent Agent Technology-Workshops*, pp. 123–128.

Wu, C.-Y., Ahmed, A., Beutel, A., Smola, A. J., and Jing, H. (2017). Recurrent recommender networks, in *Proceedings of the 10th ACM International Conference on Web Search and Data Mining*, pp. 495–503.

*Wu, D., Lu, J., Hussain, F., Doumouras, C., and Zhang, G. (2018). A workforce health insurance plan recommender system, in *Data Science and Knowledge Engineering for Sensing Decision Support: Proceedings of the 13th International FLINS Conference*, Vol. 11 (World Scientific), p. 355.

*Wu, D., Lu, J., and Zhang, G. (2010a). A hybrid recommendation approach for hierarchical items, in *2010 IEEE International Conference on Intelligent Systems and Knowledge Engineering*, pp. 492–497.

*Wu, D., Lu, J., and Zhang, G. (2011). Similarity measure models and algorithms for hierarchical cases, *Expert Systems with Applications* **38**, 12, pp. 15049–15056.

*Wu, D., Lu, J., and Zhang, G. (2014a). A fuzzy tree matching-based personalized e-learning recommender system, in *2014 IEEE International Conference on Fuzzy Systems* (IEEE).

*Wu, D., Lu, J., and Zhang, G. (2015). A fuzzy tree matching-based personalized e-learning recommender system, *IEEE Transactions on Fuzzy Systems* **23**, 6, pp. 2412–2426.

*Wu, D., Lu, J., Zhang, G., and Lin, H. (2010b). A fuzzy matching based recommendation approach for mobile products/services, in *2010 10th International Conference on Intelligent Systems Design and Applications*, pp. 645–650.

*Wu, D., Zhang, G., and Lu, J. (2013a). A fuzzy tree similarity based recommendation approach for telecom products, in *2013 Joint IFSA World Congress and NAFIPS Annual Meeting* (IEEE), pp. 813–818.

*Wu, D., Zhang, G., and Lu, J. (2013b). A fuzzy tree similarity measure and its application in telecom product recommendation, in *2013 IEEE International Conference on Systems, Man, and Cybernetics* (IEEE), pp. 3483–3488.

*Wu, D., Zhang, G., and Lu, J. (2014b). A fuzzy preference tree-based recommender system for personalized business-to-business e-services, *IEEE Transactions on Fuzzy Systems* **23**, 1, pp. 29–43.

*Wu, D., Zhang, G., Lu, J., and Halang, W. A. (2012). A similarity measure on tree structured business data, in *Proceedings of the 23rd Australasian Conference on Information Systems* (ACIS), pp. 1–10.

Wu, J., Chen, L., Feng, Y., Zheng, Z., Zhou, M. C., and Wu, Z. (2013). Predicting quality of service for selection by neighborhood-based collaborative filtering, *IEEE Transactions on Systems, Man, and Cybernetics: Systems* **43**, 2, pp. 428–439.

Wu, S., Ren, W., Yu, C., Chen, G., Zhang, D., and Zhu, J. (2016). Personal recommendation using deep recurrent neural networks in NetEase, in *2016 IEEE 32nd International Conference on Data Engineering*, pp. 1218–1229.

Wu, X., Zhu, X., Wu, G.-Q., and Ding, W. (2014). Data mining with big data, *IEEE Transactions on Knowledge and Data Engineering* **26**, 1, pp. 97–107.

Xiang, L., Yuan, Q., Zhao, S., Chen, L., Zhang, X., Yang, Q., and Sun, J. (2010). Temporal recommendation on graphs via long-and short-term preference fusion, in *Proceedings of the 16th ACM SIGKDD International Conference on Knowledge Discovery and Data Mining*, pp. 723–732.

Xiao, W., Zhao, H., Pan, H., Song, Y., Zheng, V. W., and Yang, Q. (2019). Beyond personalization: social content recommendation for creator equality and consumer satisfaction, in *Proceedings of the 25th ACM SIGKDD International Conference on Knowledge Discovery & Data Mining* (ACM), pp. 235–245.

Xu, C., Xu, L., Lu, Y., Xu, H., and Zhu, Z. (2019). E-government recommendation algorithm based on probabilistic semantic cluster analysis in combination of improved collaborative filtering in big-data environment of government affairs, *Personal and Ubiquitous Computing*, pp. 1–11.

Xu, J., Yao, Y., Tong, H., Tao, X., and Lu, J. (2017). Rapare: a generic strategy for cold-start rating prediction problem, *IEEE Transactions on Knowledge and Data Engineering* **29**, 6, pp. 1296–1309.

Xu, S. and Watada, J. (2014). A method for hybrid personalized recommender based on clustering of fuzzy user profiles, in *2014 IEEE International Conference on Fuzzy Systems*, pp. 2171–2177.

*Xuan, J., Lu, J., and Zhang, G. (2019). Cooperative hierarchical dirichlet processes: superposition vs. maximization, *Artificial Intelligence* **271**, pp. 43–73.

Yager, R. R. (1988). On ordered weighted averaging aggregation operators in multicriteria decisionmaking, *IEEE Transactions on Systems, Man, and Cybernetics* **18**, 1, pp. 183–190.

Yager, R. R. (2003). Fuzzy logic methods in recommender systems, *Fuzzy Sets and Systems* **136**, 2, pp. 133–149.

Yan, Q. (2008). Modeling and simulation of instant messageing on Internet, in *2008*

International Conference on Computer Science and Information Technology, pp. 841–844.

Yang, B., Lei, Y., Liu, J., and Li, W. (2017a). Social collaborative filtering by trust, *IEEE Transactions on Pattern Analysis and Machine Intelligence* **39**, 8, pp. 1633–1647.

Yang, D., He, J., Qin, H., Xiao, Y., and Wang, W. (2015). A graph-based recommendation across heterogeneous domains, in *Proceedings of the 24th ACM International on Conference on Information and Knowledge Management*, pp. 463–472.

Yang, D., Xiao, Y., Song, Y., Zhang, J., Zhang, K., and Wang, W. (2014). Tag propagation based recommendation across diverse social media, in *Proceedings of the 23rd International Conference on World Wide Web*, pp. 407–408.

Yang, J., Liu, C., Teng, M., Chen, J., and Xiong, H. (2017b). A unified view of social and temporal modeling for b2b marketing campaign recommendation, *IEEE Transactions on Knowledge and Data Engineering* **30**, 5, pp. 810–823.

Yang, Q. (2019). Federated recommendation systems, in *2019 IEEE International Conference on Big Data* (IEEE), p. 1.

Yang, W.-S., Cheng, H.-C., and Dia, J.-B. (2008). A location-aware recommender system for mobile shopping environments, *Expert Systems with Applications* **34**, 1, pp. 437–445.

Yang, W.-S. and Hwang, S.-Y. (2013). itravel: a recommender system in mobile peer-to-peer environment, *Journal of Systems and Software* **86**, 1, pp. 12–20.

Ye, M., Liu, X., and Lee, W.-C. (2012). Exploring social influence for recommendation: a generative model approach, in *Proceedings of the 35th International ACM SIGIR Conference on Research and Development in Information Retrieval*, pp. 671–680.

Yera, R., Castro, J., and Martínez, L. (2016). A fuzzy model for managing natural noise in recommender systems, *Applied Soft Computing Journal* **40**, pp. 187–198.

Yera, R. and Martinez, L. (2017). Fuzzy tools in recommender systems: a survey, *International Journal of Computational Intelligence Systems* **10**, 1, pp. 776–803.

Yildirim, H. and Krishnamoorthy, M. S. (2008). A random walk method for alleviating the sparsity problem in collaborative filtering, in *Proceedings of the 2008 ACM Conference on Recommender Systems*, pp. 131–138.

Yin, H., Cui, B., Chen, L., Hu, Z., and Zhou, X. (2015). Dynamic user modeling in social media systems, *ACM Transactions on Information Systems* **33**, 3, p. 10.

*Yin, R., Li, K., Lu, J., and Zhang, G. (2019a). Enhancing fashion recommendation with visual compatibility relationship, in *The World Wide Web Conference*, pp. 3434–3440.

*Yin, R., Li, K., Lu, J., and Zhang, G. (2019b). Rsygan: generative adversarial network for recommender systems, in *2019 International Joint Conference on Neural Networks* (IEEE), pp. 1–7.

Yoon, V. Y., Hostler, R. E., Guo, Z., and Guimaraes, T. (2013). Assessing the moderating effect of consumer product knowledge and online shopping experience on using recommendation agents for customer loyalty, *Decision Support Systems* **55**, 4, pp. 883–893.

Yu, Z., Zhou, X., Hao, Y., and Gu, J. (2006). Tv program recommendation for multiple viewers based on user profile merging, *User Modeling and User-Adapted Interaction* **16**, 1, pp. 63–82.

Yuan, W., Shu, L., Chao, H.-C., Guan, D., Lee, Y.-K., and Lee, S. (2010). Itars: trust-aware recommender system using implicit trust networks, *IET Communications* **4**, 14, pp. 1709–1721.

Zadeh, L. A. (1965). Fuzzy sets, *Information and Control* **8**, 3, pp. 338–353.

Zadeh, L. A. (1975). The concept of a linguistic variable and its application to approximate reasoning, *Information Sciences* **8**, 3, pp. 199–249.

Zaíane, O. R. (2002). Building a recommender agent for e-learning systems, in *Proceedings of the International Conference on Computers in Education*, pp. 55–59.

Zenebe, A. and Norcio, A. F. (2009). Representation, similarity measures and aggregation methods using fuzzy sets for content-based recommender systems, *Fuzzy Sets and Systems* **160**, 1, pp. 76–94.

Zenebe, A., Zhou, L., and Norcio, A. F. (2010). User preferences discovery using fuzzy models, *Fuzzy Sets and Systems* **161**, 23, pp. 3044–3063.

Zhang, C., Wang, K., Yu, H., Sun, J., and Lim, E.-P. (2014). Latent factor transition for dynamic collaborative filtering, in *Proceedings of the 2014 SIAM International Conference on Data Mining*, pp. 452–460.

Zhang, F., Yuan, N. J., Lian, D., Xie, X., and Ma, W.-Y. (2016). Collaborative knowledge base embedding for recommender systems, in *Proceedings of the 22nd ACM SIGKDD International Conference on Knowledge Discovery and Data Mining*, pp. 353–362.

*Zhang, G. and Lu, J. (2003). An integrated group decision-making method dealing with fuzzy preferences for alternatives and individual judgments for selection criteria, *Group Decision and Negotiation* **12**, 6, pp. 501–515.

*Zhang, G. and Lu, J. (2004). Using general fuzzy number to handle uncertainty and imprecision in group decision-making, in *Intelligent Sensory Evaluation* (Springer), pp. 51–70.

*Zhang, G. and Lu, J. (2009). A linguistic intelligent user guide for method selection in multi-objective decision support systems, *Information Sciences* **179**, 14, pp. 2299–2308.

Zhang, K. (1996). A constrained edit distance between unordered labeled trees, *Algorithmica* **15**, 3, pp. 205–222.

Zhang, L., Zhu, M., and Huang, W. (2009). A framework for an ontology-based e-commerce product information retrieval system, *Journal of Computers* **4**, 6, pp. 436–443.

*Zhang, Q., Hao, P., Lu, J., and Zhang, G. (2019). Cross-domain recommendation with semantic correlation in tagging systems, in *2019 International Joint Conference on Neural Networks* (IEEE), pp. 1–8.

*Zhang, Q., Lu, J., Wu, D., and Zhang, G. (2018a). Cross-domain recommendation with consistent knowledge transfer by subspace alignment, in *International Conference on Web Information Systems Engineering* (Springer), pp. 67–82.

*Zhang, Q., Lu, J., Wu, D., and Zhang, G. (2018b). A cross-domain recommender system with kernel-induced knowledge transfer for overlapping entities, *IEEE Transactions on Neural Networks and Learning Systems* **30**, 7, pp. 1998–2012.

*Zhang, Q., Wu, D., Lu, J., Liu, F., and Zhang, G. (2017). A cross-domain recommender system with consistent information transfer, *Decision Support Systems* **104**, pp. 49–63.

*Zhang, Q., Wu, D., Lu, J., and Zhang, G. (2018c). Cross-domain recommendation with probabilistic knowledge transfer, in *International Conference on Neural Information Processing* (Springer), pp. 208–219.

*Zhang, Q., Wu, D., Zhang, G., and Lu, J. (2016). Fuzzy user-interest drift detection based recommender systems, in *IEEE International Conference on Fuzzy Systems*, pp. 1274–1281.

*Zhang, Q., Zhang, G., Lu, J., and Wu, D. (2015). A framework of hybrid recommender system for personalized clinical prescription, in *2015 10th International Conference on Intelligent Systems and Knowledge Engineering* (IEEE), pp. 189–195.

Zhang, S., Yao, L., and Xu, X. (2017). Autosvd++: an efficient hybrid collaborative filtering model via contractive auto-encoders, in *Proceedings of the 40th International ACM SIGIR Conference on Research and Development in Information Retrieval*, pp. 957–960.

Zhang, Z., Jin, X., Li, L., Ding, G., and Yang, Q. (2016). Multi-domain active learning for recommendation, in *Proceedings of the 30th AAAI Conference on Artificial Intelligence*, pp. 2358–2364.

*Zhang, Z., Lin, H., Liu, K., Wu, D., Zhang, G., and Lu, J. (2013). A hybrid fuzzy-based personalized recommender system for telecom products/services, *Information Sciences* **235**, pp. 117–129.

Zhang, Z.-K., Zhou, T., and Zhang, Y.-C. (2010). Personalized recommendation via integrated diffusion on user-item-tag tripartite graphs, *Physica A: Statistical Mechanics and its Applications* **389**, 1, pp. 179–186.

Zhao, D., Li, L., Peng, H., Luo, Q., and Yang, Y. (2014). Multiple routes transmitted epidemics on multiplex networks, *Physics Letters A* **378**, 10, pp. 770–776.

Zhao, L., Lu, Z., Pan, S. J., and Yang, Q. (2016). Matrix factorization+ for movie recommendation. in *Proceedings of the 25th International Joint Conference on Artificial Intelligence*, pp. 3945–3951.

Zhao, L., Pan, S. J., Xiang, E. W., Zhong, E., Lu, Z., and Yang, Q. (2013). Active transfer learning for cross-system recommendation, in *Proceedings of the 27th AAAI Conference on Artificial Intelligence*.

Zhao, L., Pan, S. J., and Yang, Q. (2017). A unified framework of active transfer learning for cross-system recommendation, *Artificial Intelligence* **245**, pp. 38–55.

Zhen, Y., Li, W.-J., and Yeung, D.-Y. (2009). Tagicofi: tag informed collaborative filtering, in *Proceedings of the 3rd ACM Conference on Recommender Systems*, pp. 69–76.

Zheng, N. and Li, Q. (2011). A recommender system based on tag and time information for social tagging systems, *Expert Systems with Applications* **38**, 4, pp. 4575–4587.

Zheng, V. W., Cao, B., Zheng, Y., Xie, X., and Yang, Q. (2010a). Collaborative filtering meets mobile recommendation: a user-centered approach, in *Proceedings of the 24th AAAI Conference on Artificial Intelligence*.

Zheng, V. W., Zheng, Y., Xie, X., and Yang, Q. (2010b). Collaborative location and activity recommendations with GPS history data, in *Proceedings of the 19th International Conference on World Wide Web*, pp. 1029–1038.

Zheng, V. W., Zheng, Y., Xie, X., and Yang, Q. (2012). Towards mobile intelligence: Learning from gps history data for collaborative recommendation, *Artificial Intelligence* **184**, pp. 17–37.

Zheng, Y., Burke, R., and Mobasher, B. (2013). Recommendation with differential context weighting, in *International Conference on User Modeling, Adaptation and Personalization*, pp. 152–164.

Zheng, Y., Mobasher, B., and Burke, R. (2014). Cslim: contextual slim recommendation algorithms, in *Proceedings of the 8th ACM Conference on Recommender Systems*, pp. 301–304.

Zhong, E., Fan, W., and Yang, Q. (2014). User behavior learning and transfer in composite social networks, *ACM Transactions on Knowledge Discovery from Data* **8**, 1, pp. 6:1–6:32.

Zhou, D., Huang, J., and Schölkopf, B. (2007). Learning with hypergraphs: clustering, classification, and embedding, in *Advances in Neural Information Processing Systems*, pp. 1601–1608.

Zhou, D. and Schölkopf, B. (2004). A regularization framework for learning from graph data, in *ICML Workshop on Statistical Relational Learning and its Connections to Other Fields*, Vol. 15, pp. 67–68.

Zhou, T., Bian, W., and Tao, D. (2013). Divide-and-conquer anchoring for near-separable nonnegative matrix factorization and completion in high dimensions, in *2013 IEEE 13th International Conference on Data Mining*, pp. 917–926.

Zhu, T., Harrington, P., Li, J., and Tang, L. (2014). Bundle recommendation in ecommerce, in *Proceedings of the 37th International ACM SIGIR Conference on Research & Development in Information Retrieval*, pp. 657–666.

Ziegler, C.-N. and Lausen, G. (2004). Analyzing correlation between trust and user similarity in online communities, in *International Conference on Trust Management*, pp. 251–265.

Zimmerman, J., Kauapati, K., Buczak, A. L., Schaffer, D., Gutta, S., and Martino, J. (2004). Tv personalization system, in *Personalized digital television* (Springer), pp. 27–51.

Žliobaitė, I., Pechenizkiy, M., and Gama, J. (2016). *An overview of concept drift applications*, book section Chapter 4, Studies in Big Data (Springer International Publishing, Cham), pp. 91–114.

Index

Printed in the United States
By Bookmasters